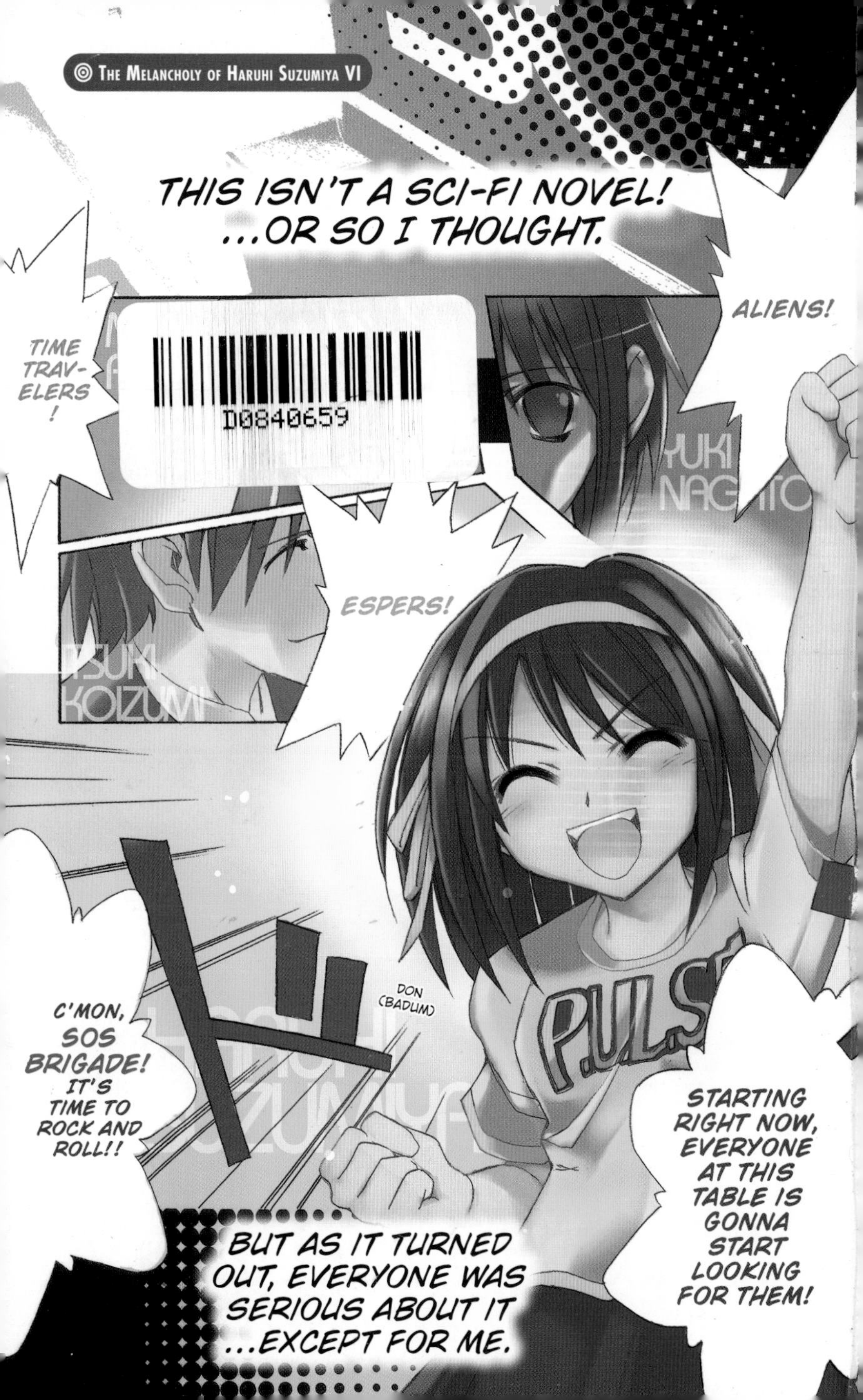

THE MELANCHOLY OF HARUHI SUZUMIYA VI
THIS ISN'T A SCI-FI NOVEL! ...OR SO I THOUGHT.
ALIENS!
TIME TRAV-ELERS!
YUKI NAGATO
ESPERS!
KOIZUMI
DON (BADUM)
C'MON, SOS BRIGADE! IT'S TIME TO ROCK AND ROLL!!
STARTING RIGHT NOW, EVERYONE AT THIS TABLE IS GONNA START LOOKING FOR THEM!
BUT AS IT TURNED OUT, EVERYONE WAS SERIOUS ABOUT IT ...EXCEPT FOR ME.

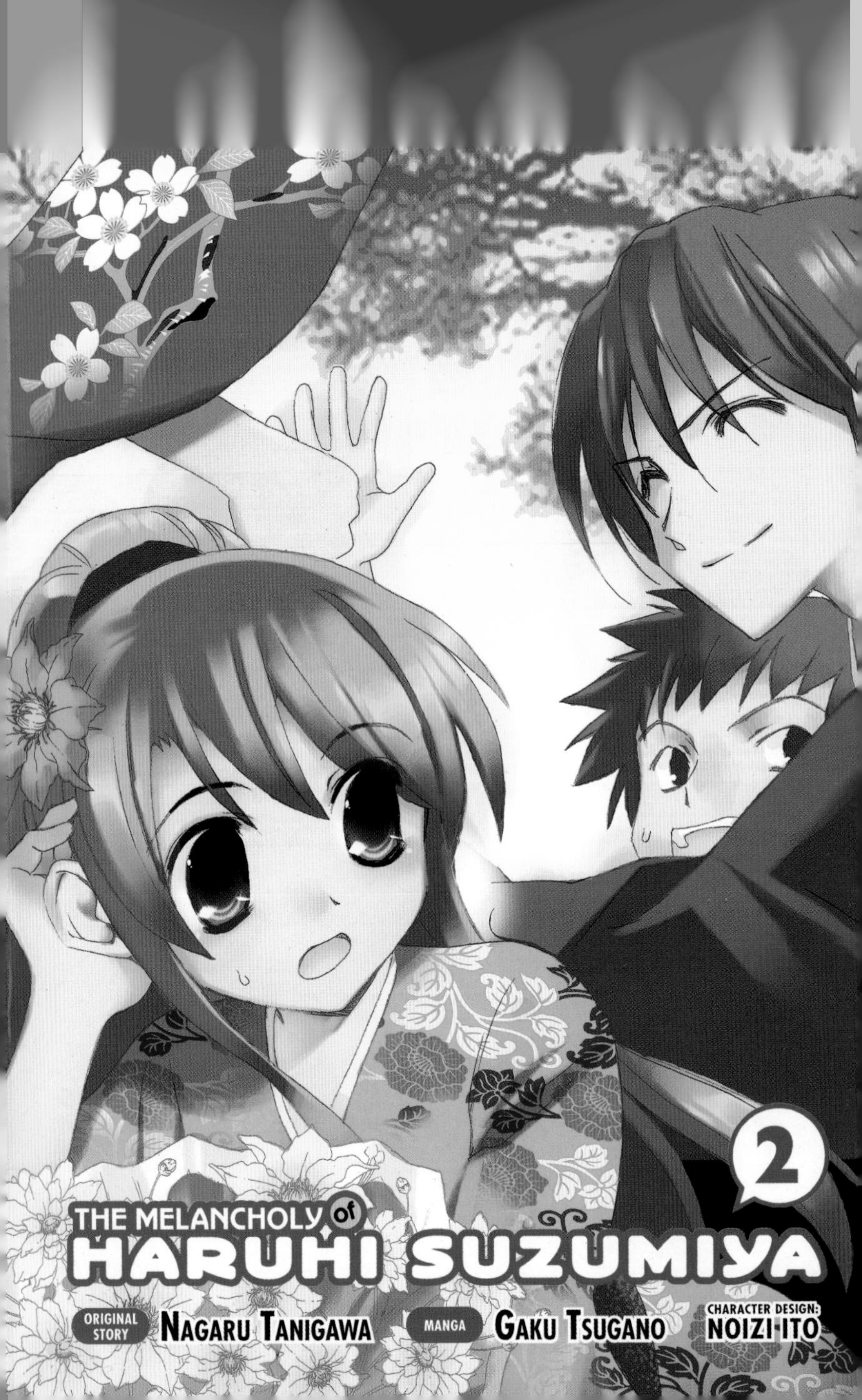
2
THE MELANCHOLY of
HARUHI SUZUMIYA
ORIGINAL STORY
NAGARU TANIGAWA
MANGA
GAKU TSUGANO
CHARACTER DESIGN:
NOIZI ITO

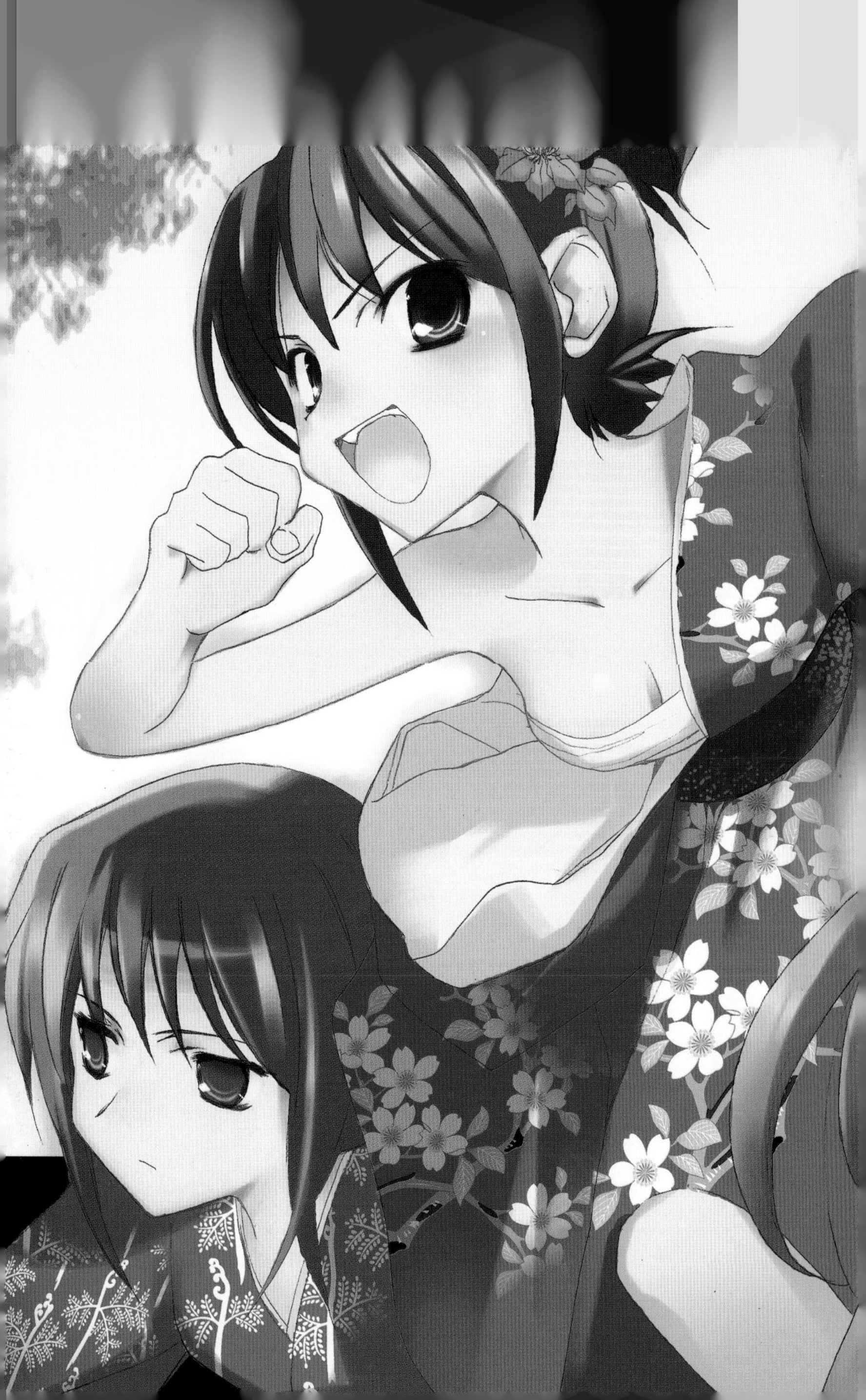

CONTENTS

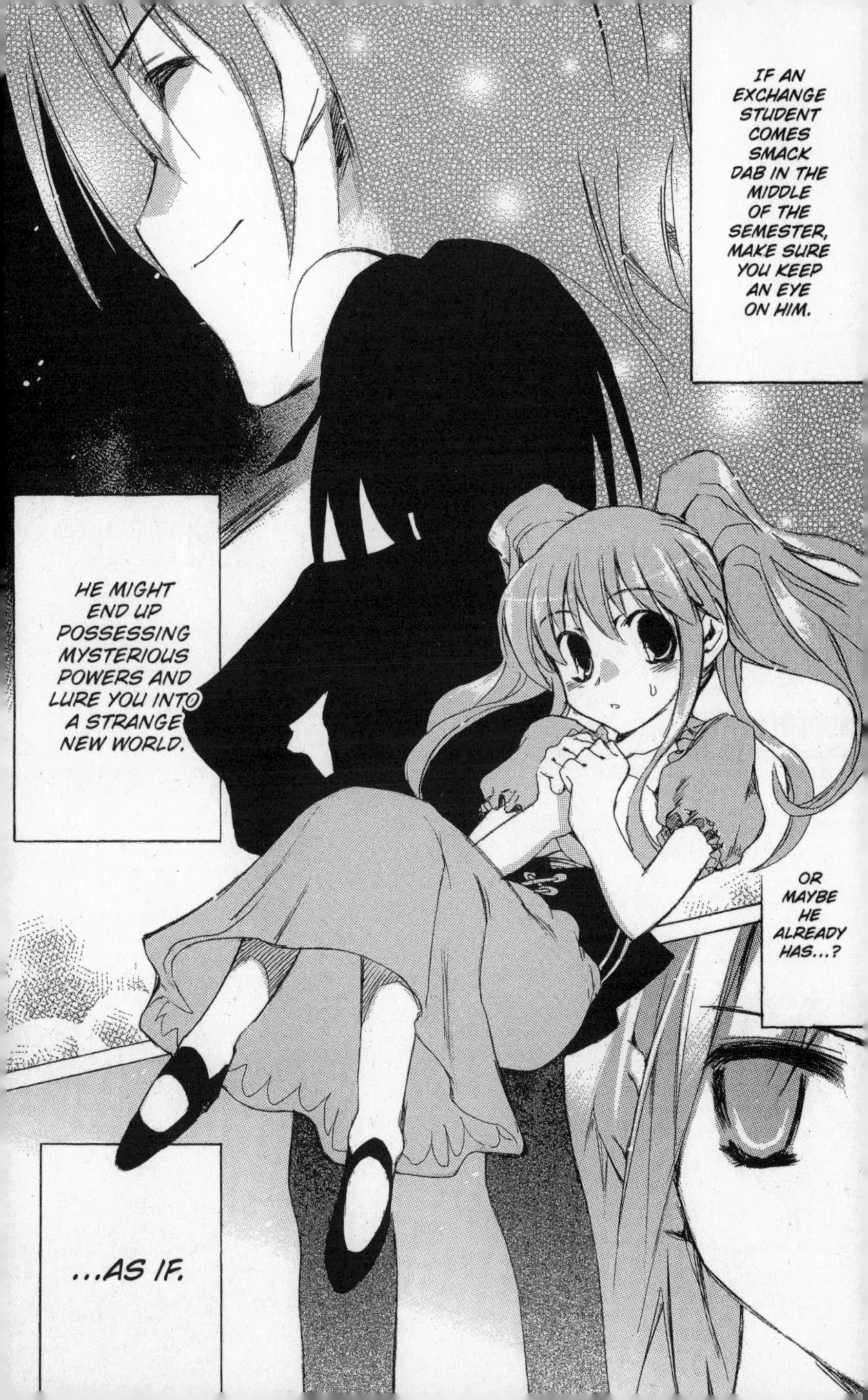
IF AN EXCHANGE STUDENT COMES SMACK DAB IN THE MIDDLE OF THE SEMESTER, MAKE SURE YOU KEEP AN EYE ON HIM.
HE MIGHT END UP POSSESSING MYSTERIOUS POWERS AND LURE YOU INTO A STRANGE NEW WORLD.
OR MAYBE HE ALREADY HAS...?
...AS IF.

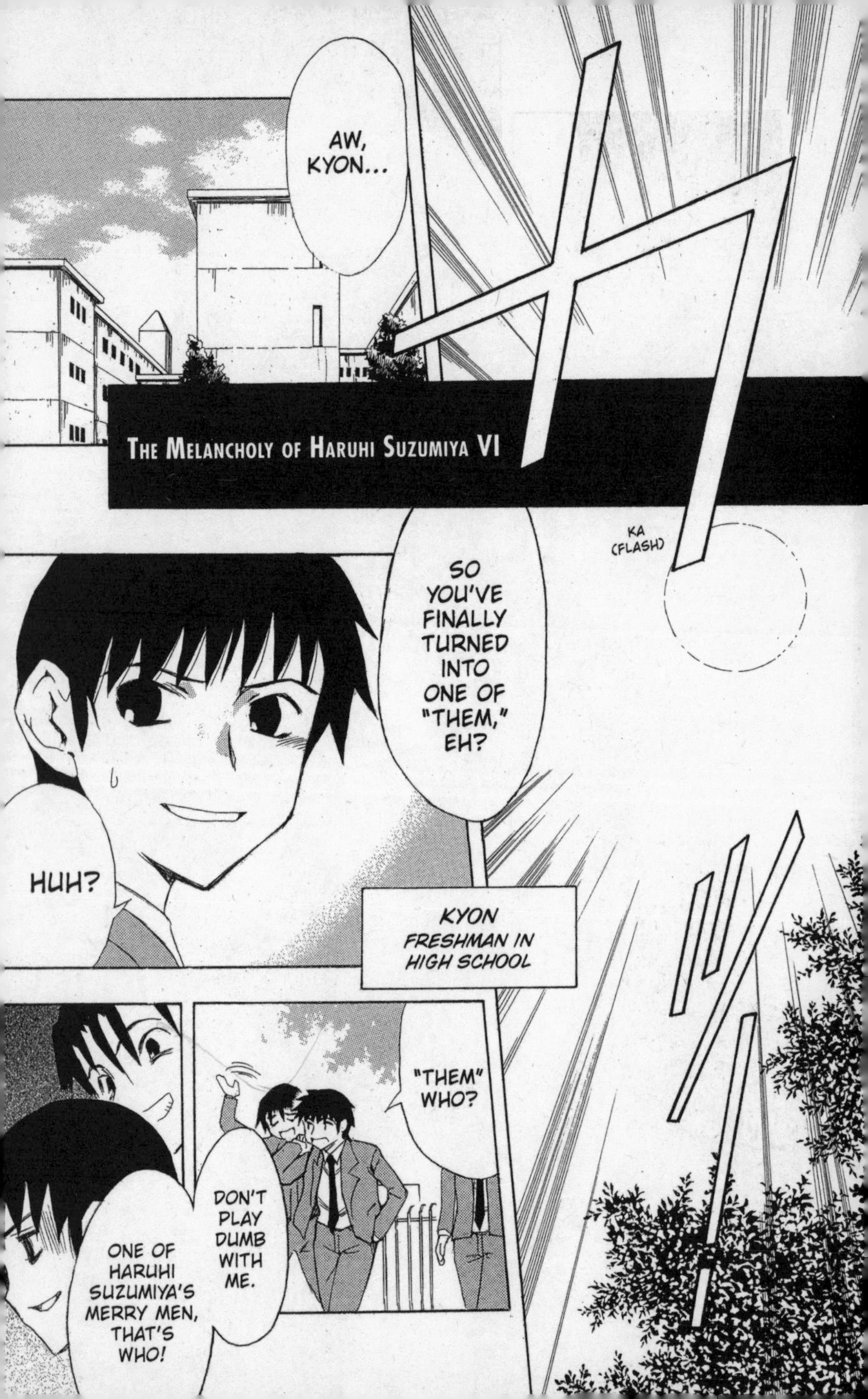
AW, KYON...
THE MELANCHOLY OF HARUHI SUZUMIYA VI
KA (FLASH)
SO YOU'VE FINALLY TURNED INTO ONE OF "THEM," EH?
HUH?
KYON FRESHMAN IN HIGH SCHOOL
"THEM" WHO?
DON'T PLAY DUMB WITH ME.
ONE OF HARUHI SUZUMIYA'S MERRY MEN, THAT'S WHO!

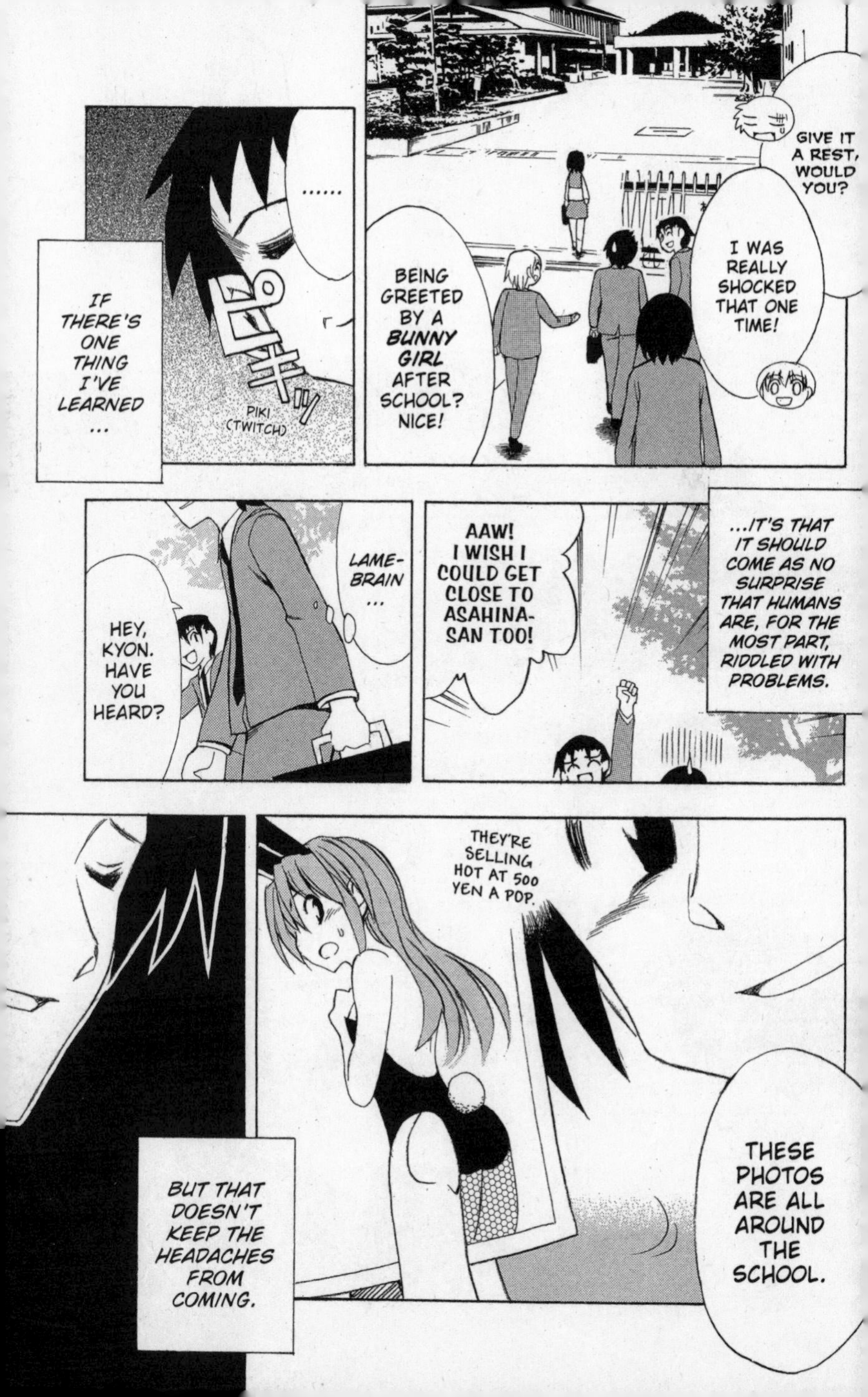
BEING GREETED BY A *BUNNY GIRL* AFTER SCHOOL? NICE!
I WAS REALLY SHOCKED THAT ONE TIME!
GIVE IT A REST, WOULD YOU?
......
PIKI (TWITCH)
IF THERE'S ONE THING I'VE LEARNED ...
...IT'S THAT IT SHOULD COME AS NO SURPRISE THAT HUMANS ARE, FOR THE MOST PART, RIDDLED WITH PROBLEMS.
AAW! I WISH I COULD GET CLOSE TO ASAHINA-SAN TOO!
LAME-BRAIN ...
HEY, KYON. HAVE YOU HEARD?
THESE PHOTOS ARE ALL AROUND THE SCHOOL.
THEY'RE SELLING HOT AT 500 YEN A POP.
BUT THAT DOESN'T KEEP THE HEADACHES FROM COMING.

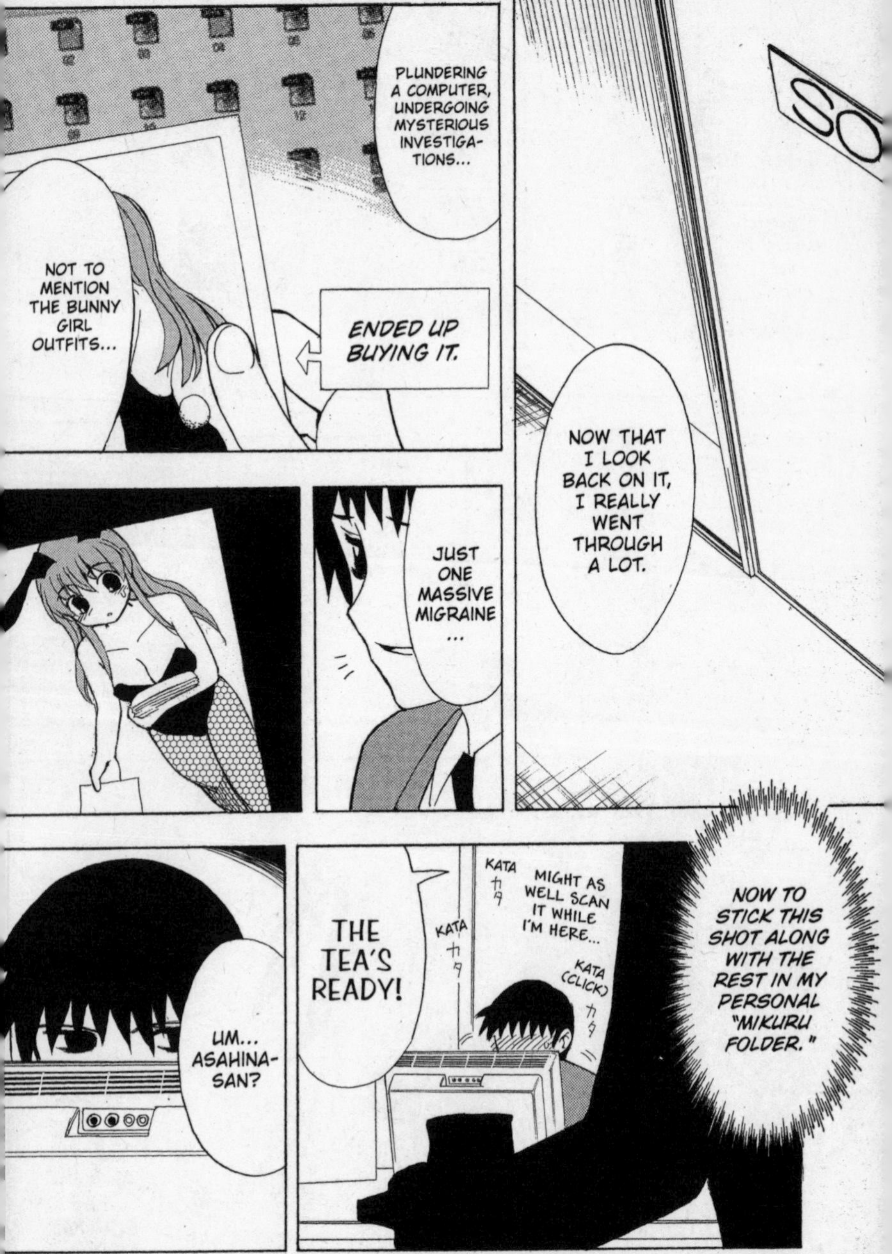
NOW THAT I LOOK BACK ON IT, I REALLY WENT THROUGH A LOT.
PLUNDERING A COMPUTER, UNDERGOING MYSTERIOUS INVESTIGA-TIONS...
NOT TO MENTION THE BUNNY GIRL OUTFITS...
ENDED UP BUYING IT.
JUST ONE MASSIVE MIGRAINE ...
NOW TO STICK THIS SHOT ALONG WITH THE REST IN MY PERSONAL "MIKURU FOLDER."
KATA
MIGHT AS WELL SCAN IT WHILE I'M HERE...
KATA
KATA (CLICK)
THE TEA'S READY!
UM... ASAHINA-SAN?

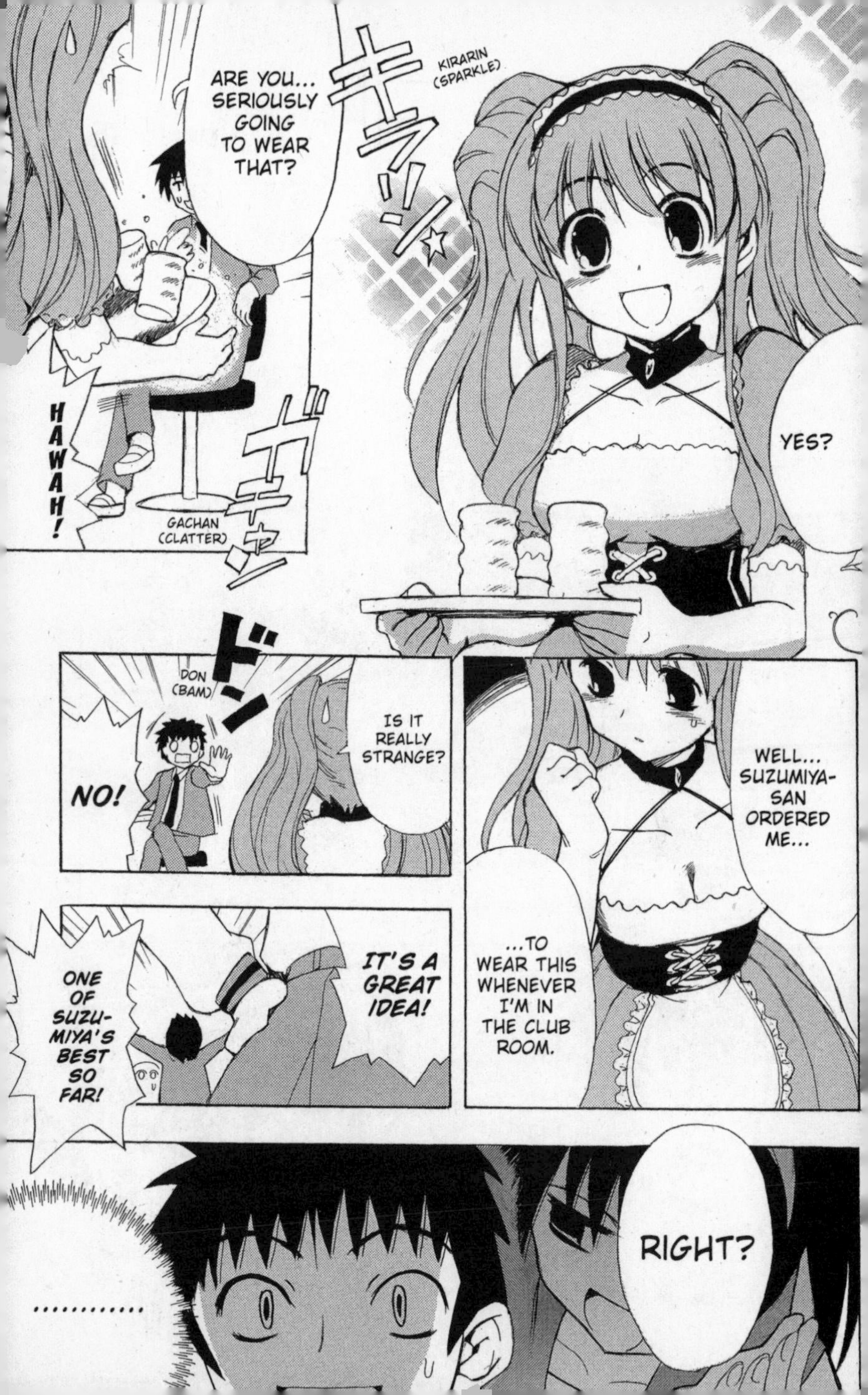
KIRARIN (SPARKLE)
YES?
ARE YOU... SERIOUSLY GOING TO WEAR THAT?
HAWAH!
GACHAN (CLATTER)
WELL... SUZUMIYA-SAN ORDERED ME...
...TO WEAR THIS WHENEVER I'M IN THE CLUB ROOM.
IS IT REALLY STRANGE?
DON (BAM)
NO!
IT'S A GREAT IDEA!
ONE OF SUZU-MIYA'S BEST SO FAR!
RIGHT?
....

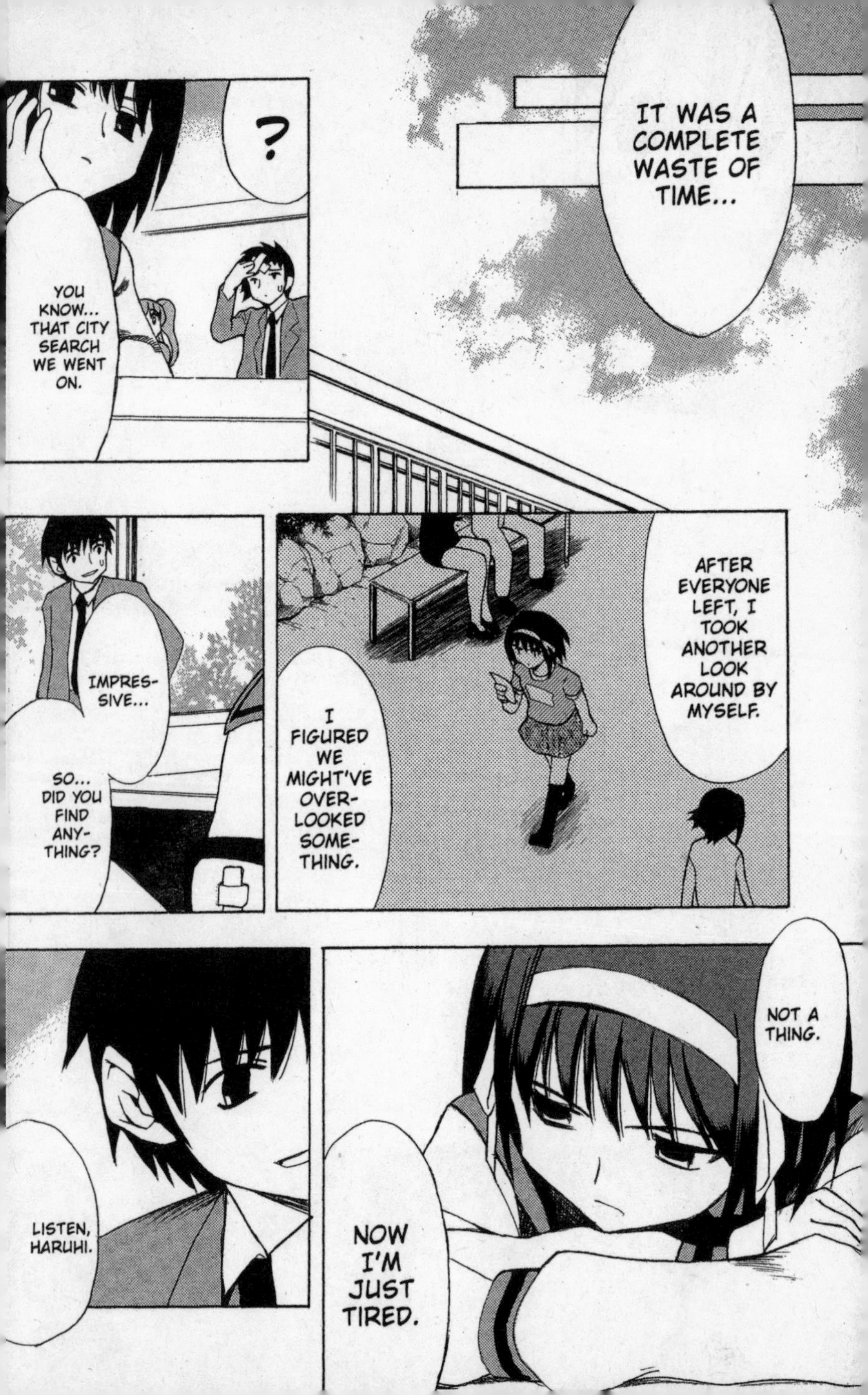
?
YOU KNOW... THAT CITY SEARCH WE WENT ON.
IT WAS A COMPLETE WASTE OF TIME...
AFTER EVERYONE LEFT, I TOOK ANOTHER LOOK AROUND BY MYSELF.
I FIGURED WE MIGHT'VE OVER-LOOKED SOME-THING.
IMPRES-SIVE...
SO... DID YOU FIND ANY-THING?
NOT A THING.
NOW I'M JUST TIRED.
LISTEN, HARUHI.

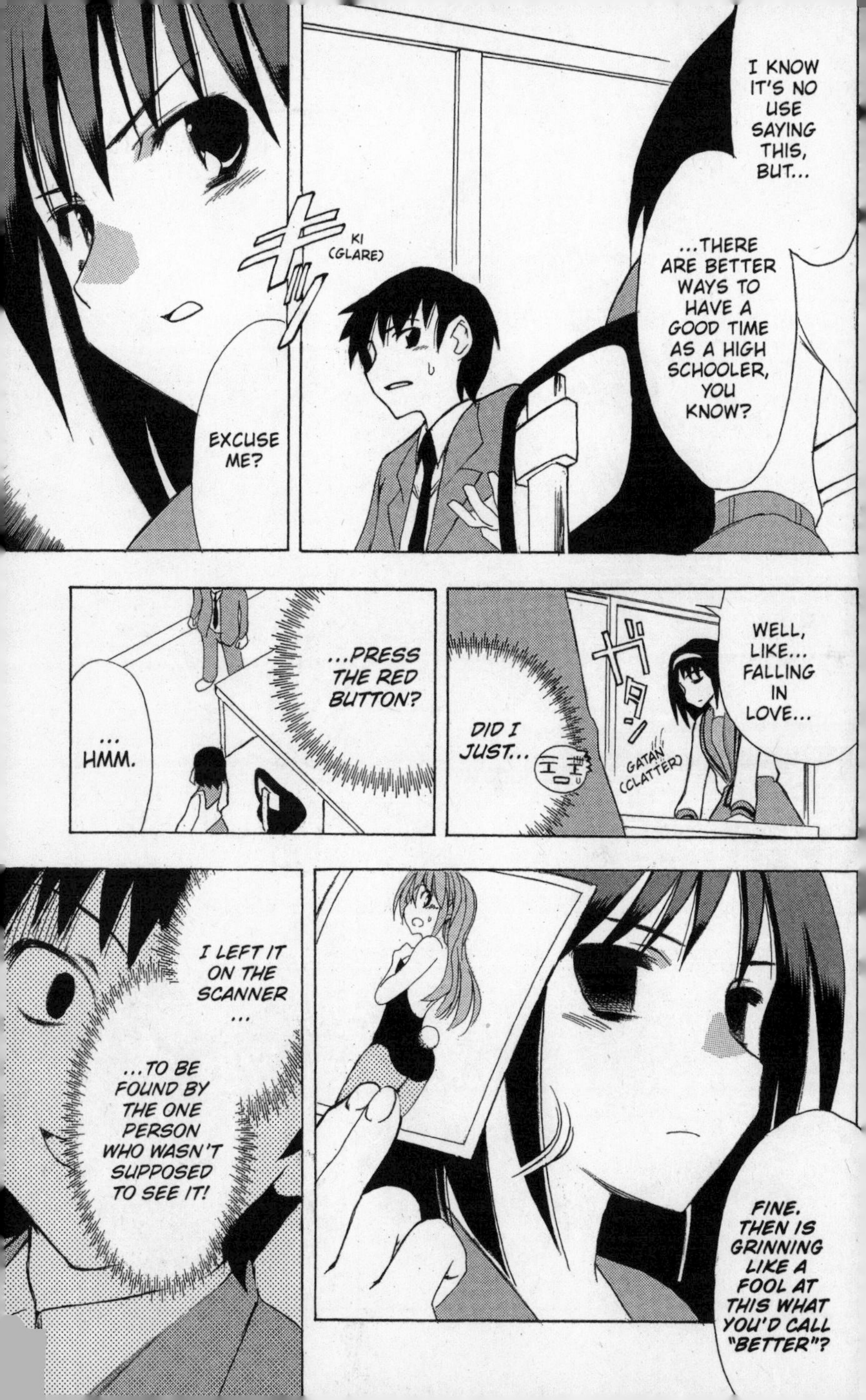
I KNOW IT'S NO USE SAYING THIS, BUT...
...THERE ARE BETTER WAYS TO HAVE A GOOD TIME AS A HIGH SCHOOLER, YOU KNOW?
KI (GLARE)
EXCUSE ME?
WELL, LIKE... FALLING IN LOVE...
GATAN (CLATTER)
DID I JUST...
...PRESS THE RED BUTTON?
... HMM.
FINE. THEN IS GRINNING LIKE A FOOL AT THIS WHAT YOU'D CALL "BETTER"?
I LEFT IT ON THE SCANNER ...
...TO BE FOUND BY THE ONE PERSON WHO WASN'T SUPPOSED TO SEE IT!

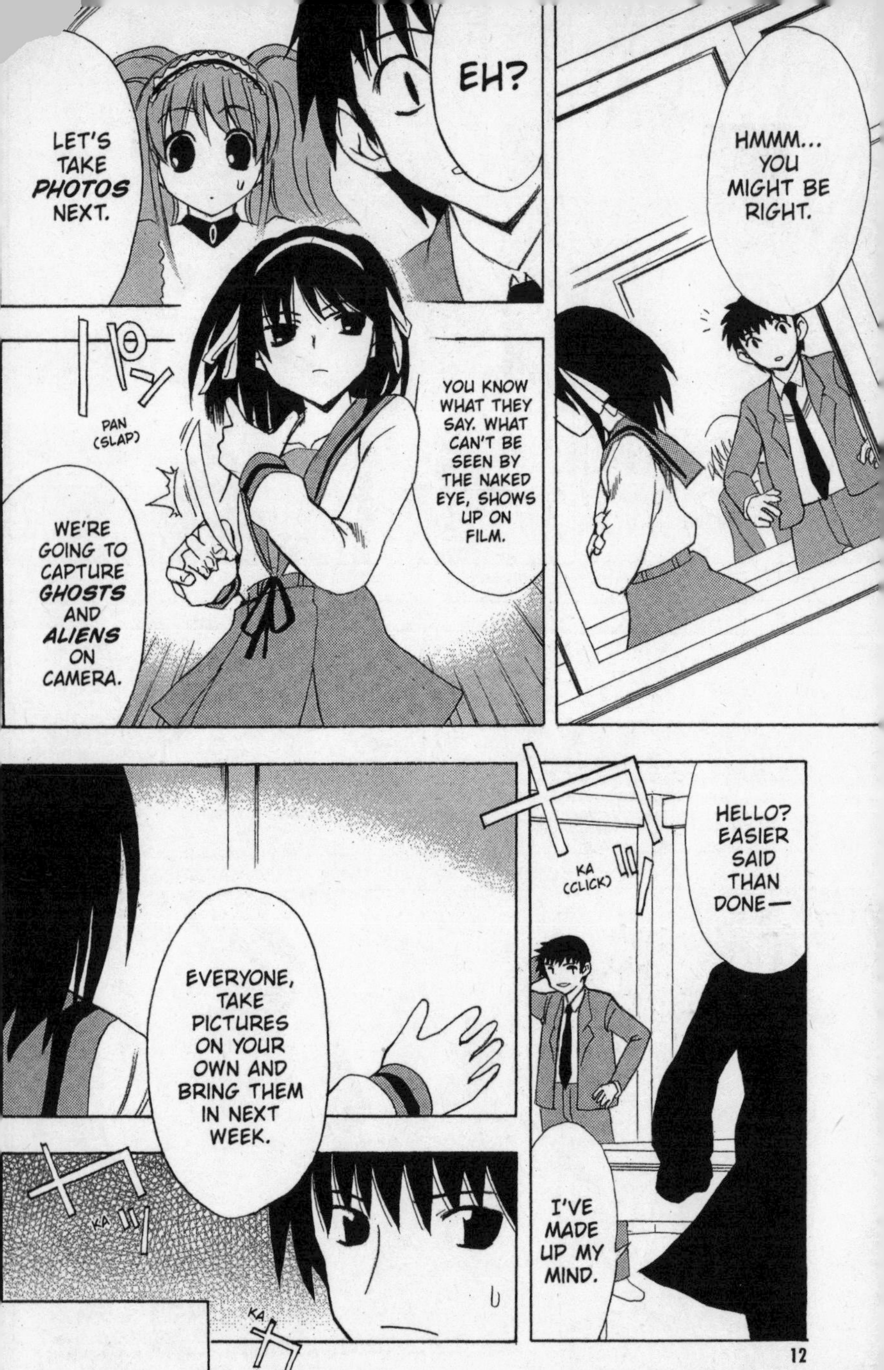
LET'S TAKE PHOTOS NEXT.
EH?
PAN (SLAP)
WE'RE GOING TO CAPTURE GHOSTS AND ALIENS ON CAMERA.
YOU KNOW WHAT THEY SAY. WHAT CAN'T BE SEEN BY THE NAKED EYE, SHOWS UP ON FILM.
HMMM... YOU MIGHT BE RIGHT.
HELLO? EASIER SAID THAN DONE—
KA (CLICK)
I'VE MADE UP MY MIND.
EVERYONE, TAKE PICTURES ON YOUR OWN AND BRING THEM IN NEXT WEEK.
KA
KA

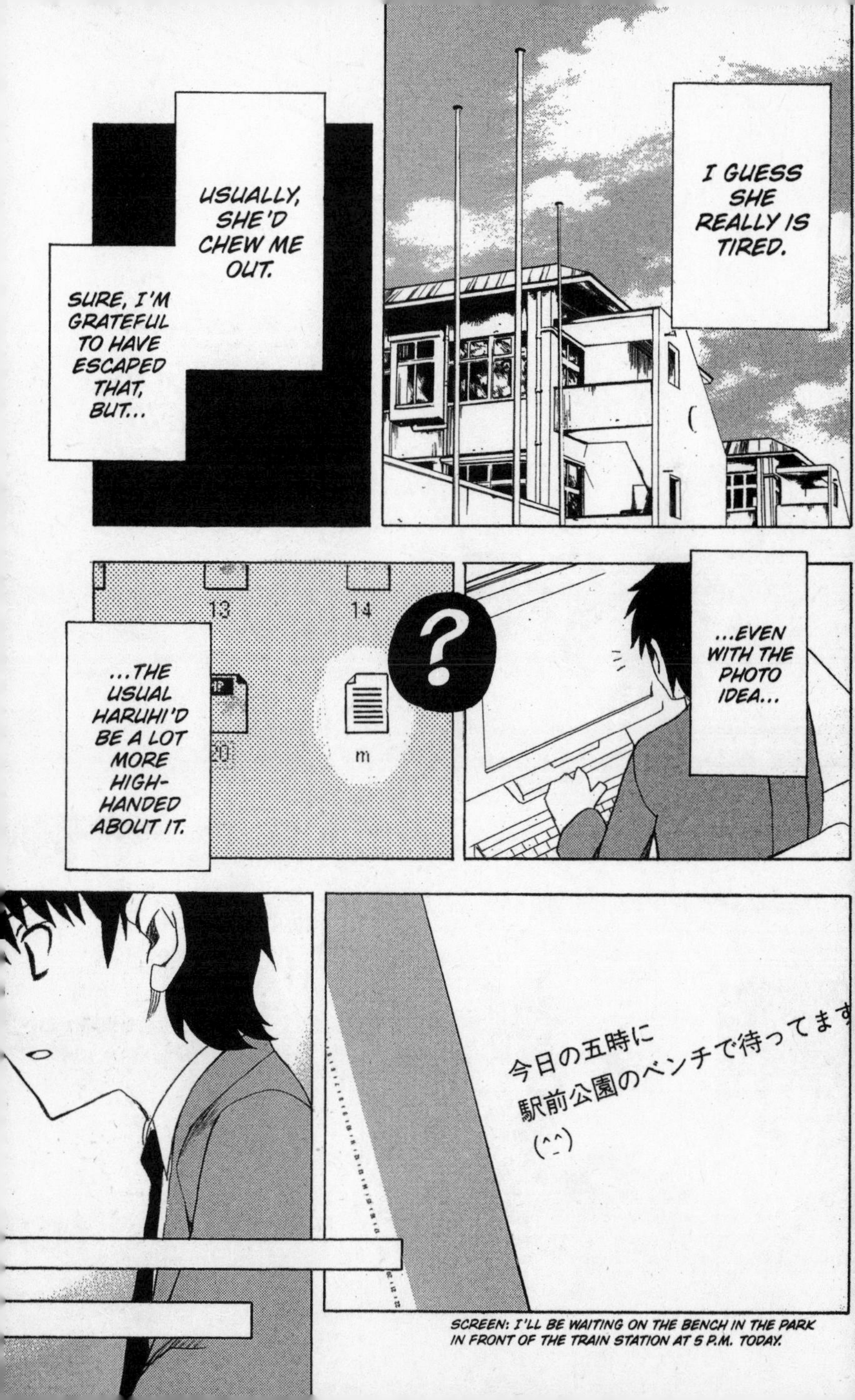
I GUESS SHE REALLY IS TIRED.
USUALLY, SHE'D CHEW ME OUT.
SURE, I'M GRATEFUL TO HAVE ESCAPED THAT, BUT...
...EVEN WITH THE PHOTO IDEA...
?
...THE USUAL HARUHI'D BE A LOT MORE HIGH-HANDED ABOUT IT.
今日の五時に
駅前公園のベンチで待ってます
(^_^)

SCREEN: I'LL BE WAITING ON THE BENCH IN THE PARK IN FRONT OF THE TRAIN STATION AT 5 P.M. TODAY.

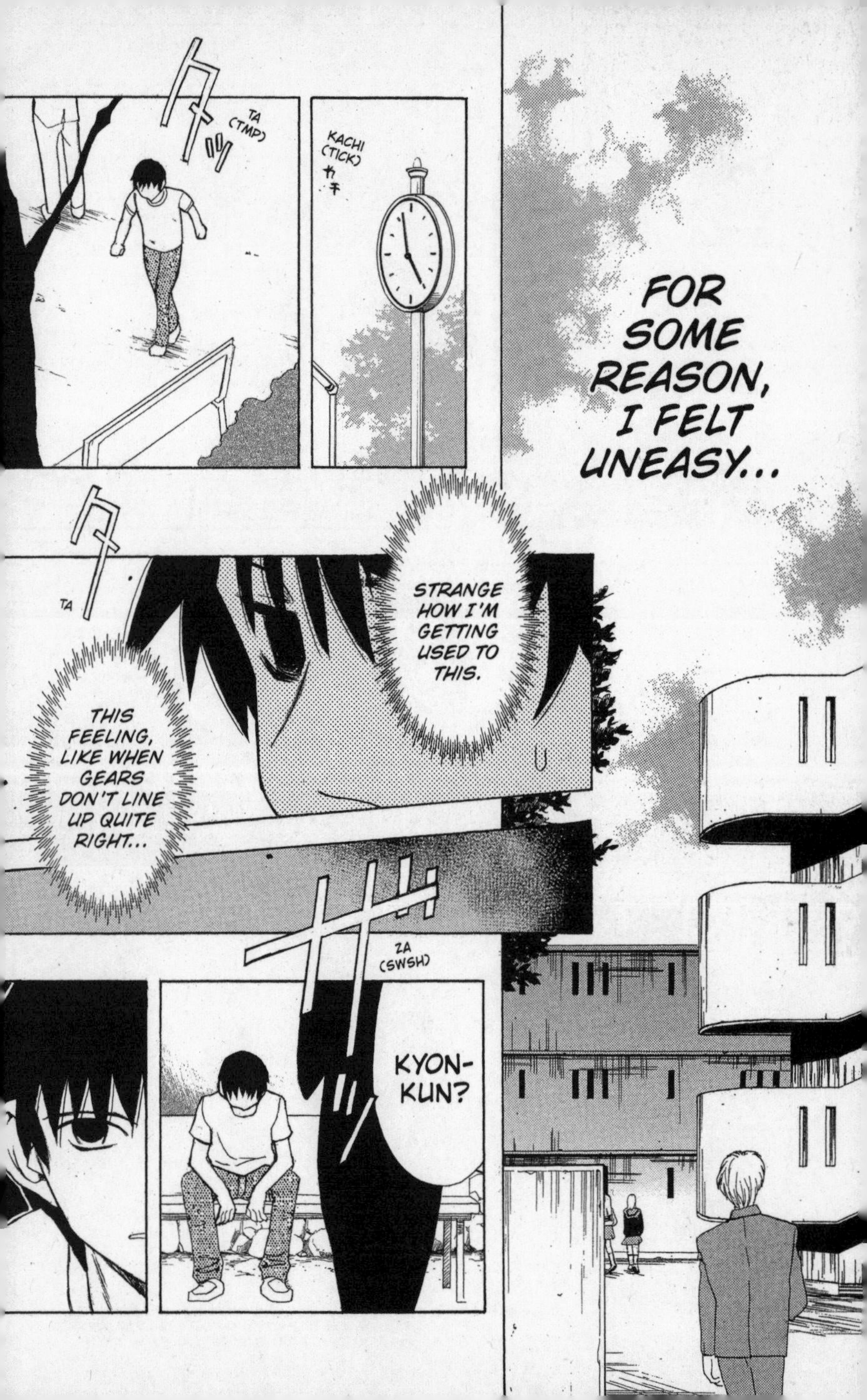
FOR SOME REASON, I FELT UNEASY...
KACHI (TICK)
TA (TMP)
TA
STRANGE HOW I'M GETTING USED TO THIS.
THIS FEELING, LIKE WHEN GEARS DON'T LINE UP QUITE RIGHT...
ZA (SWSH)
KYON-KUN?

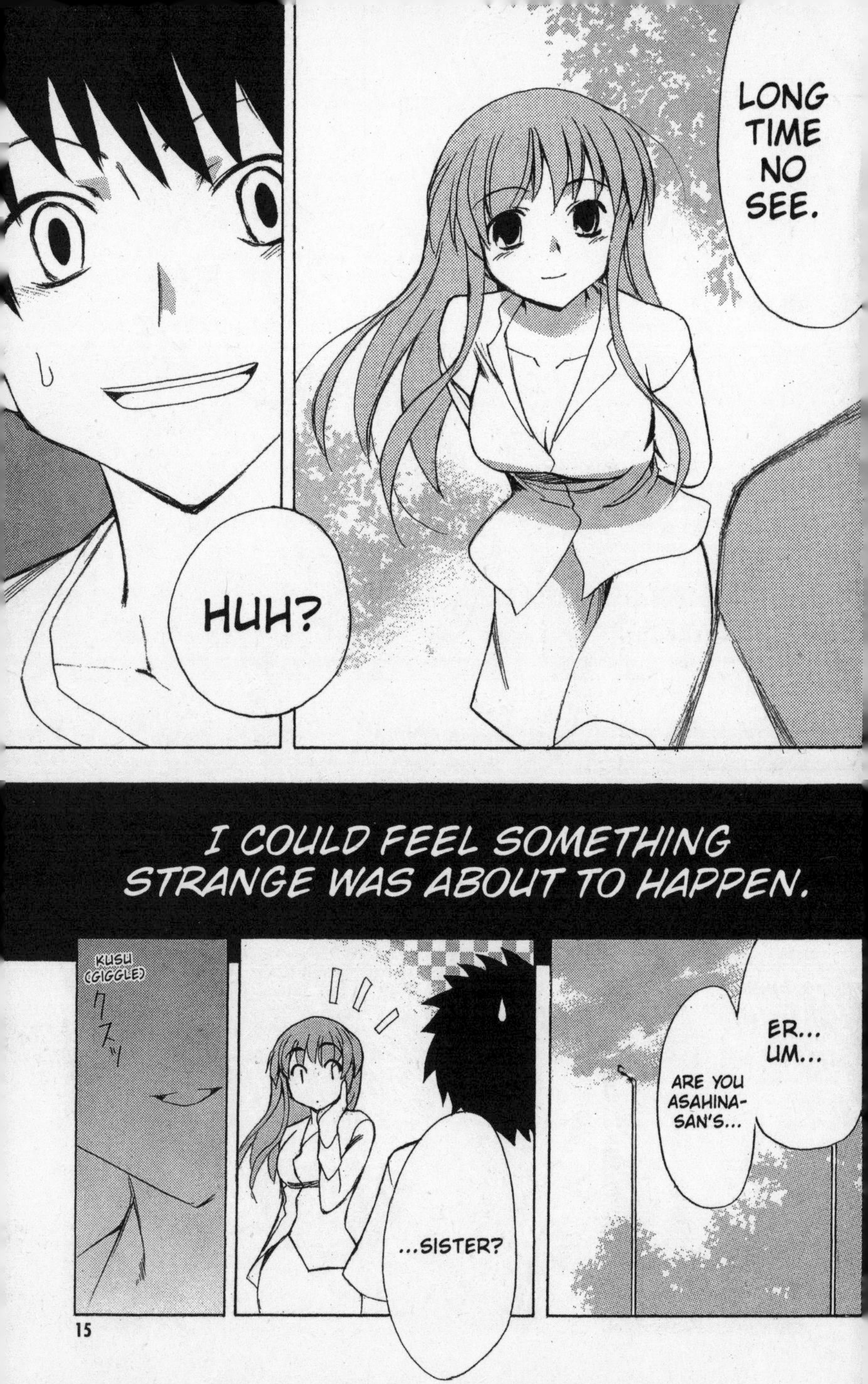
LONG TIME NO SEE.
HUH?
I COULD FEEL SOMETHING STRANGE WAS ABOUT TO HAPPEN.
ER... UM...
ARE YOU ASAHINA-SAN'S...
...SISTER?
KUSU (GIGGLE)
クスッ

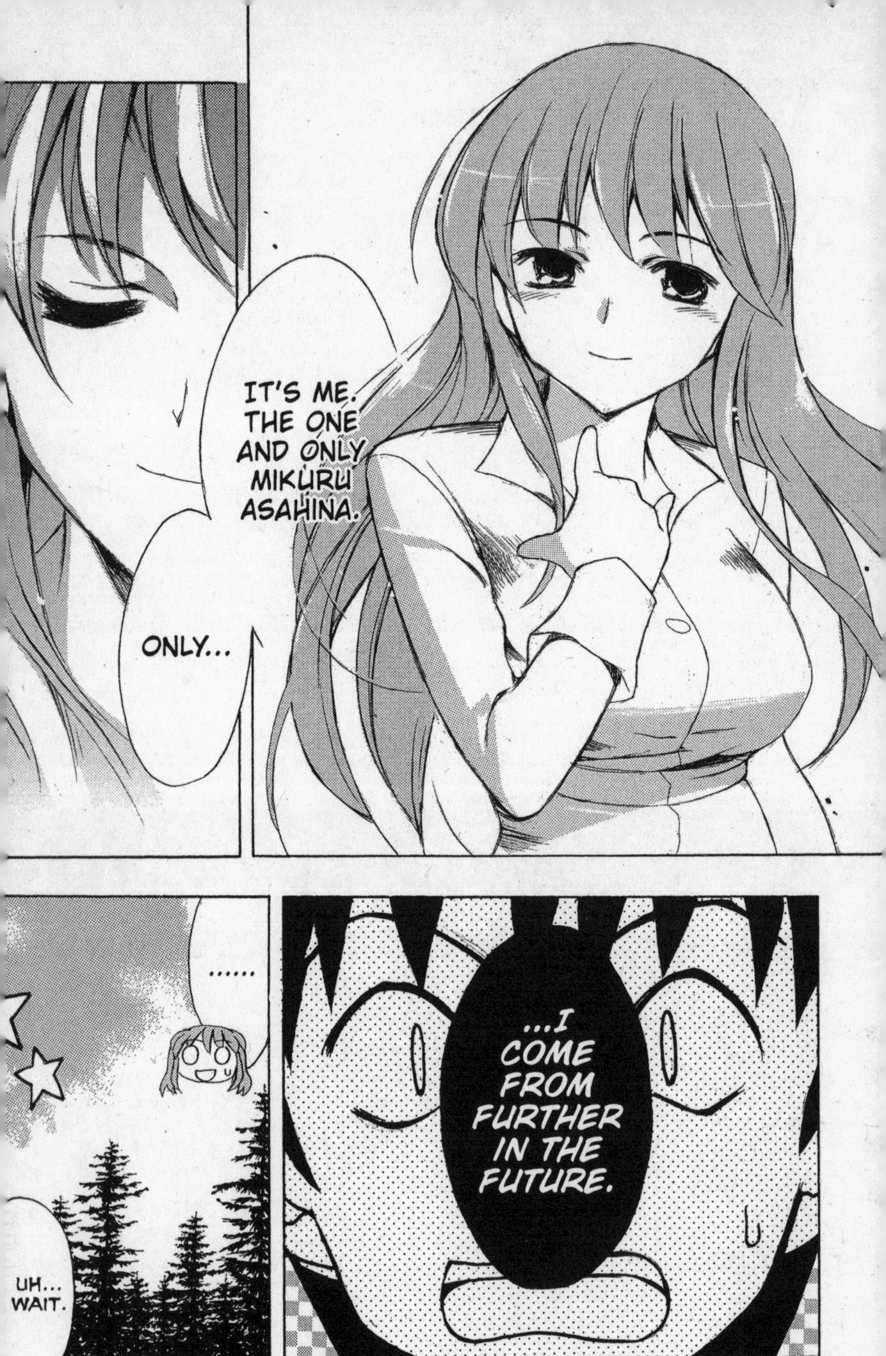
IT'S ME. THE ONE AND ONLY MIKURU ASAHINA.
ONLY...
...I COME FROM FURTHER IN THE FUTURE.
......
UH... WAIT.

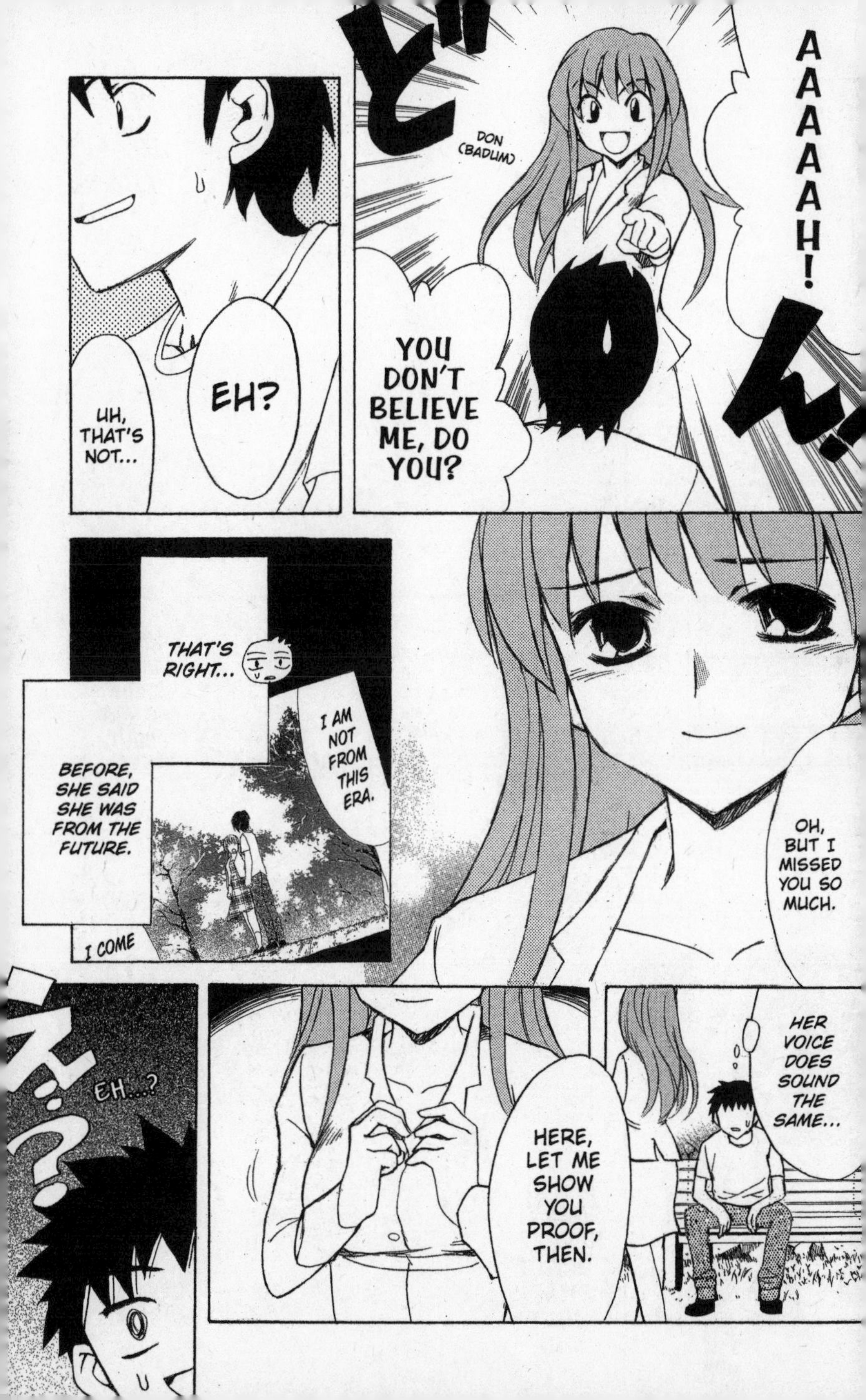
AAAAAAH!
どん!!
DON (BADUM)
YOU DON'T BELIEVE ME, DO YOU?
EH?
UH, THAT'S NOT...
OH, BUT I MISSED YOU SO MUCH.
THAT'S RIGHT...
I AM NOT FROM THIS ERA.
BEFORE, SHE SAID SHE WAS FROM THE FUTURE.
I COME
HER VOICE DOES SOUND THE SAME...
HERE, LET ME SHOW YOU PROOF, THEN.
EH...?

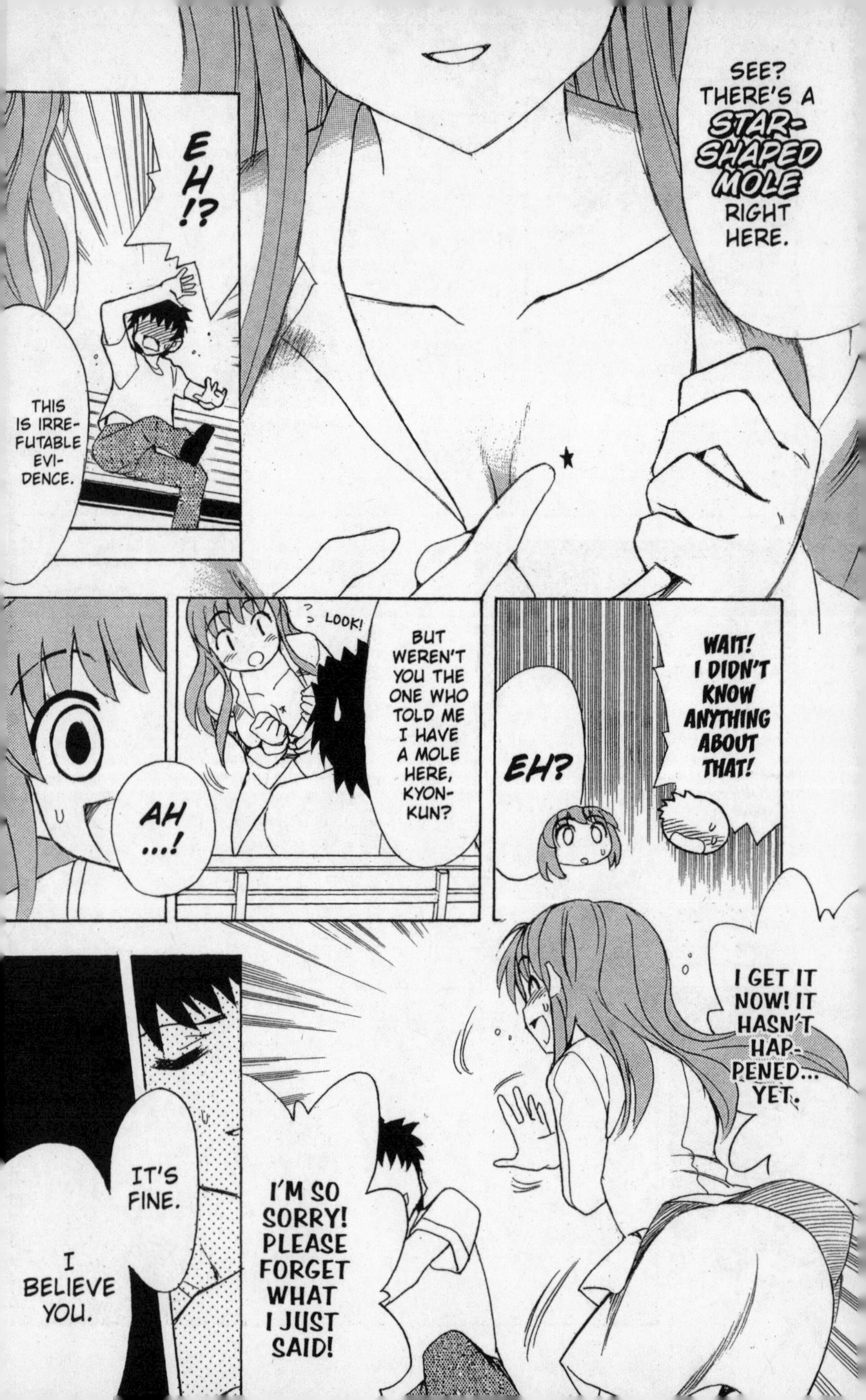
SEE? THERE'S A STAR-SHAPED MOLE RIGHT HERE.
EH!?
THIS IS IRREFUTABLE EVIDENCE.
WAIT! I DIDN'T KNOW ANYTHING ABOUT THAT!
EH?
LOOK!
BUT WEREN'T YOU THE ONE WHO TOLD ME I HAVE A MOLE HERE, KYON-KUN?
AH ...!
I GET IT NOW! IT HASN'T HAPPENED... YET.
I'M SO SORRY! PLEASE FORGET WHAT I JUST SAID!
IT'S FINE.
I BELIEVE YOU.

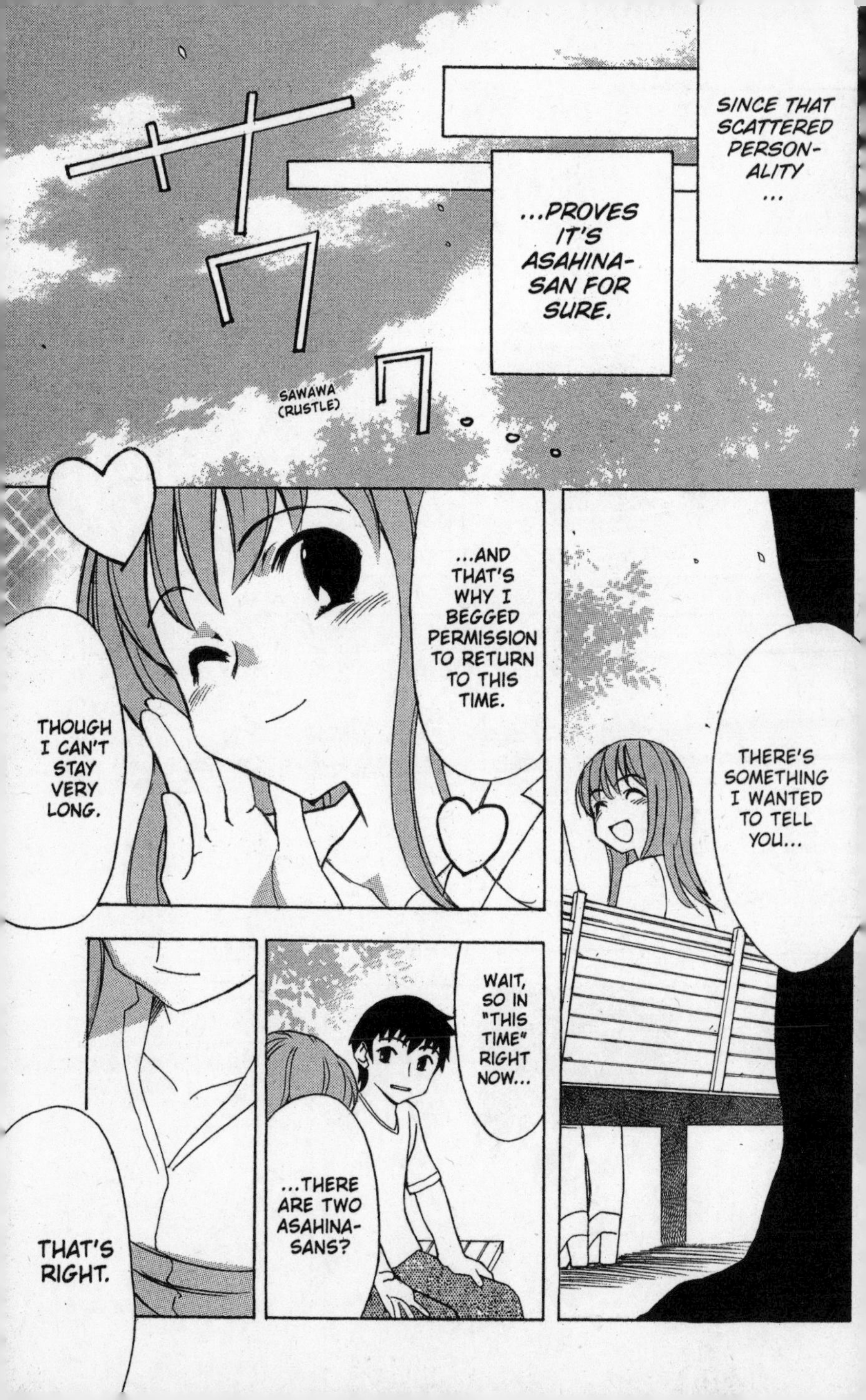
SINCE THAT SCATTERED PERSON-ALITY ...
...PROVES IT'S ASAHINA-SAN FOR SURE.
SAWAWA (RUSTLE)
THERE'S SOMETHING I WANTED TO TELL YOU...
...AND THAT'S WHY I BEGGED PERMISSION TO RETURN TO THIS TIME.
THOUGH I CAN'T STAY VERY LONG.
WAIT, SO IN "THIS TIME" RIGHT NOW...
...THERE ARE TWO ASAHINA-SANS?
THAT'S RIGHT.

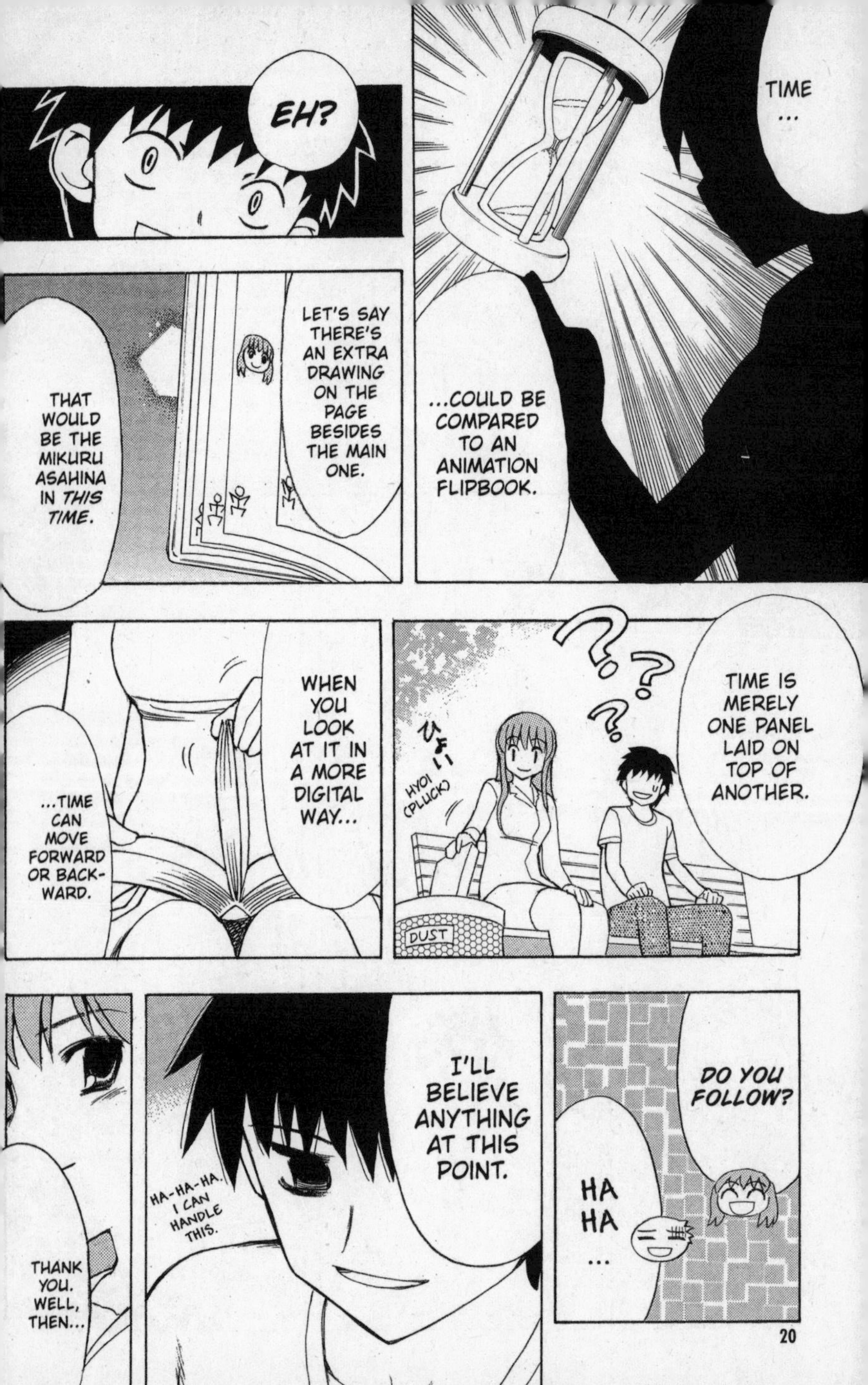
TIME ...
...COULD BE COMPARED TO AN ANIMATION FLIPBOOK.
EH?
LET'S SAY THERE'S AN EXTRA DRAWING ON THE PAGE BESIDES THE MAIN ONE.
THAT WOULD BE THE MIKURU ASAHINA IN *THIS TIME*.
TIME IS MERELY ONE PANEL LAID ON TOP OF ANOTHER.
ひょい
HYOI (PLUCK)
DUST
WHEN YOU LOOK AT IT IN A MORE DIGITAL WAY...
...TIME CAN MOVE FORWARD OR BACK-WARD.
DO YOU FOLLOW?
HA HA ...
I'LL BELIEVE ANYTHING AT THIS POINT.
HA-HA-HA. I CAN HANDLE THIS.
THANK YOU. WELL, THEN...

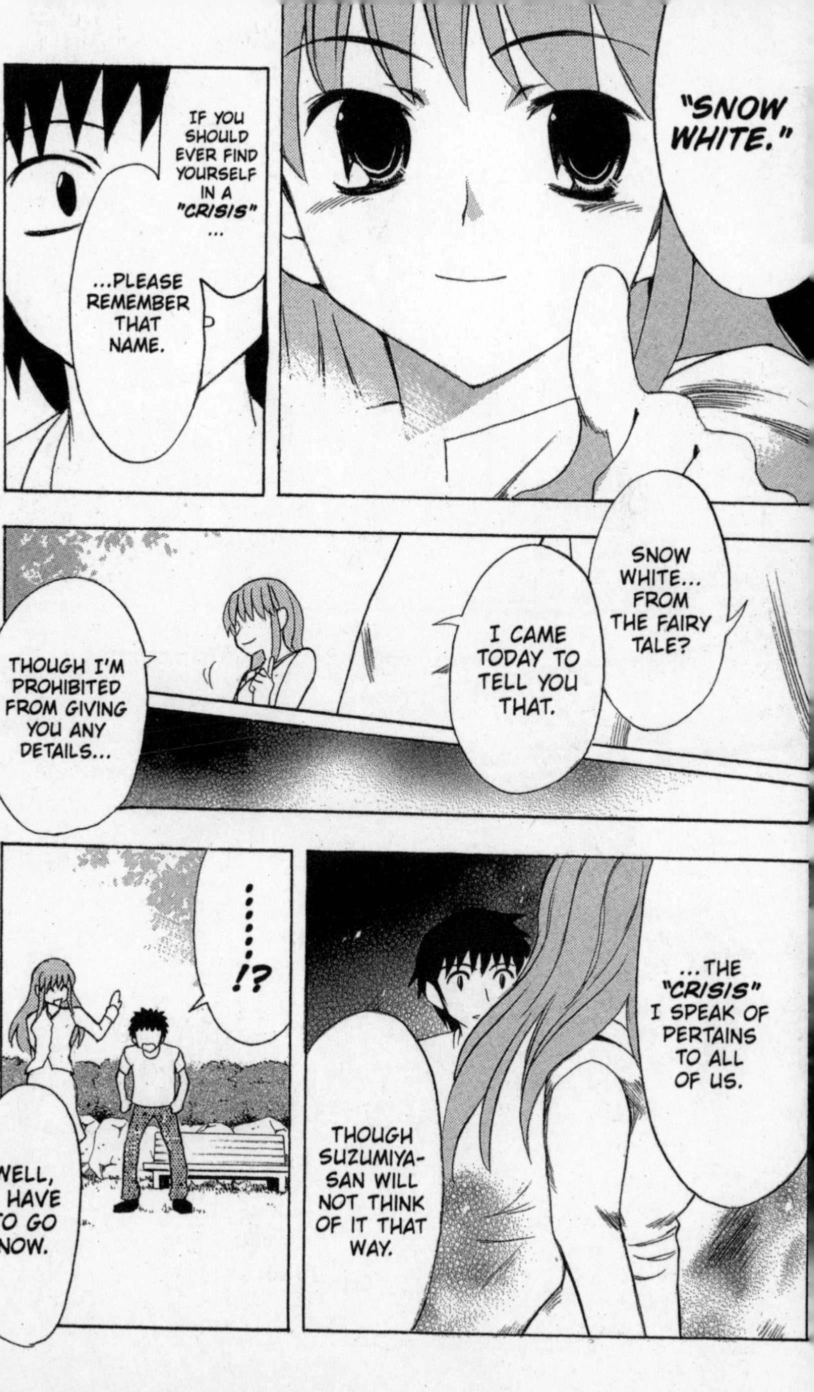
"SNOW WHITE."
IF YOU SHOULD EVER FIND YOURSELF IN A "CRISIS"...
...PLEASE REMEMBER THAT NAME.
SNOW WHITE... FROM THE FAIRY TALE?
I CAME TODAY TO TELL YOU THAT.
THOUGH I'M PROHIBITED FROM GIVING YOU ANY DETAILS...
...THE "CRISIS" I SPEAK OF PERTAINS TO ALL OF US.
THOUGH SUZUMIYA-SAN WILL NOT THINK OF IT THAT WAY.
......!?
WELL, I HAVE TO GO NOW.

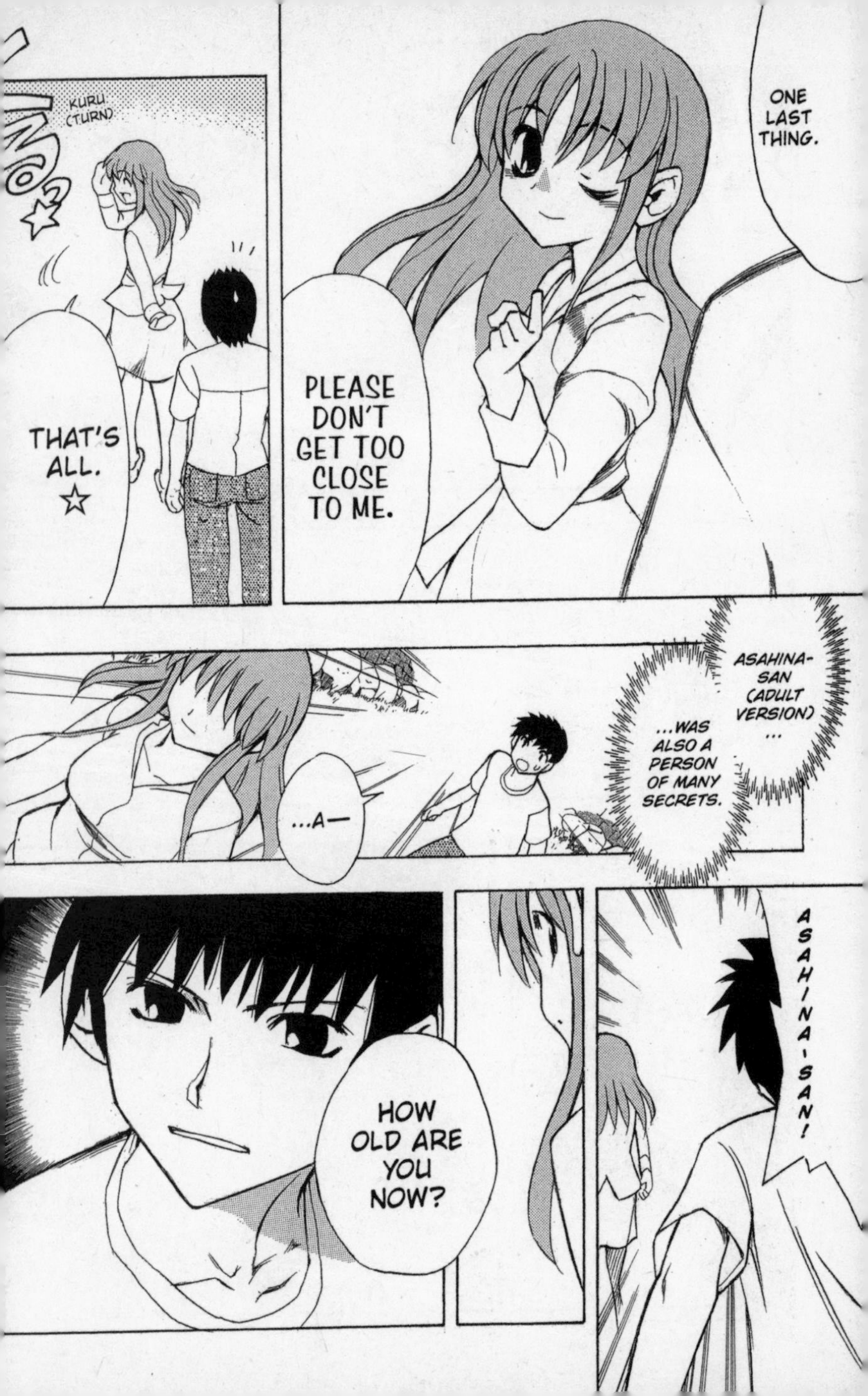
ONE LAST THING.
PLEASE DON'T GET TOO CLOSE TO ME.
KURU (TURN)
THAT'S ALL. ☆
ASAHINA-SAN (ADULT VERSION) ...
...WAS ALSO A PERSON OF MANY SECRETS.
...A—
ASAHINA-SAN!
HOW OLD ARE YOU NOW?

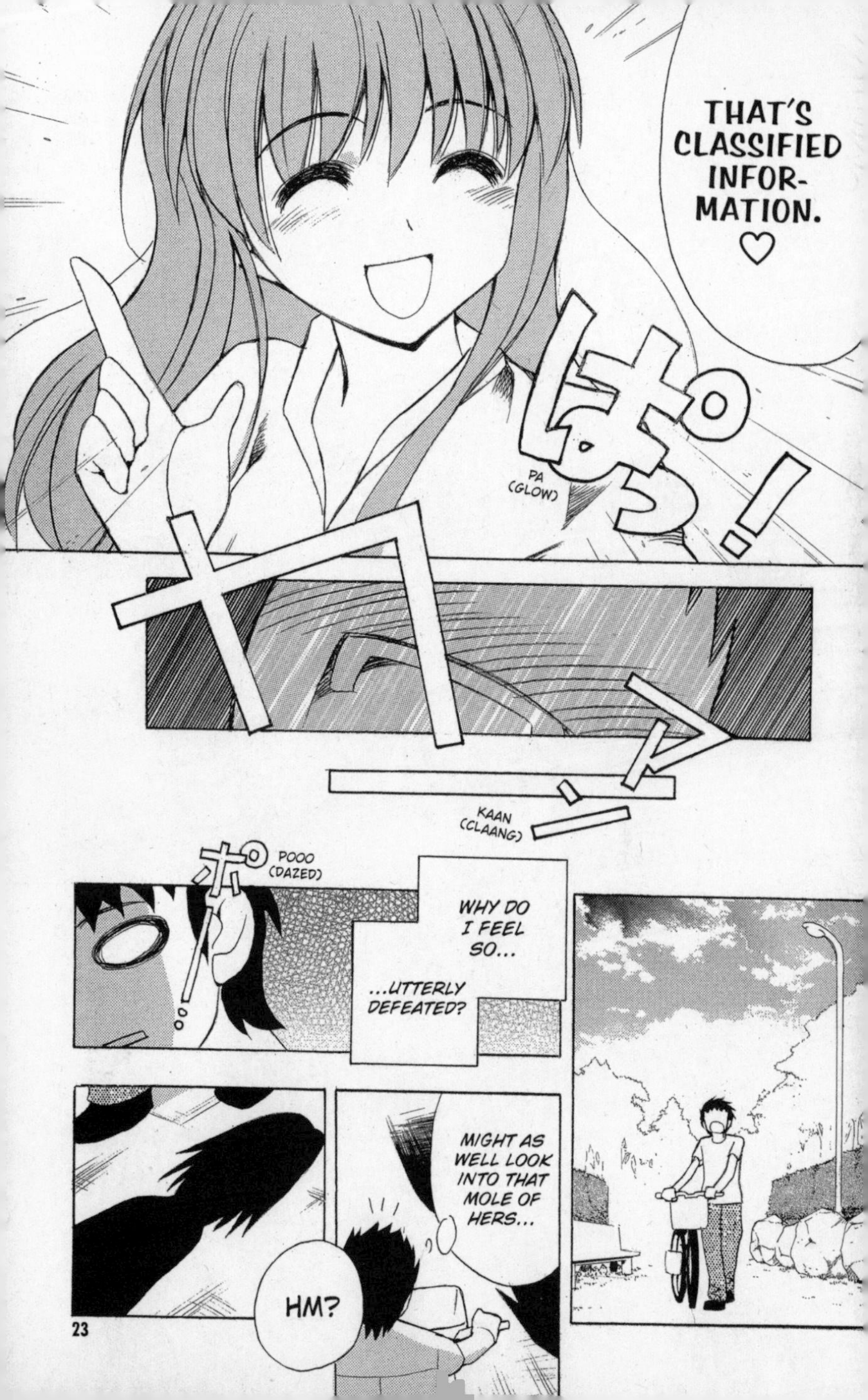
THAT'S CLASSIFIED INFOR-MATION. ♡
PA (GLOW)
KAAN (CLAANG)
POOO (DAZED)
WHY DO I FEEL SO...
...UTTERLY DEFEATED?
MIGHT AS WELL LOOK INTO THAT MOLE OF HERS...
HM?

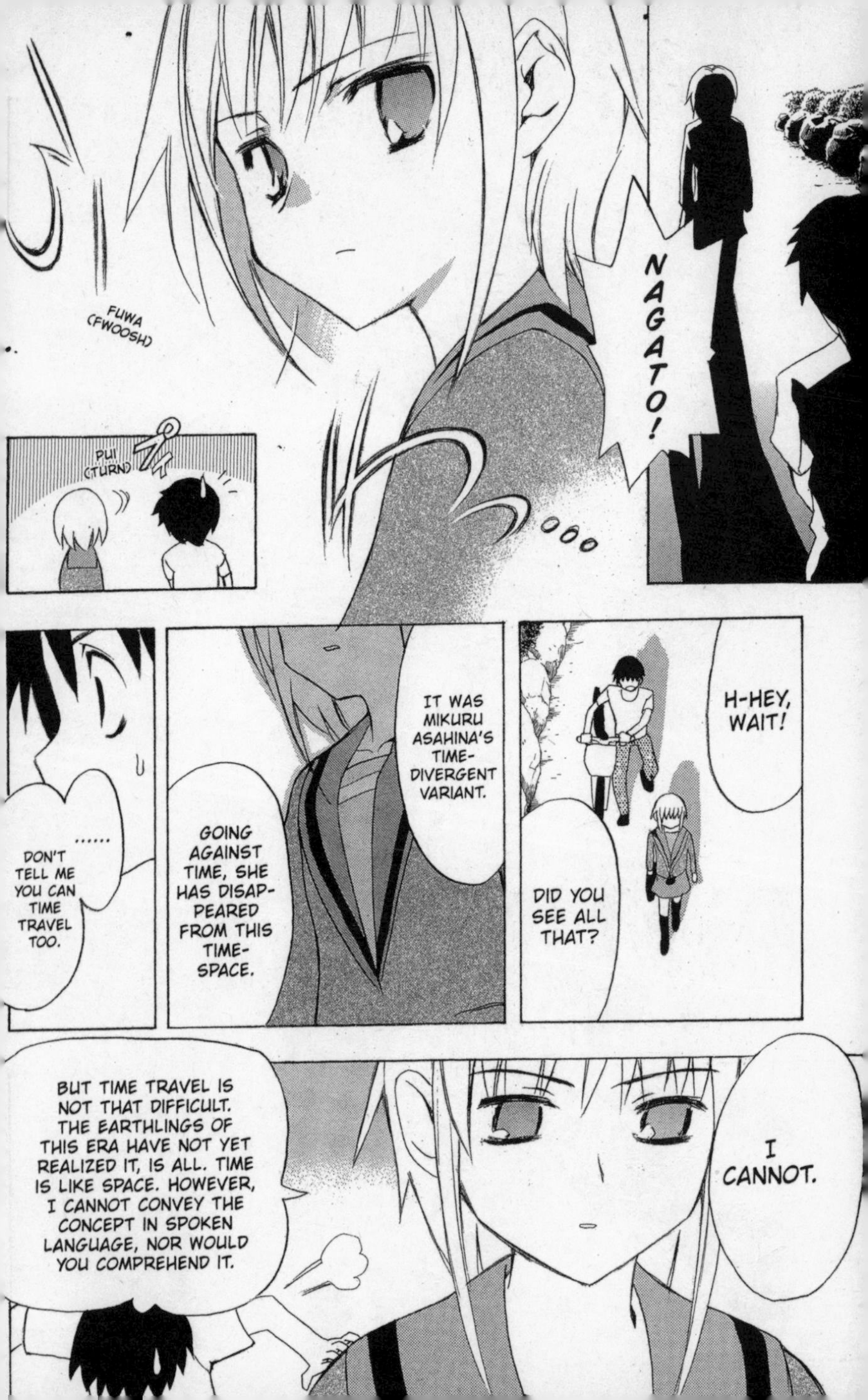
NAGATO!
FUWA (FWOOSH)
PUI (TURN)
H-HEY, WAIT!
DID YOU SEE ALL THAT?
IT WAS MIKURU ASAHINA'S TIME-DIVERGENT VARIANT.
GOING AGAINST TIME, SHE HAS DISAPPEARED FROM THIS TIME-SPACE.
......
DON'T TELL ME YOU CAN TIME TRAVEL TOO.
I CANNOT.
BUT TIME TRAVEL IS NOT THAT DIFFICULT. THE EARTHLINGS OF THIS ERA HAVE NOT YET REALIZED IT, IS ALL. TIME IS LIKE SPACE. HOWEVER, I CANNOT CONVEY THE CONCEPT IN SPOKEN LANGUAGE, NOR WOULD YOU COMPREHEND IT.

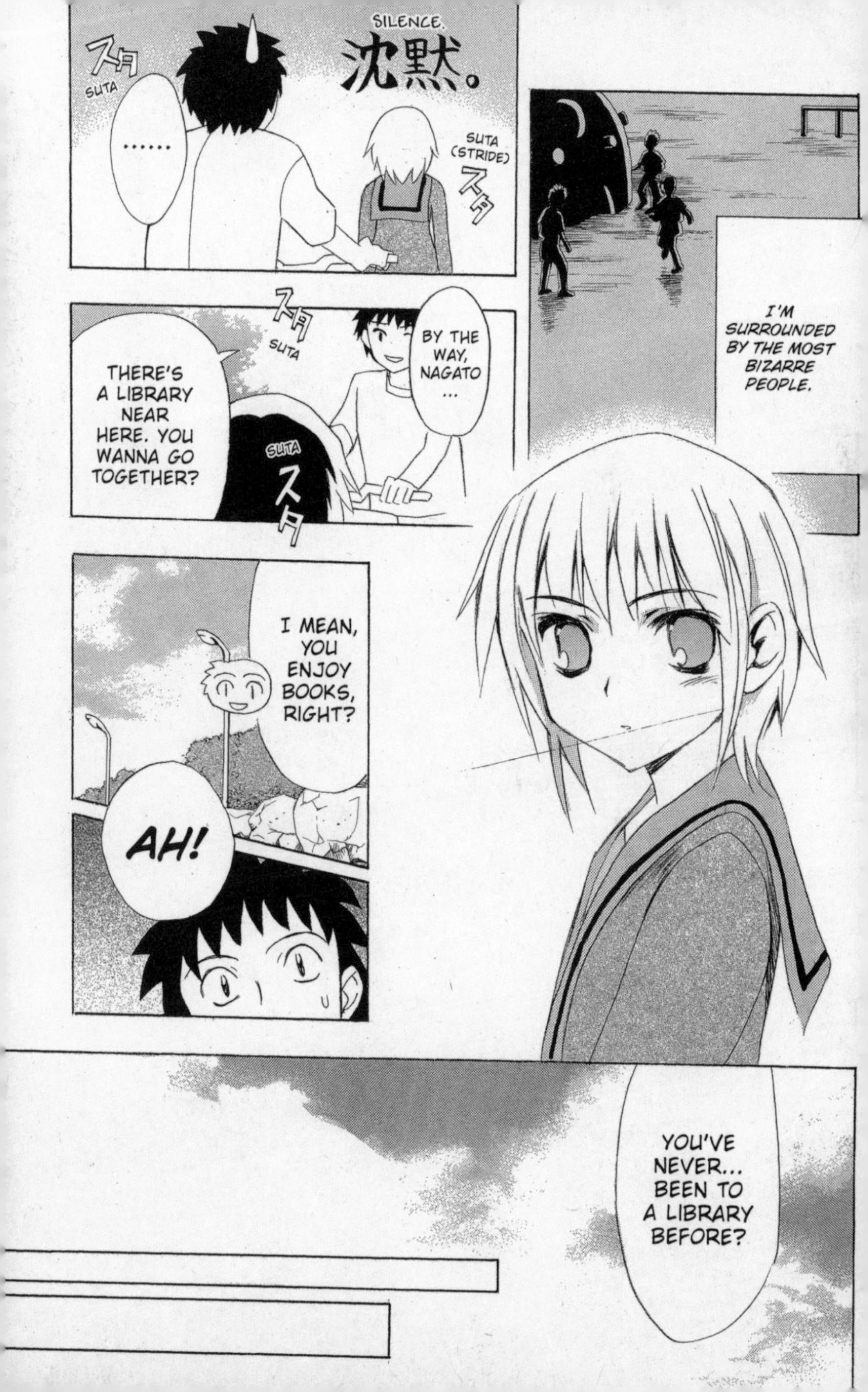
I'M SURROUNDED BY THE MOST BIZARRE PEOPLE.
沈黙。
SILENCE.
スタ
SUTA
......
SUTA (STRIDE)
スタ
スタ
SUTA
BY THE WAY, NAGATO ...
THERE'S A LIBRARY NEAR HERE. YOU WANNA GO TOGETHER?
SUTA
スタ
I MEAN, YOU ENJOY BOOKS, RIGHT?
AH!
YOU'VE NEVER... BEEN TO A LIBRARY BEFORE?

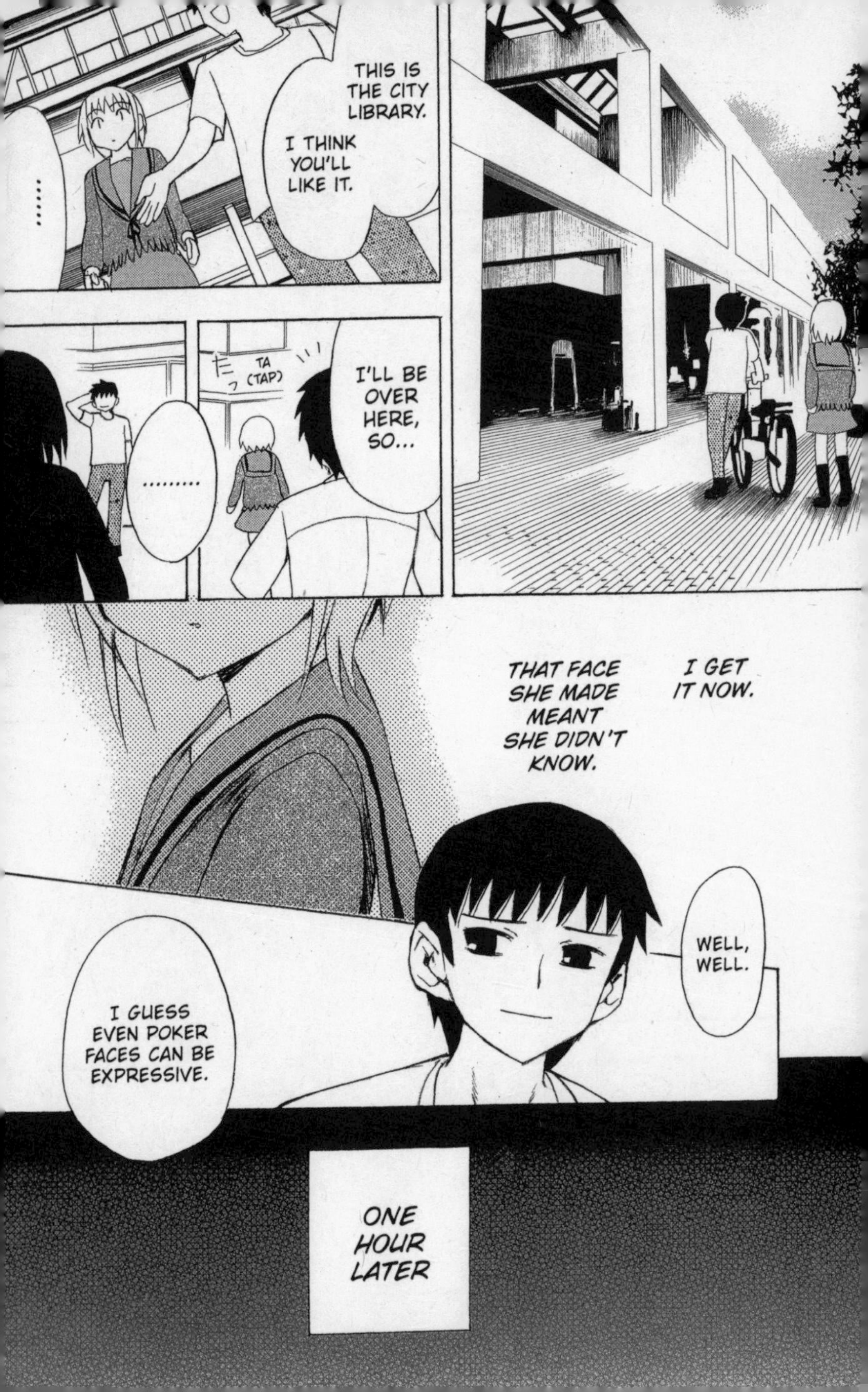
THIS IS THE CITY LIBRARY.
I THINK YOU'LL LIKE IT.
......
TA (TAP)
I'LL BE OVER HERE, SO...
....
I GET IT NOW.
THAT FACE SHE MADE MEANT SHE DIDN'T KNOW.
WELL, WELL.
I GUESS EVEN POKER FACES CAN BE EXPRESSIVE.
ONE HOUR LATER

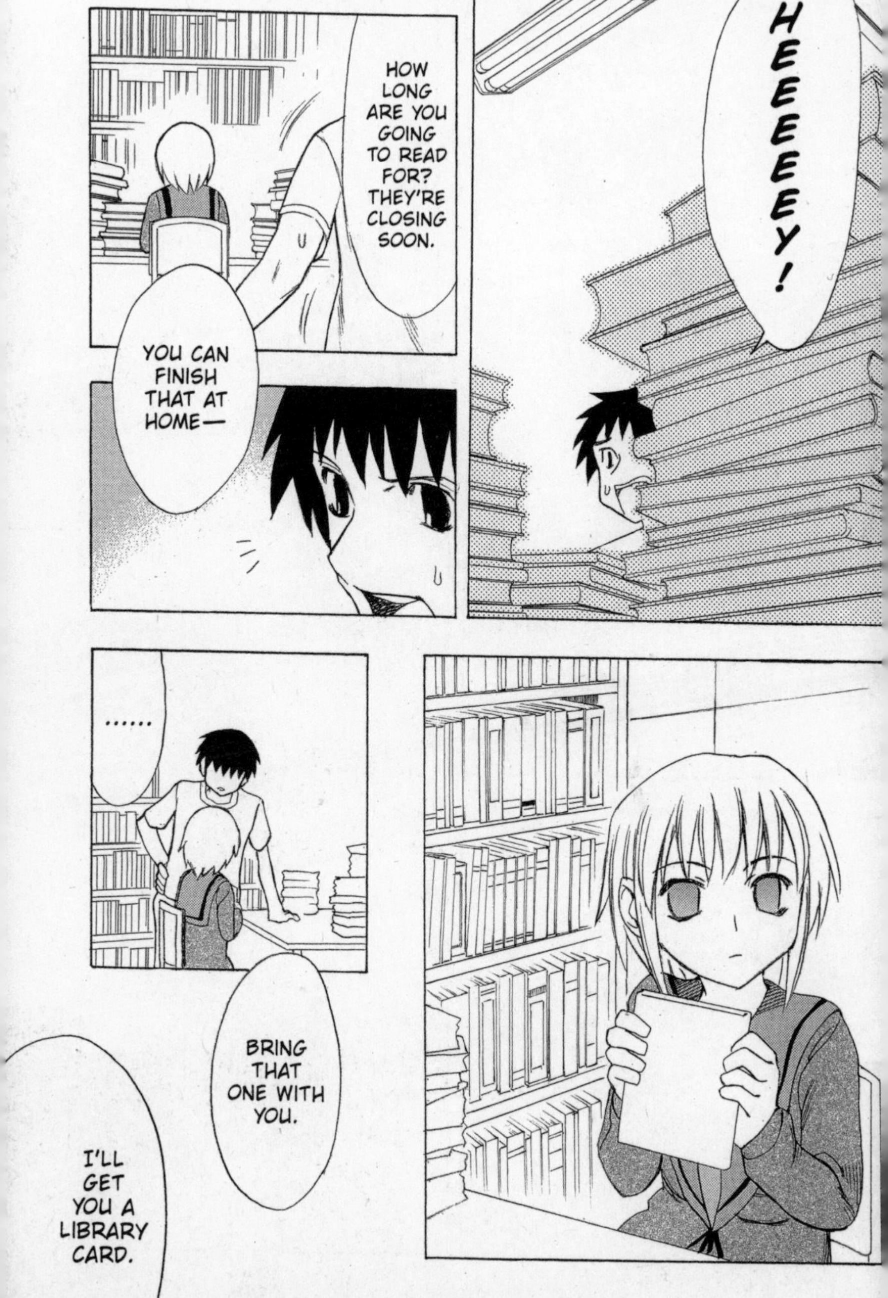
HEEEEEEY!
HOW LONG ARE YOU GOING TO READ FOR? THEY'RE CLOSING SOON.
YOU CAN FINISH THAT AT HOME—
......
BRING THAT ONE WITH YOU.
I'LL GET YOU A LIBRARY CARD.

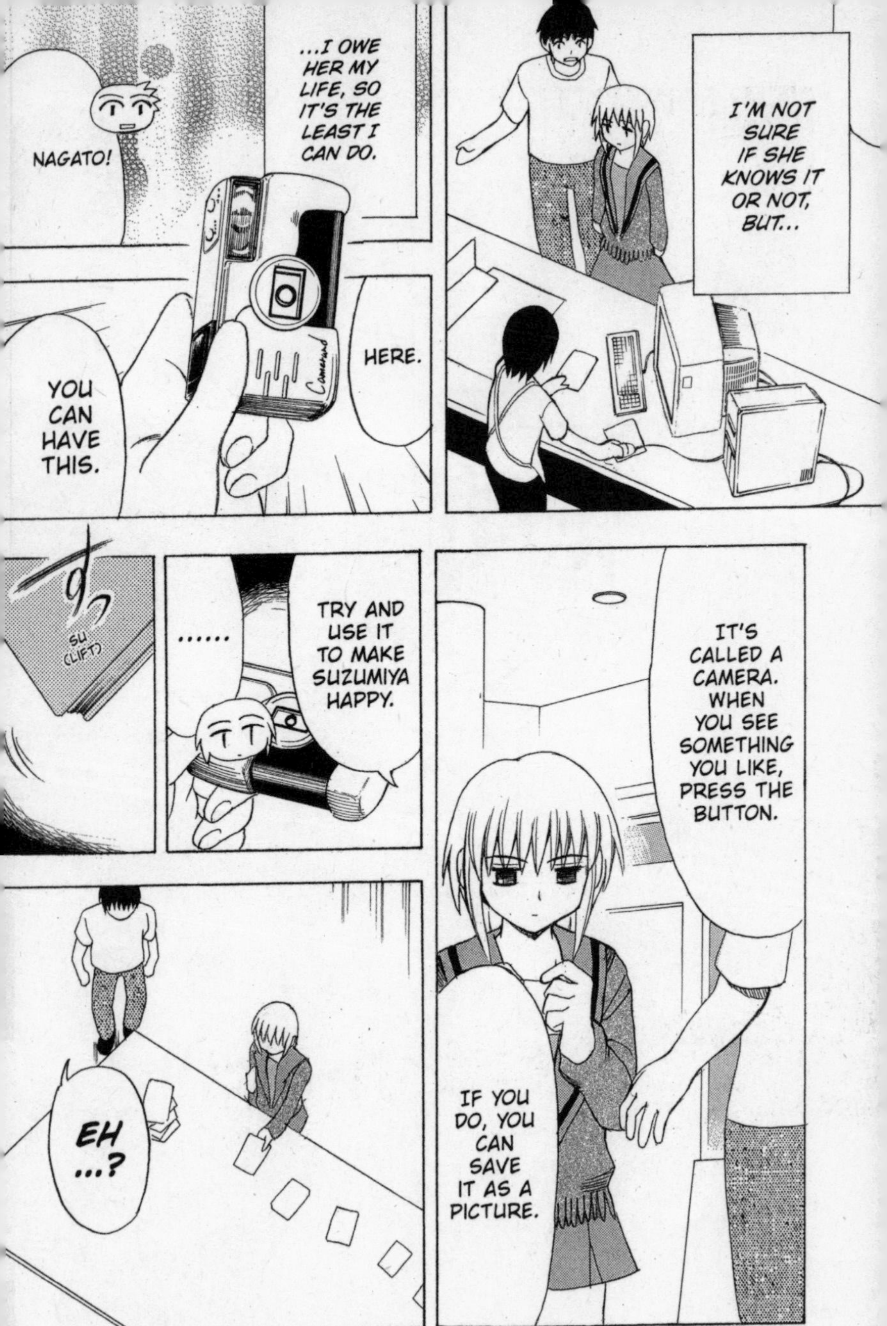

I'M NOT SURE IF SHE KNOWS IT OR NOT, BUT...
...I OWE HER MY LIFE, SO IT'S THE LEAST I CAN DO.
NAGATO!
HERE.
YOU CAN HAVE THIS.
TRY AND USE IT TO MAKE SUZUMIYA HAPPY.
......
SU (LIFT)
IT'S CALLED A CAMERA. WHEN YOU SEE SOMETHING YOU LIKE, PRESS THE BUTTON.
IF YOU DO, YOU CAN SAVE IT AS A PICTURE.
EH ...?

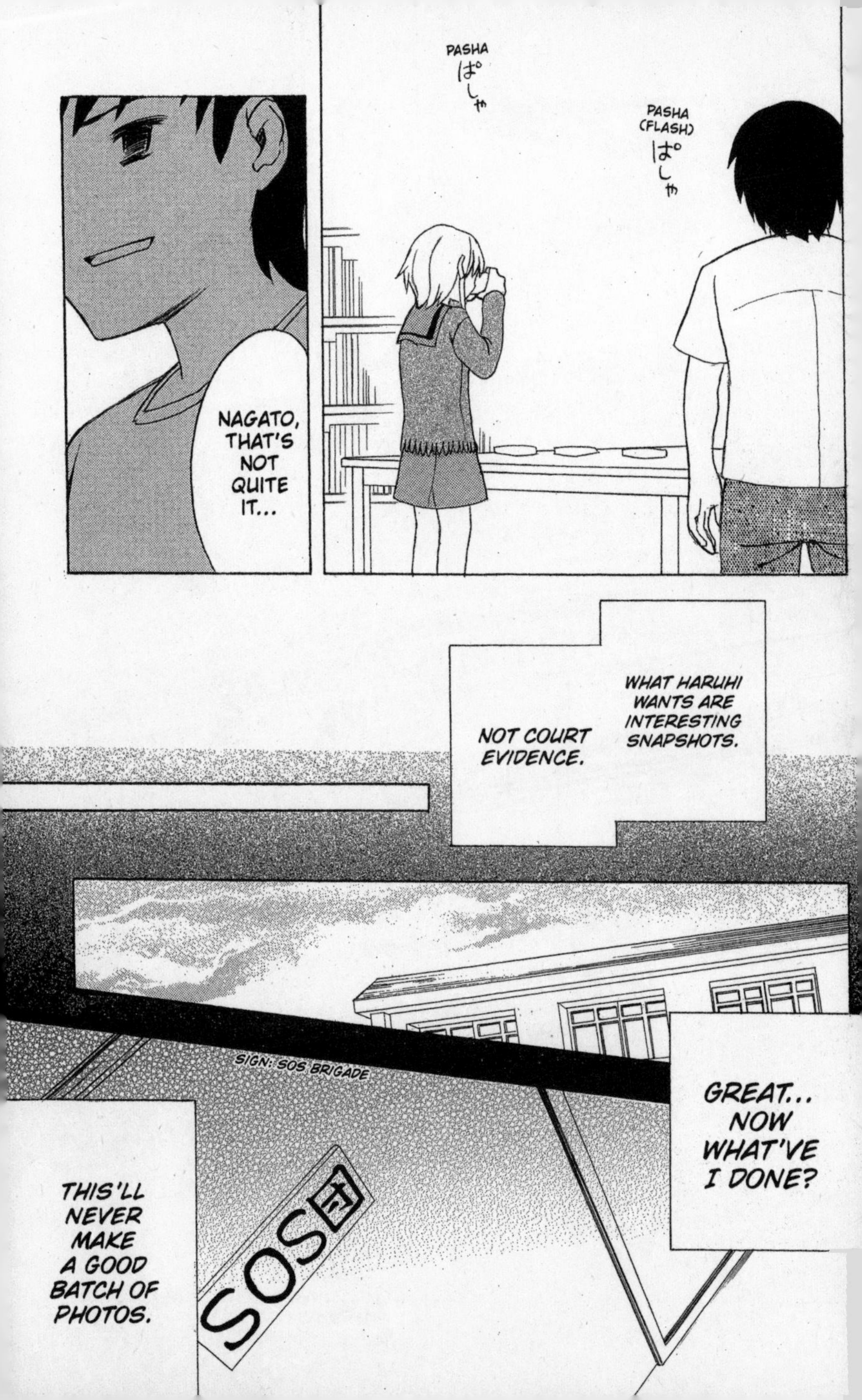
PASHA
ぱしゃ
PASHA (FLASH)
ぱしゃ
NAGATO, THAT'S NOT QUITE IT...
WHAT HARUHI WANTS ARE INTERESTING SNAPSHOTS.
NOT COURT EVIDENCE.
GREAT... NOW WHAT'VE I DONE?
SIGN: SOS BRIGADE
SOS団
THIS'LL NEVER MAKE A GOOD BATCH OF PHOTOS.

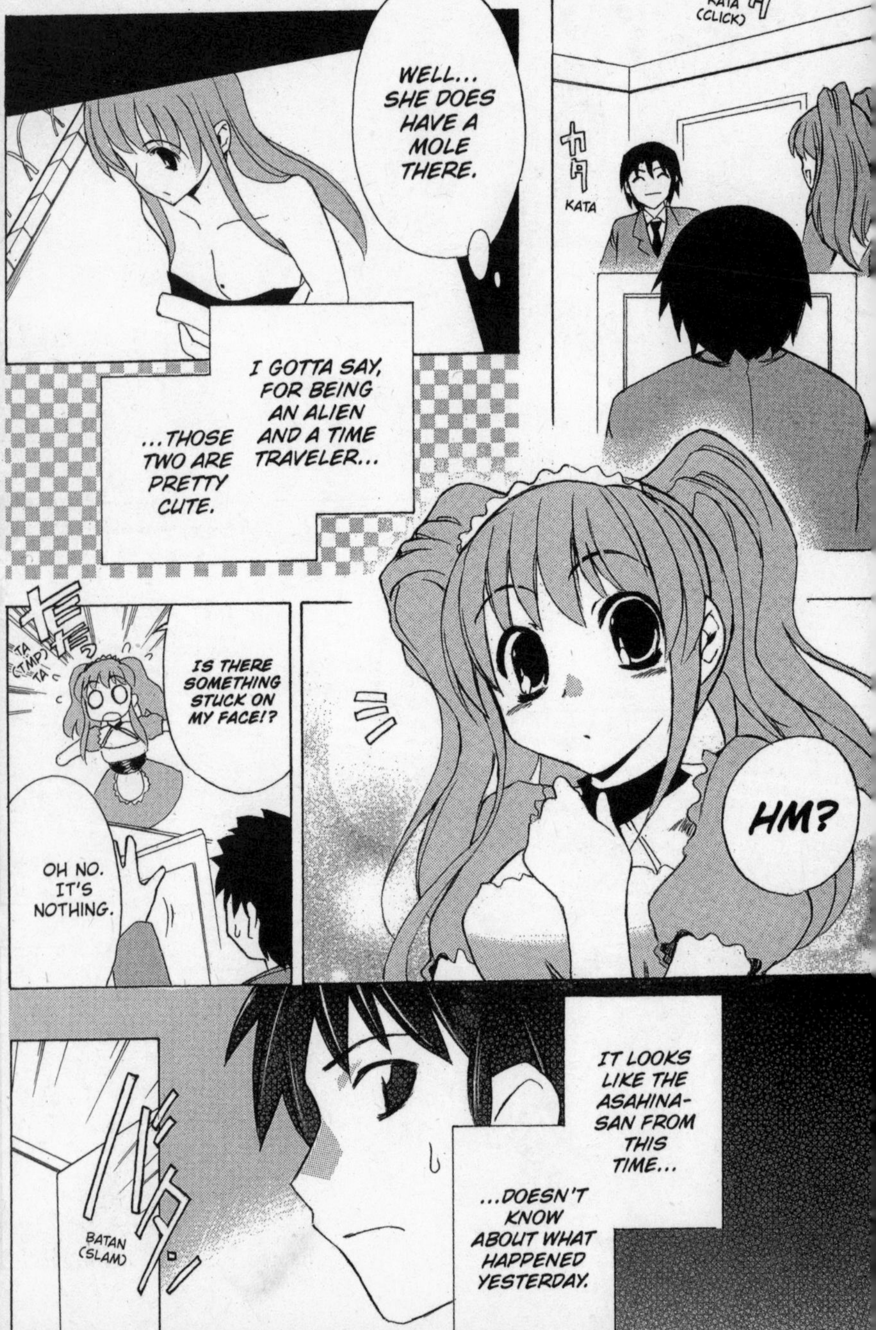
KATA (CLICK)
KATA
WELL... SHE DOES HAVE A MOLE THERE.
I GOTTA SAY, FOR BEING AN ALIEN AND A TIME TRAVELER...
...THOSE TWO ARE PRETTY CUTE.
HM?
IS THERE SOMETHING STUCK ON MY FACE!?
TA (TMP) TA
OH NO. IT'S NOTHING.
IT LOOKS LIKE THE ASAHINA-SAN FROM THIS TIME...
...DOESN'T KNOW ABOUT WHAT HAPPENED YESTERDAY.
BATAN (SLAM)

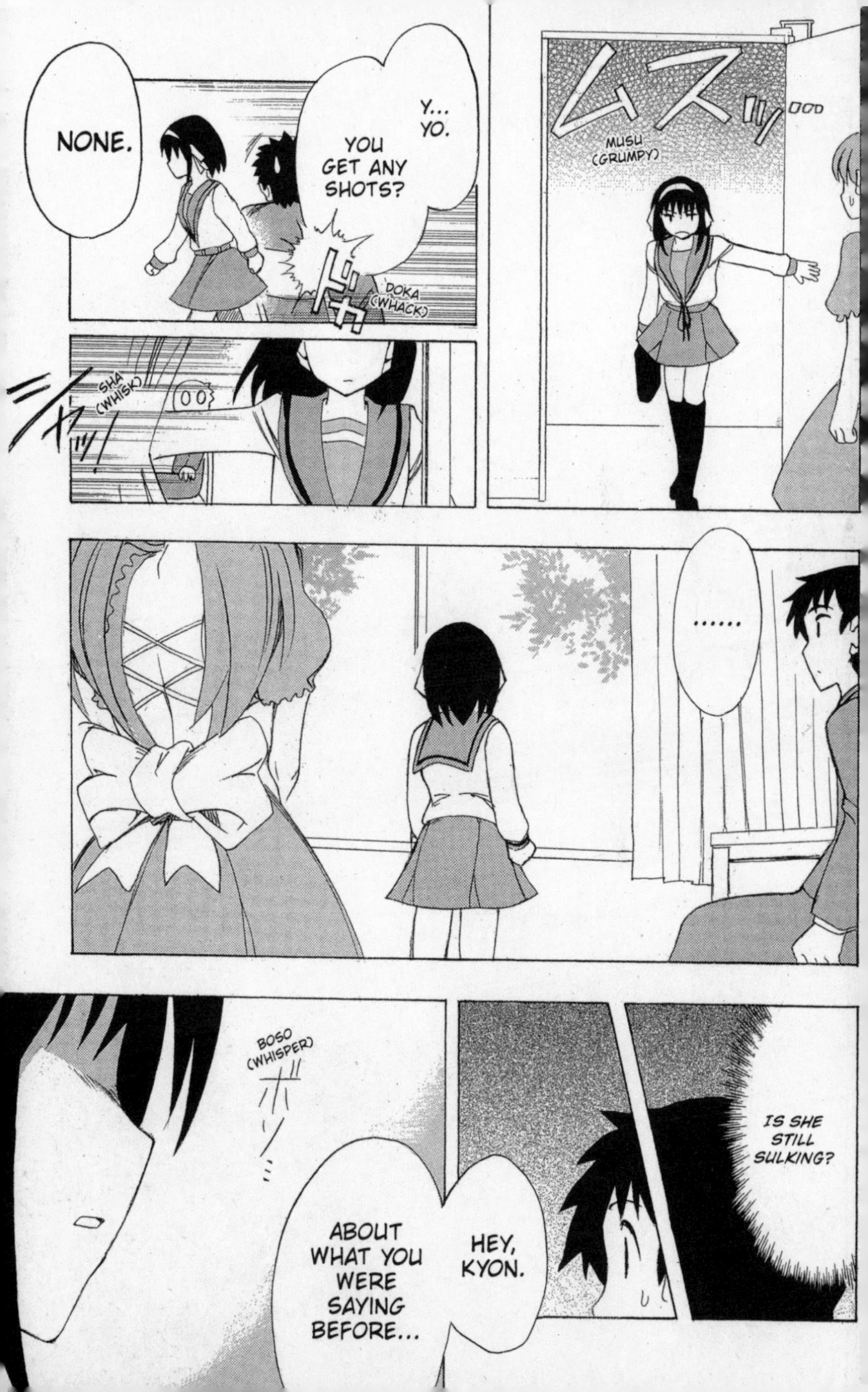
MUSU (GRUMPY)
Y... YO.
YOU GET ANY SHOTS?
DOKA (WHACK)
NONE.
SHA (WHISK)
......
IS SHE STILL SULKING?
HEY, KYON.
ABOUT WHAT YOU WERE SAYING BEFORE...
BOSO (WHISPER)

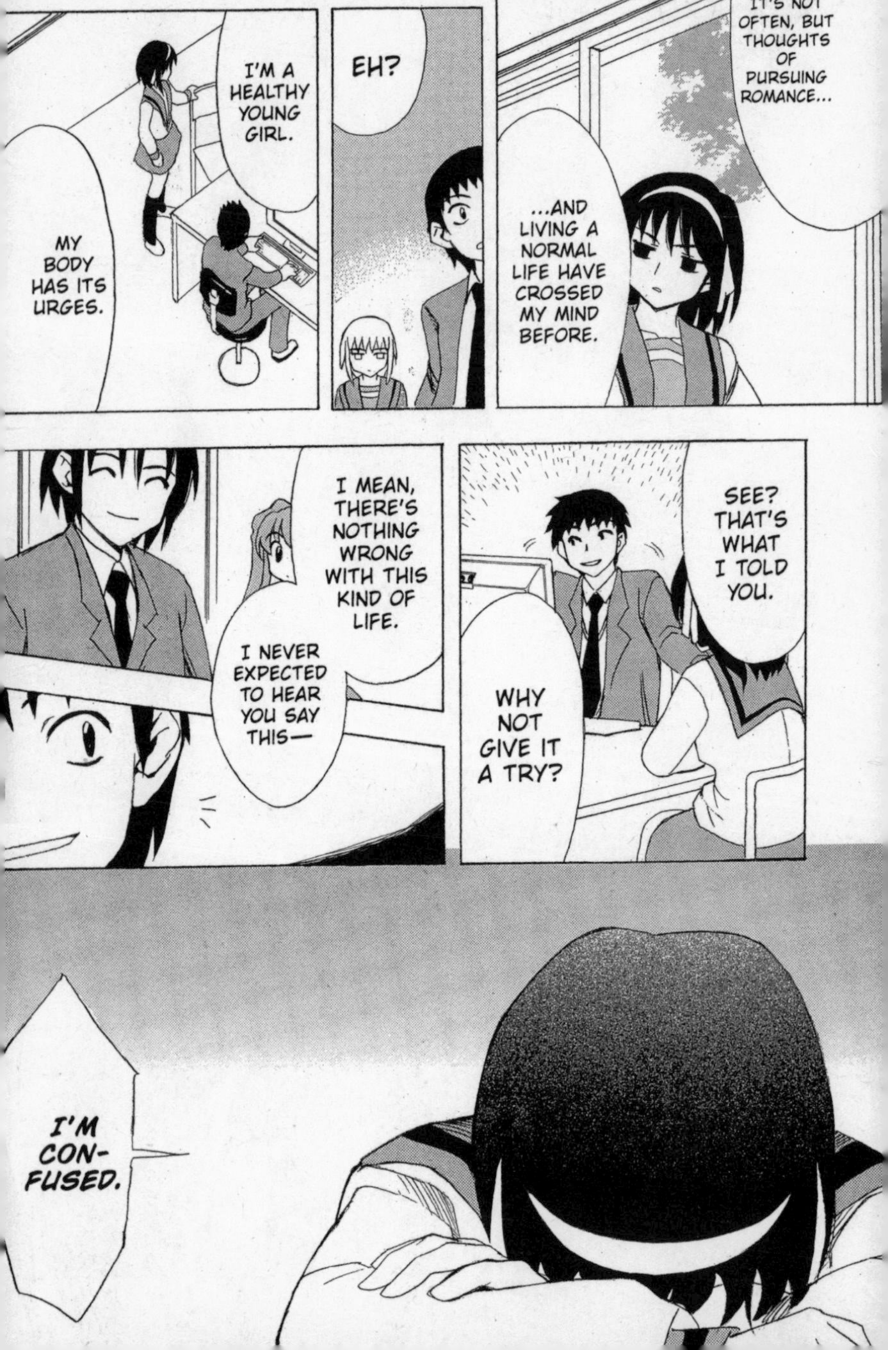
IT'S NOT OFTEN, BUT THOUGHTS OF PURSUING ROMANCE...
...AND LIVING A NORMAL LIFE HAVE CROSSED MY MIND BEFORE.
EH?
I'M A HEALTHY YOUNG GIRL.
MY BODY HAS ITS URGES.
SEE? THAT'S WHAT I TOLD YOU.
WHY NOT GIVE IT A TRY?
I MEAN, THERE'S NOTHING WRONG WITH THIS KIND OF LIFE.
I NEVER EXPECTED TO HEAR YOU SAY THIS—
I'M CON-FUSED.

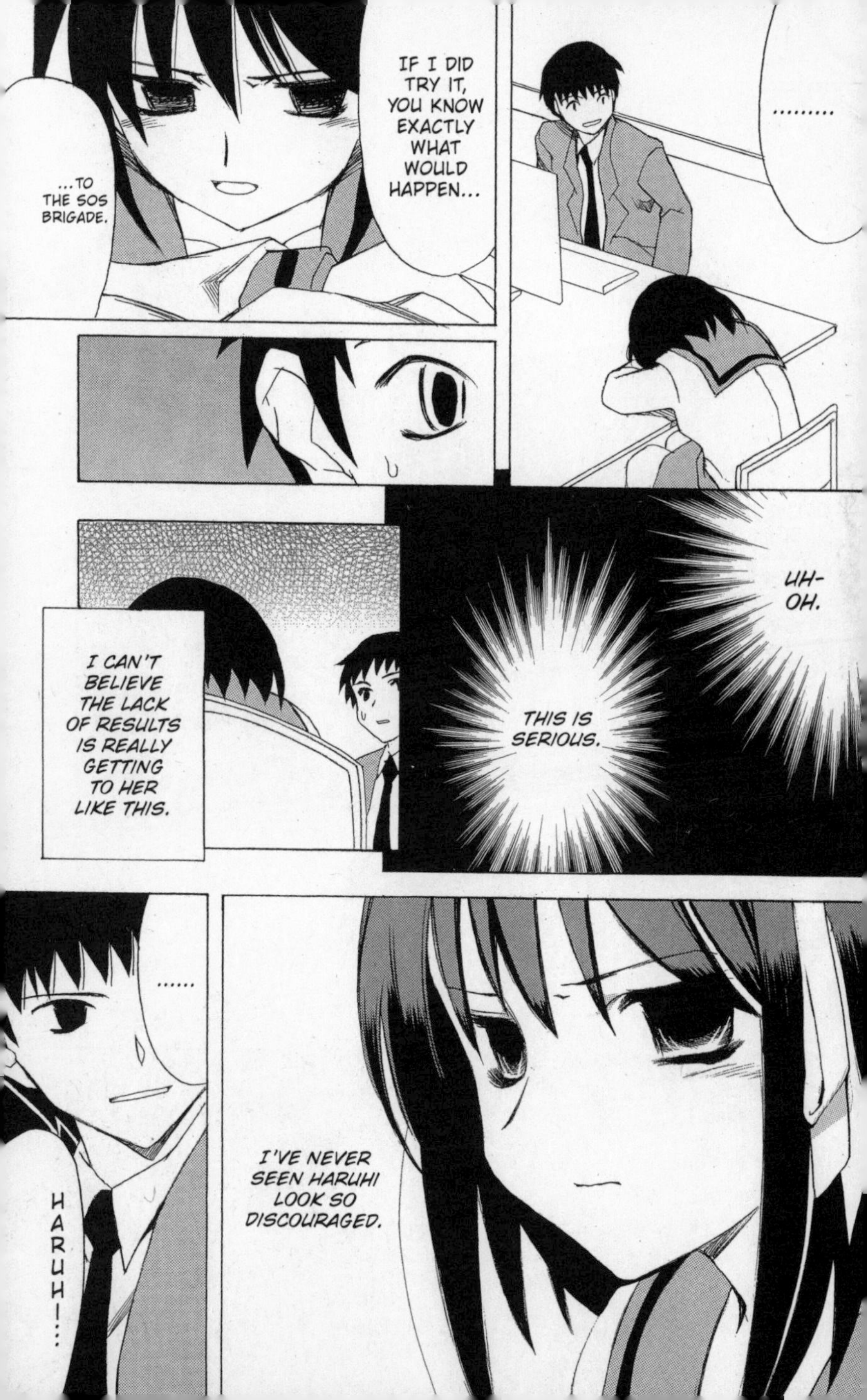
....
IF I DID TRY IT, YOU KNOW EXACTLY WHAT WOULD HAPPEN...
...TO THE SOS BRIGADE.
UH-OH.
THIS IS SERIOUS.
I CAN'T BELIEVE THE LACK OF RESULTS IS REALLY GETTING TO HER LIKE THIS.
I'VE NEVER SEEN HARUHI LOOK SO DISCOURAGED.
......
HARUHI...!

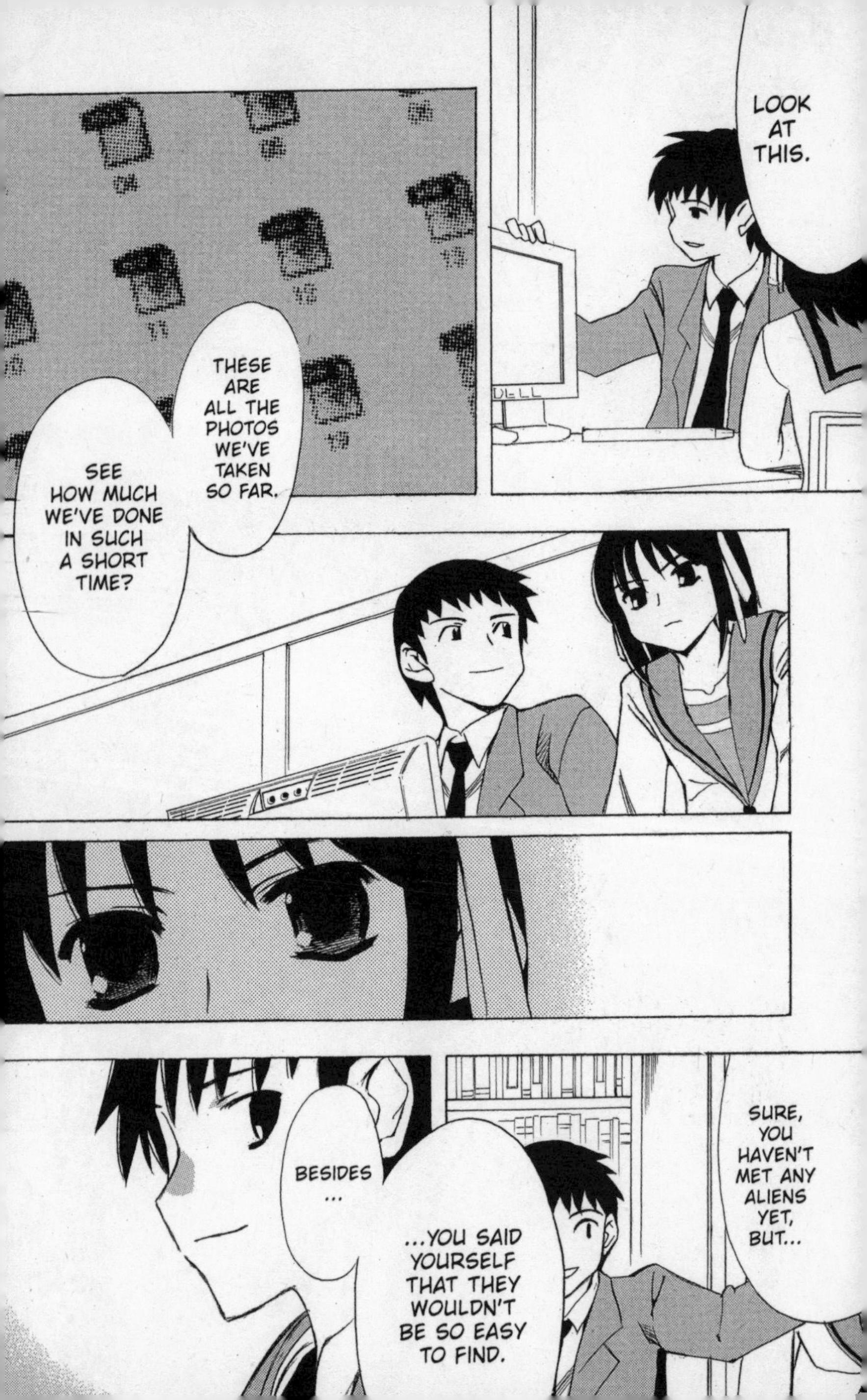
LOOK AT THIS.
THESE ARE ALL THE PHOTOS WE'VE TAKEN SO FAR.
SEE HOW MUCH WE'VE DONE IN SUCH A SHORT TIME?
SURE, YOU HAVEN'T MET ANY ALIENS YET, BUT...
BESIDES...
...YOU SAID YOURSELF THAT THEY WOULDN'T BE SO EASY TO FIND.

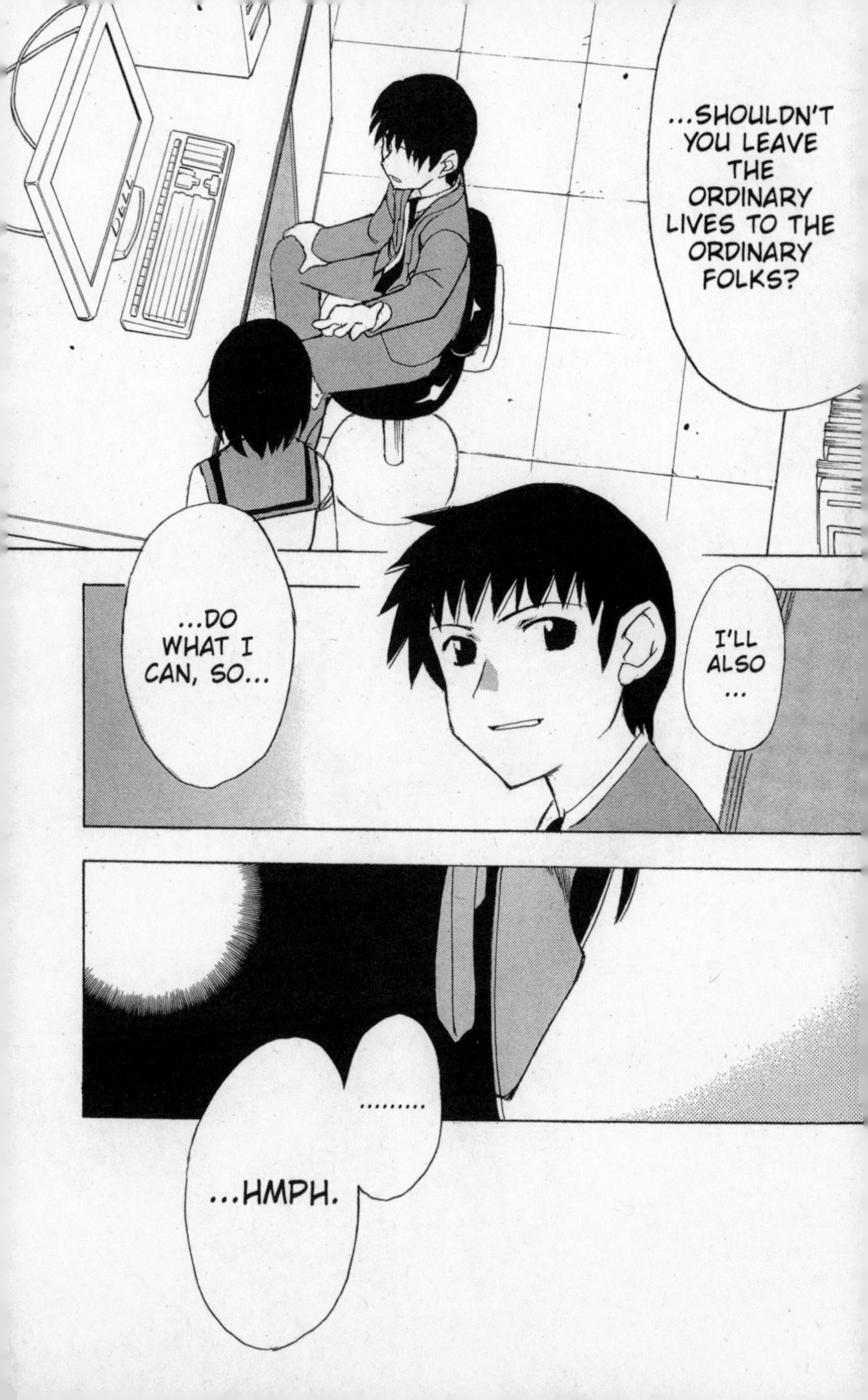
...SHOULDN'T YOU LEAVE THE ORDINARY LIVES TO THE ORDINARY FOLKS?
I'LL ALSO ...
...DO WHAT I CAN, SO...
....
...HMPH.

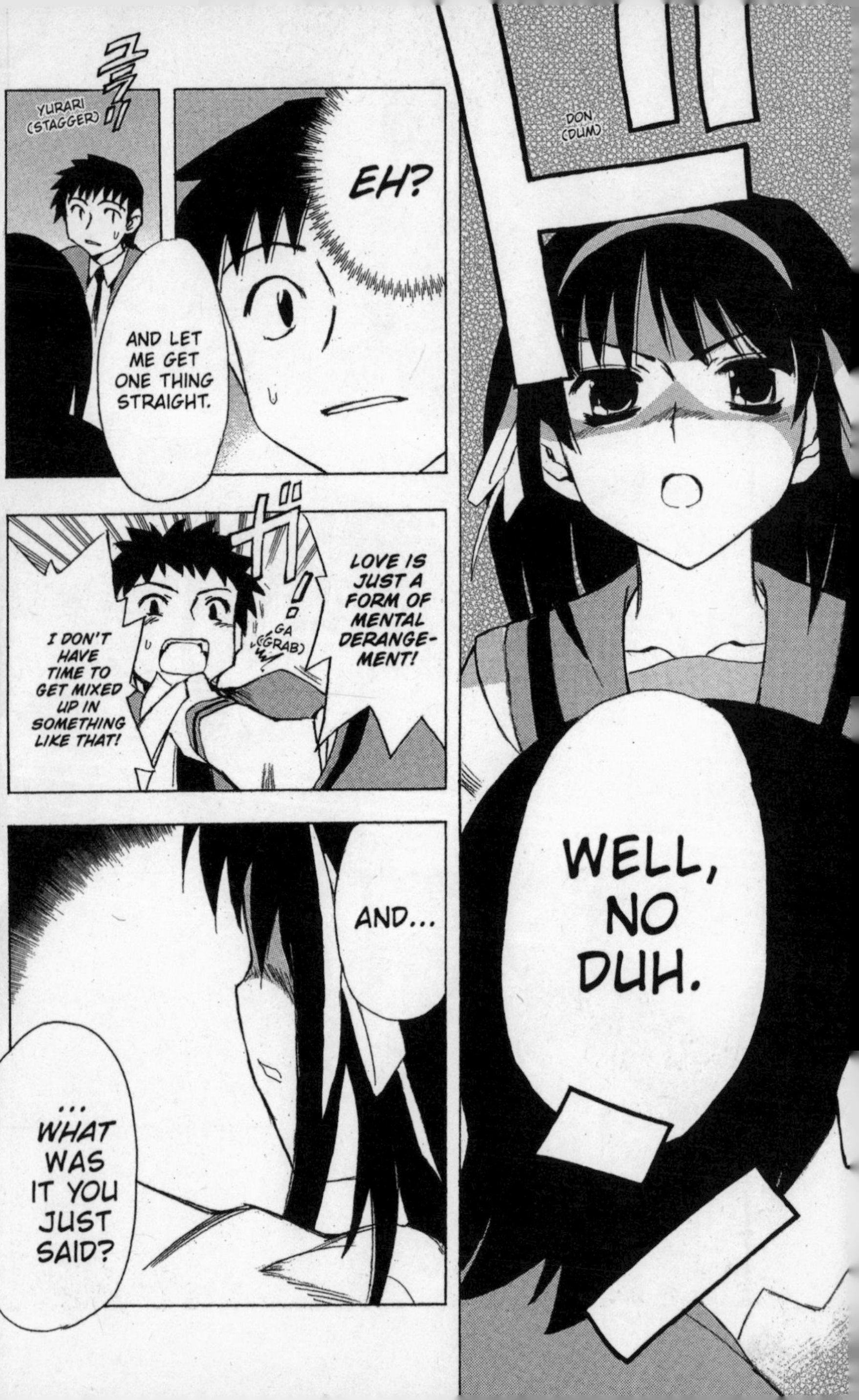
DON (DUM)
WELL, NO DUH.
EH?
AND LET ME GET ONE THING STRAIGHT.
YURARI (STAGGER)
LOVE IS JUST A FORM OF MENTAL DERANGE-MENT!
GA (GRAB)
I DON'T HAVE TIME TO GET MIXED UP IN SOMETHING LIKE THAT!
AND...
... WHAT WAS IT YOU JUST SAID?

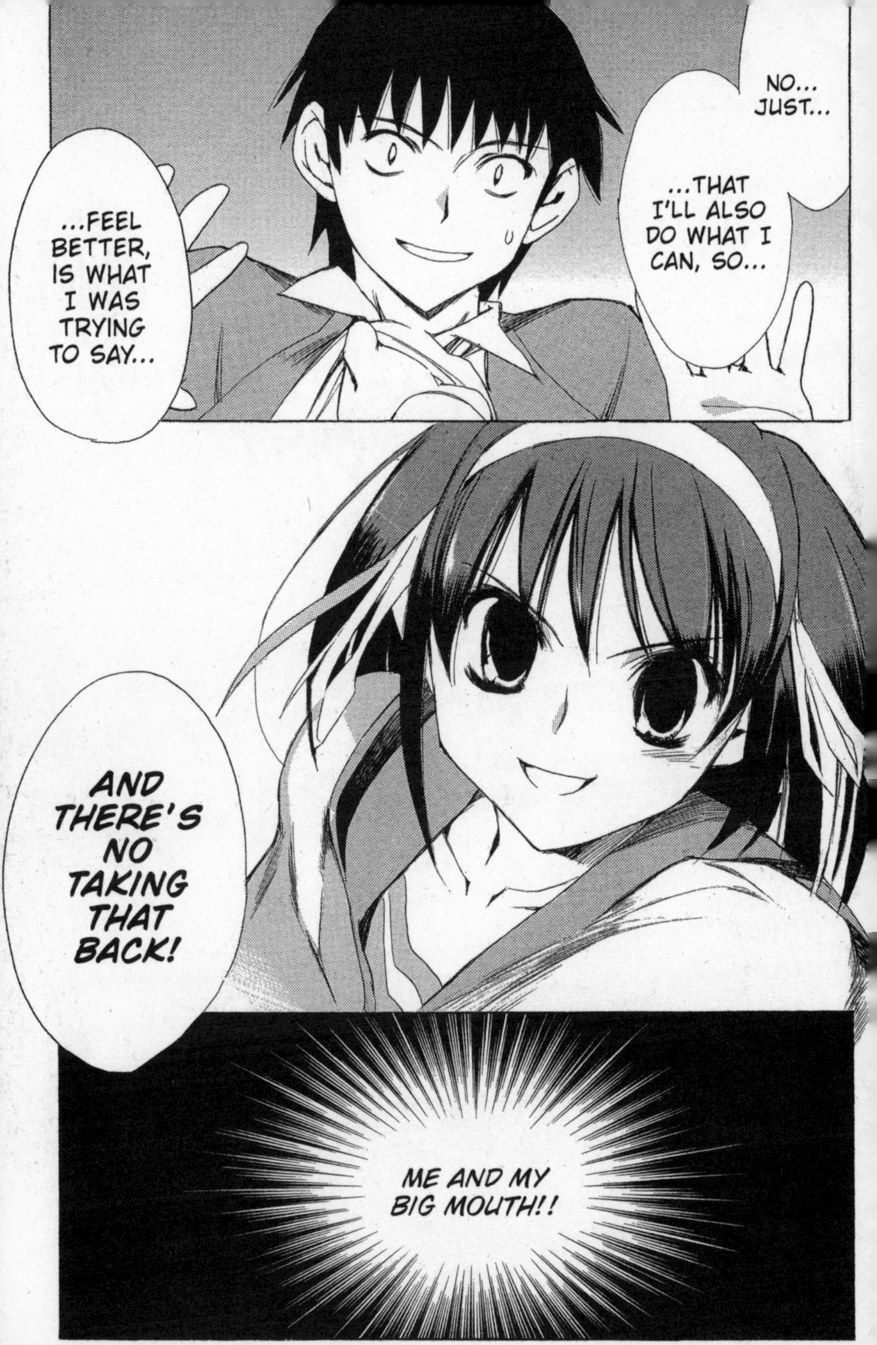
NO... JUST...
...THAT I'LL ALSO DO WHAT I CAN, SO...
...FEEL BETTER, IS WHAT I WAS TRYING TO SAY...
AND THERE'S NO TAKING THAT BACK!
ME AND MY BIG MOUTH!!

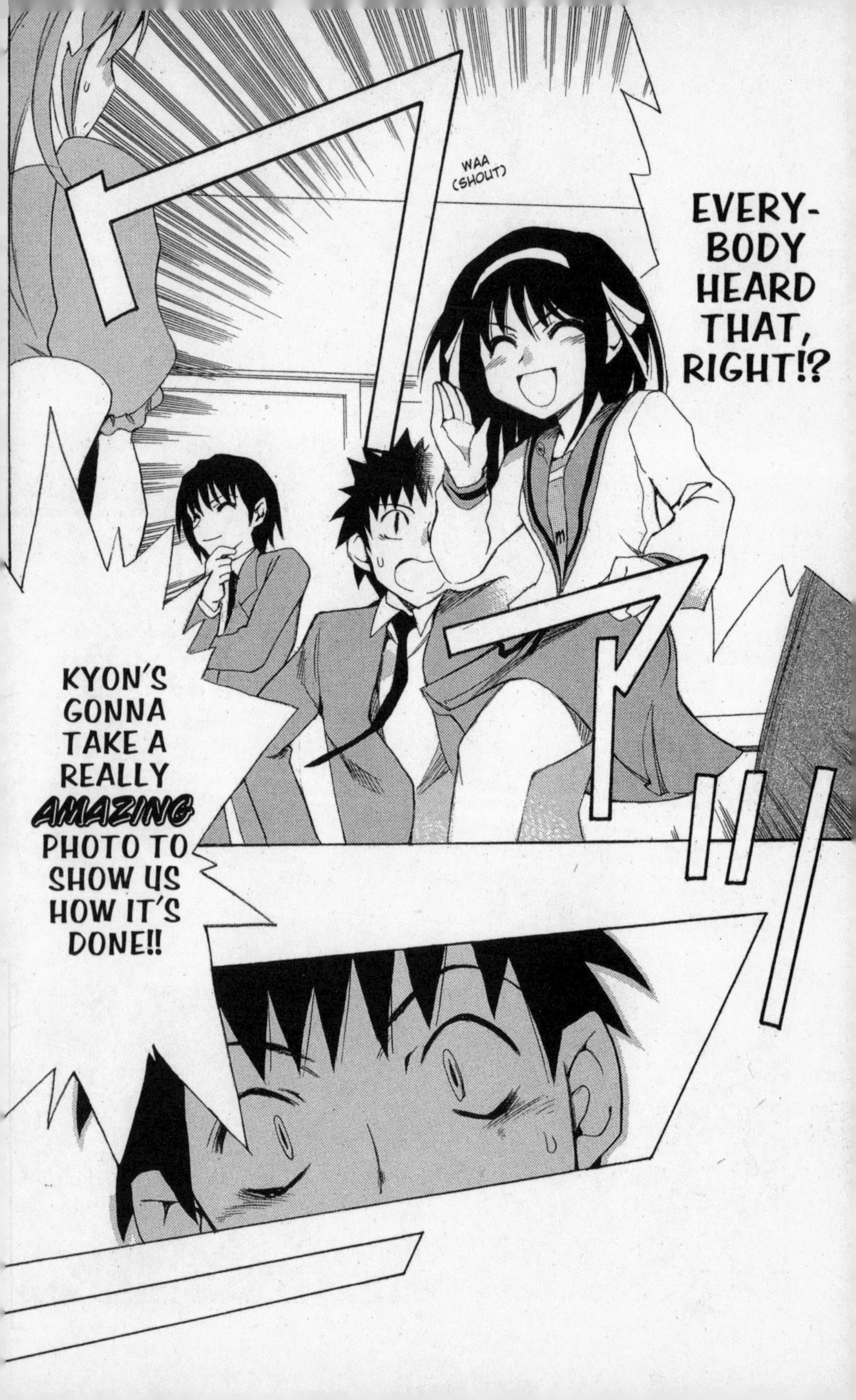
WAA (SHOUT)
EVERY-BODY HEARD THAT, RIGHT!?
KYON'S GONNA TAKE A REALLY AMAZING PHOTO TO SHOW US HOW IT'S DONE!!

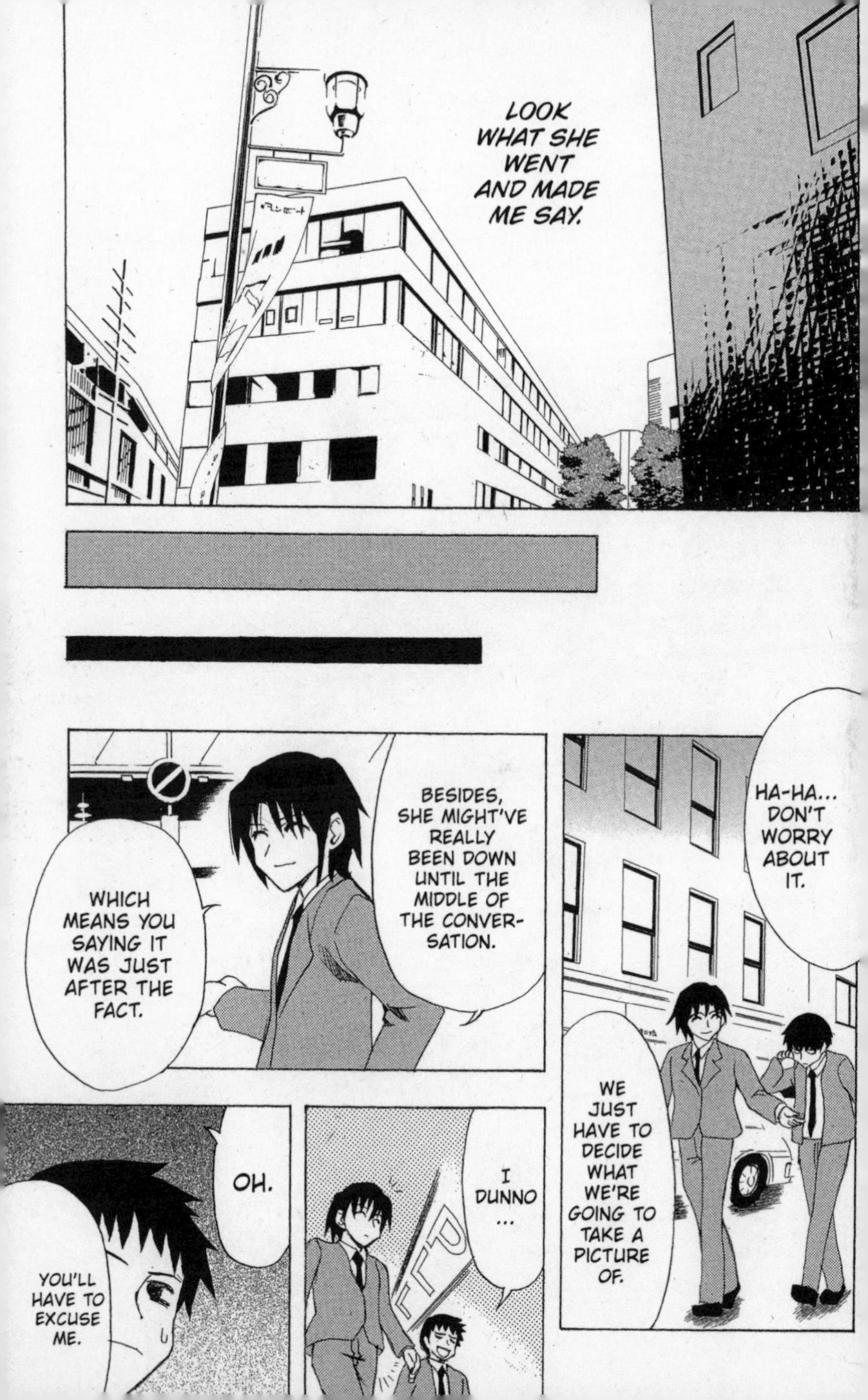
LOOK WHAT SHE WENT AND MADE ME SAY.
BESIDES, SHE MIGHT'VE REALLY BEEN DOWN UNTIL THE MIDDLE OF THE CONVER-SATION.
WHICH MEANS YOU SAYING IT WAS JUST AFTER THE FACT.
HA-HA... DON'T WORRY ABOUT IT.
WE JUST HAVE TO DECIDE WHAT WE'RE GOING TO TAKE A PICTURE OF.
I DUNNO ...
OH.
YOU'LL HAVE TO EXCUSE ME.

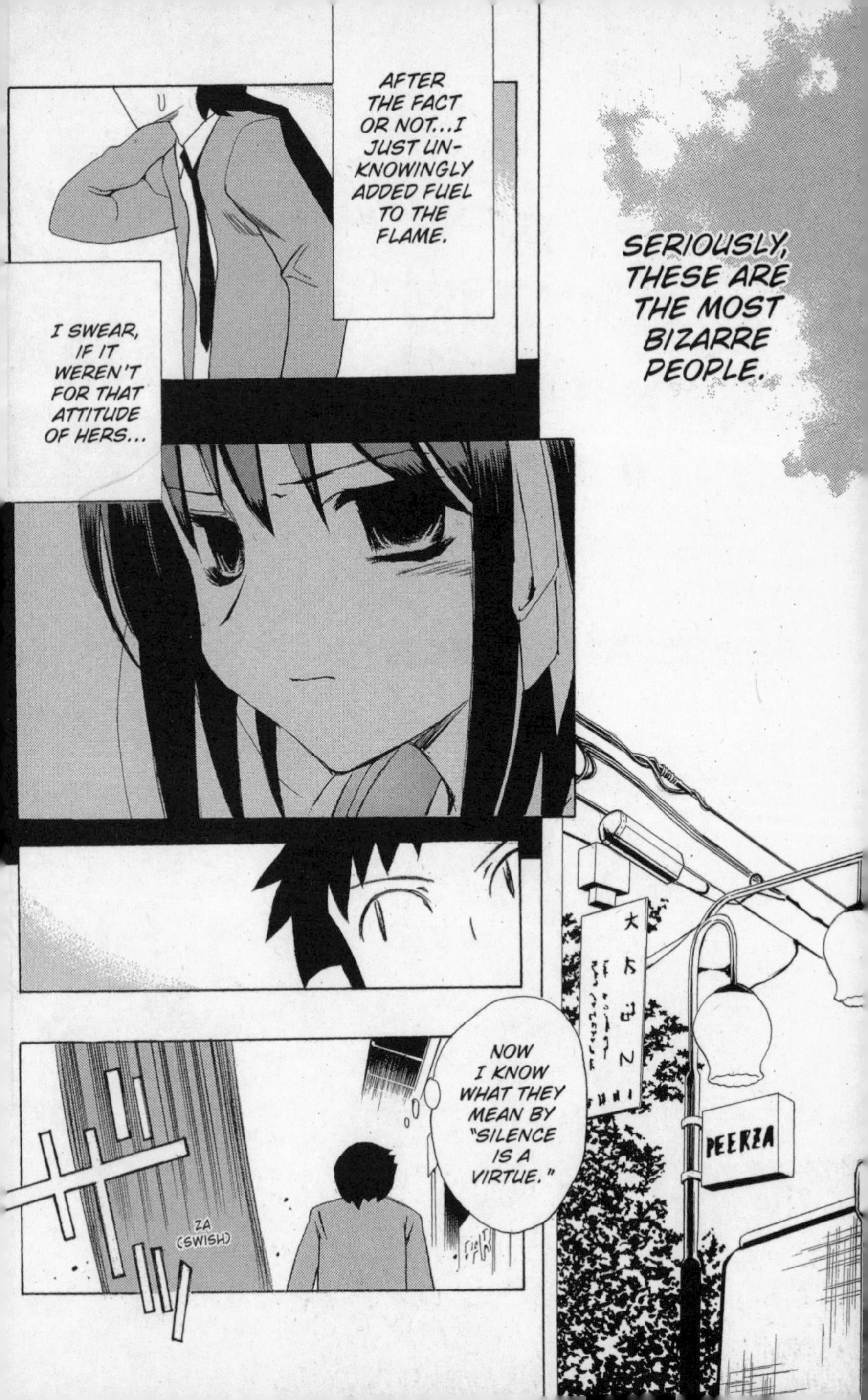
AFTER THE FACT OR NOT...I JUST UN-KNOWINGLY ADDED FUEL TO THE FLAME.
I SWEAR, IF IT WEREN'T FOR THAT ATTITUDE OF HERS...
ZA (SWISH)
NOW I KNOW WHAT THEY MEAN BY "SILENCE IS A VIRTUE."
SERIOUSLY, THESE ARE THE MOST BIZARRE PEOPLE.
PEERZA

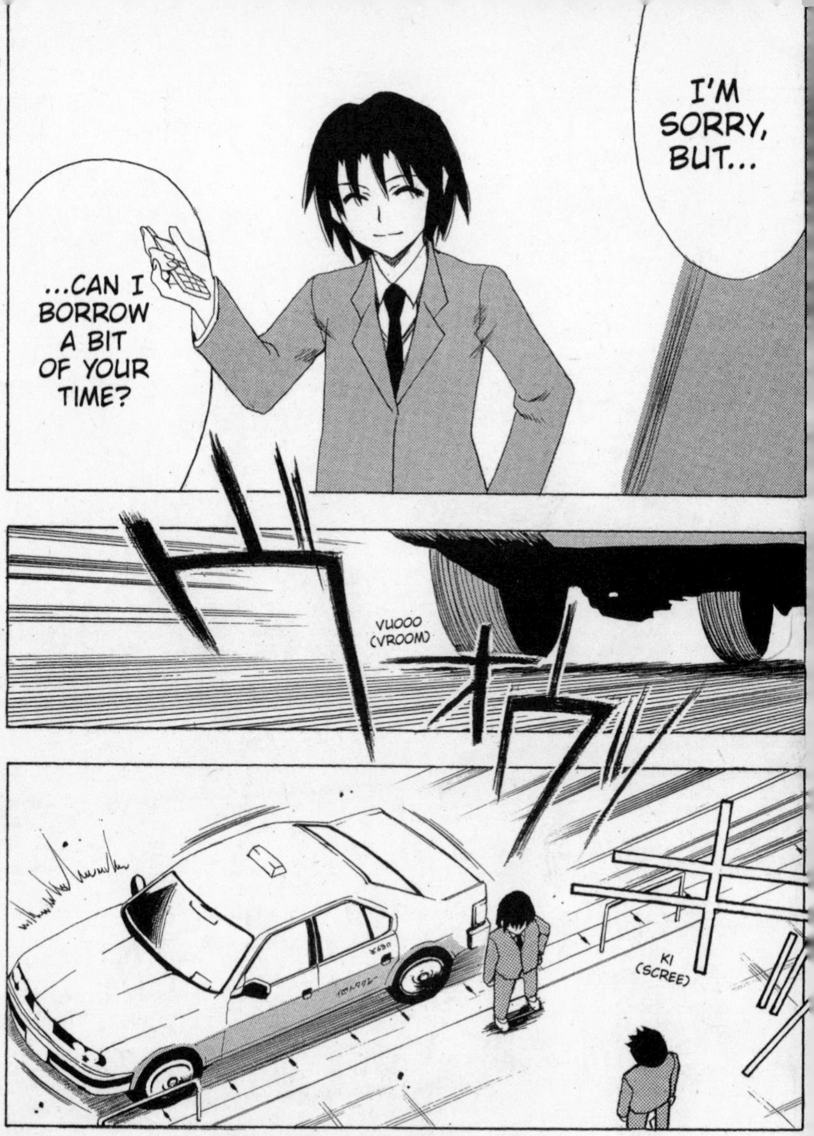
I'M SORRY, BUT...
...CAN I BORROW A BIT OF YOUR TIME?
VUOOO (VROOM)
KI (SCREE)

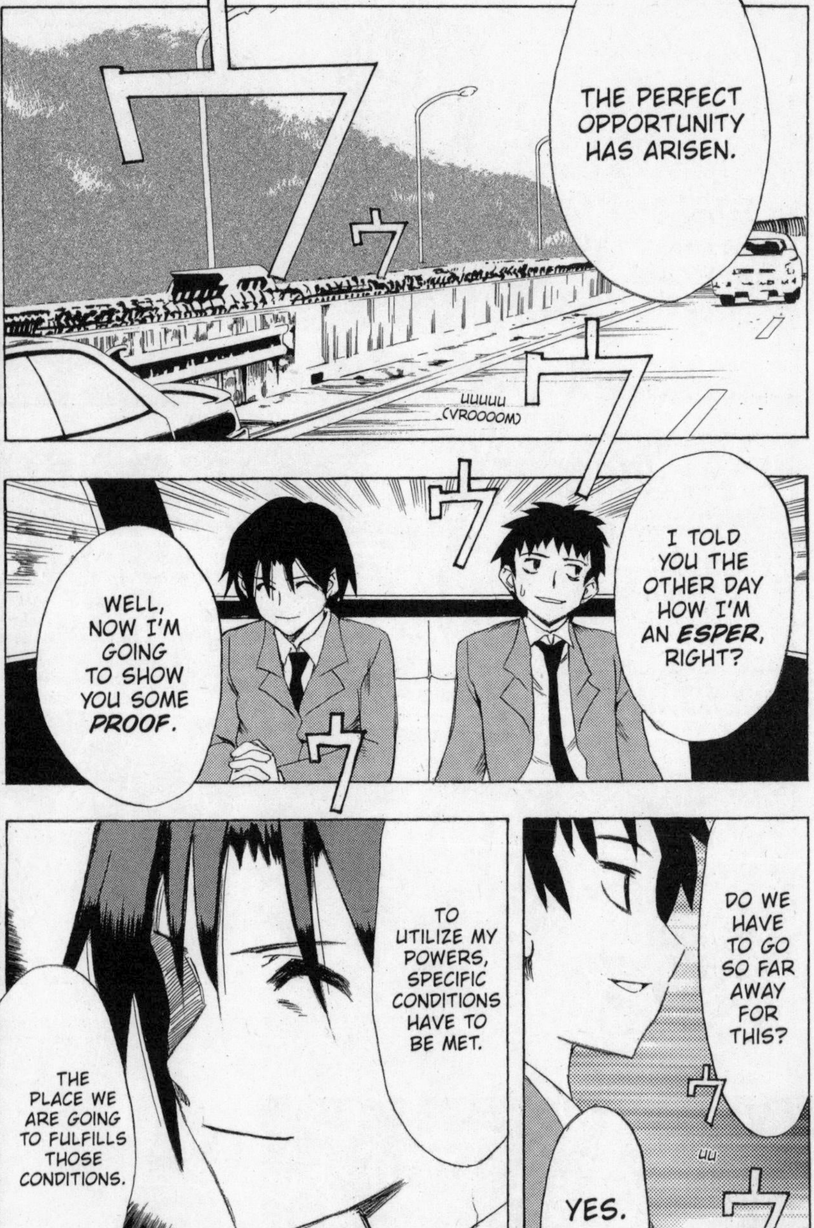
THE PERFECT OPPORTUNITY HAS ARISEN.
uuuuu (VROOOOM)
I TOLD YOU THE OTHER DAY HOW I'M AN ESPER, RIGHT?
WELL, NOW I'M GOING TO SHOW YOU SOME PROOF.
DO WE HAVE TO GO SO FAR AWAY FOR THIS?
uu
YES.
TO UTILIZE MY POWERS, SPECIFIC CONDITIONS HAVE TO BE MET.
THE PLACE WE ARE GOING TO FULFILLS THOSE CONDITIONS.

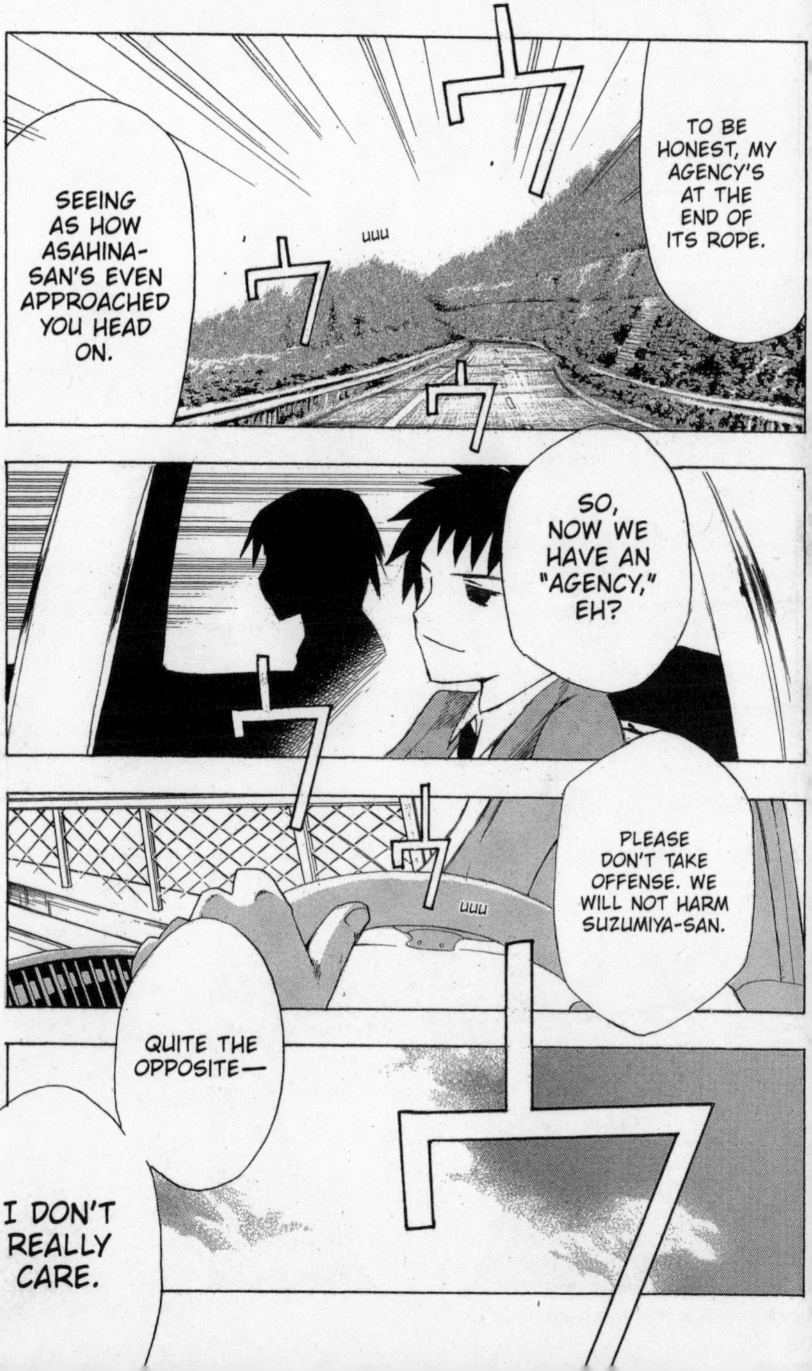
TO BE HONEST, MY AGENCY'S AT THE END OF ITS ROPE.
SEEING AS HOW ASAHINA-SAN'S EVEN APPROACHED YOU HEAD ON.
uuu
SO, NOW WE HAVE AN "AGENCY," EH?
PLEASE DON'T TAKE OFFENSE. WE WILL NOT HARM SUZUMIYA-SAN.
uuu
QUITE THE OPPOSITE—
I DON'T REALLY CARE.

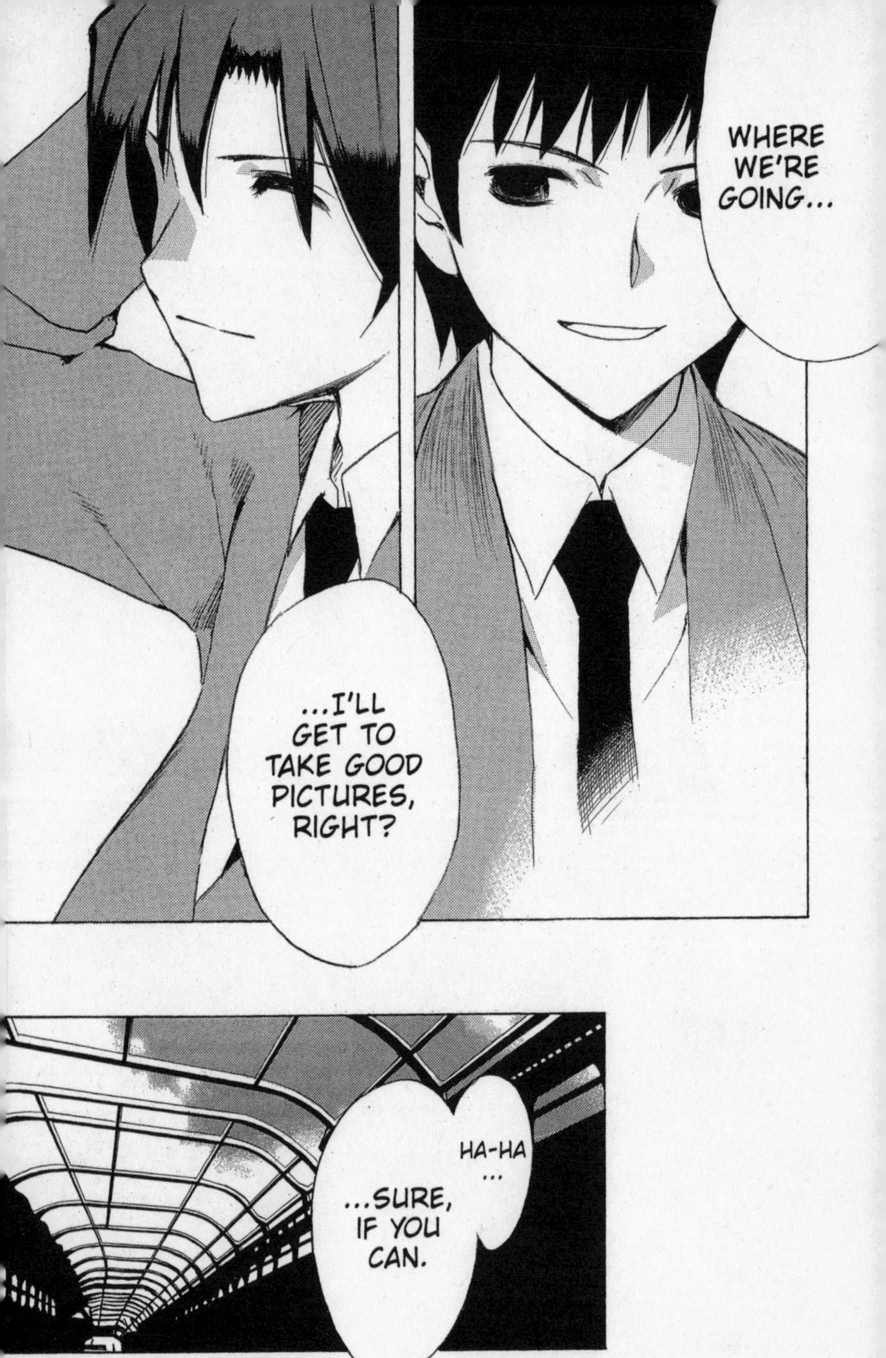
WHERE WE'RE GOING...
...I'LL GET TO TAKE GOOD PICTURES, RIGHT?
HA-HA ...
...SURE, IF YOU CAN.

THE MELANCHOLY OF HARUHI SUZUMIYA VI : END

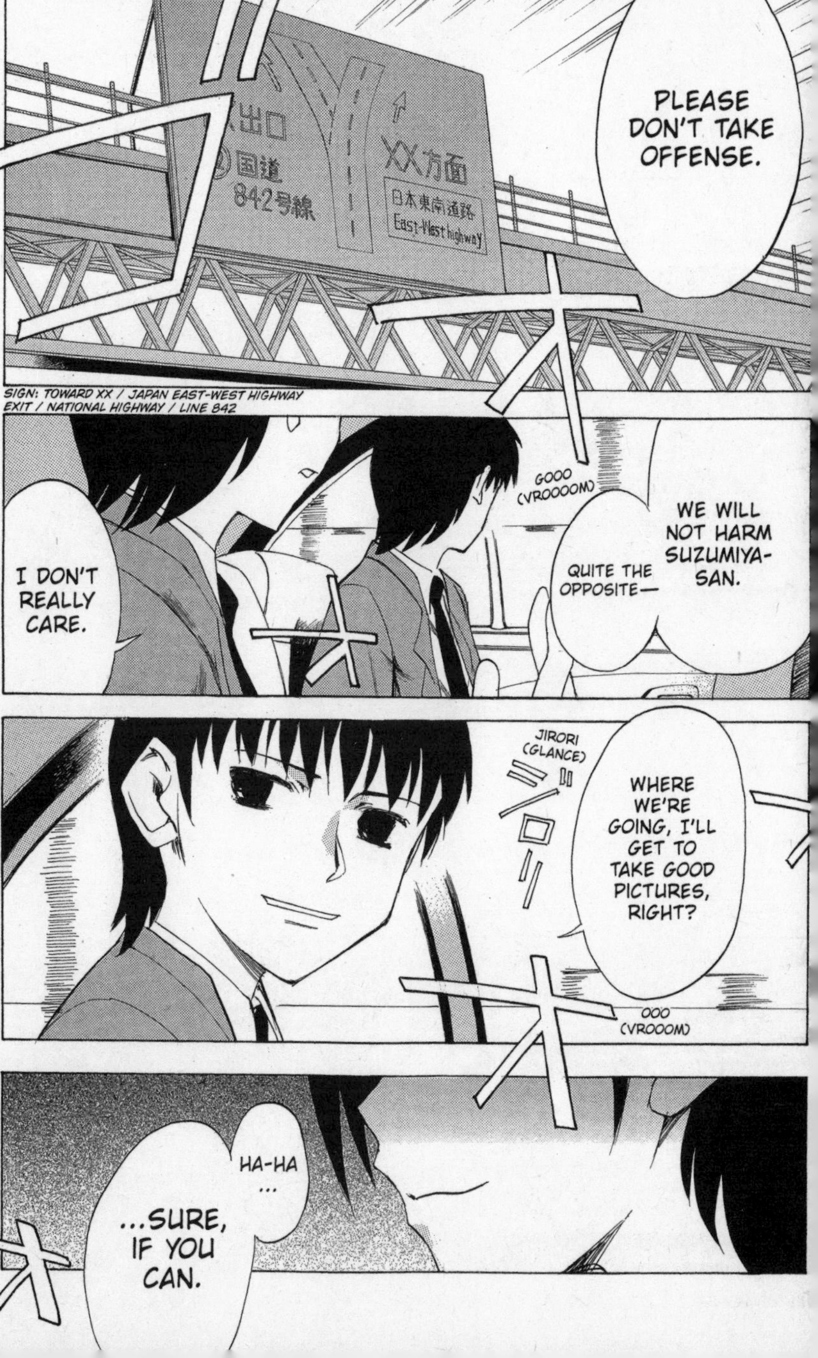
PLEASE DON'T TAKE OFFENSE.
出口
国道
842号線
XX方面
日本東西道路
East-West highway
SIGN: TOWARD XX / JAPAN EAST-WEST HIGHWAY
EXIT / NATIONAL HIGHWAY / LINE 842
GOOO (VROOOOM)
WE WILL NOT HARM SUZUMIYA-SAN.
QUITE THE OPPOSITE—
I DON'T REALLY CARE.
JIRORI (GLANCE)
WHERE WE'RE GOING, I'LL GET TO TAKE GOOD PICTURES, RIGHT?
OOO (VROOOM)
HA-HA ...
...SURE, IF YOU CAN.

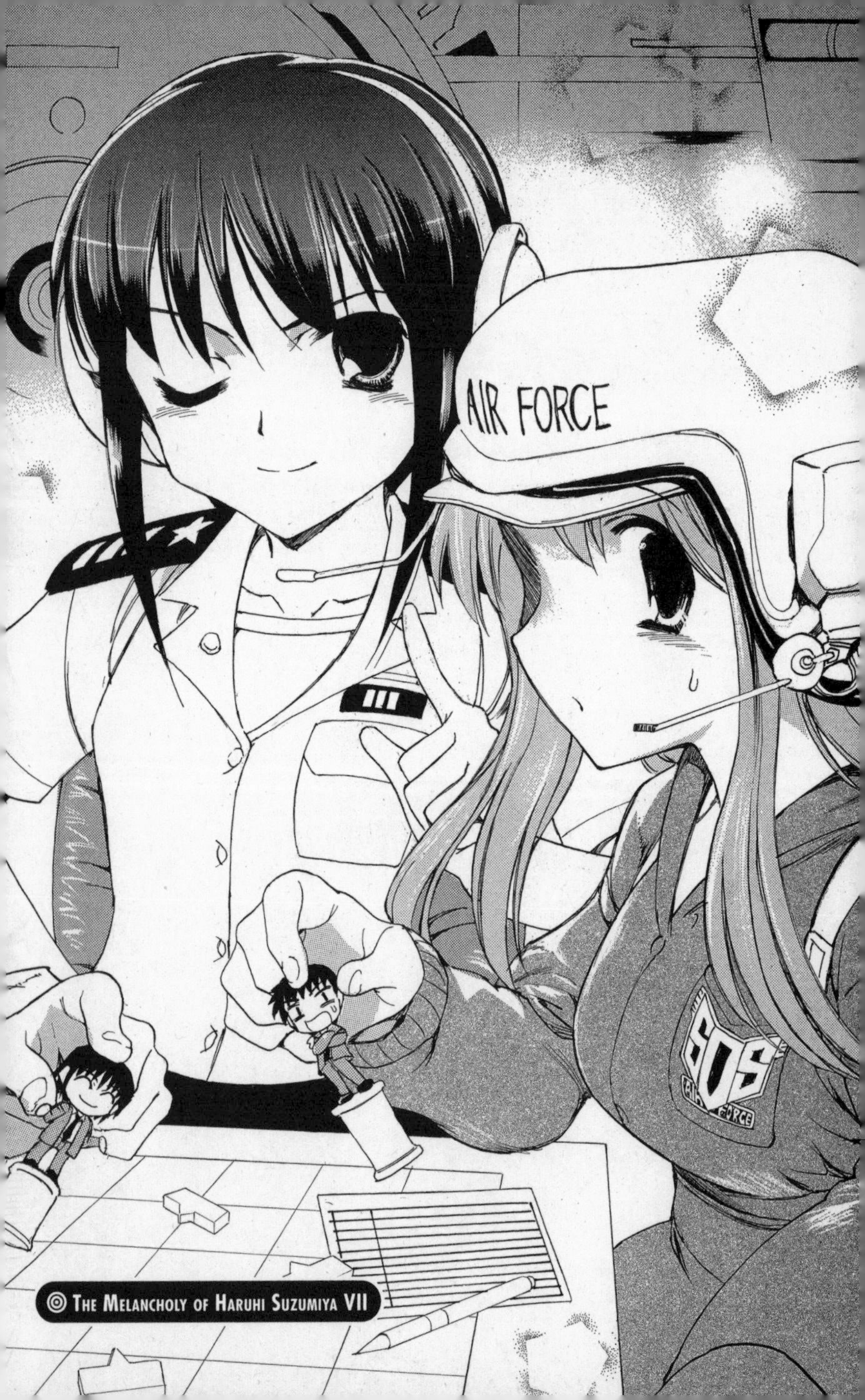
AIR FORCE
SOS
AIR FORCE
© THE MELANCHOLY OF HARUHI SUZUMIYA VII

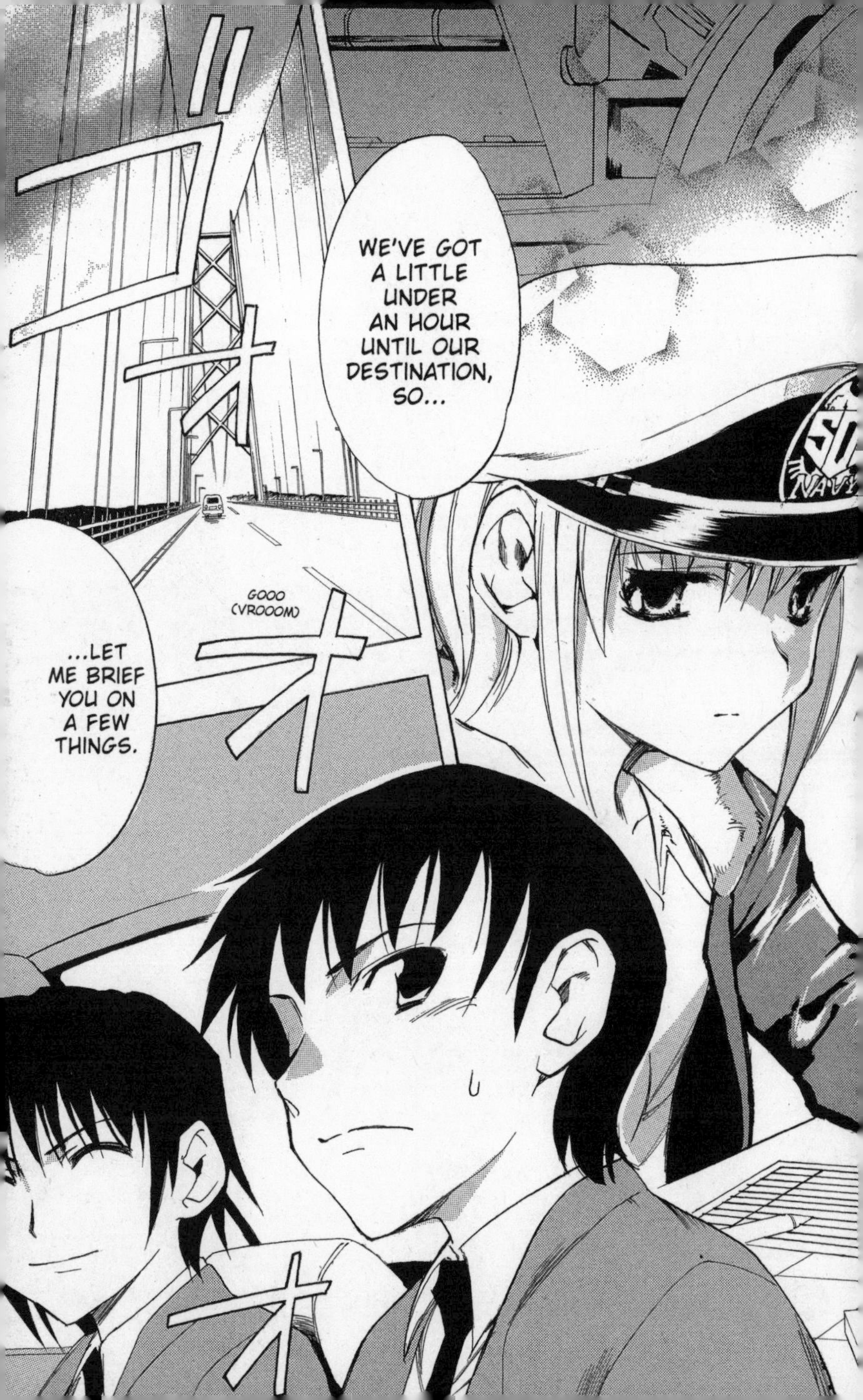
WE'VE GOT A LITTLE UNDER AN HOUR UNTIL OUR DESTINATION, SO...
GOOO (VROOOM)
...LET ME BRIEF YOU ON A FEW THINGS.

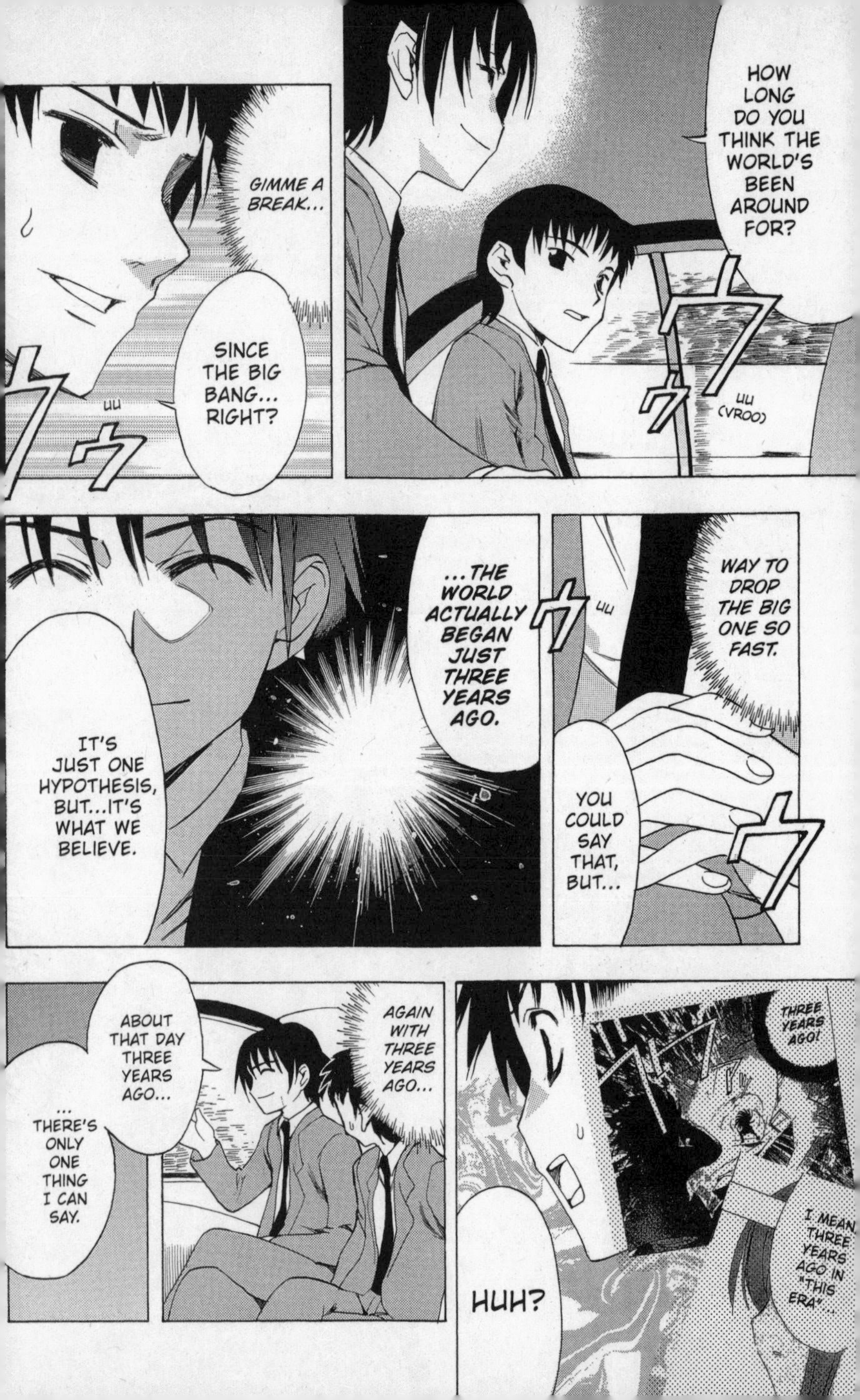
HOW LONG DO YOU THINK THE WORLD'S BEEN AROUND FOR?
UU (VROO)
GIMME A BREAK...
SINCE THE BIG BANG... RIGHT?
UU
WAY TO DROP THE BIG ONE SO FAST.
UU
YOU COULD SAY THAT, BUT...
...THE WORLD ACTUALLY BEGAN JUST THREE YEARS AGO.
IT'S JUST ONE HYPOTHESIS, BUT...IT'S WHAT WE BELIEVE.
THREE YEARS AGO!
I MEAN, THREE YEARS AGO IN "THIS ERA"...
HUH?
AGAIN WITH THREE YEARS AGO...
ABOUT THAT DAY THREE YEARS AGO...
... THERE'S ONLY ONE THING I CAN SAY.

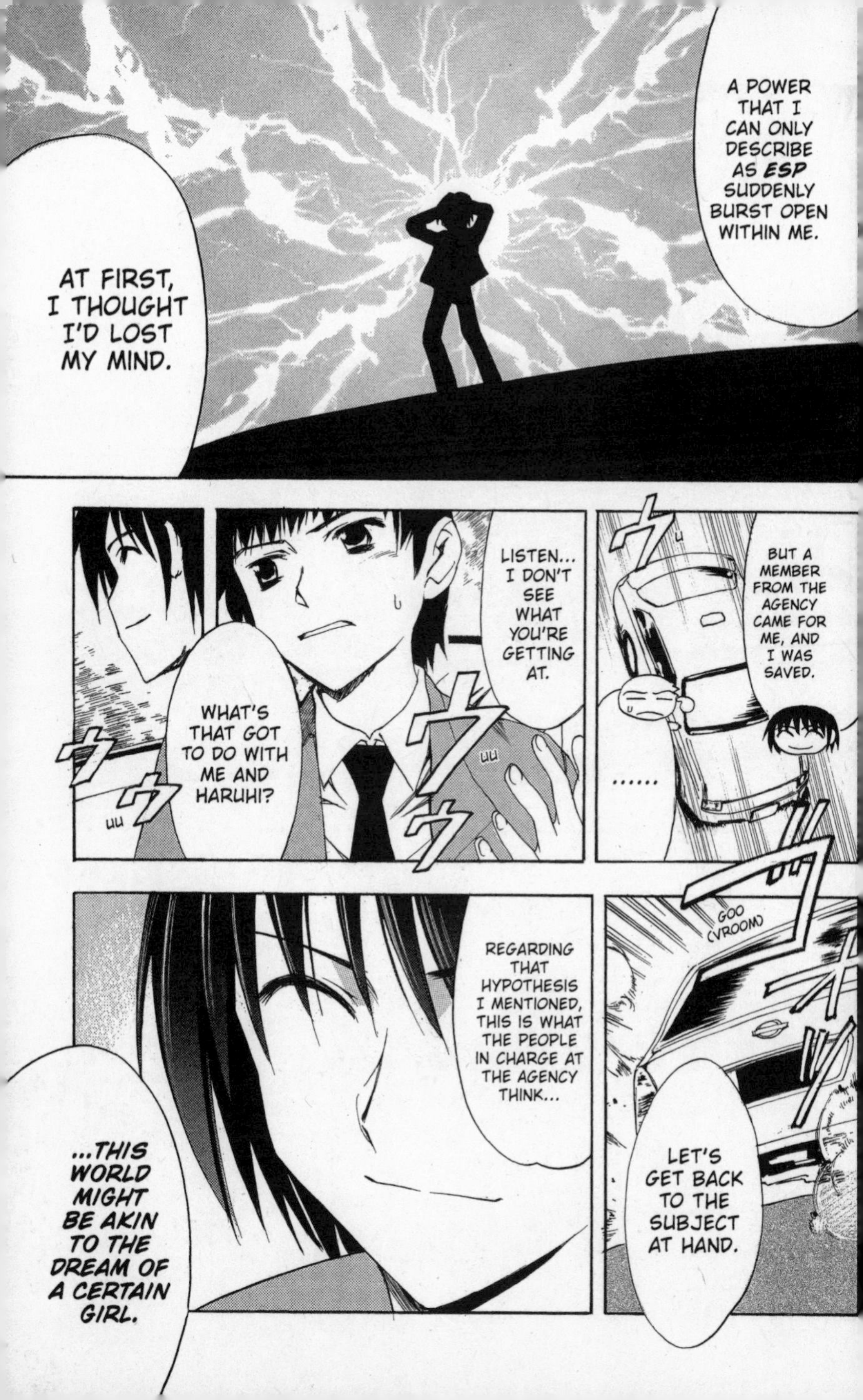
A POWER THAT I CAN ONLY DESCRIBE AS ESP SUDDENLY BURST OPEN WITHIN ME.
AT FIRST, I THOUGHT I'D LOST MY MIND.
u
BUT A MEMBER FROM THE AGENCY CAME FOR ME, AND I WAS SAVED.
......
uu
LISTEN... I DON'T SEE WHAT YOU'RE GETTING AT.
uu
WHAT'S THAT GOT TO DO WITH ME AND HARUHI?
uu
GOO (VROOM)
LET'S GET BACK TO THE SUBJECT AT HAND.
REGARDING THAT HYPOTHESIS I MENTIONED, THIS IS WHAT THE PEOPLE IN CHARGE AT THE AGENCY THINK...
...THIS WORLD MIGHT BE AKIN TO THE DREAM OF A CERTAIN GIRL.

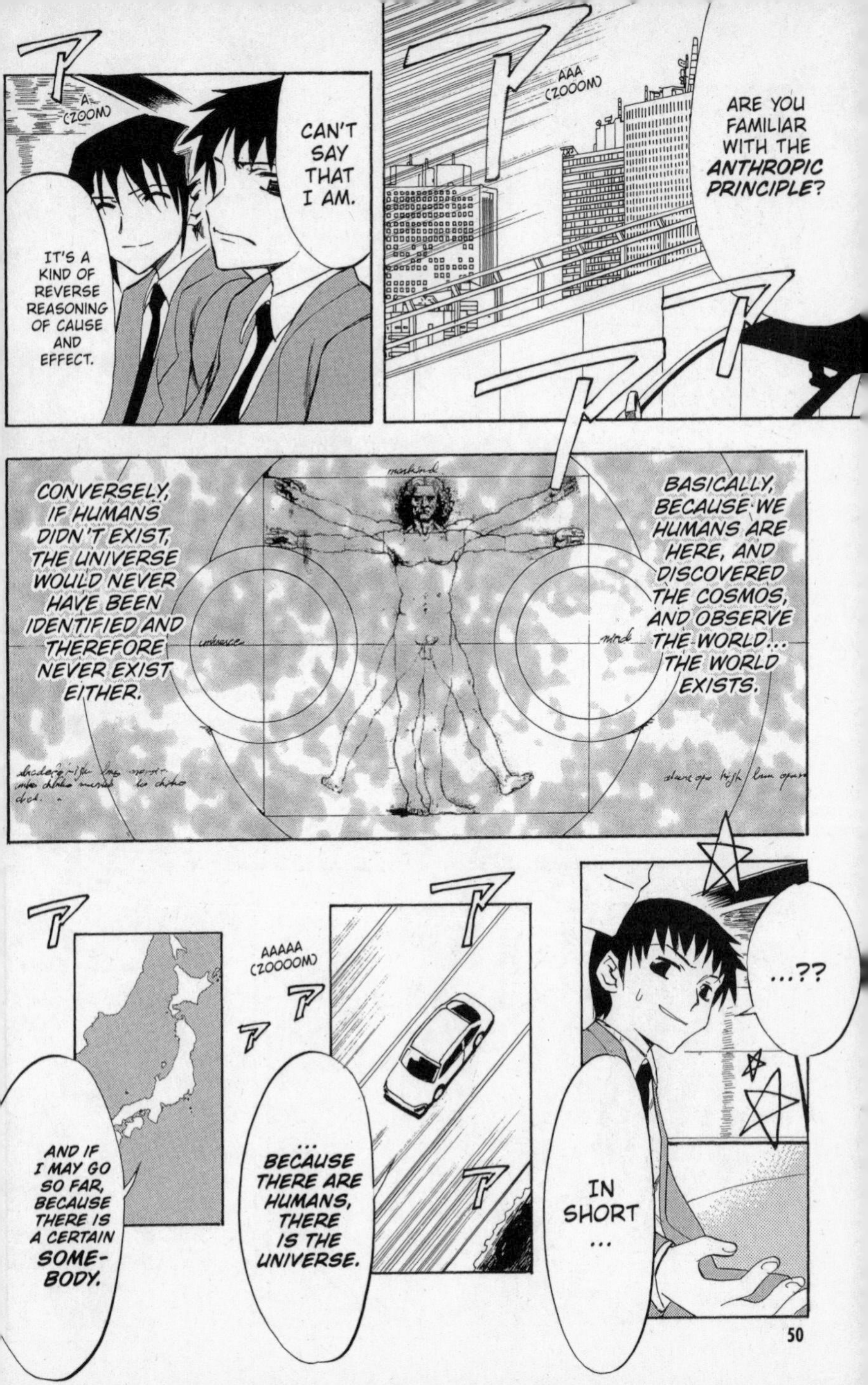
AAA (ZOOOM)
ARE YOU FAMILIAR WITH THE ANTHROPIC PRINCIPLE?
A (ZOOOM)
CAN'T SAY THAT I AM.
IT'S A KIND OF REVERSE REASONING OF CAUSE AND EFFECT.
BASICALLY, BECAUSE WE HUMANS ARE HERE, AND DISCOVERED THE COSMOS, AND OBSERVE THE WORLD... THE WORLD EXISTS.
CONVERSELY, IF HUMANS DIDN'T EXIST, THE UNIVERSE WOULD NEVER HAVE BEEN IDENTIFIED AND THEREFORE NEVER EXIST EITHER.
...??
IN SHORT ...
AAAAA (ZOOOOM)
... BECAUSE THERE ARE HUMANS, THERE IS THE UNIVERSE.
AND IF I MAY GO SO FAR, BECAUSE THERE IS A CERTAIN SOME-BODY.

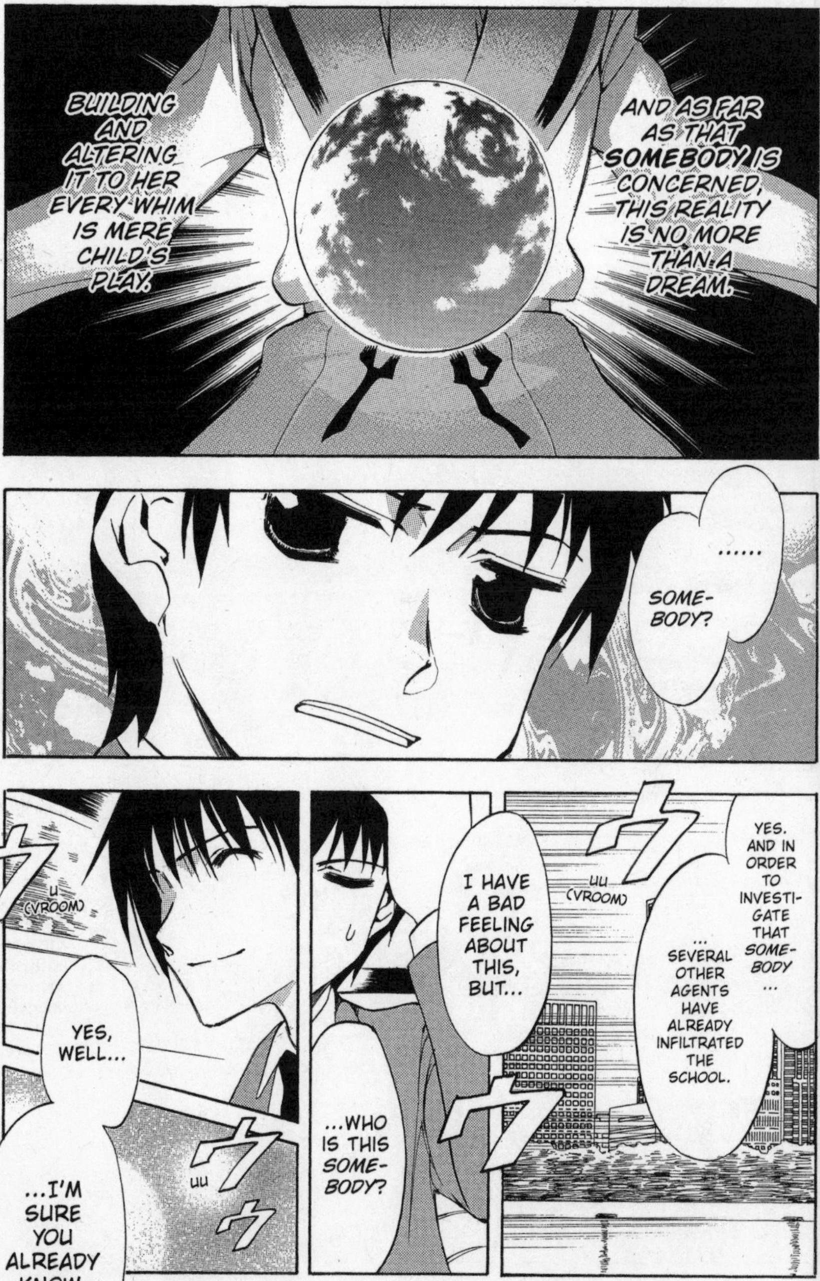
AND AS FAR AS THAT SOMEBODY IS CONCERNED, THIS REALITY IS NO MORE THAN A DREAM.
BUILDING AND ALTERING IT TO HER EVERY WHIM IS MERE CHILD'S PLAY.
...... SOME-BODY?
UU (VROOM)
YES. AND IN ORDER TO INVESTI-GATE THAT SOME-BODY ...
... SEVERAL OTHER AGENTS HAVE ALREADY INFILTRATED THE SCHOOL.
I HAVE A BAD FEELING ABOUT THIS, BUT...
...WHO IS THIS SOME-BODY?
U (VROOM)
YES, WELL...
UU
...I'M SURE YOU ALREADY KNOW.

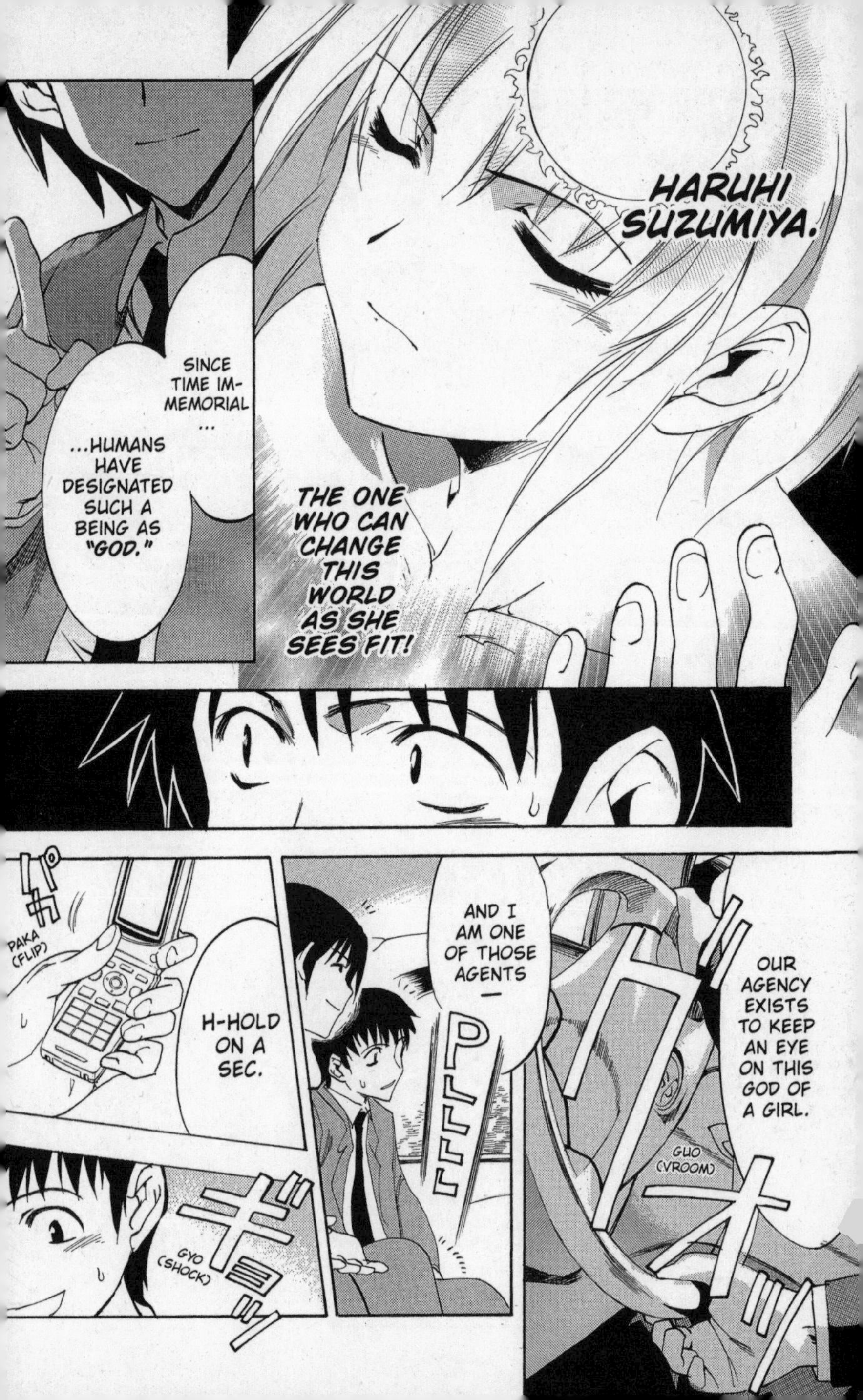
HARUHI SUZUMIYA.
THE ONE WHO CAN CHANGE THIS WORLD AS SHE SEES FIT!
SINCE TIME IM-MEMORIAL ...
...HUMANS HAVE DESIGNATED SUCH A BEING AS "GOD."
OUR AGENCY EXISTS TO KEEP AN EYE ON THIS GOD OF A GIRL.
GUO (VROOM)
AND I AM ONE OF THOSE AGENTS —
PLLLL
PAKA (FLIP)
H-HOLD ON A SEC.
GYO (SHOCK)

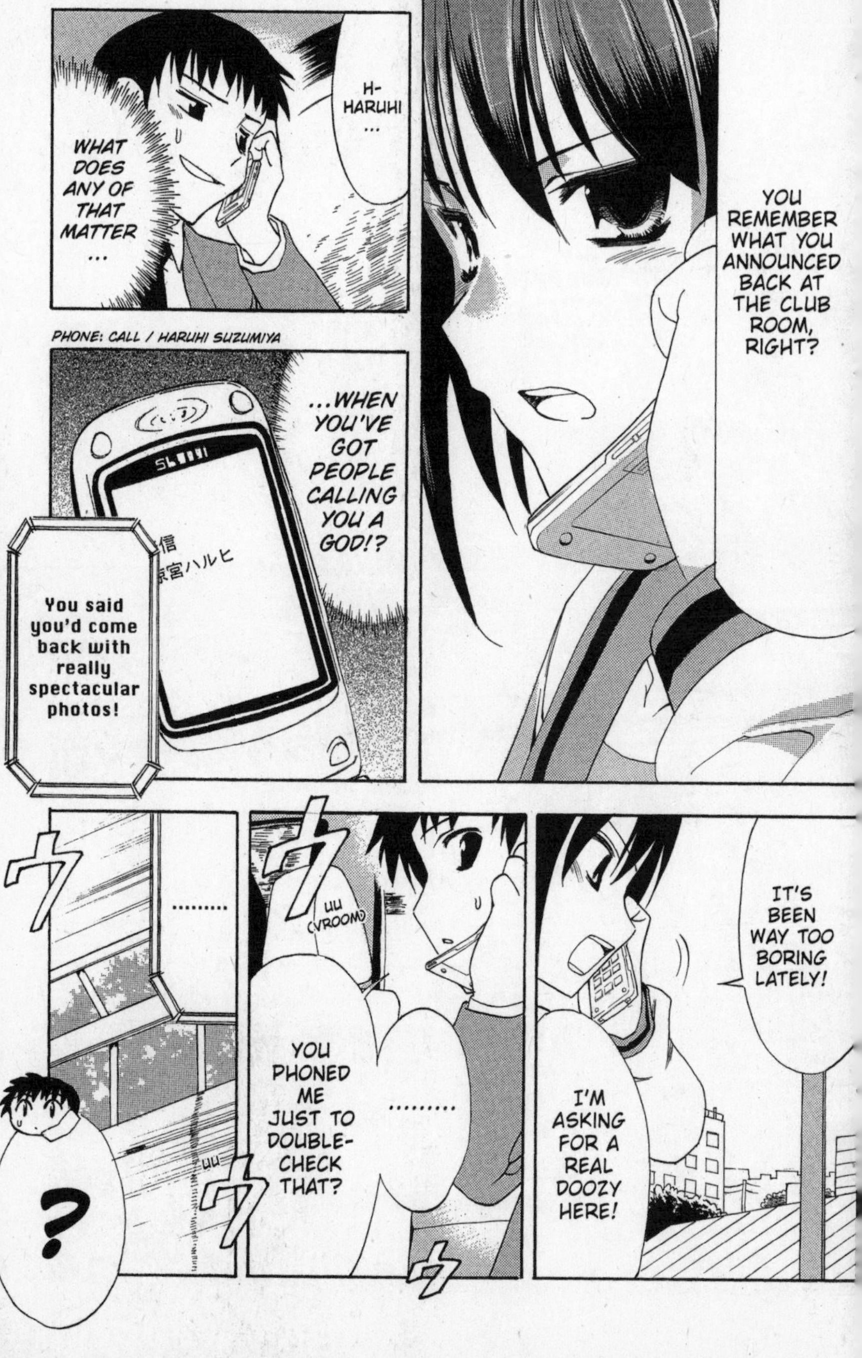
YOU REMEMBER WHAT YOU ANNOUNCED BACK AT THE CLUB ROOM, RIGHT?
H-HARUHI ...
WHAT DOES ANY OF THAT MATTER ...
PHONE: CALL / HARUHI SUZUMIYA
...WHEN YOU'VE GOT PEOPLE CALLING YOU A GOD!?
You said you'd come back with really spectacular photos!
IT'S BEEN WAY TOO BORING LATELY!
I'M ASKING FOR A REAL DOOZY HERE!
UU (VROOM)
YOU PHONED ME JUST TO DOUBLE-CHECK THAT?
....
....
UU
?

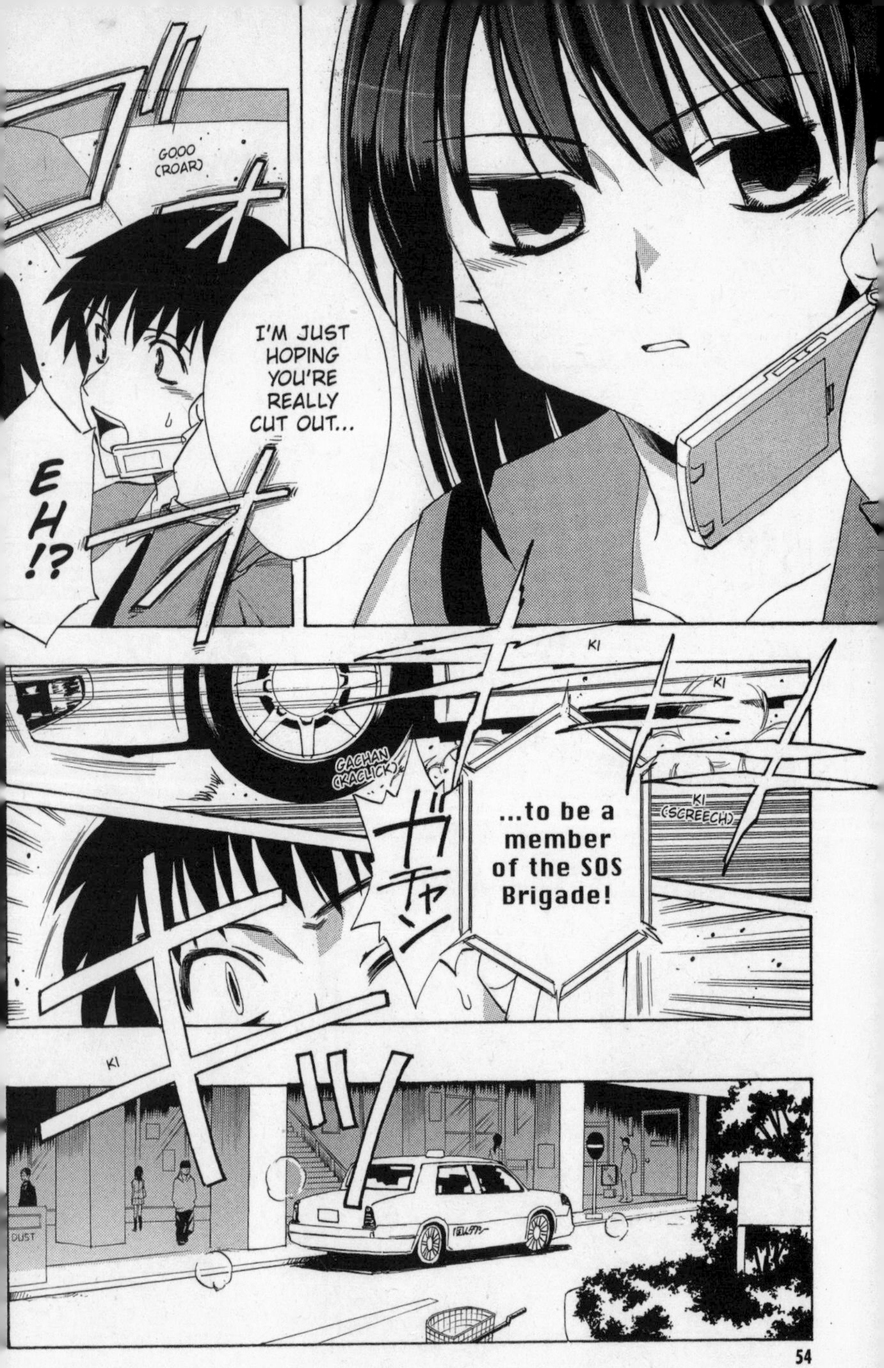
I'M JUST HOPING YOU'RE REALLY CUT OUT...
GOOO (ROAR)
EH!?
KI
KI
KI (SCREECH)
...to be a member of the SOS Brigade!
GACHAN (KACLICK)
KI
DUST

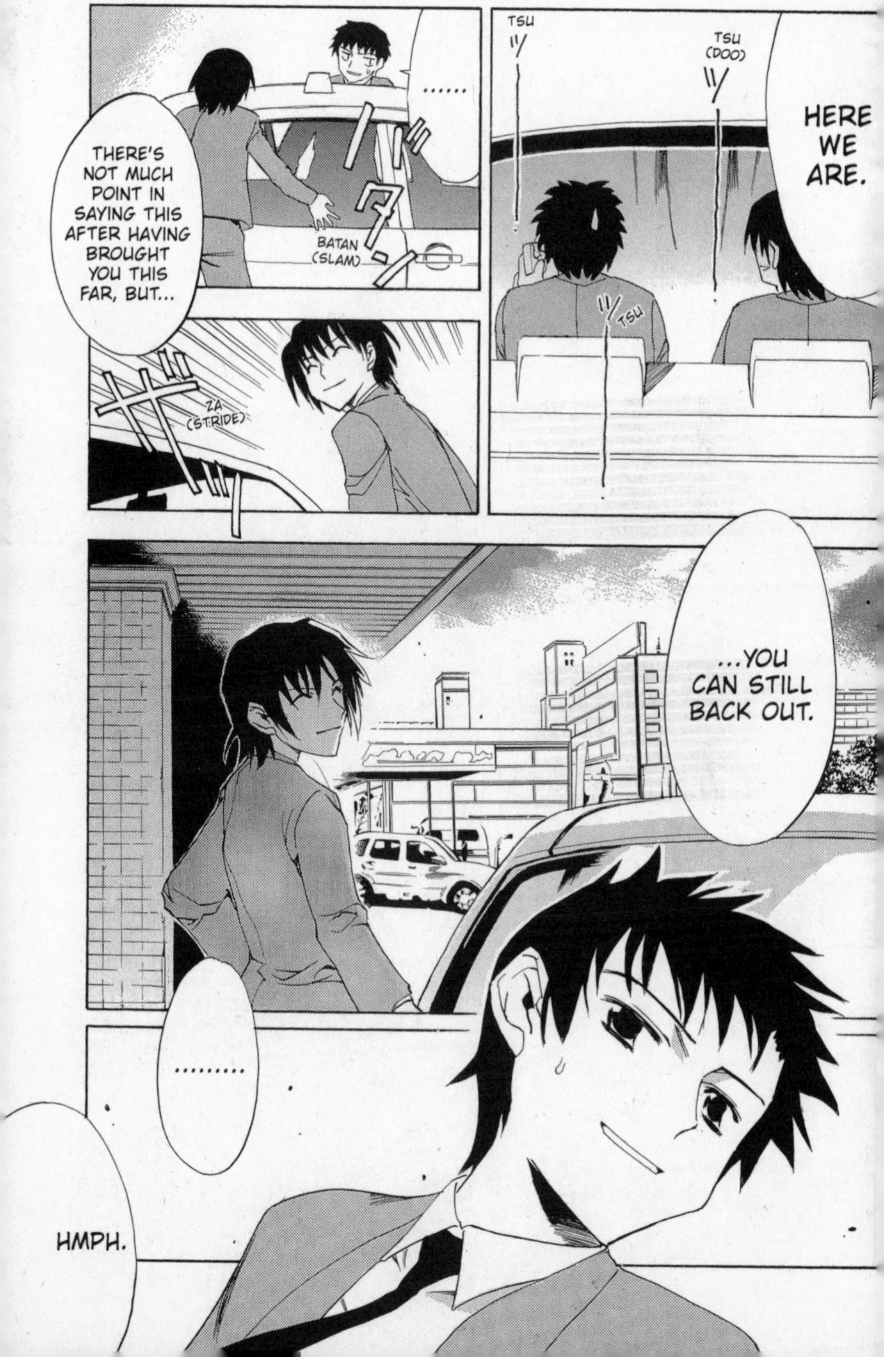
TSU
TSU (DOO)
HERE WE ARE.
TSU
......
BATAN (SLAM)
THERE'S NOT MUCH POINT IN SAYING THIS AFTER HAVING BROUGHT YOU THIS FAR, BUT...
ZA (STRIDE)
...YOU CAN STILL BACK OUT.
....
HMPH.

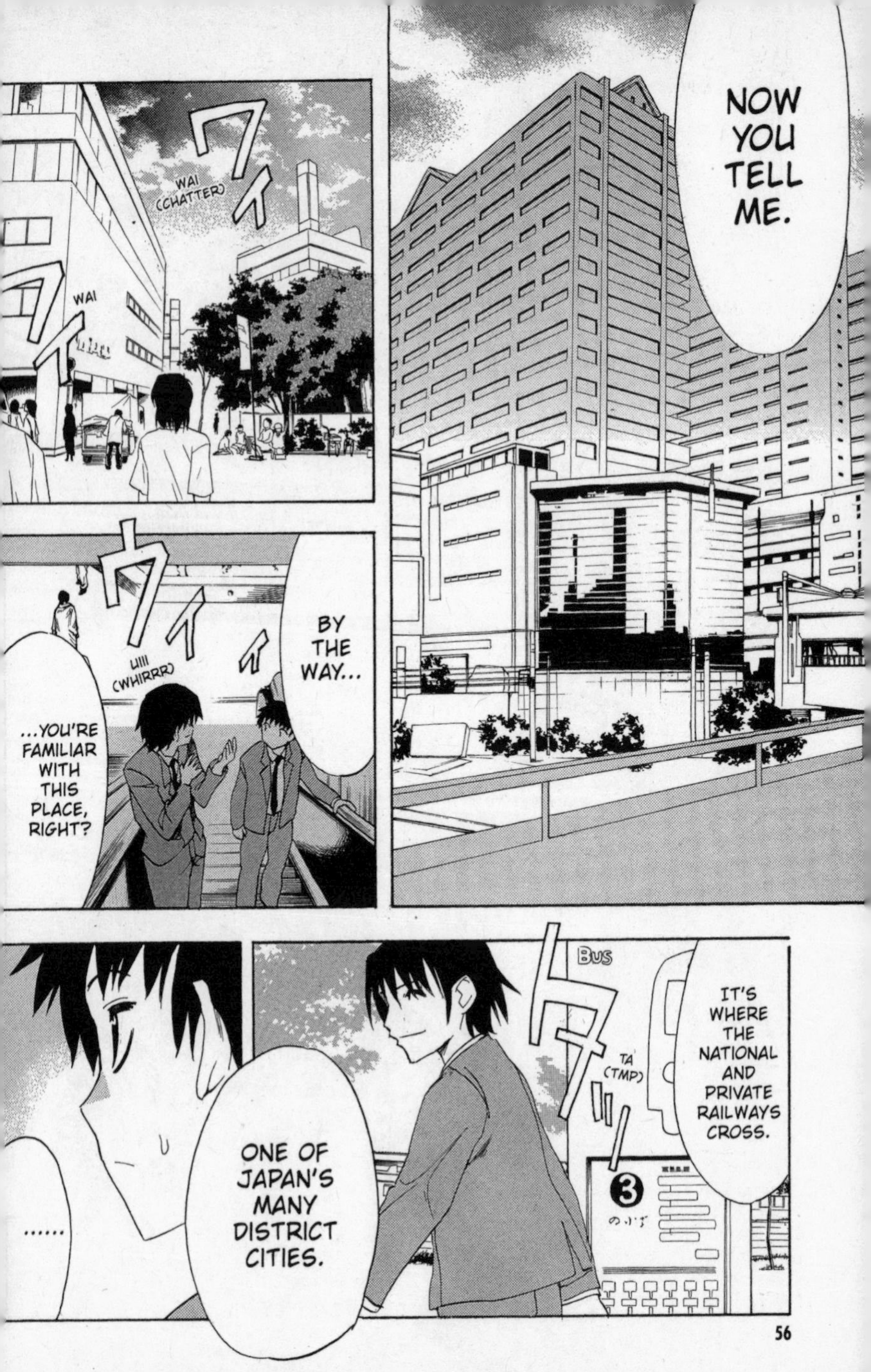
NOW YOU TELL ME.
WAI (CHATTER)
WAI
BY THE WAY...
UIII (WHIRRR)
...YOU'RE FAMILIAR WITH THIS PLACE, RIGHT?
BUS
TA (TMP)
IT'S WHERE THE NATIONAL AND PRIVATE RAILWAYS CROSS.
ONE OF JAPAN'S MANY DISTRICT CITIES.
......

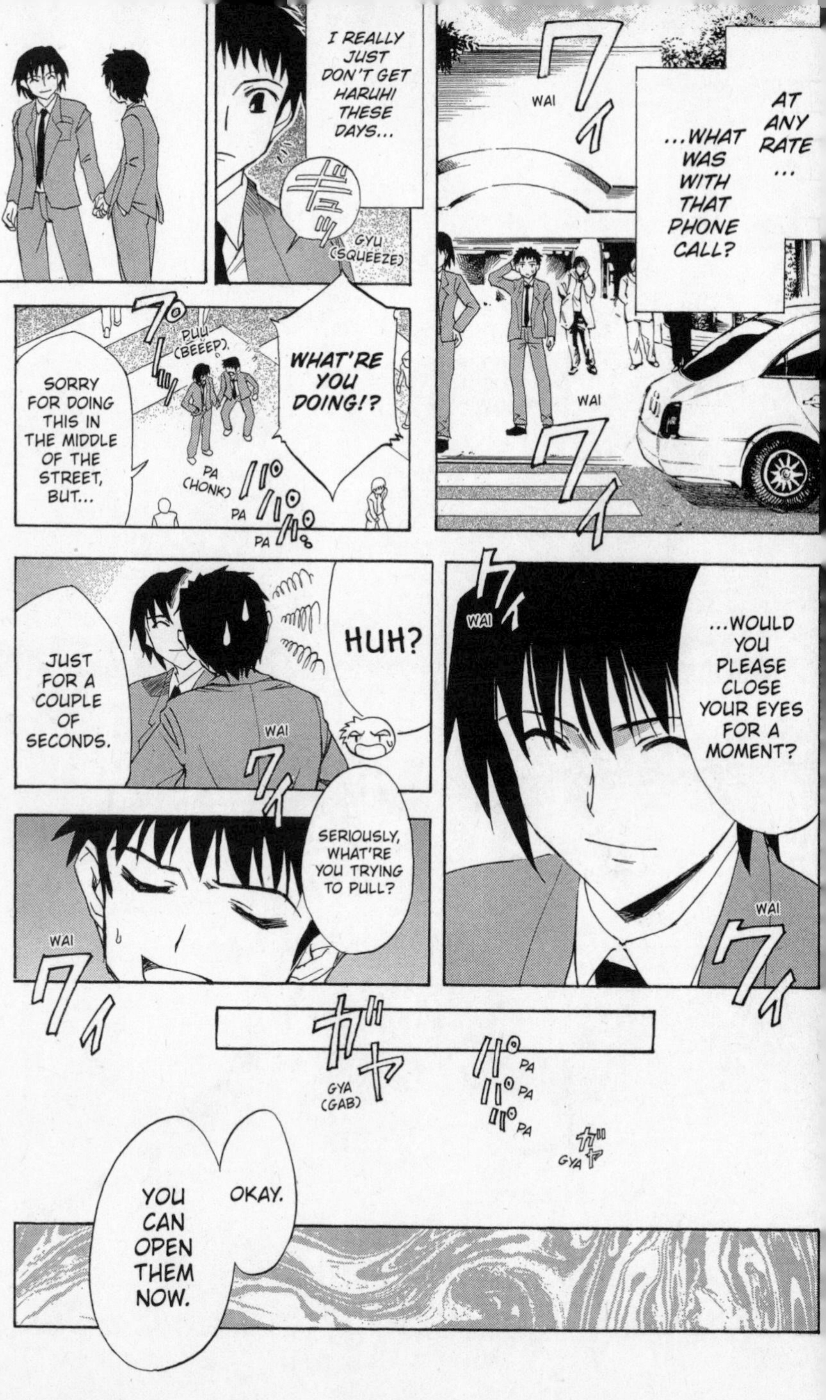
WAI
AT ANY RATE...
...WHAT WAS WITH THAT PHONE CALL?
WAI
I REALLY JUST DON'T GET HARUHI THESE DAYS...
GYU (SQUEEZE)
WHAT'RE YOU DOING!?
PUU (BEEEP)
SORRY FOR DOING THIS IN THE MIDDLE OF THE STREET, BUT...
PA (HONK)
PA
PA
WAI
...WOULD YOU PLEASE CLOSE YOUR EYES FOR A MOMENT?
WAI
HUH?
JUST FOR A COUPLE OF SECONDS.
WAI
SERIOUSLY, WHAT'RE YOU TRYING TO PULL?
WAI
GYA
PA
PA
PA
GYA (GAB)
OKAY.
YOU CAN OPEN THEM NOW.

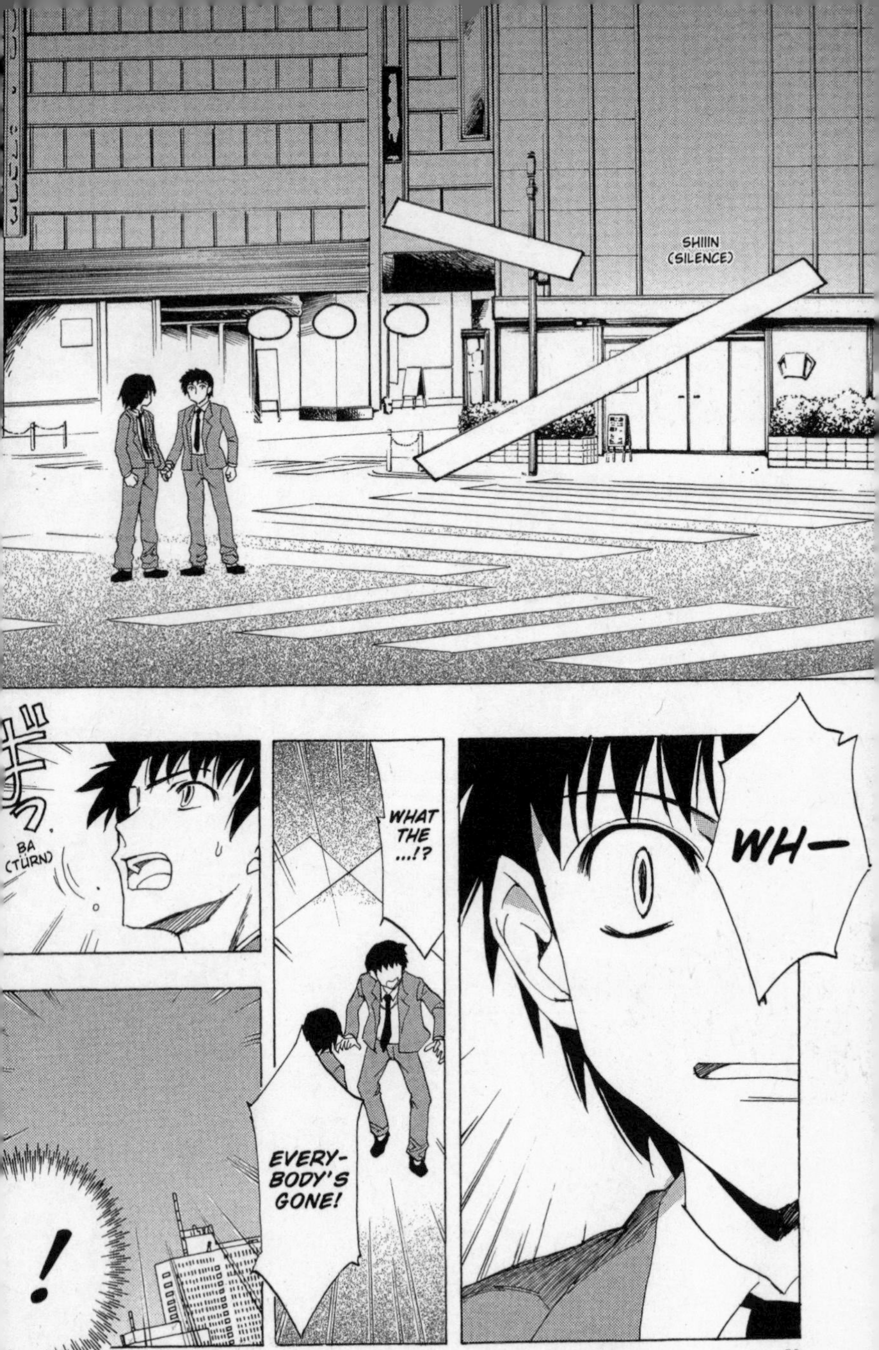
SHIIIN (SILENCE)
WH—
WHAT THE ...!?
EVERY-BODY'S GONE!
BA (TURN)
!

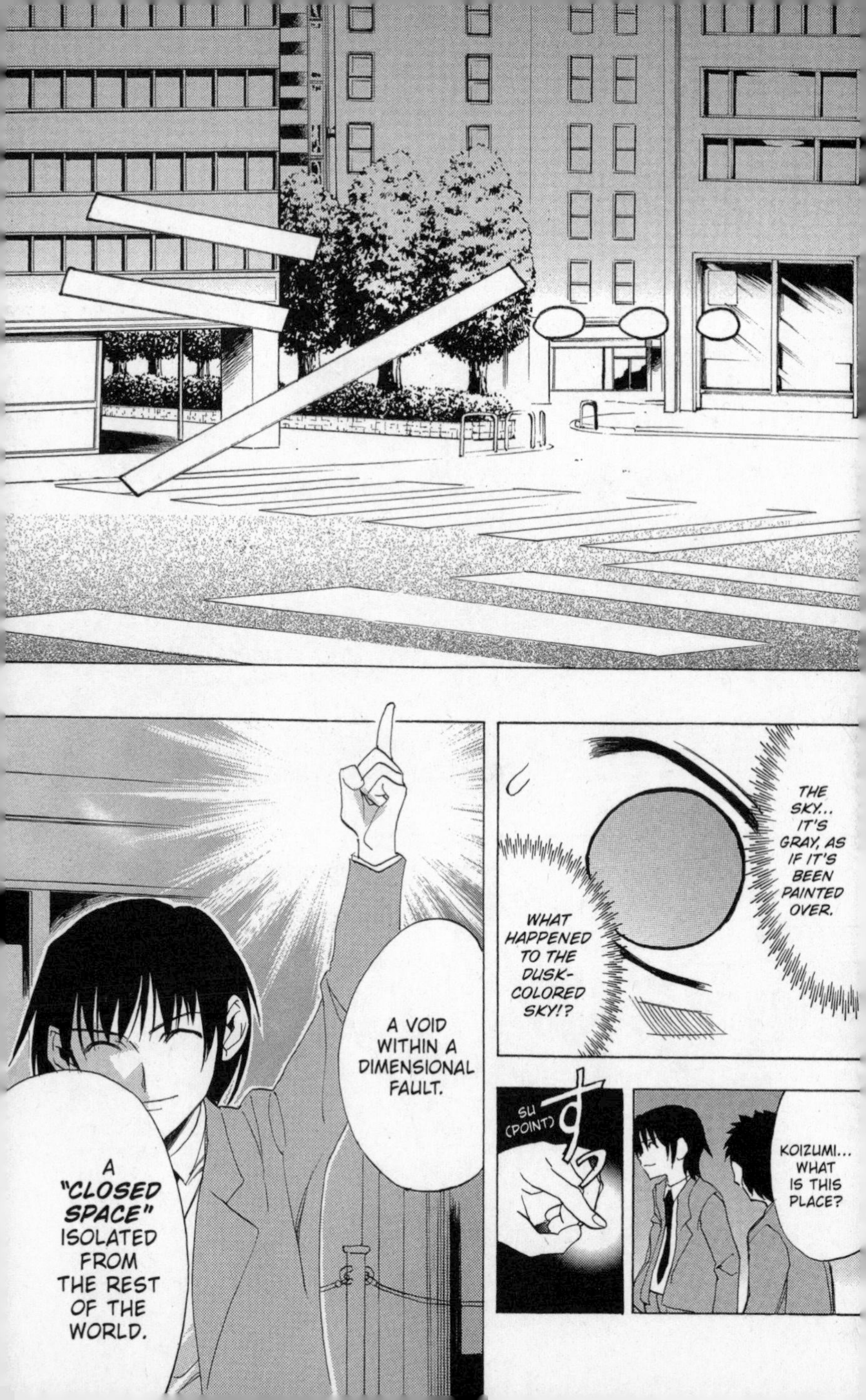
THE SKY... IT'S GRAY, AS IF IT'S BEEN PAINTED OVER.
WHAT HAPPENED TO THE DUSK-COLORED SKY!?
KOIZUMI... WHAT IS THIS PLACE?
SU (POINT)
A VOID WITHIN A DIMENSIONAL FAULT.
A "CLOSED SPACE" ISOLATED FROM THE REST OF THE WORLD.

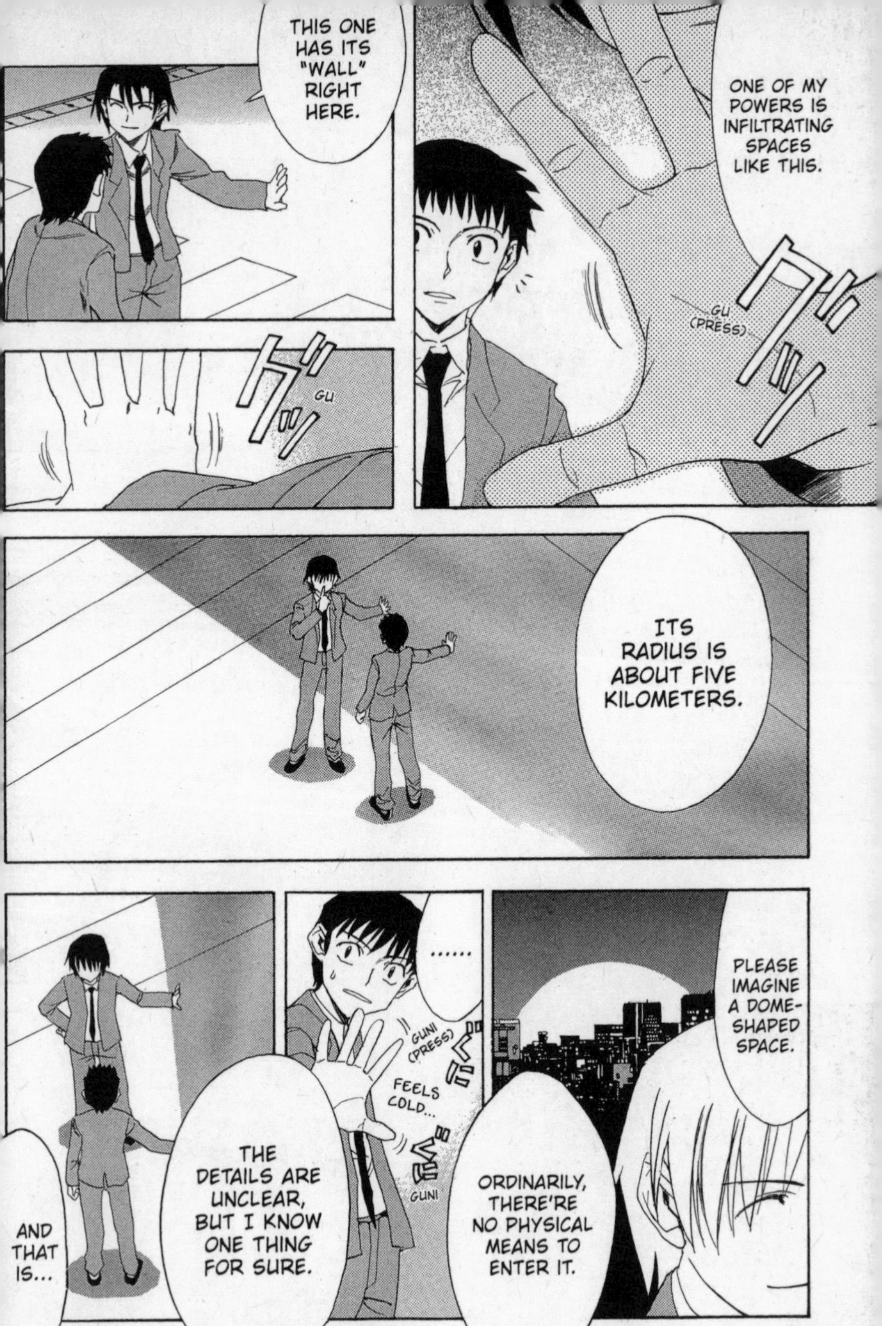
ONE OF MY POWERS IS INFILTRATING SPACES LIKE THIS.
GU (PRESS)
THIS ONE HAS ITS "WALL" RIGHT HERE.
GU
ITS RADIUS IS ABOUT FIVE KILOMETERS.
PLEASE IMAGINE A DOME-SHAPED SPACE.
ORDINARILY, THERE'RE NO PHYSICAL MEANS TO ENTER IT.
......
GUNI (PRESS)
FEELS COLD...
GUNI
THE DETAILS ARE UNCLEAR, BUT I KNOW ONE THING FOR SURE.
AND THAT IS...

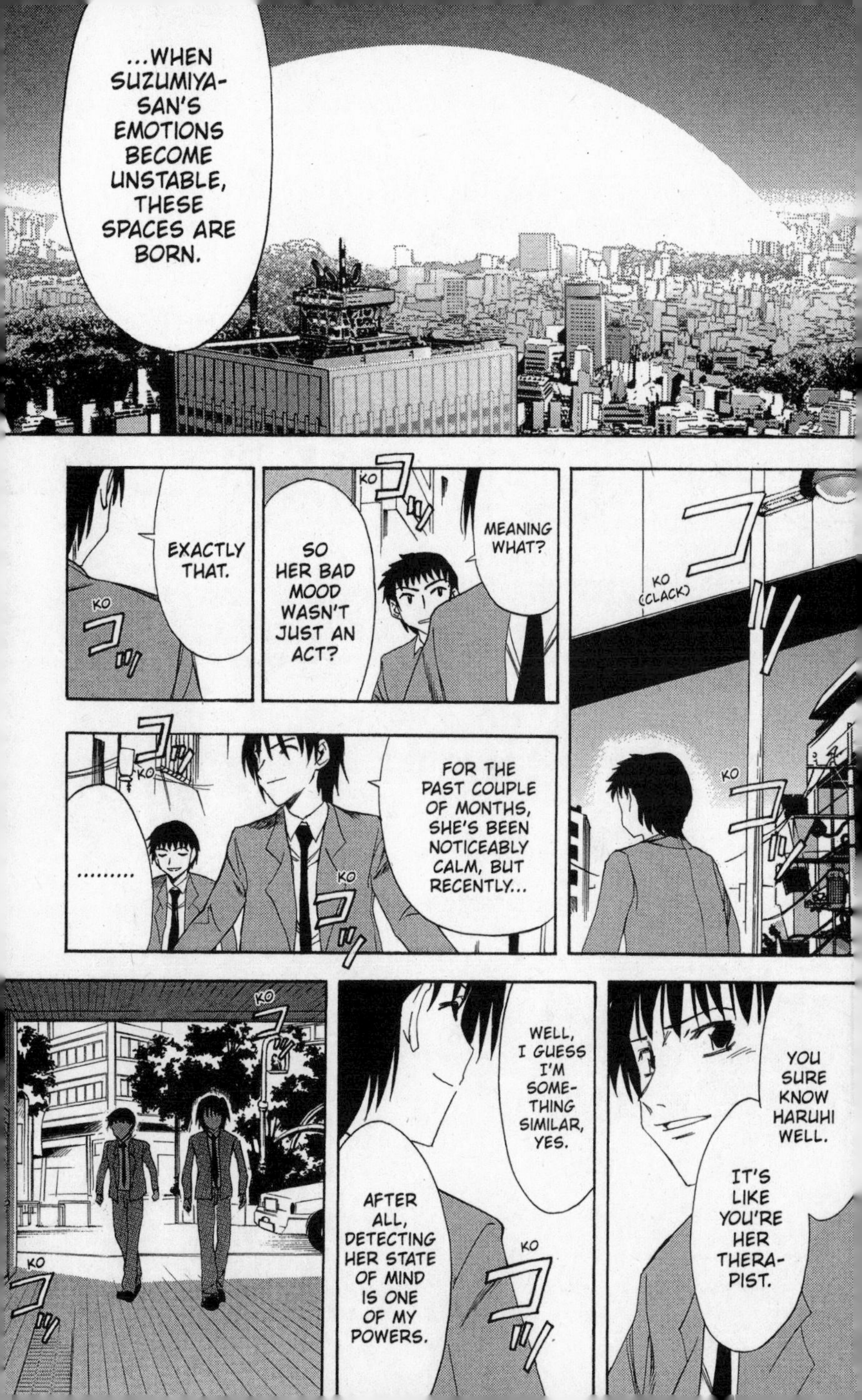
...WHEN SUZUMIYA-SAN'S EMOTIONS BECOME UNSTABLE, THESE SPACES ARE BORN.
KO (CLACK)
KO
MEANING WHAT?
SO HER BAD MOOD WASN'T JUST AN ACT?
KO
EXACTLY THAT.
KO
FOR THE PAST COUPLE OF MONTHS, SHE'S BEEN NOTICEABLY CALM, BUT RECENTLY...
KO
....
KO
YOU SURE KNOW HARUHI WELL.
IT'S LIKE YOU'RE HER THERAPIST.
WELL, I GUESS I'M SOME-THING SIMILAR, YES.
AFTER ALL, DETECTING HER STATE OF MIND IS ONE OF MY POWERS.
KO
KO
KO

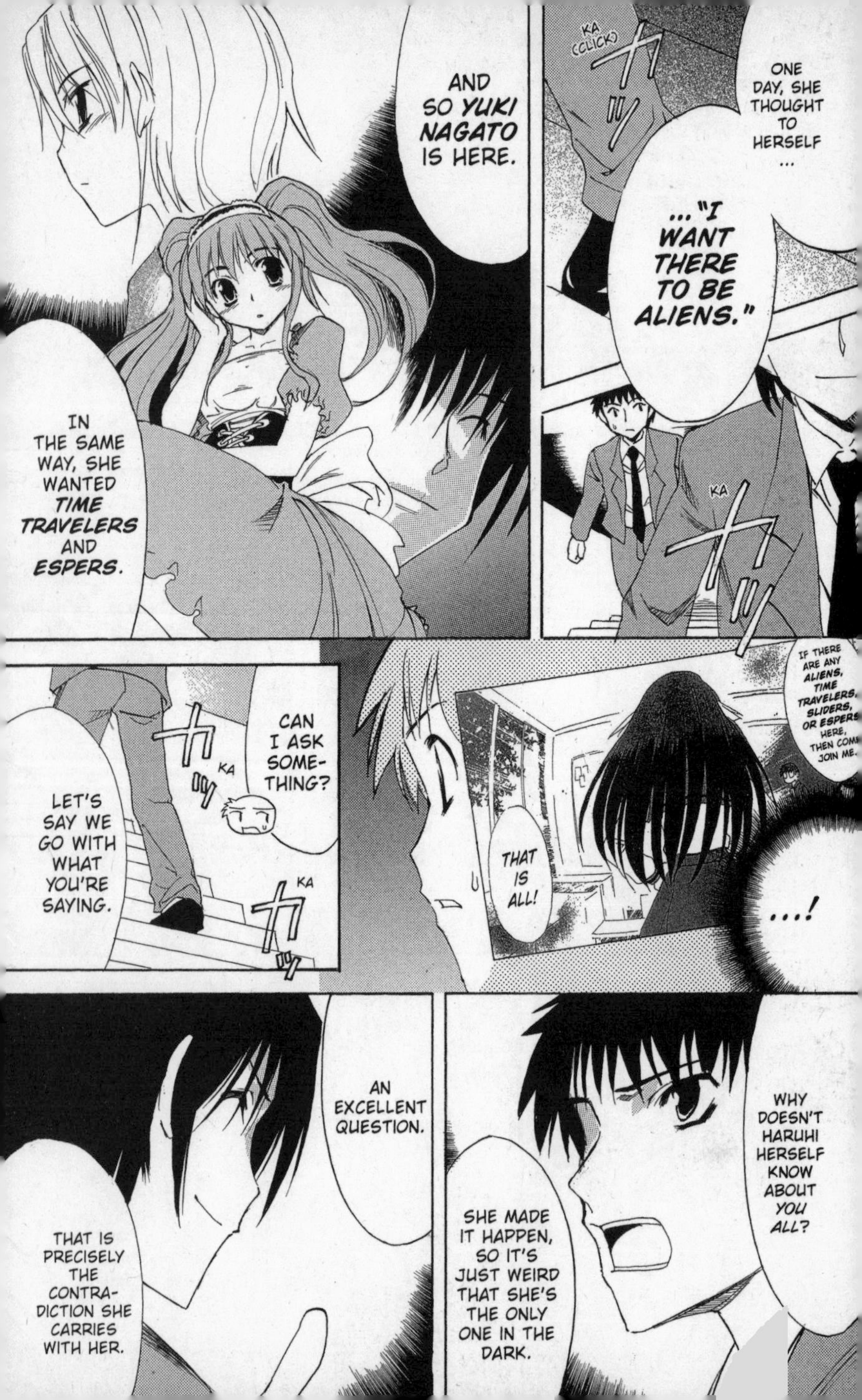
KA (CLICK)
ONE DAY, SHE THOUGHT TO HERSELF ...
..."I WANT THERE TO BE ALIENS."
KA
AND SO YUKI NAGATO IS HERE.
IN THE SAME WAY, SHE WANTED TIME TRAVELERS AND ESPERS.
IF THERE ARE ANY ALIENS, TIME TRAVELERS, SLIDERS, OR ESPERS HERE, THEN COM JOIN ME.
THAT IS ALL!
...!
CAN I ASK SOME-THING?
KA
LET'S SAY WE GO WITH WHAT YOU'RE SAYING.
KA
WHY DOESN'T HARUHI HERSELF KNOW ABOUT YOU ALL?
SHE MADE IT HAPPEN, SO IT'S JUST WEIRD THAT SHE'S THE ONLY ONE IN THE DARK.
AN EXCELLENT QUESTION.
THAT IS PRECISELY THE CONTRA-DICTION SHE CARRIES WITH HER.

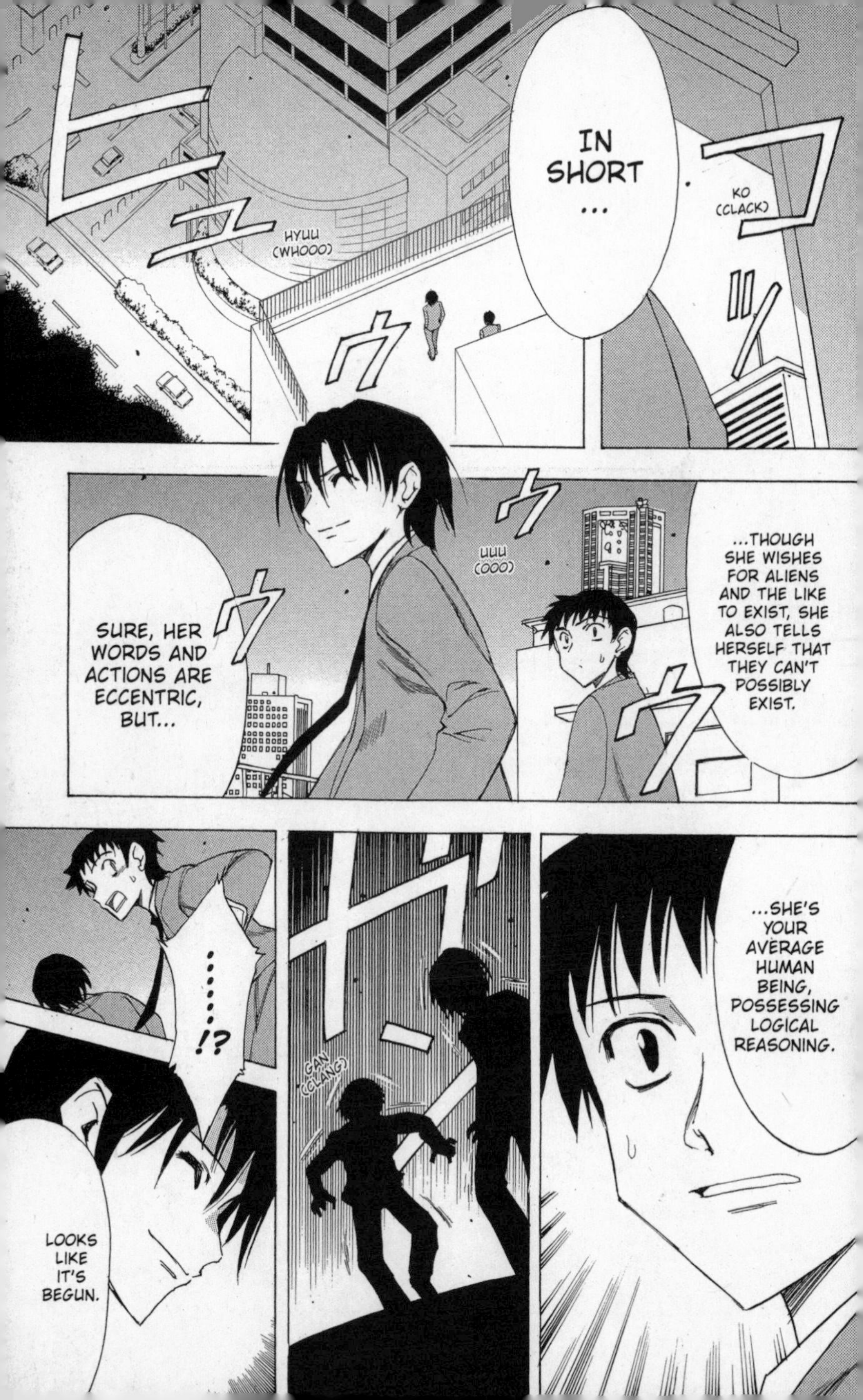
KO (CLACK)
IN SHORT ...
HYUU (WHOOO)
...THOUGH SHE WISHES FOR ALIENS AND THE LIKE TO EXIST, SHE ALSO TELLS HERSELF THAT THEY CAN'T POSSIBLY EXIST.
UUU (OOO)
SURE, HER WORDS AND ACTIONS ARE ECCENTRIC, BUT...
...SHE'S YOUR AVERAGE HUMAN BEING, POSSESSING LOGICAL REASONING.
GAN (CLANG)
......!?
LOOKS LIKE IT'S BEGUN.

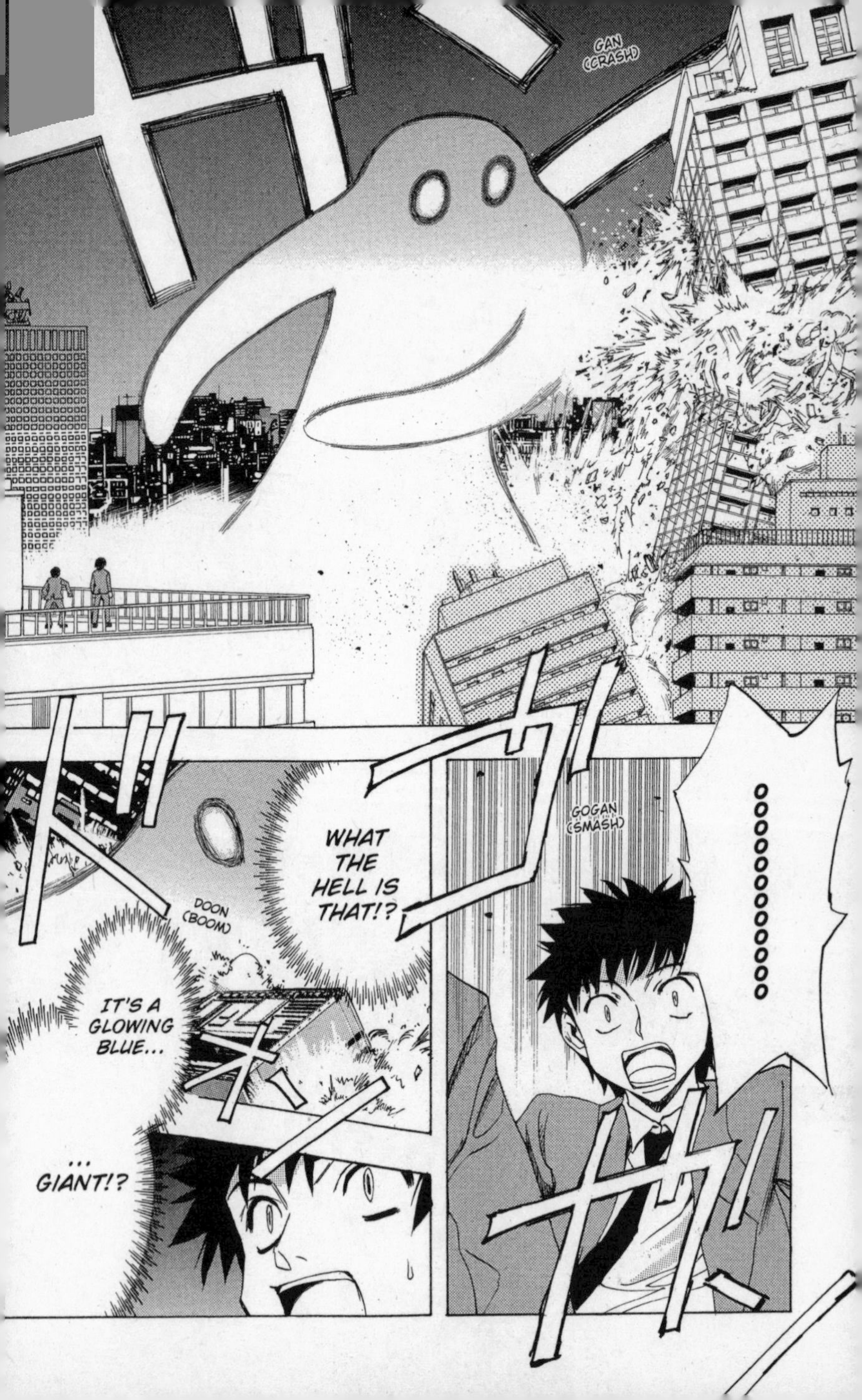

GAN (CRASH)
GOGAN (SMASH)
OOOOOOOOOOOOO
WHAT THE HELL IS THAT!?
DOON (BOOM)
IT'S A GLOWING BLUE...
... GIANT!?

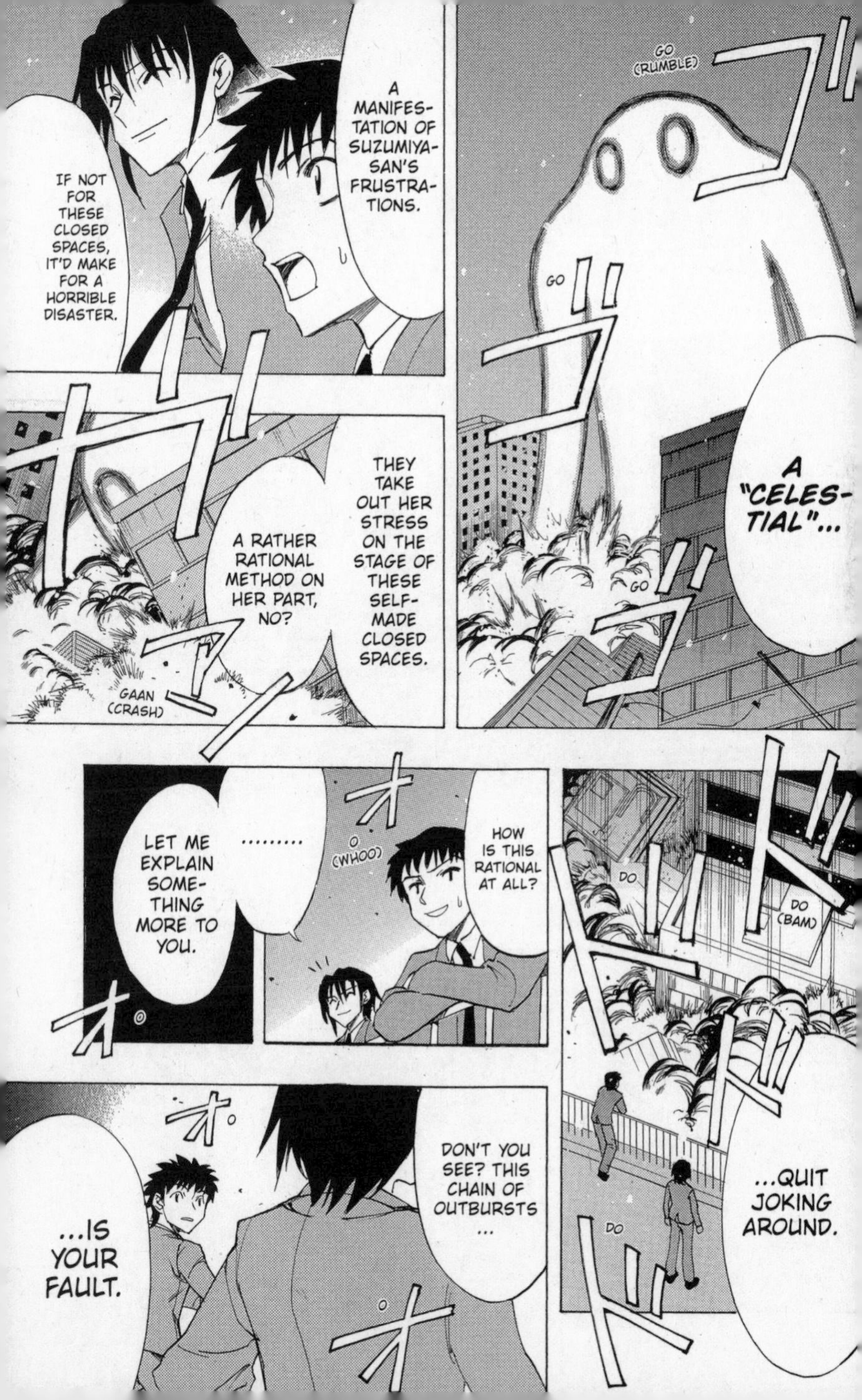
GO (RUMBLE)
GO
GO
A "CELESTIAL"...
A MANIFESTATION OF SUZUMIYA-SAN'S FRUSTRATIONS.
IF NOT FOR THESE CLOSED SPACES, IT'D MAKE FOR A HORRIBLE DISASTER.
THEY TAKE OUT HER STRESS ON THE STAGE OF THESE SELF-MADE CLOSED SPACES.
A RATHER RATIONAL METHOD ON HER PART, NO?
GAAN (CRASH)
DO
DO (BAM)
HOW IS THIS RATIONAL AT ALL?
O (WHOO)
....
LET ME EXPLAIN SOMETHING MORE TO YOU.
DO
...QUIT JOKING AROUND.
DON'T YOU SEE? THIS CHAIN OF OUTBURSTS ...
...IS YOUR FAULT.

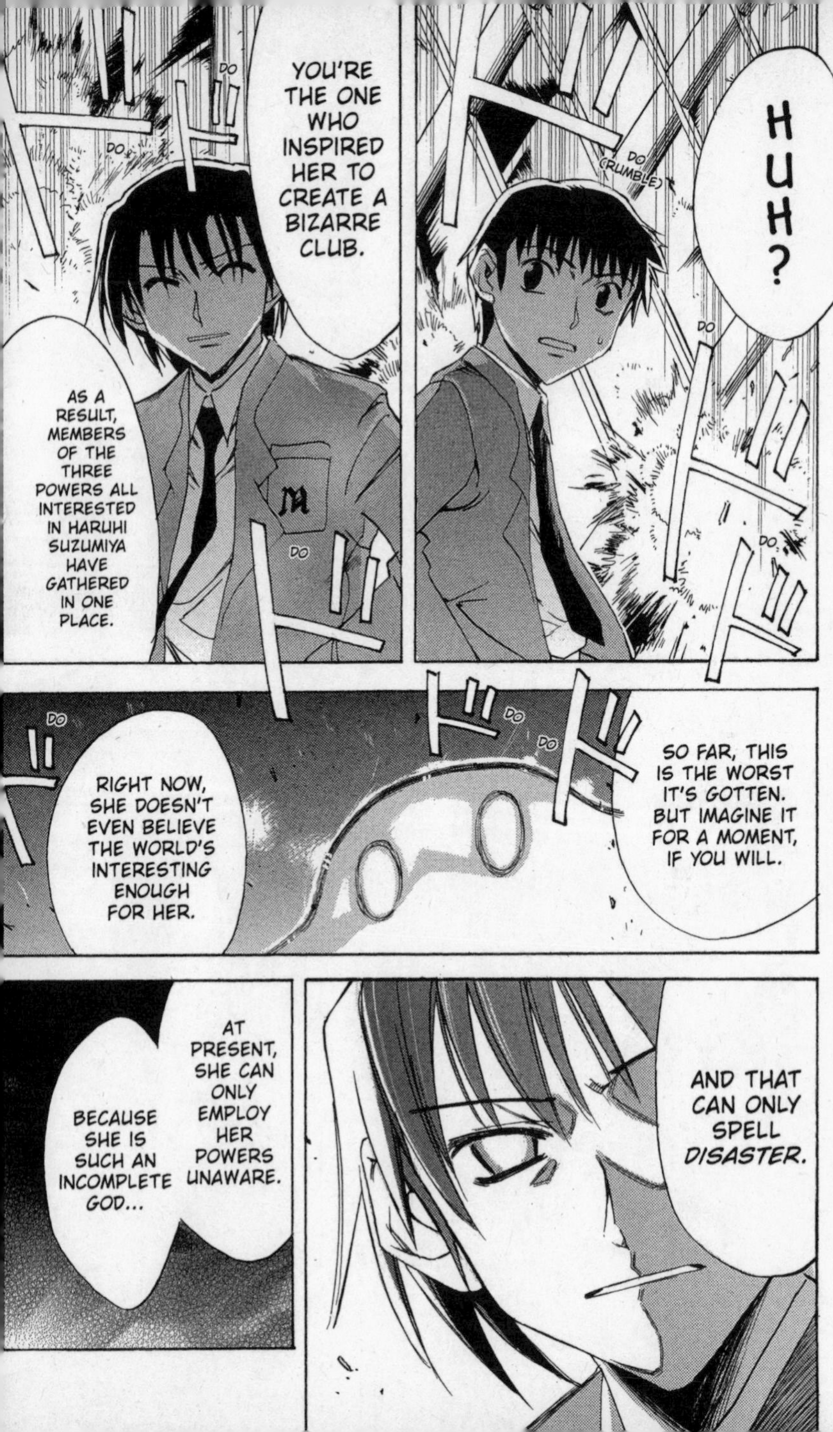
HUH?
DO (RUMBLE)
DO
DO
YOU'RE THE ONE WHO INSPIRED HER TO CREATE A BIZARRE CLUB.
AS A RESULT, MEMBERS OF THE THREE POWERS ALL INTERESTED IN HARUHI SUZUMIYA HAVE GATHERED IN ONE PLACE.
DO
DO
DO
SO FAR, THIS IS THE WORST IT'S GOTTEN. BUT IMAGINE IT FOR A MOMENT, IF YOU WILL.
DO
DO
DO
RIGHT NOW, SHE DOESN'T EVEN BELIEVE THE WORLD'S INTERESTING ENOUGH FOR HER.
AND THAT CAN ONLY SPELL DISASTER.
AT PRESENT, SHE CAN ONLY EMPLOY HER POWERS UNAWARE.
BECAUSE SHE IS SUCH AN INCOMPLETE GOD...

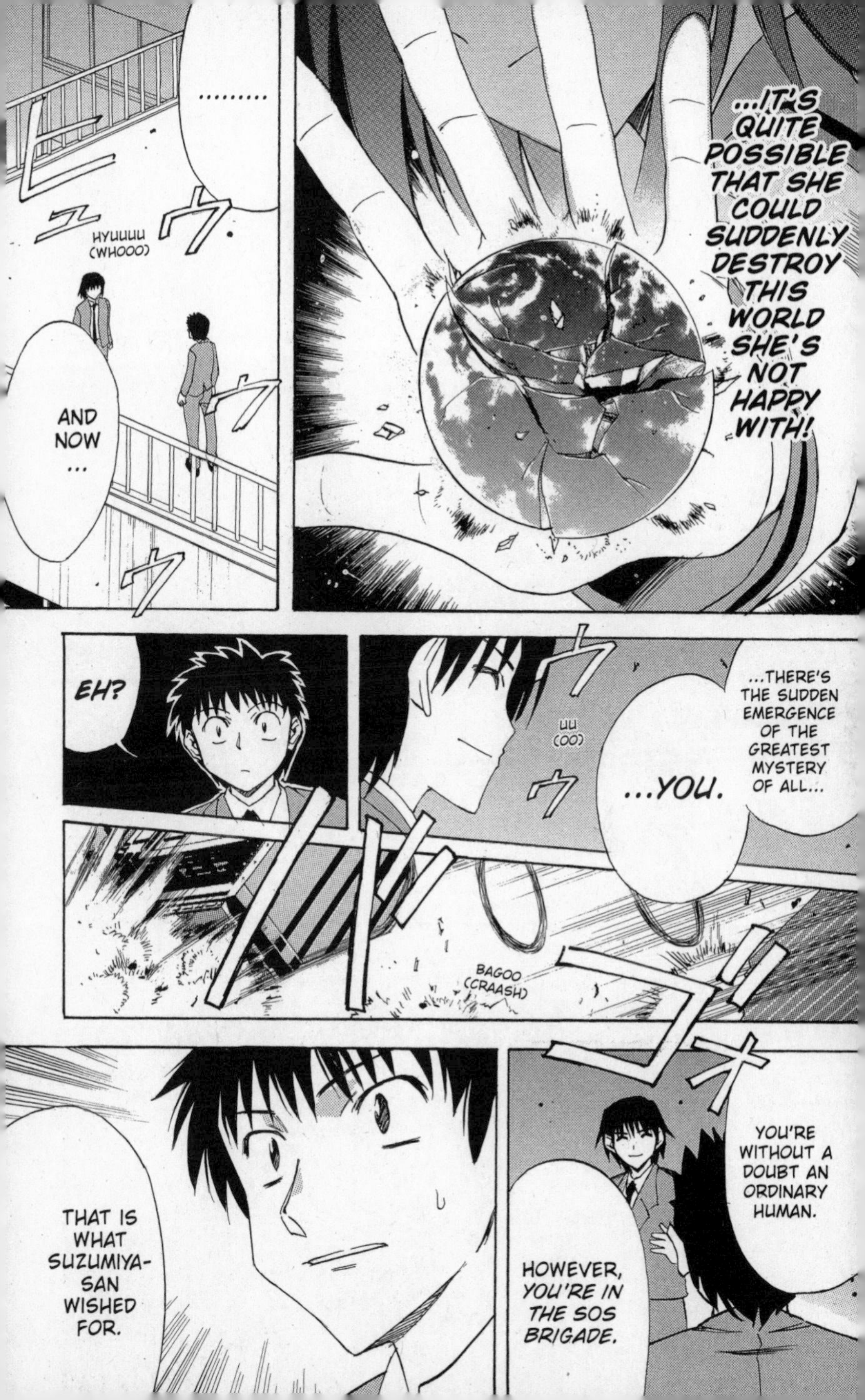
...IT'S QUITE POSSIBLE THAT SHE COULD SUDDENLY DESTROY THIS WORLD SHE'S NOT HAPPY WITH!
....
HYUUUU (WHOOO)
AND NOW ...
...THERE'S THE SUDDEN EMERGENCE OF THE GREATEST MYSTERY OF ALL...
UU (OO)
...YOU.
EH?
BAGOO (CRAASH)
YOU'RE WITHOUT A DOUBT AN ORDINARY HUMAN.
HOWEVER, YOU'RE IN THE SOS BRIGADE.
THAT IS WHAT SUZUMIYA-SAN WISHED FOR.

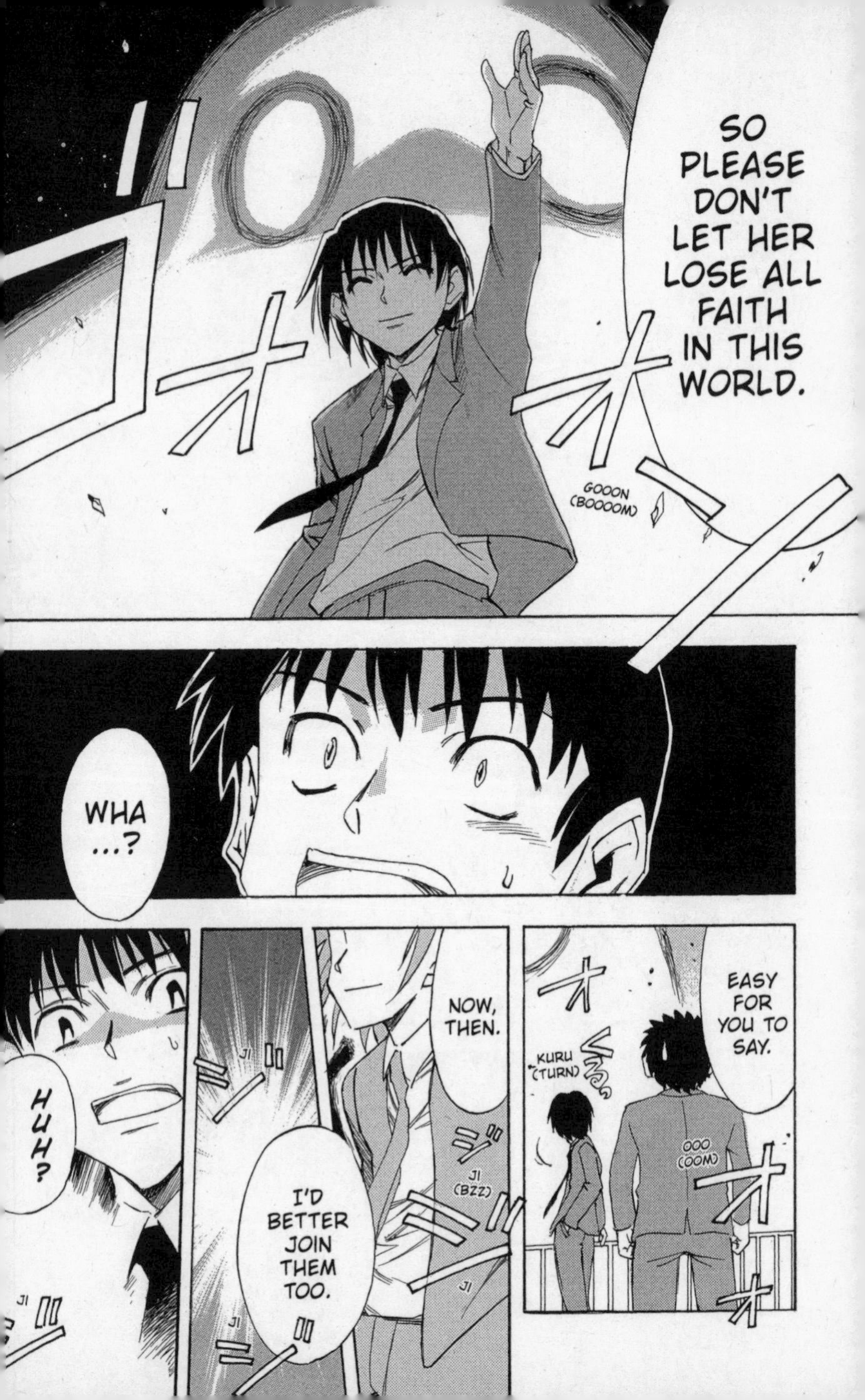
SO PLEASE DON'T LET HER LOSE ALL FAITH IN THIS WORLD.
GOOON (BOOOOM)
WHA ...?
EASY FOR YOU TO SAY.
OOO (OOM)
KURU (TURN)
NOW, THEN.
JI (BZZ)
I'D BETTER JOIN THEM TOO.
JI
JI
HUH?
JI

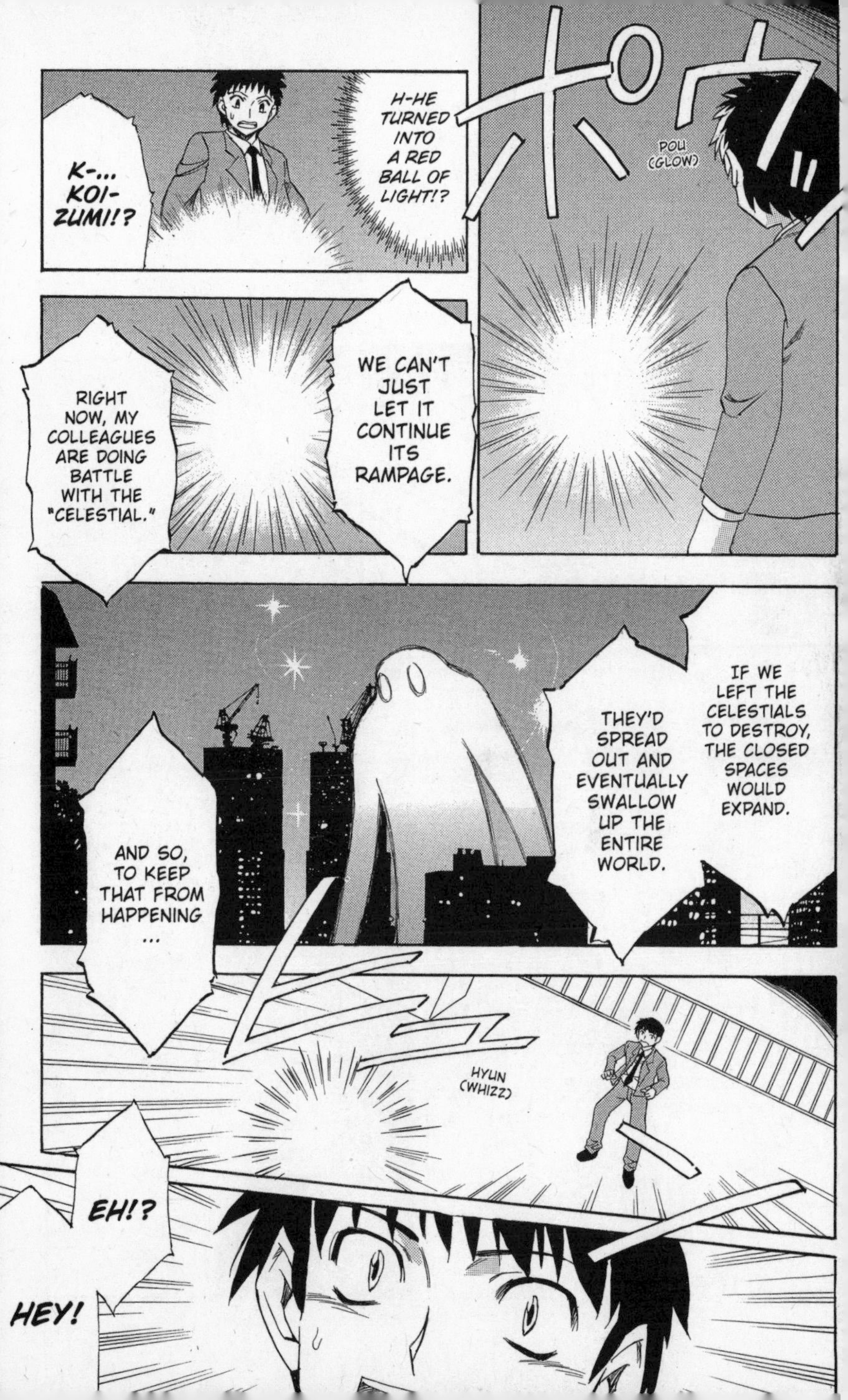
POU
(GLOW)
H-HE TURNED INTO A RED BALL OF LIGHT!?
K-... KOI-ZUMI!?
WE CAN'T JUST LET IT CONTINUE ITS RAMPAGE.
RIGHT NOW, MY COLLEAGUES ARE DOING BATTLE WITH THE "CELESTIAL."
IF WE LEFT THE CELESTIALS TO DESTROY, THE CLOSED SPACES WOULD EXPAND.
THEY'D SPREAD OUT AND EVENTUALLY SWALLOW UP THE ENTIRE WORLD.
AND SO, TO KEEP THAT FROM HAPPENING ...
HYUN
(WHIZZ)
EH!?
HEY!

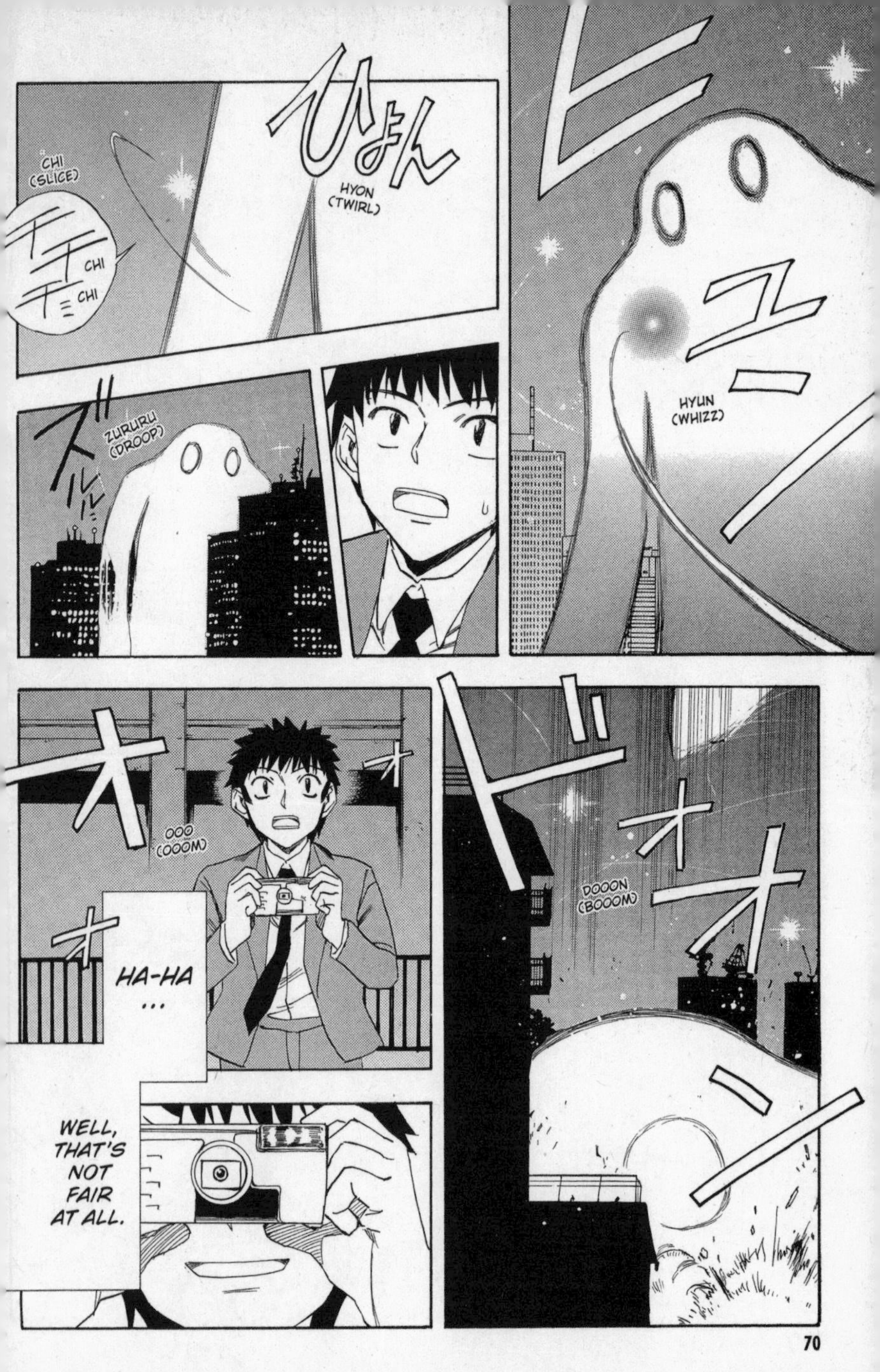
HYUN
(WHIZZ)
HYON
(TWIRL)
CHI
(SLICE)
CHI
CHI
ZURURU
(DROOP)
DOOON
(BOOOM)
OOO
(OOOM)
HA-HA ...
WELL, THAT'S NOT FAIR AT ALL.

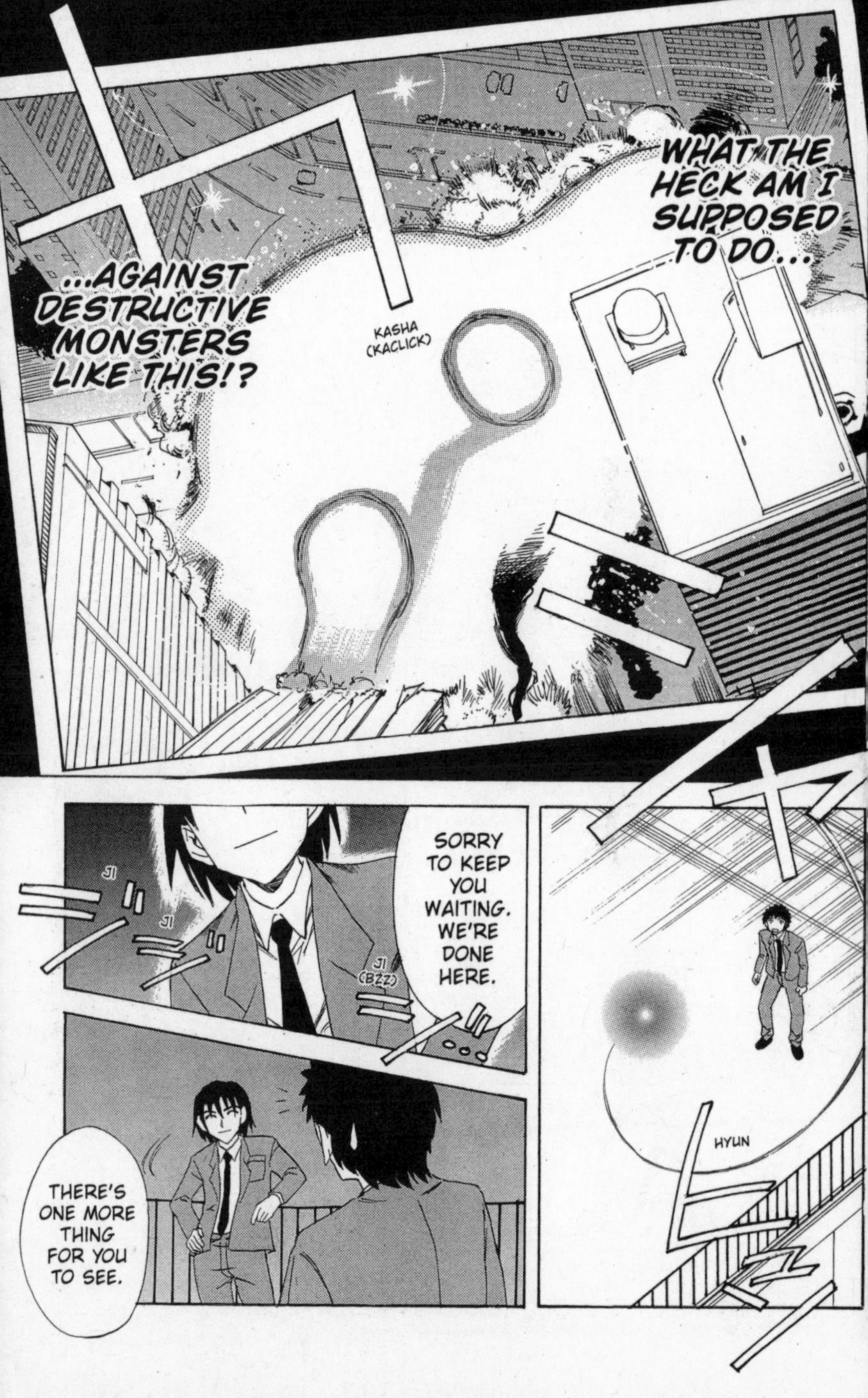
WHAT THE HECK AM I SUPPOSED TO DO...
...AGAINST DESTRUCTIVE MONSTERS LIKE THIS!?
KASHA (KACLICK)
HYUN
JI
JI
JI (BZZ)
SORRY TO KEEP YOU WAITING. WE'RE DONE HERE.
THERE'S ONE MORE THING FOR YOU TO SEE.

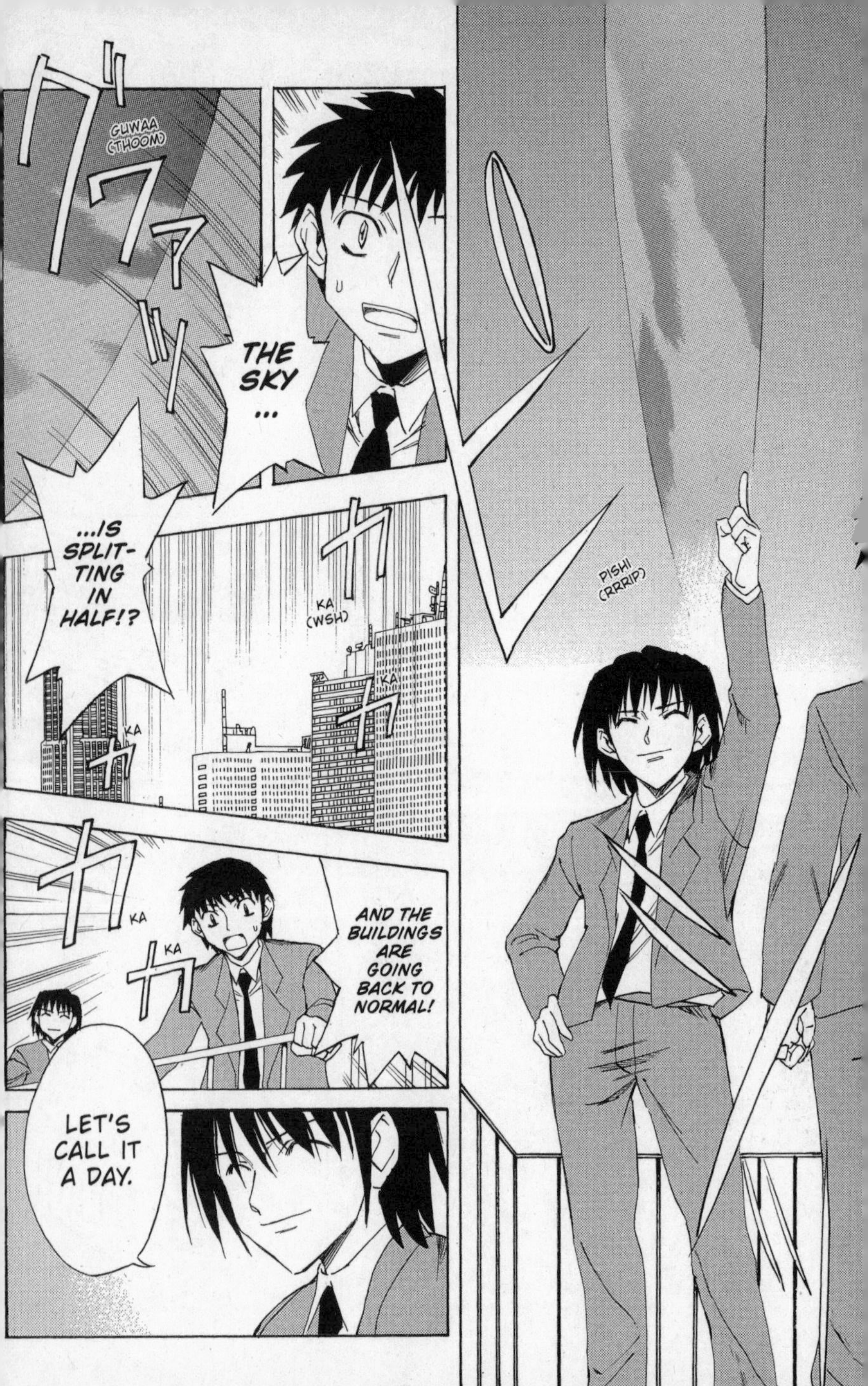
PISHI (RRRIP)
THE SKY ...
GUWAA (THOOM)
...IS SPLIT-TING IN HALF!?
KA (WSH)
KA
KA
AND THE BUILDINGS ARE GOING BACK TO NORMAL!
KA
KA
LET'S CALL IT A DAY.

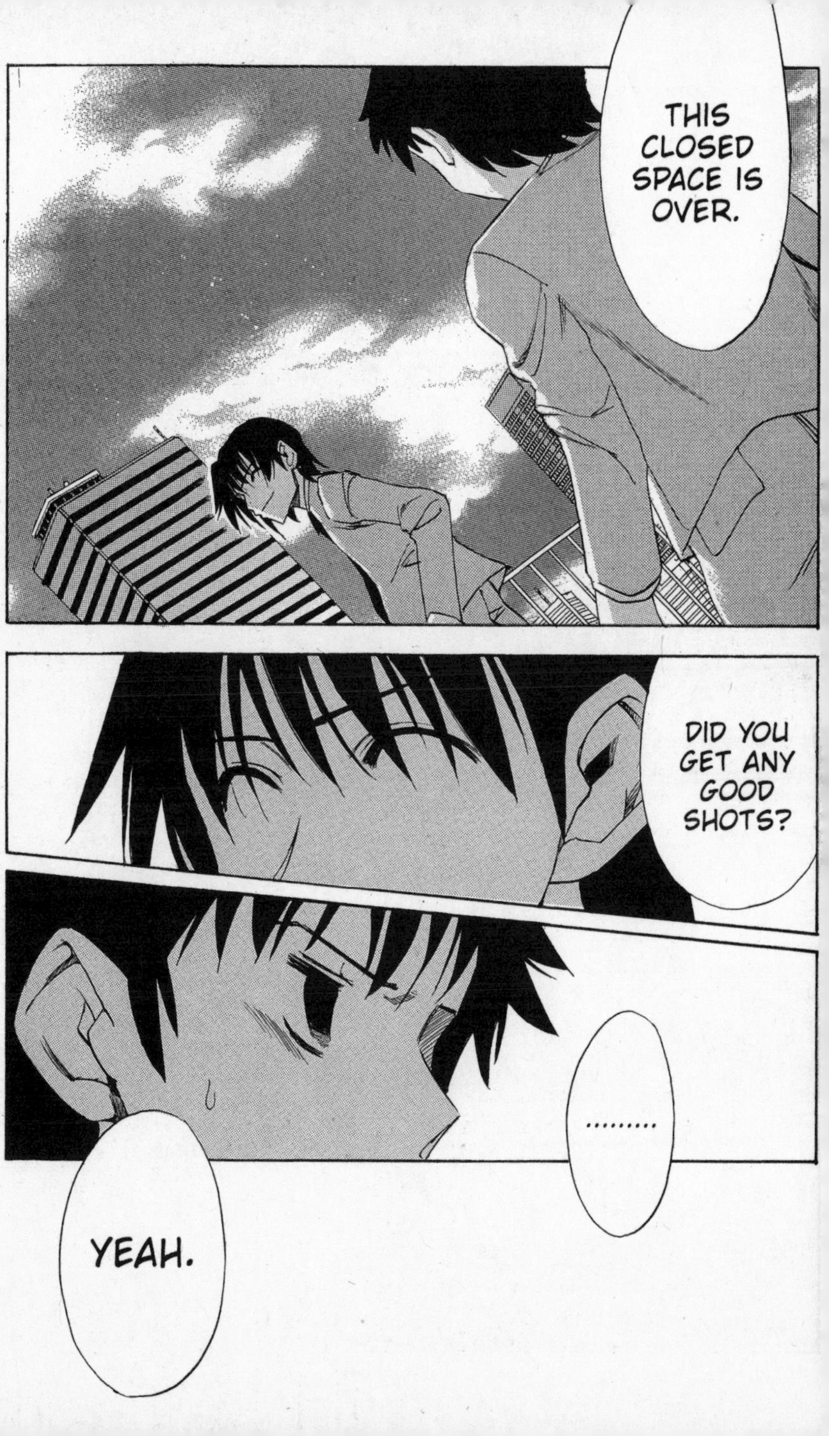
THIS CLOSED SPACE IS OVER.
DID YOU GET ANY GOOD SHOTS?
....
YEAH.

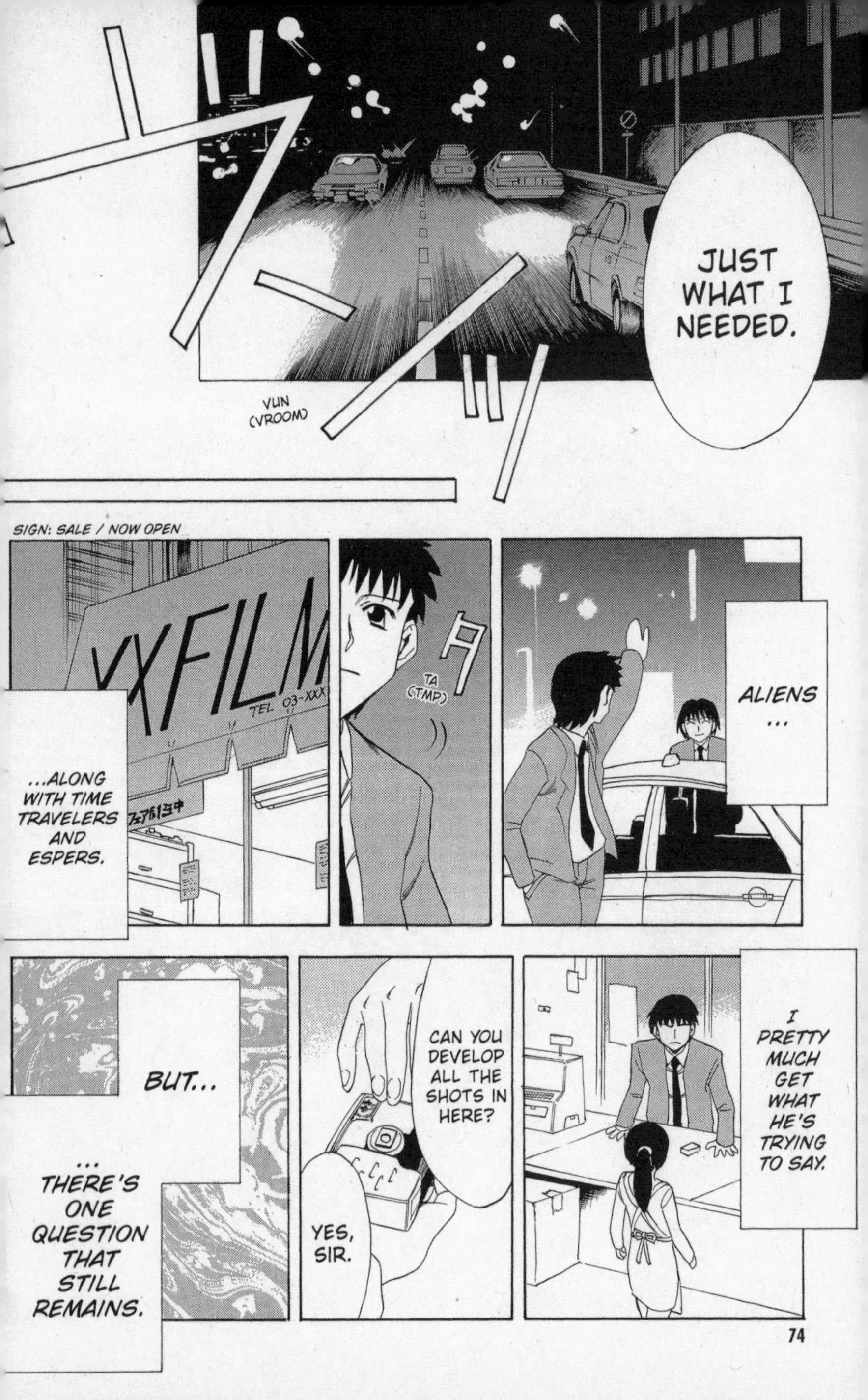
JUST WHAT I NEEDED.
VUN (VROOM)
ALIENS...
TA (TMP)
SIGN: SALE / NOW OPEN
VXFILM
TEL 03-XXX
...ALONG WITH TIME TRAVELERS AND ESPERS.
I PRETTY MUCH GET WHAT HE'S TRYING TO SAY.
CAN YOU DEVELOP ALL THE SHOTS IN HERE?
YES, SIR.
BUT...
...THERE'S ONE QUESTION THAT STILL REMAINS.

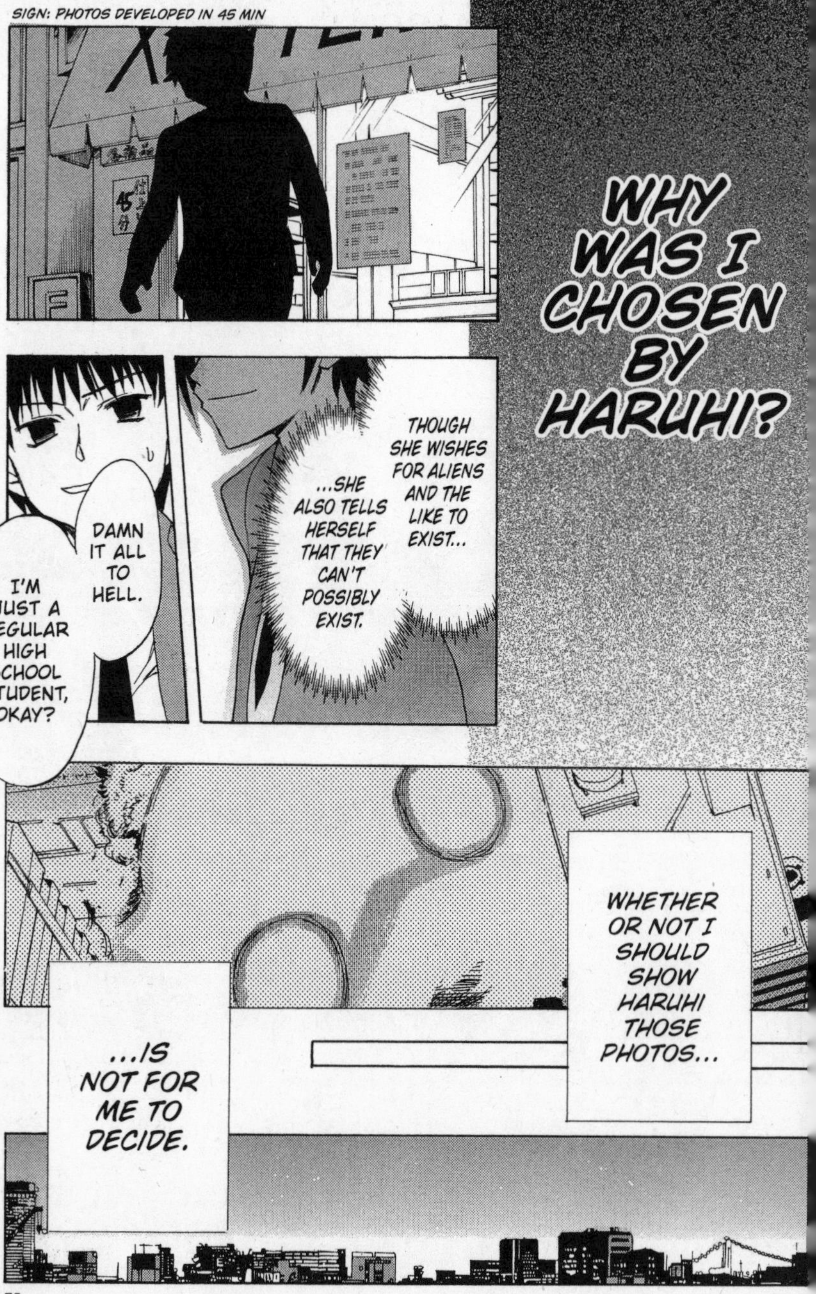
SIGN: PHOTOS DEVELOPED IN 45 MIN
WHY WAS I CHOSEN BY HARUHI?
THOUGH SHE WISHES FOR ALIENS AND THE LIKE TO EXIST...
...SHE ALSO TELLS HERSELF THAT THEY CAN'T POSSIBLY EXIST.
DAMN IT ALL TO HELL.
I'M JUST A REGULAR HIGH SCHOOL STUDENT, OKAY?
WHETHER OR NOT I SHOULD SHOW HARUHI THOSE PHOTOS...
...IS NOT FOR ME TO DECIDE.

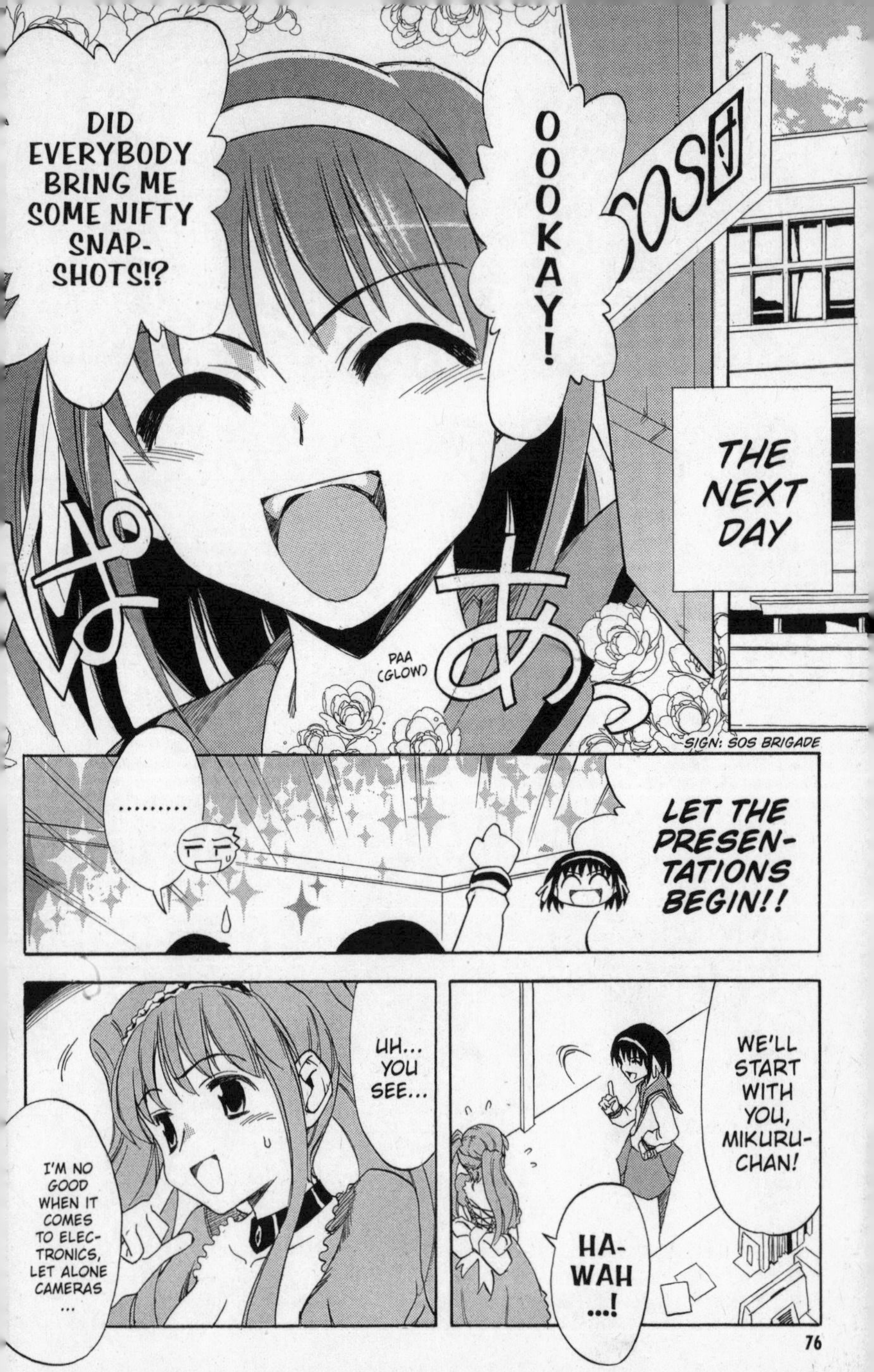
SOS団
THE NEXT DAY
OOOKAY!
DID EVERYBODY BRING ME SOME NIFTY SNAP-SHOTS!?
ぱあっ
PAA (GLOW)
SIGN: SOS BRIGADE
LET THE PRESEN-TATIONS BEGIN!!
....
WE'LL START WITH YOU, MIKURU-CHAN!
HA-WAH ...!
UH... YOU SEE...
I'M NO GOOD WHEN IT COMES TO ELEC-TRONICS, LET ALONE CAMERAS ...

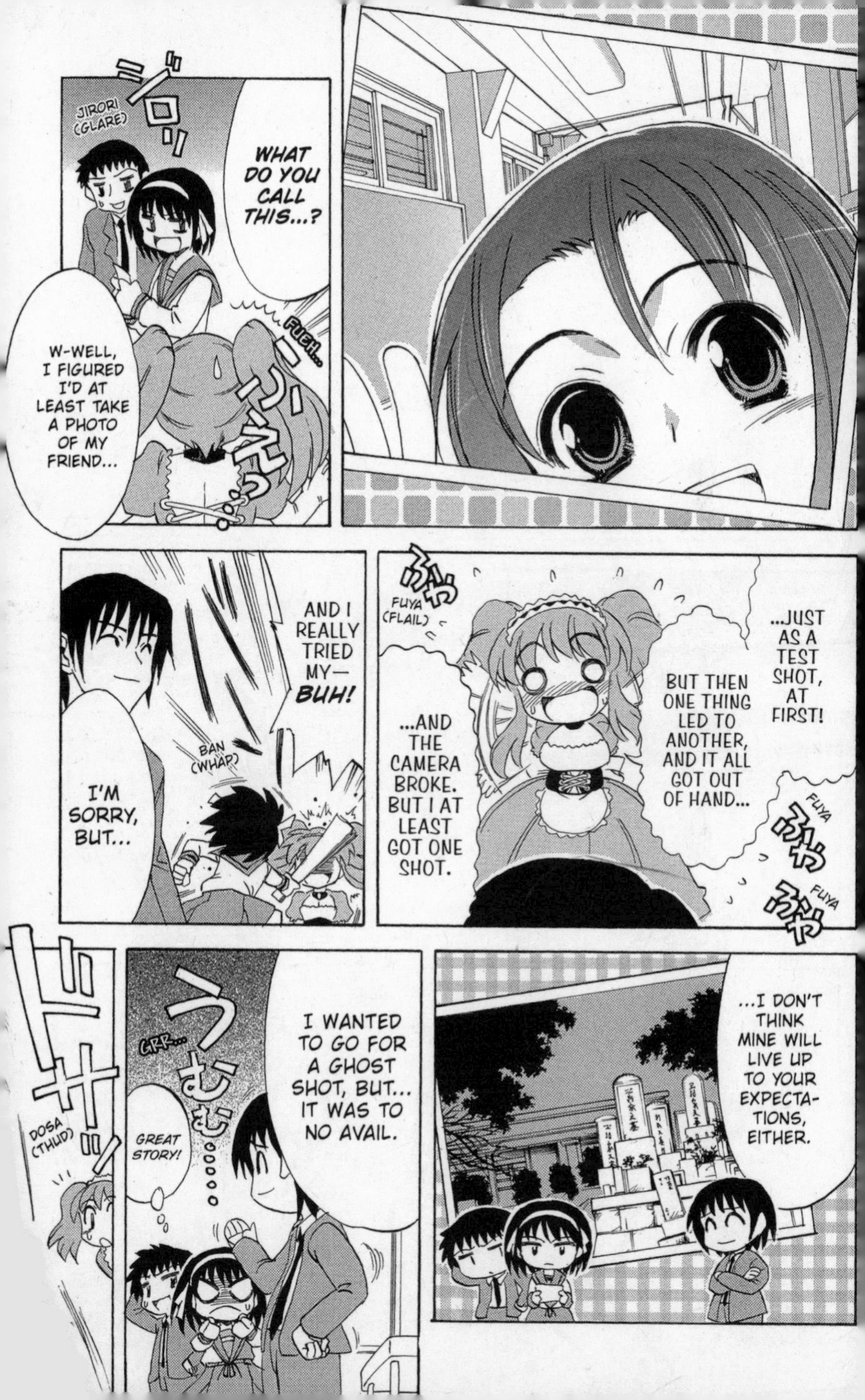
JIRORI (GLARE)
WHAT DO YOU CALL THIS...?
FUEH...
W-WELL, I FIGURED I'D AT LEAST TAKE A PHOTO OF MY FRIEND...
...JUST AS A TEST SHOT, AT FIRST!
BUT THEN ONE THING LED TO ANOTHER, AND IT ALL GOT OUT OF HAND...
FUYA (FLAIL)
...AND THE CAMERA BROKE. BUT I AT LEAST GOT ONE SHOT.
FUYA
FUYA
AND I REALLY TRIED MY— BUH!
BAN (WHAP)
I'M SORRY, BUT...
...I DON'T THINK MINE WILL LIVE UP TO YOUR EXPECTATIONS, EITHER.
I WANTED TO GO FOR A GHOST SHOT, BUT... IT WAS TO NO AVAIL.
GRR...
GREAT STORY!
DOSA (THUD)

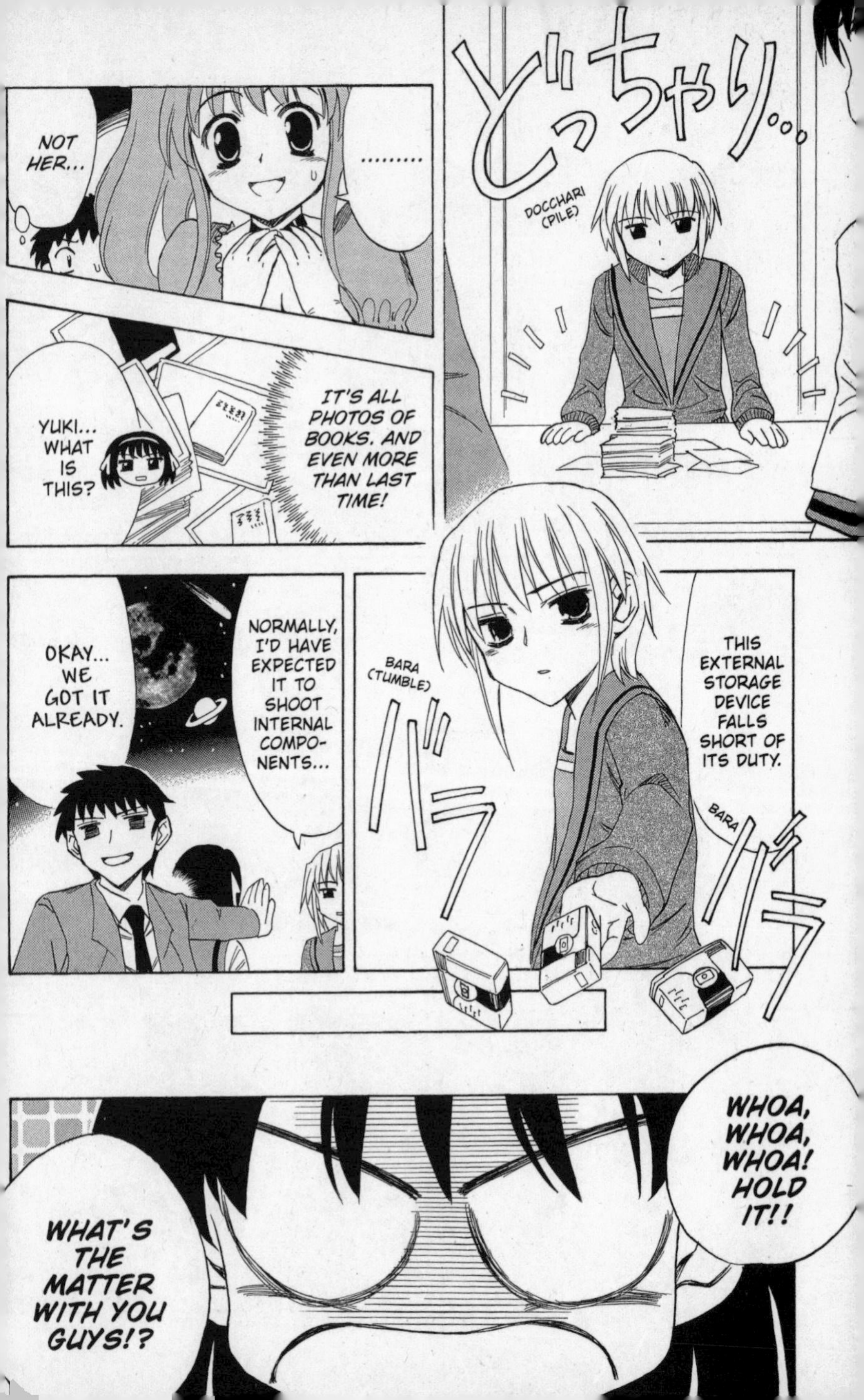
どっちゃり…
DOCCHARI (PILE)
....
NOT HER...
IT'S ALL PHOTOS OF BOOKS. AND EVEN MORE THAN LAST TIME!
YUKI... WHAT IS THIS?
THIS EXTERNAL STORAGE DEVICE FALLS SHORT OF ITS DUTY.
BARA
バラ
BARA (TUMBLE)
バラ
NORMALLY, I'D HAVE EXPECTED IT TO SHOOT INTERNAL COMPONENTS...
OKAY... WE GOT IT ALREADY.
WHOA, WHOA, WHOA! HOLD IT!!
WHAT'S THE MATTER WITH YOU GUYS!?

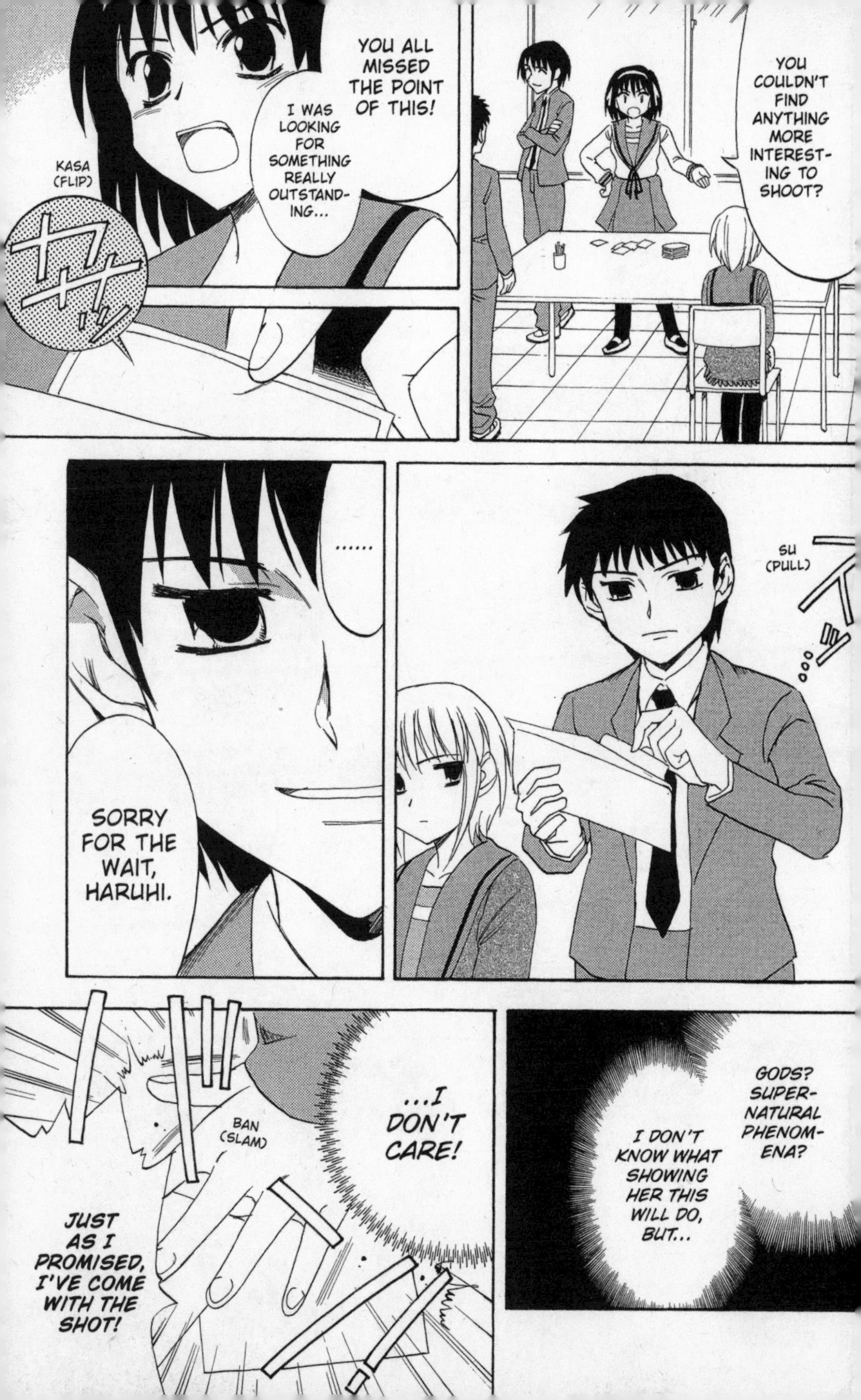

YOU COULDN'T FIND ANYTHING MORE INTERESTING TO SHOOT?
YOU ALL MISSED THE POINT OF THIS!
I WAS LOOKING FOR SOMETHING REALLY OUTSTANDING...
KASA (FLIP)
SU (PULL)
......
SORRY FOR THE WAIT, HARUHI.
GODS? SUPERNATURAL PHENOMENA?
I DON'T KNOW WHAT SHOWING HER THIS WILL DO, BUT...
...I DON'T CARE!
BAN (SLAM)
JUST AS I PROMISED, I'VE COME WITH THE SHOT!

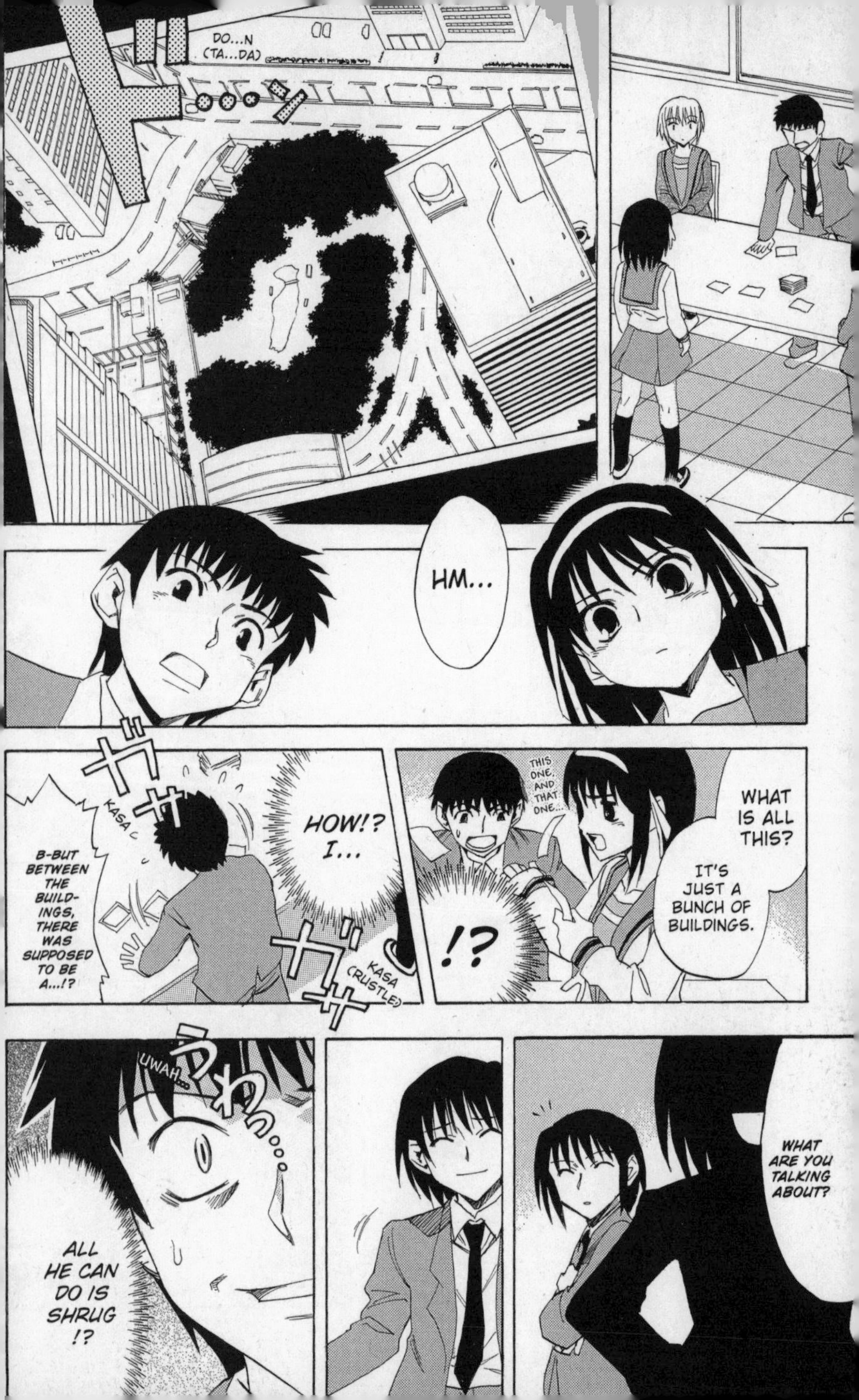
DO...N
(TA...DA)
HM...
WHAT IS ALL THIS?
IT'S JUST A BUNCH OF BUILDINGS.
THIS ONE, AND THAT ONE...
!?
HOW!? I...
KASA (RUSTLE)
KASA
B-BUT BETWEEN THE BUILDINGS, THERE WAS SUPPOSED TO BE A...!?
WHAT ARE YOU TALKING ABOUT?
UWAH...
ALL HE CAN DO IS SHRUG !?

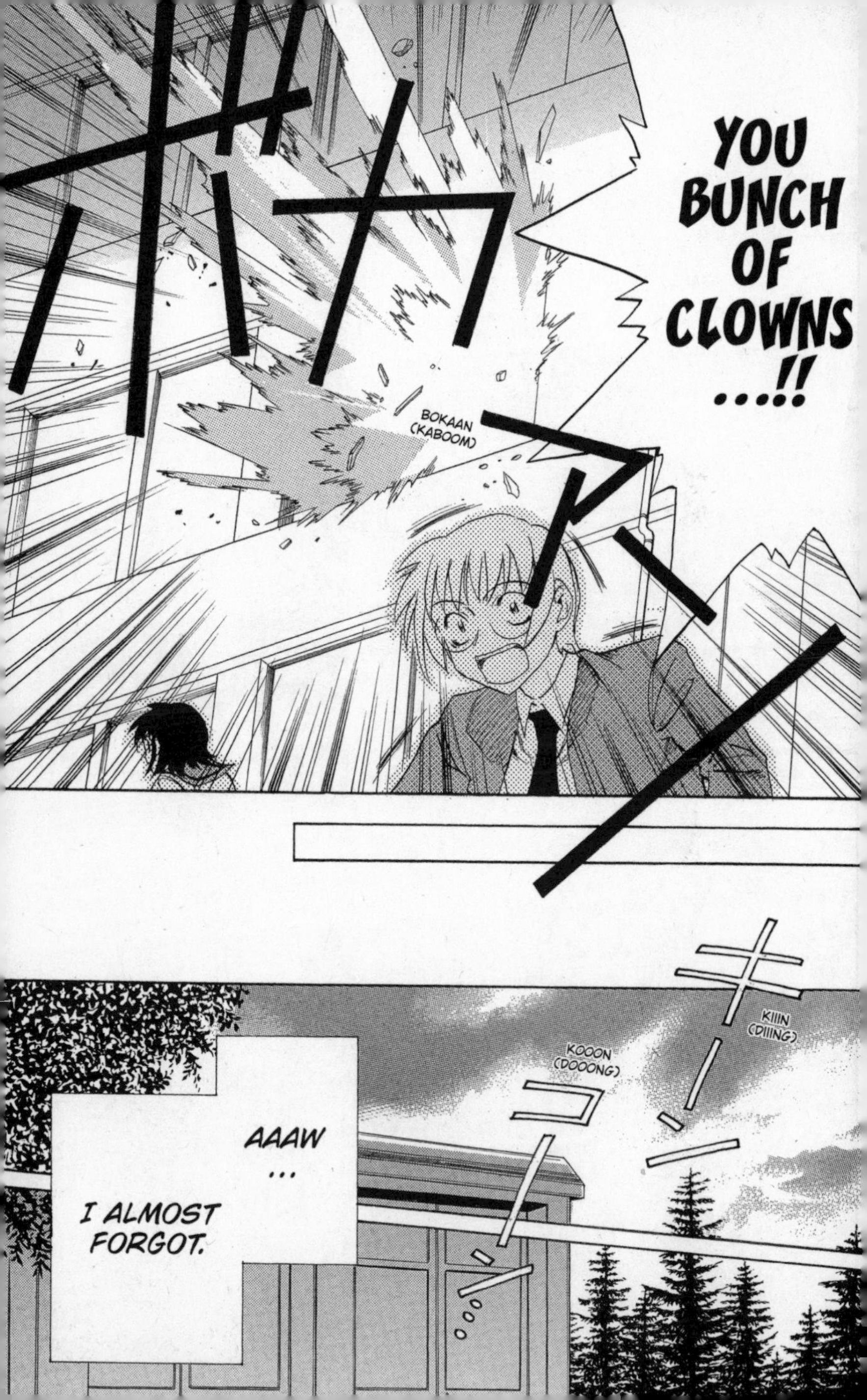
YOU BUNCH OF CLOWNS ....!!
BOKAAN (KABOOM)
KIIN (DIIING)
KOOON (DOOONG)
AAAW ... I ALMOST FORGOT.

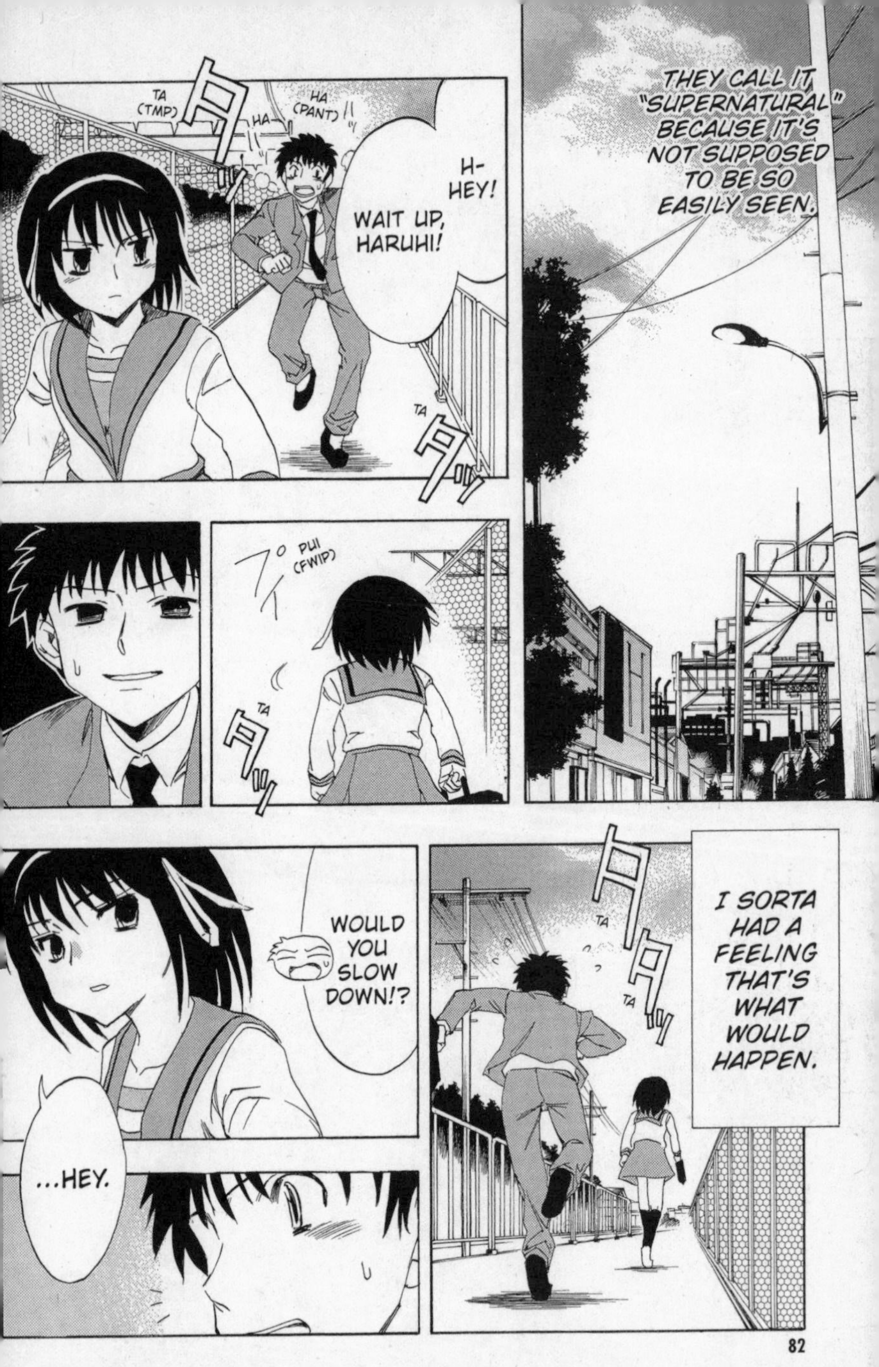
THEY CALL IT "SUPERNATURAL" BECAUSE IT'S NOT SUPPOSED TO BE SO EASILY SEEN.
H- HEY! WAIT UP, HARUHI!
HA (PANT)
HA-
TA (TMP)
TA
PUI (FWIP)
TA
I SORTA HAD A FEELING THAT'S WHAT WOULD HAPPEN.
TA
TA
WOULD YOU SLOW DOWN!?
...HEY.

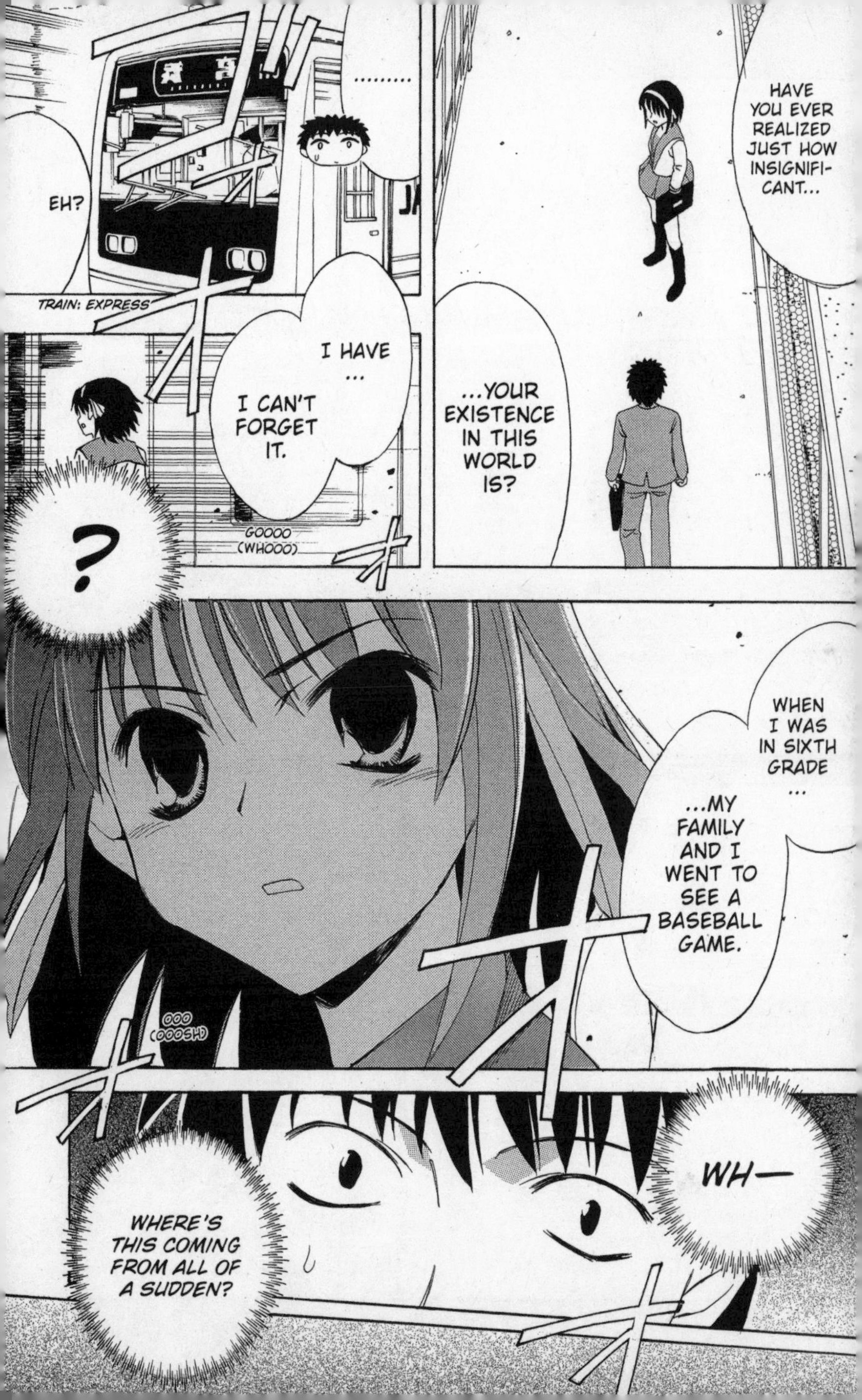
HAVE YOU EVER REALIZED JUST HOW INSIGNIFICANT...
...YOUR EXISTENCE IN THIS WORLD IS?
....
EH?
TRAIN: EXPRESS
I HAVE ...
I CAN'T FORGET IT.
GOOOO (WHOOO)
?
WHEN I WAS IN SIXTH GRADE ...
...MY FAMILY AND I WENT TO SEE A BASEBALL GAME.
OOO (OOOSH)
WH—
WHERE'S THIS COMING FROM ALL OF A SUDDEN?

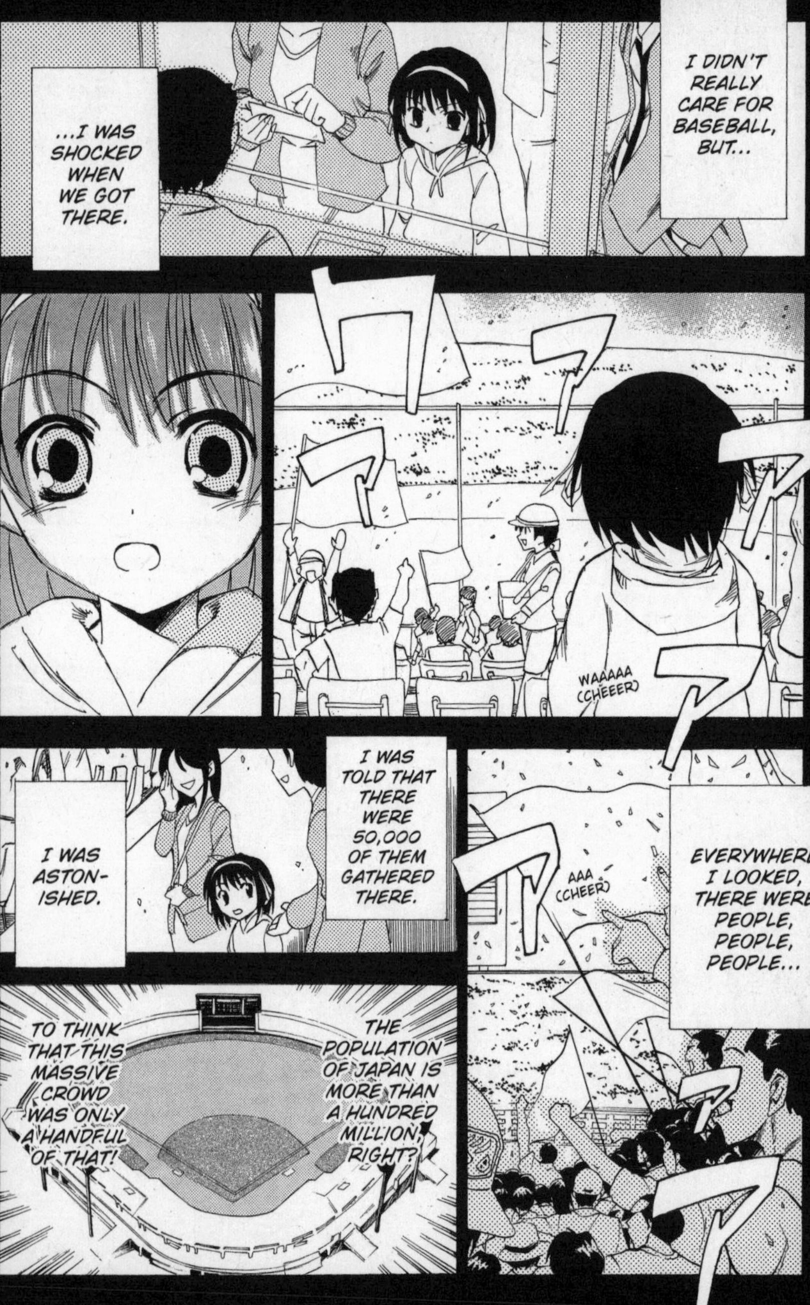
I DIDN'T REALLY CARE FOR BASEBALL, BUT...
...I WAS SHOCKED WHEN WE GOT THERE.
WAAAAA (CHEEER)
EVERYWHERE I LOOKED, THERE WERE PEOPLE, PEOPLE, PEOPLE...
AAA (CHEER)
I WAS TOLD THAT THERE WERE 50,000 OF THEM GATHERED THERE.
I WAS ASTON-ISHED.
THE POPULATION OF JAPAN IS MORE THAN A HUNDRED MILLION, RIGHT?
TO THINK THAT THIS MASSIVE CROWD WAS ONLY A HANDFUL OF THAT!

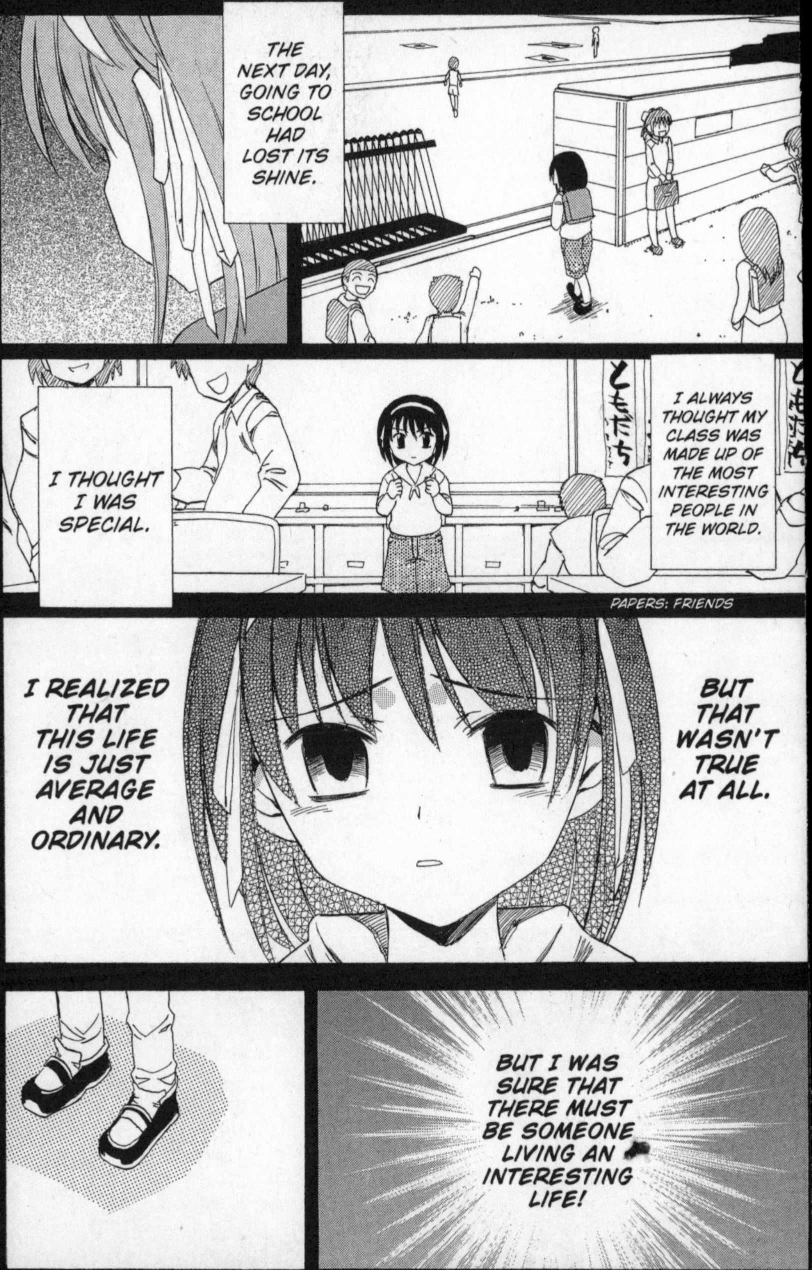
THE NEXT DAY, GOING TO SCHOOL HAD LOST ITS SHINE.
I ALWAYS THOUGHT MY CLASS WAS MADE UP OF THE MOST INTERESTING PEOPLE IN THE WORLD.
ともだち
I THOUGHT I WAS SPECIAL.
PAPERS: FRIENDS
BUT THAT WASN'T TRUE AT ALL.
I REALIZED THAT THIS LIFE IS JUST AVERAGE AND ORDINARY.
BUT I WAS SURE THAT THERE MUST BE SOMEONE LIVING AN INTERESTING LIFE!

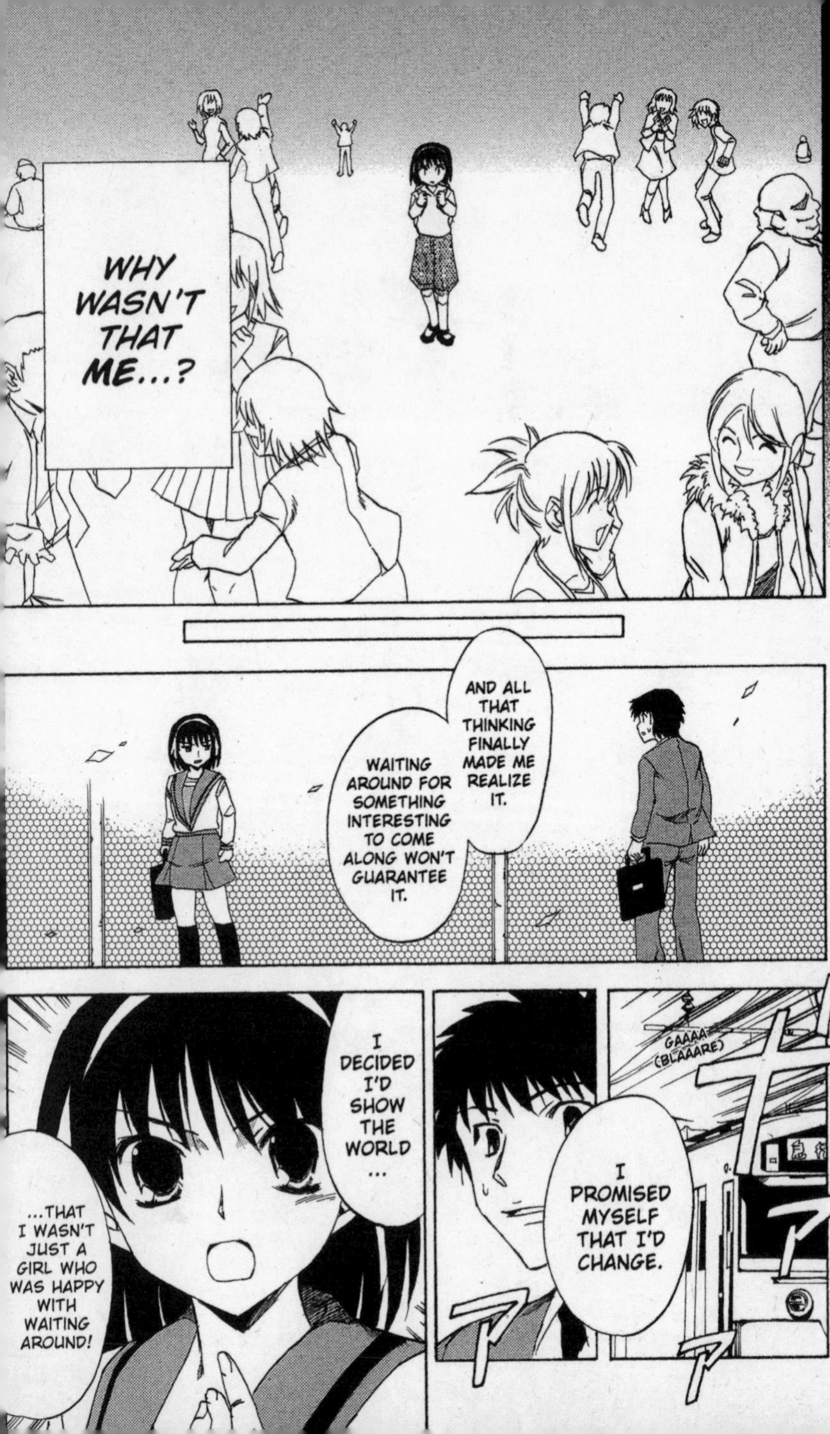
WHY WASN'T THAT ME...?
AND ALL THAT THINKING FINALLY MADE ME REALIZE IT.
WAITING AROUND FOR SOMETHING INTERESTING TO COME ALONG WON'T GUARANTEE IT.
GAAAA (BLAAARE)
I PROMISED MYSELF THAT I'D CHANGE.
I DECIDED I'D SHOW THE WORLD...
...THAT I WASN'T JUST A GIRL WHO WAS HAPPY WITH WAITING AROUND!

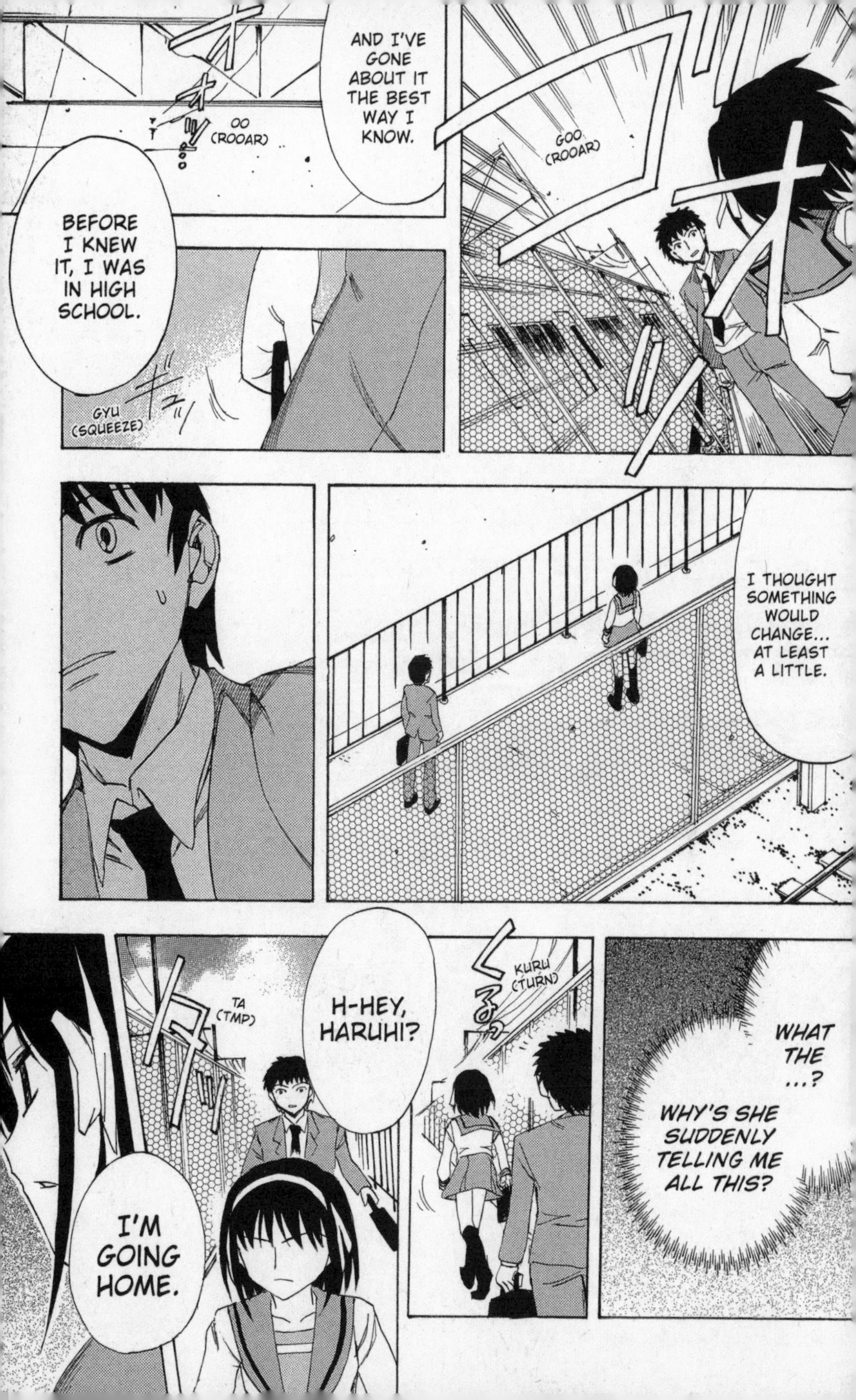
GOO (ROOAR)
AND I'VE GONE ABOUT IT THE BEST WAY I KNOW.
OO (ROOAR)
BEFORE I KNEW IT, I WAS IN HIGH SCHOOL.
GYU (SQUEEZE)
I THOUGHT SOMETHING WOULD CHANGE... AT LEAST A LITTLE.
WHAT THE ...?
WHY'S SHE SUDDENLY TELLING ME ALL THIS?
KURU (TURN)
H-HEY, HARUHI?
TA (TMP)
I'M GOING HOME.

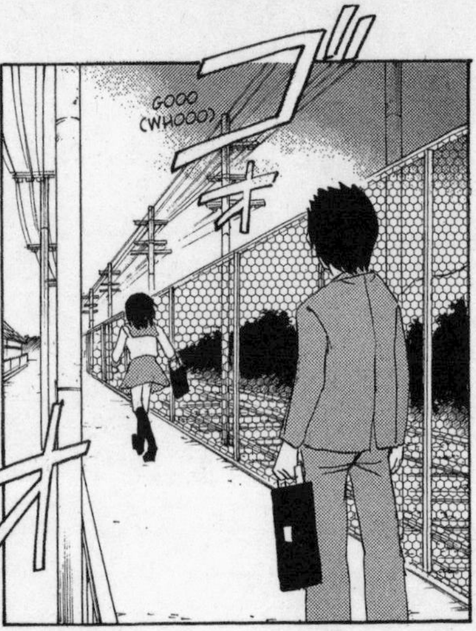
GOOO
(WHOOO)

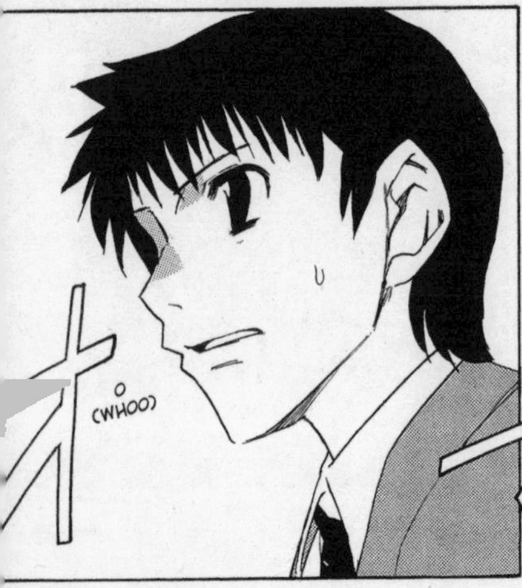
O
(WHOO)

IS IT JUST ME OR IS SHE REALLY ODD LATELY?

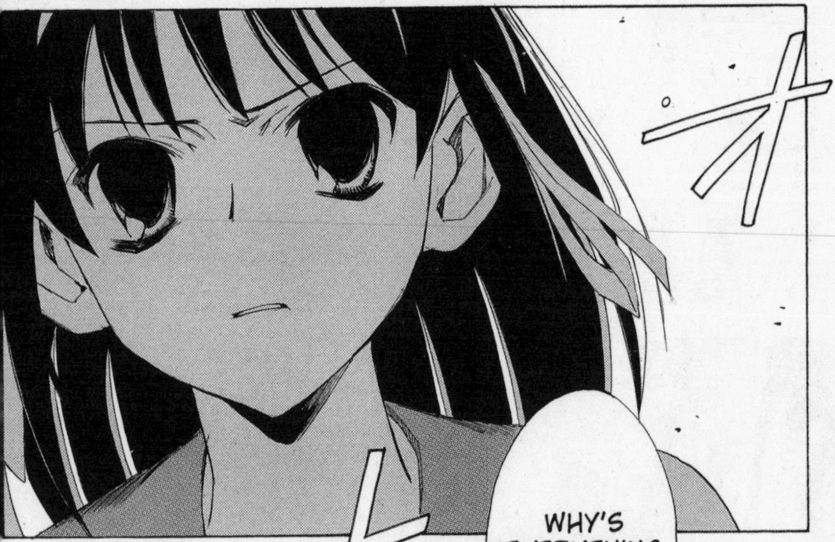
WHY'S EVERYTHING SO DAMN BORING?

THE MELANCHOLY OF HARUHI SUZUMIYA VII : END

THE MELANCHOLY OF HARUHI SUZUMIYA

SOS Brigade Break Time

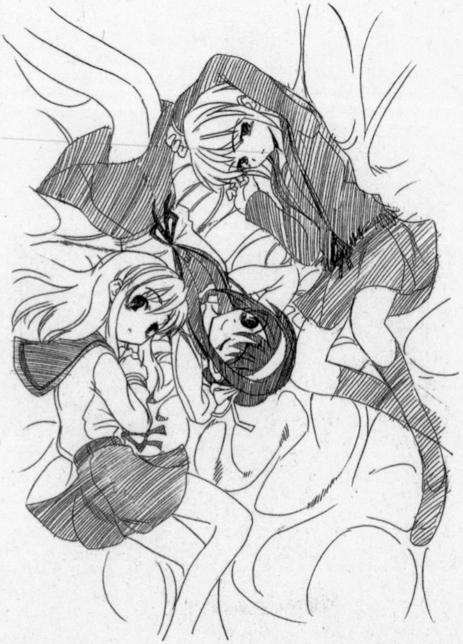

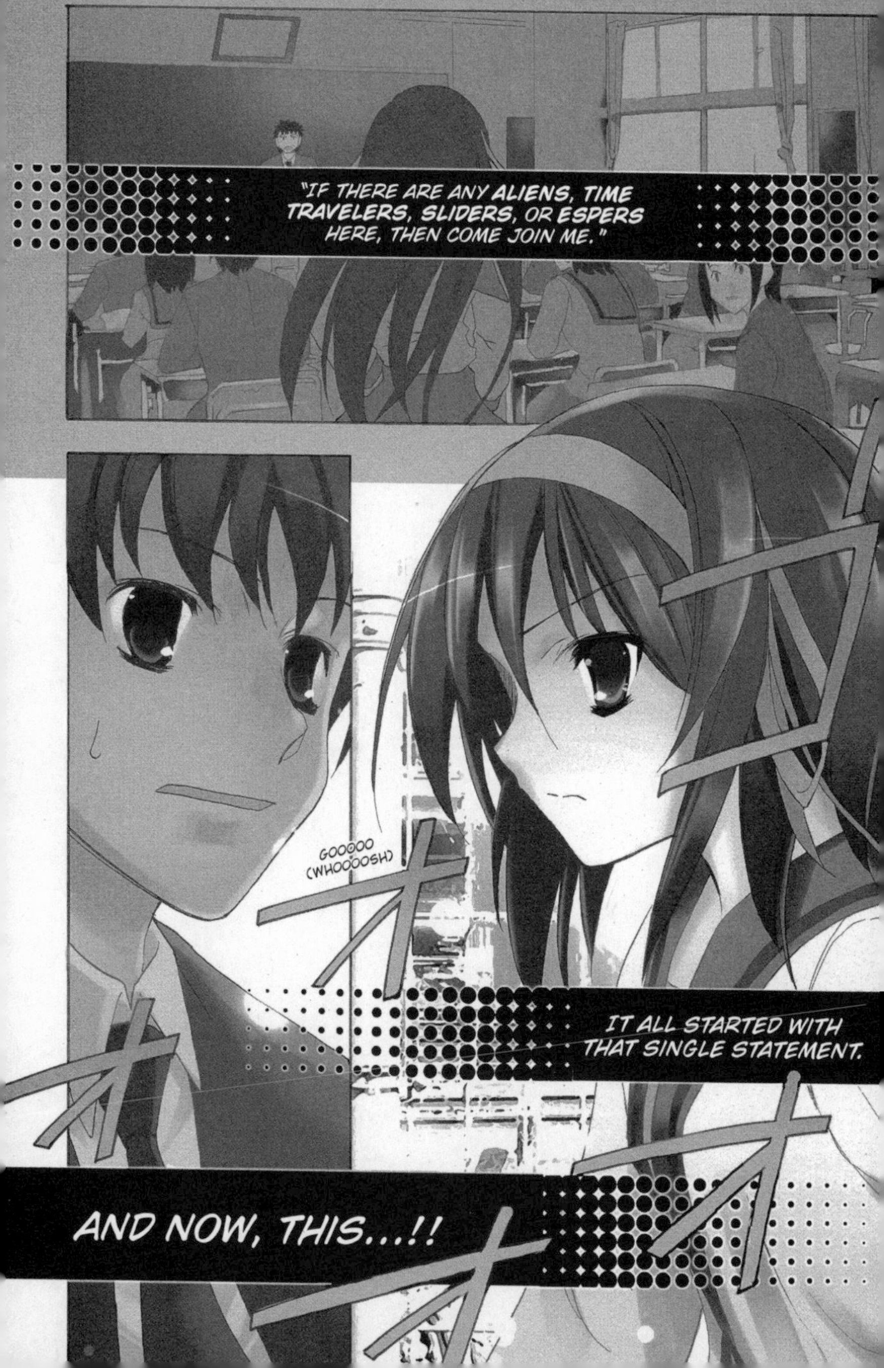
"IF THERE ARE ANY ALIENS, TIME TRAVELERS, SLIDERS, OR ESPERS HERE, THEN COME JOIN ME."
GOOOOO (WHOOOOSH)
IT ALL STARTED WITH THAT SINGLE STATEMENT.
AND NOW, THIS...!!

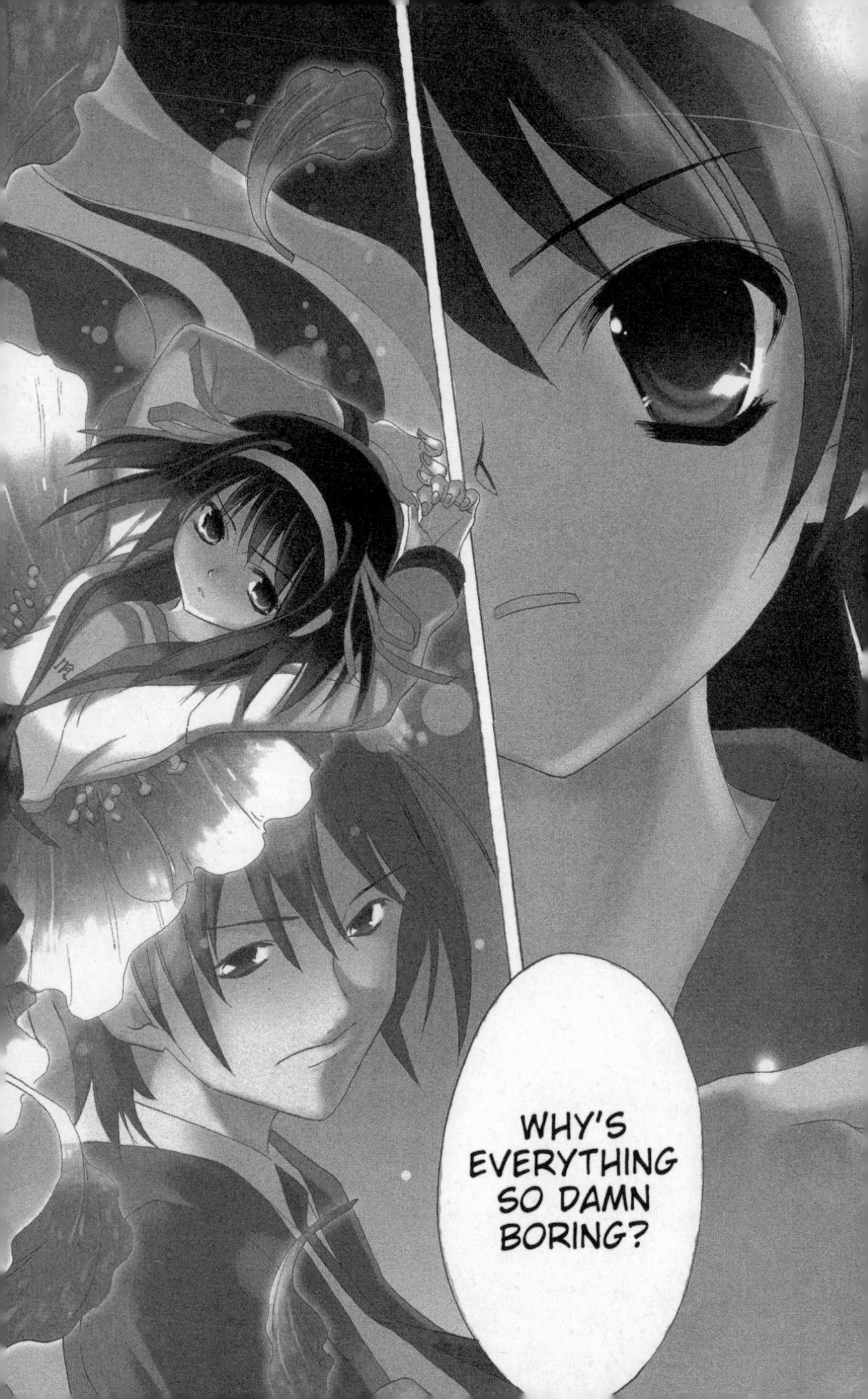
WHY'S EVERYTHING SO DAMN BORING?

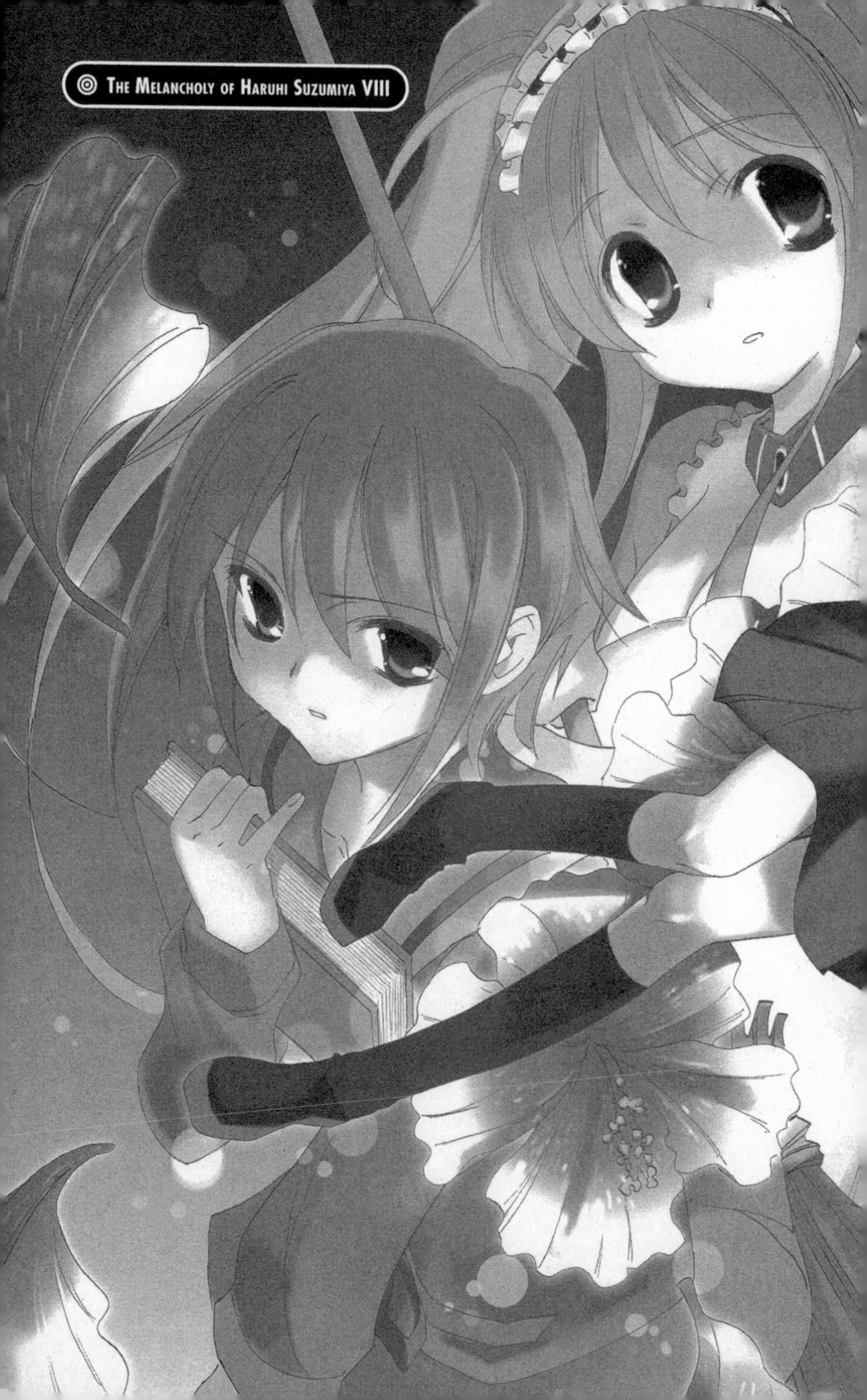
The Melancholy of Haruhi Suzumiya VIII

THE MELANCHOLY OF HARUHI SUZUMIYA

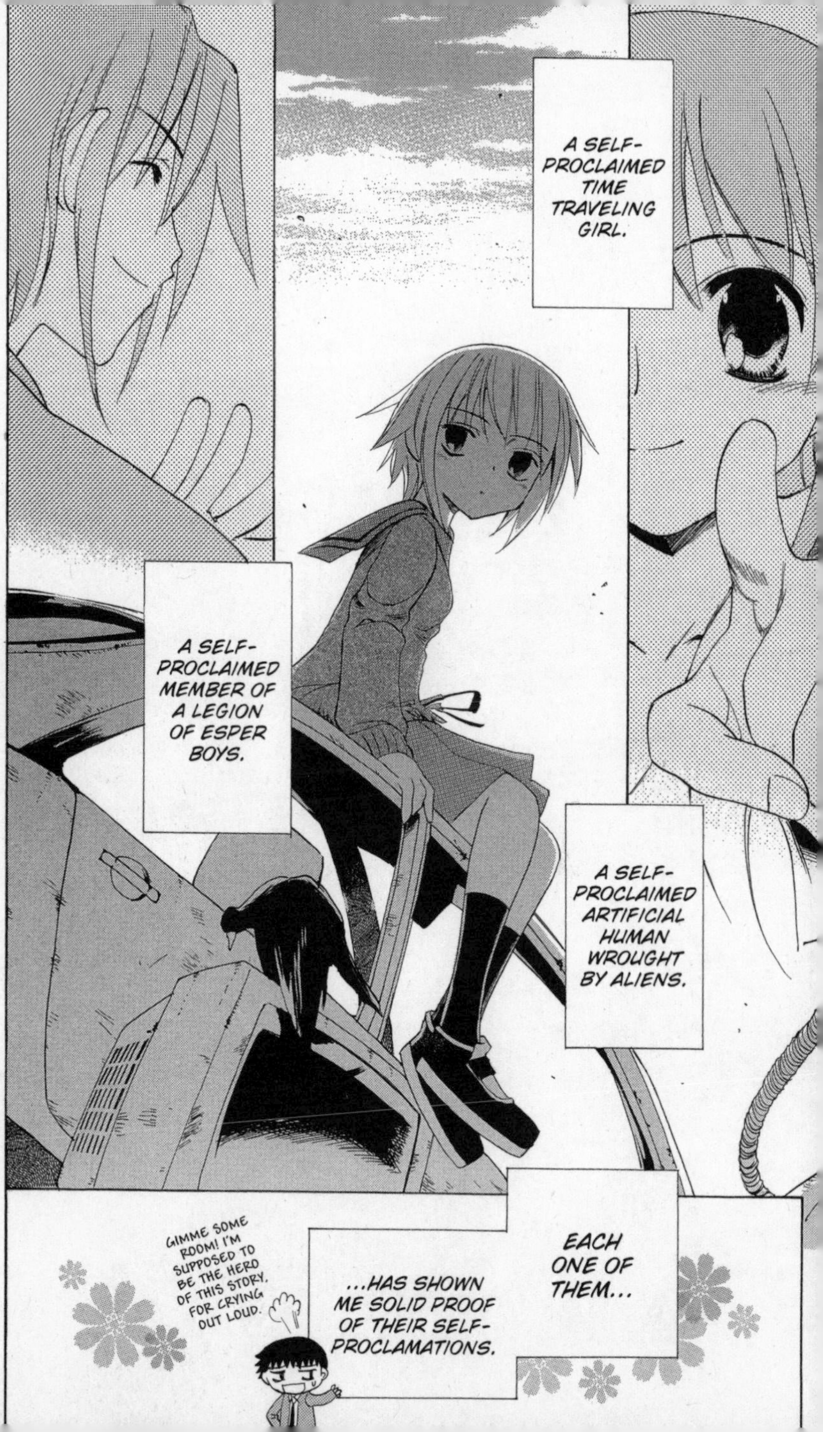
A SELF-PROCLAIMED TIME TRAVELING GIRL.
A SELF-PROCLAIMED MEMBER OF A LEGION OF ESPER BOYS.
A SELF-PROCLAIMED ARTIFICIAL HUMAN WROUGHT BY ALIENS.
EACH ONE OF THEM...
...HAS SHOWN ME SOLID PROOF OF THEIR SELF-PROCLAMATIONS.
GIMME SOME ROOM! I'M SUPPOSED TO BE THE HERO OF THIS STORY, FOR CRYING OUT LOUD.

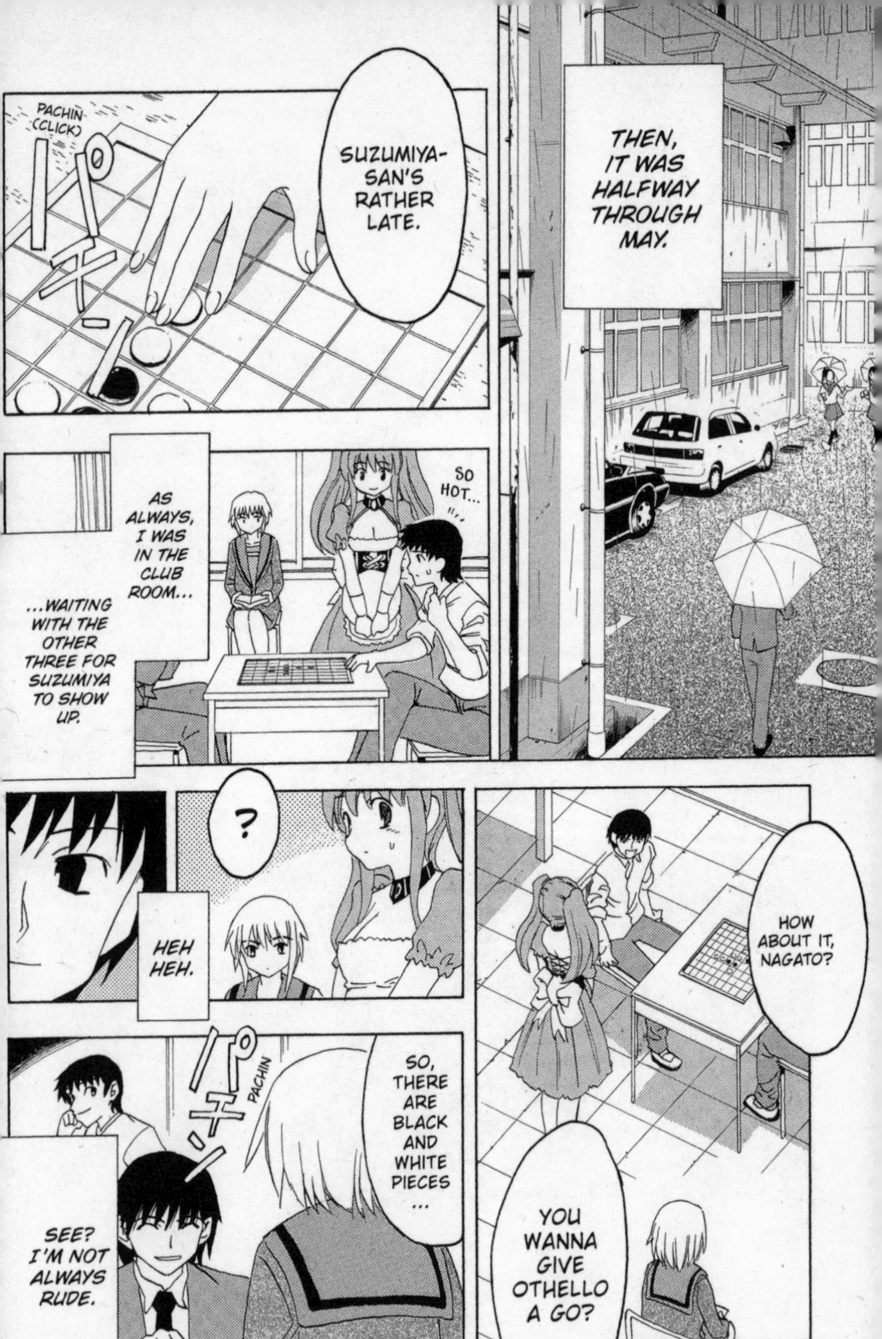
THEN, IT WAS HALFWAY THROUGH MAY.
SUZUMIYA-SAN'S RATHER LATE.
PACHIN (CLICK)
SO HOT...
AS ALWAYS, I WAS IN THE CLUB ROOM...
...WAITING WITH THE OTHER THREE FOR SUZUMIYA TO SHOW UP.
HOW ABOUT IT, NAGATO?
YOU WANNA GIVE OTHELLO A GO?
?
HEH HEH.
SO, THERE ARE BLACK AND WHITE PIECES...
PACHIN
SEE? I'M NOT ALWAYS RUDE.

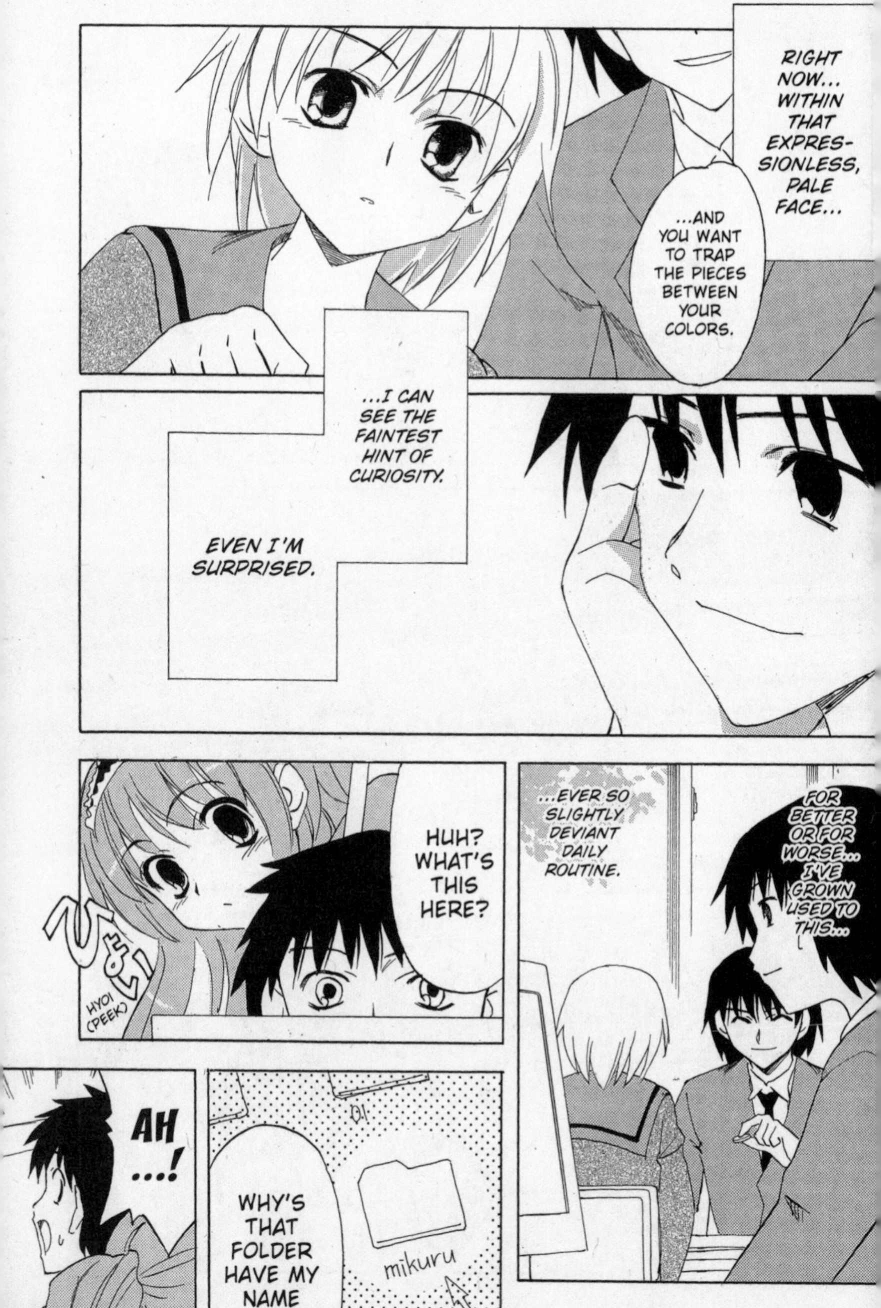
RIGHT NOW... WITHIN THAT EXPRES-SIONLESS, PALE FACE...
...AND YOU WANT TO TRAP THE PIECES BETWEEN YOUR COLORS.
...I CAN SEE THE FAINTEST HINT OF CURIOSITY.
EVEN I'M SURPRISED.
FOR BETTER OR FOR WORSE... I'VE GROWN USED TO THIS...
...EVER SO SLIGHTLY DEVIANT DAILY ROUTINE.
HUH? WHAT'S THIS HERE?
ひょい
HYOI (PEEK)
WHY'S THAT FOLDER HAVE MY NAME ON IT?
mikuru
AH ...!

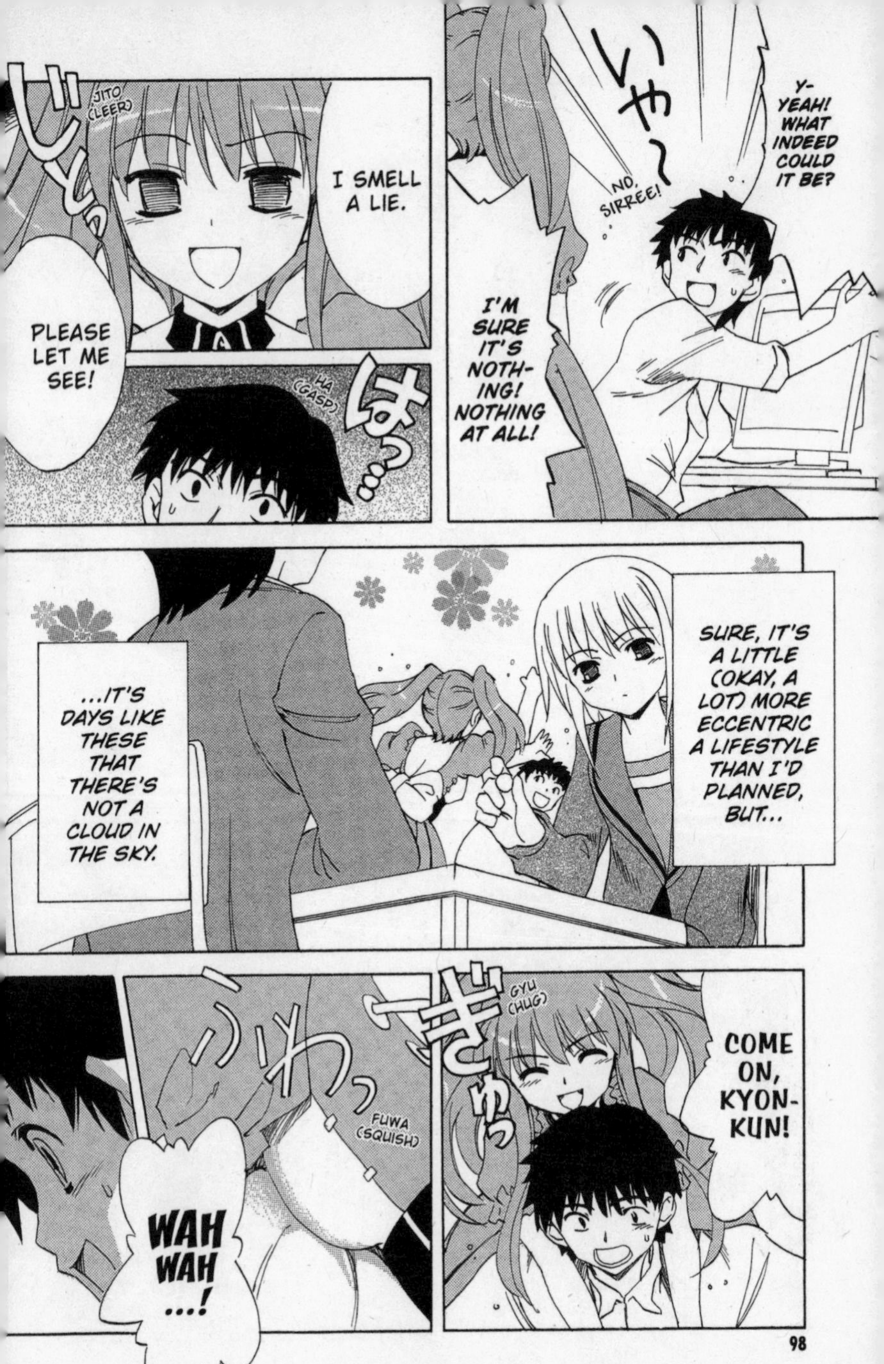
いや~
NO, SIRREE!
Y-YEAH! WHAT INDEED COULD IT BE?
I'M SURE IT'S NOTHING! NOTHING AT ALL!
じとっ
JITO (LEER)
I SMELL A LIE.
PLEASE LET ME SEE!
はっ…
HA (GASP)
SURE, IT'S A LITTLE (OKAY, A LOT) MORE ECCENTRIC A LIFESTYLE THAN I'D PLANNED, BUT...
...IT'S DAYS LIKE THESE THAT THERE'S NOT A CLOUD IN THE SKY.
ぎゅっ
GYU (HUG)
COME ON, KYON-KUN!
ふわっ
FUWA (SQUISH)
WAH WAH ...!

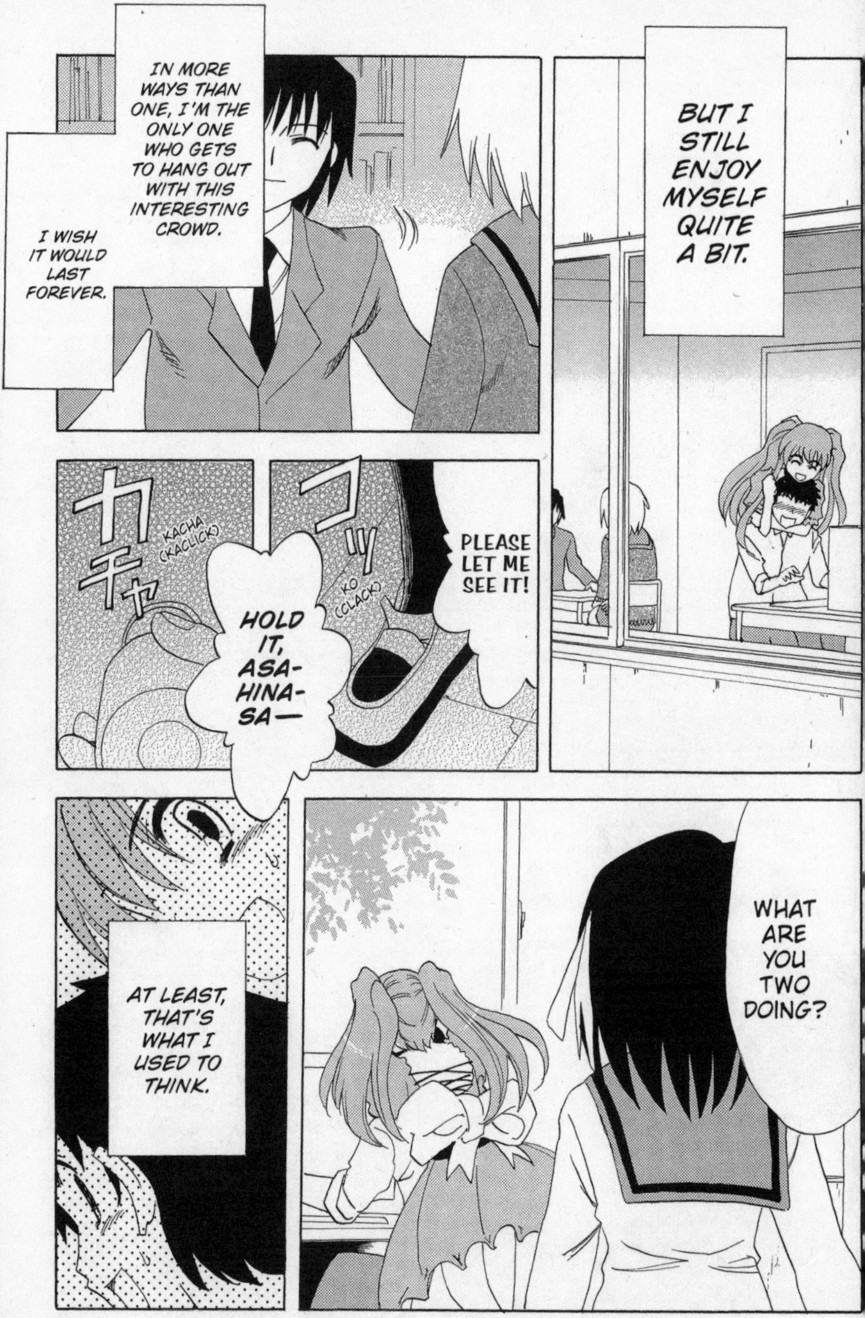
BUT I STILL ENJOY MYSELF QUITE A BIT.
IN MORE WAYS THAN ONE, I'M THE ONLY ONE WHO GETS TO HANG OUT WITH THIS INTERESTING CROWD.
I WISH IT WOULD LAST FOREVER.
PLEASE LET ME SEE IT!
KO (CLACK)
KACHA (KACLICK)
HOLD IT, ASA-HINA-SA—
WHAT ARE YOU TWO DOING?
AT LEAST, THAT'S WHAT I USED TO THINK.

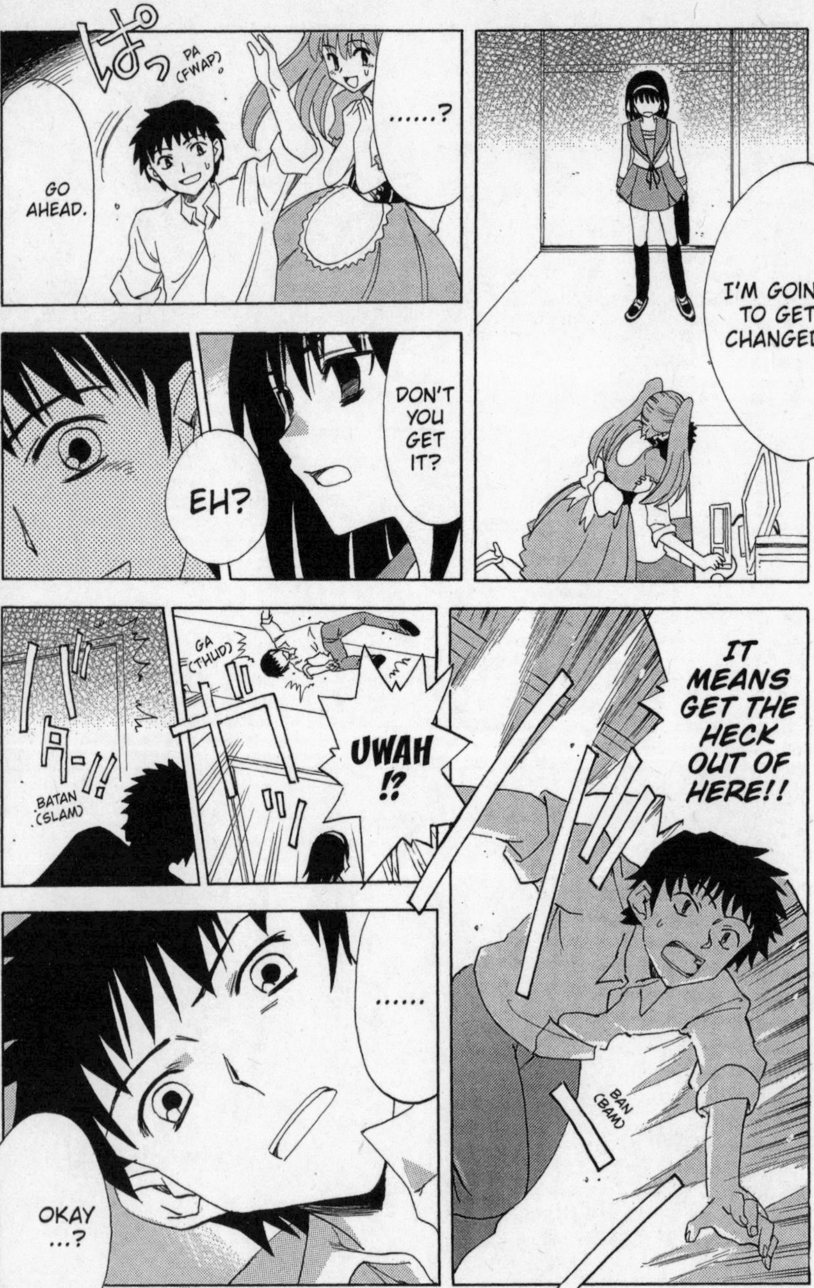
I'M GOING TO GET CHANGED.
......?
PA (FWAP)
GO AHEAD.
DON'T YOU GET IT?
EH?
IT MEANS GET THE HECK OUT OF HERE!!
BAN (BAM)
UWAH !?
GA (THUD)
BATAN (SLAM)
......
OKAY ...?

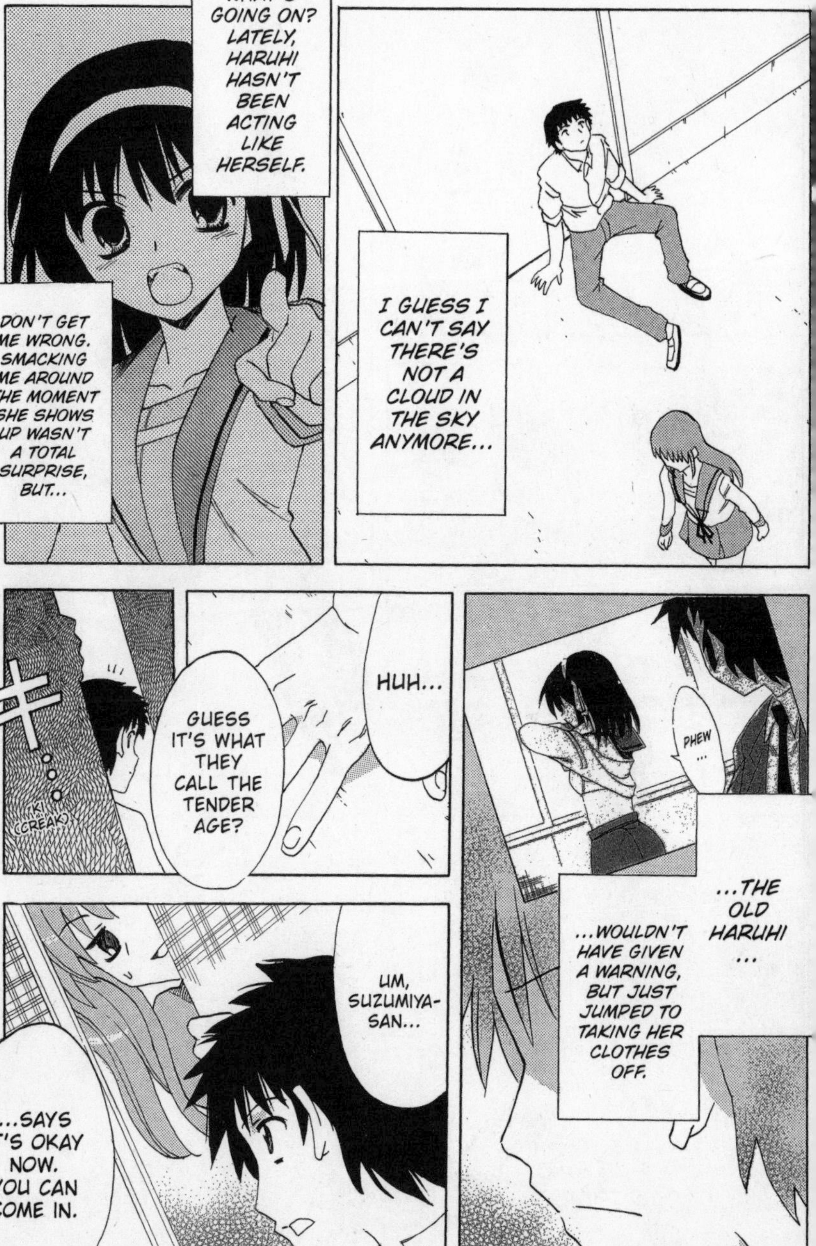
I GUESS I CAN'T SAY THERE'S NOT A CLOUD IN THE SKY ANYMORE...
WHAT'S GOING ON? LATELY, HARUHI HASN'T BEEN ACTING LIKE HERSELF.
DON'T GET ME WRONG. SMACKING ME AROUND THE MOMENT SHE SHOWS UP WASN'T A TOTAL SURPRISE, BUT...
PHEW ...
...THE OLD HARUHI ...
...WOULDN'T HAVE GIVEN A WARNING, BUT JUST JUMPED TO TAKING HER CLOTHES OFF.
HUH...
GUESS IT'S WHAT THEY CALL THE TENDER AGE?
KI (CREAK)
UM, SUZUMIYA-SAN...
...SAYS IT'S OKAY NOW. YOU CAN COME IN.

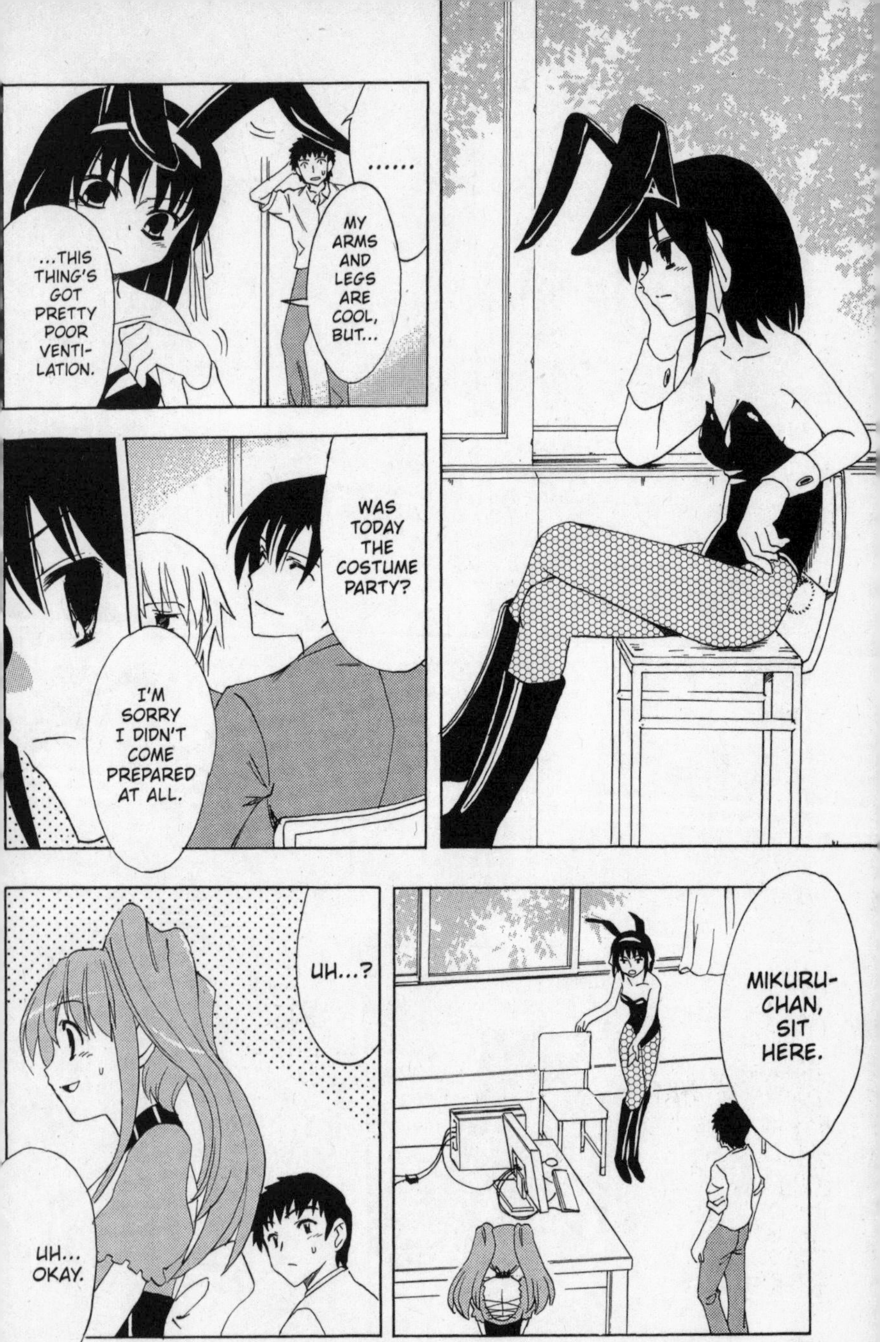
......
MY ARMS AND LEGS ARE COOL, BUT...
...THIS THING'S GOT PRETTY POOR VENTI-LATION.
WAS TODAY THE COSTUME PARTY?
I'M SORRY I DIDN'T COME PREPARED AT ALL.
MIKURU-CHAN, SIT HERE.
UH...?
UH... OKAY.

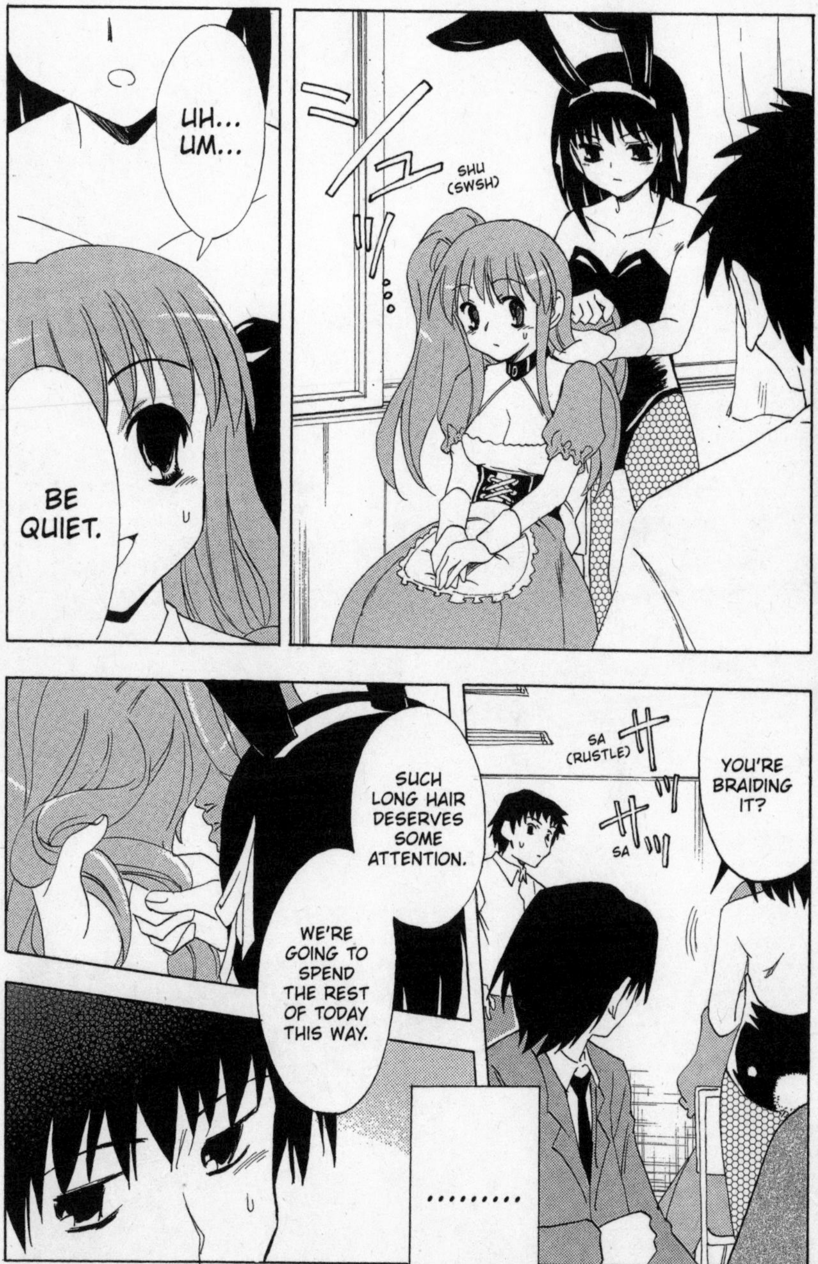
SHU (SWSH)
UH... UM...
BE QUIET.
SA (RUSTLE)
SA
YOU'RE BRAIDING IT?
SUCH LONG HAIR DESERVES SOME ATTENTION.
WE'RE GOING TO SPEND THE REST OF TODAY THIS WAY.
....

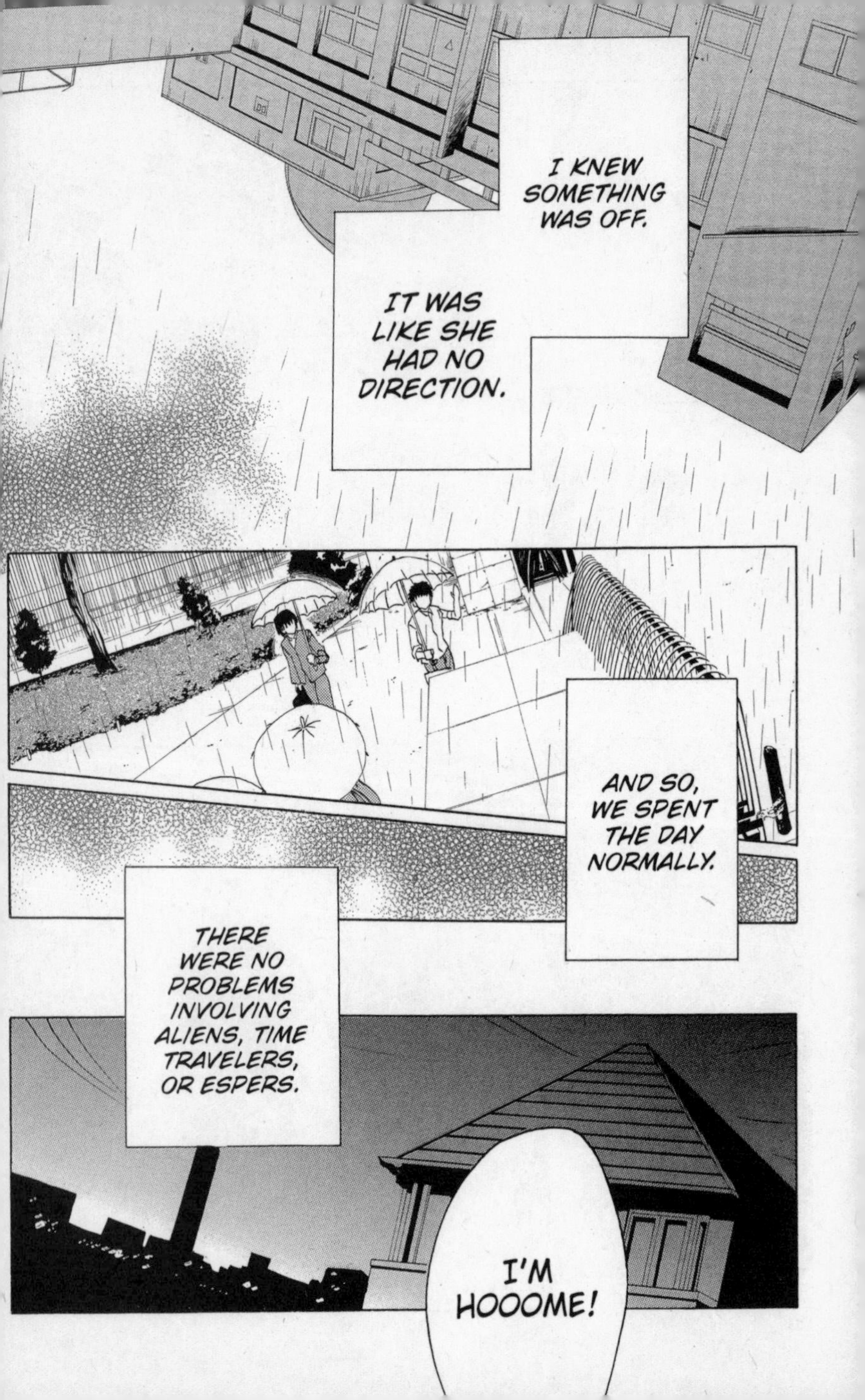
I KNEW SOMETHING WAS OFF.
IT WAS LIKE SHE HAD NO DIRECTION.
AND SO, WE SPENT THE DAY NORMALLY.
THERE WERE NO PROBLEMS INVOLVING ALIENS, TIME TRAVELERS, OR ESPERS.
I'M HOOOME!

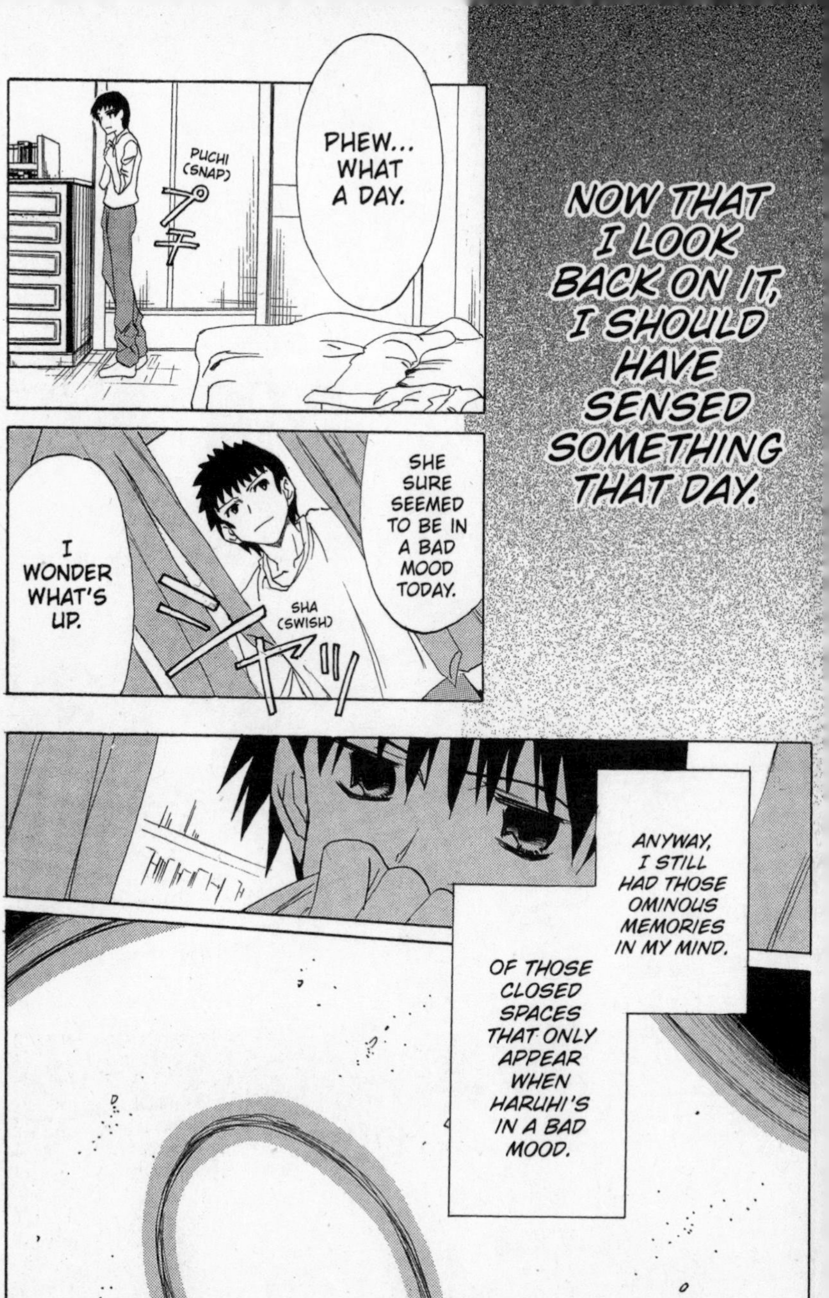
NOW THAT I LOOK BACK ON IT, I SHOULD HAVE SENSED SOMETHING THAT DAY.
PHEW... WHAT A DAY.
PUCHI (SNAP)
SHE SURE SEEMED TO BE IN A BAD MOOD TODAY.
SHA (SWISH)
I WONDER WHAT'S UP.
ANYWAY, I STILL HAD THOSE OMINOUS MEMORIES IN MY MIND.
OF THOSE CLOSED SPACES THAT ONLY APPEAR WHEN HARUHI'S IN A BAD MOOD.

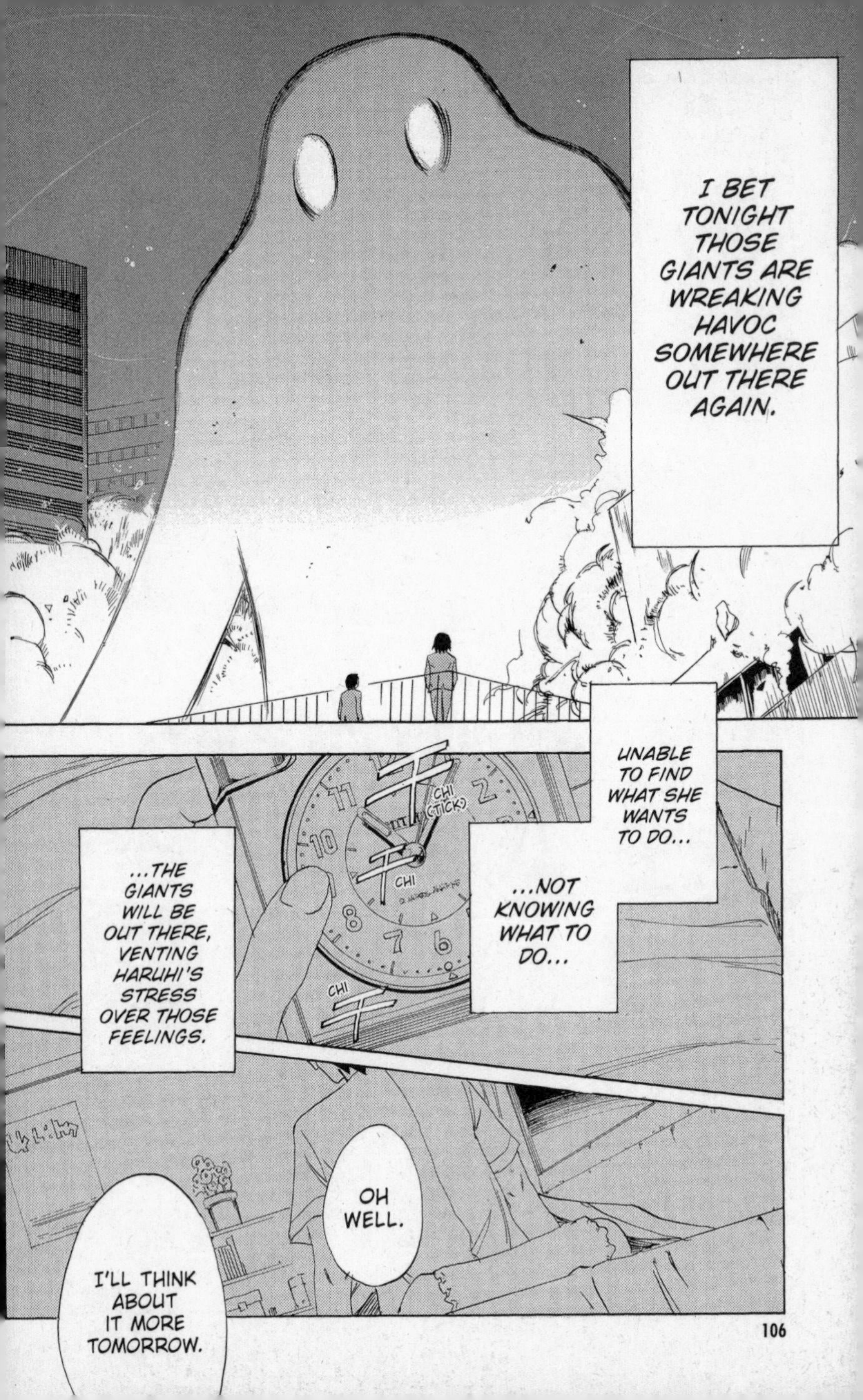
I BET TONIGHT THOSE GIANTS ARE WREAKING HAVOC SOMEWHERE OUT THERE AGAIN.
UNABLE TO FIND WHAT SHE WANTS TO DO...
...NOT KNOWING WHAT TO DO...
CHI (TICK)
CHI
CHI
...THE GIANTS WILL BE OUT THERE, VENTING HARUHI'S STRESS OVER THOSE FEELINGS.
OH WELL.
I'LL THINK ABOUT IT MORE TOMORROW.

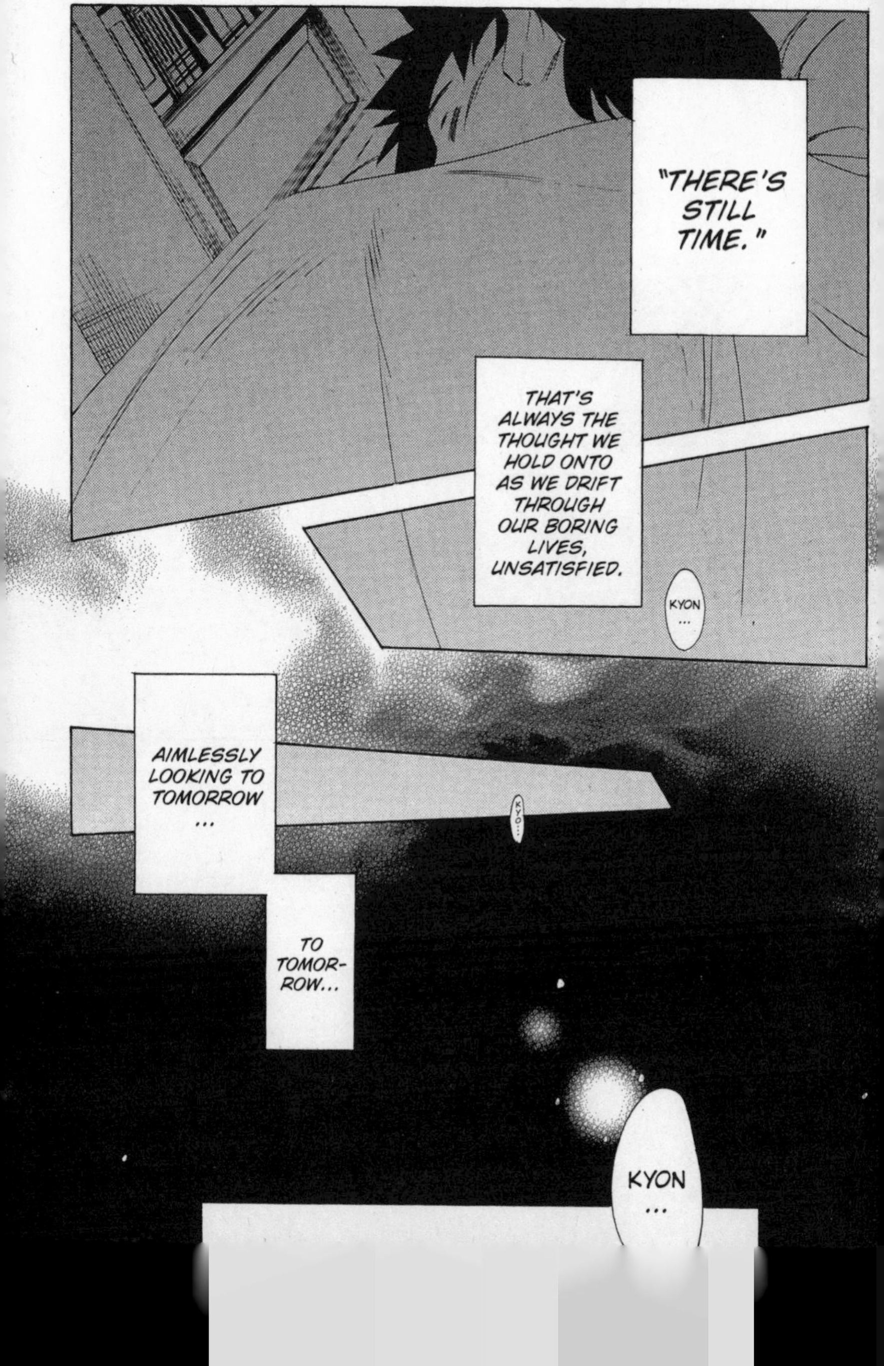
"THERE'S STILL TIME."
THAT'S ALWAYS THE THOUGHT WE HOLD ONTO AS WE DRIFT THROUGH OUR BORING LIVES, UNSATISFIED.
KYON ...
AIMLESSLY LOOKING TO TOMORROW ...
KYO...
TO TOMOR-ROW...
KYON ...

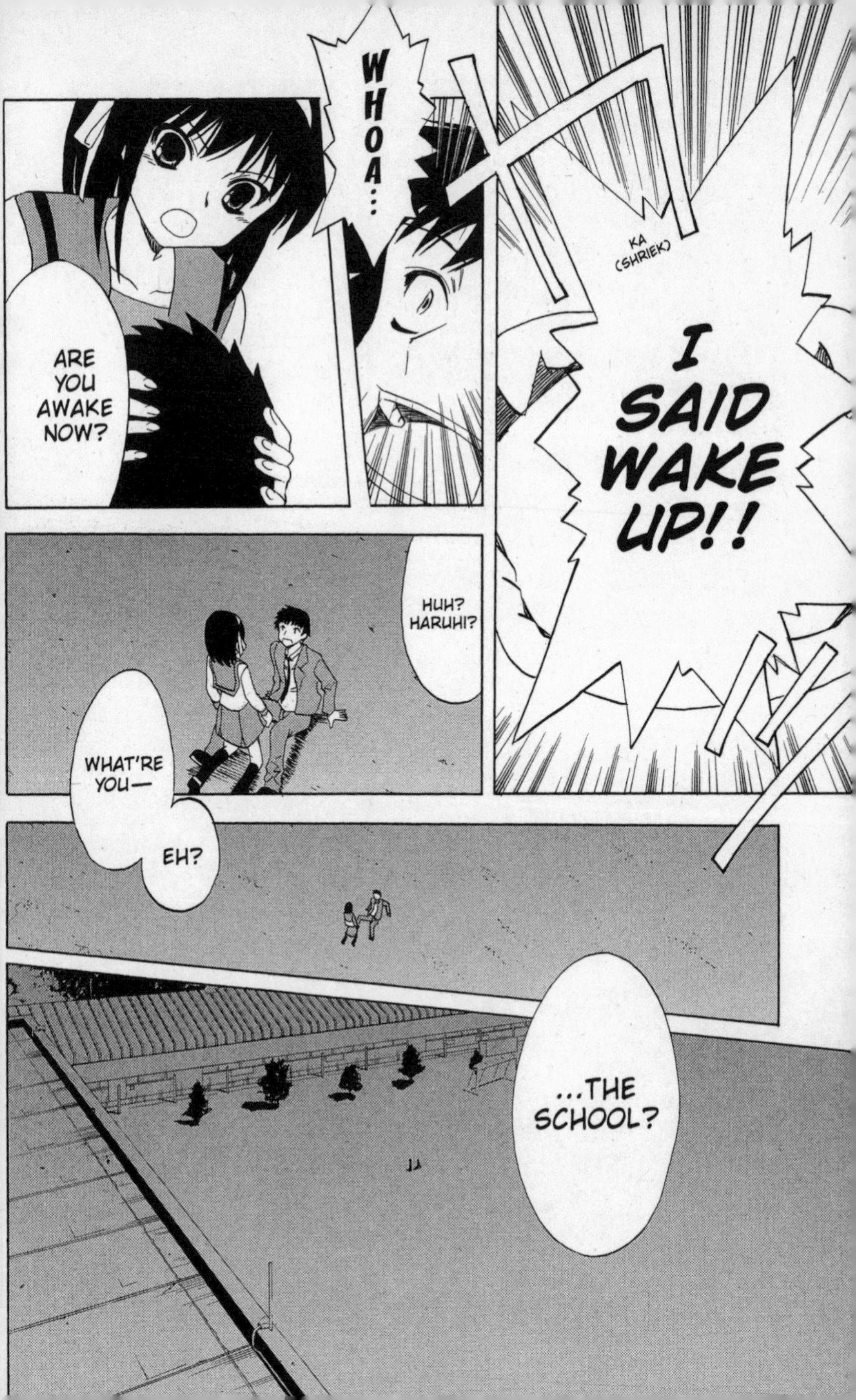
KA (SHRIEK)
I SAID WAKE UP!!
WHOA...
ARE YOU AWAKE NOW?
HUH? HARUHI?
WHAT'RE YOU—
EH?
...THE SCHOOL?

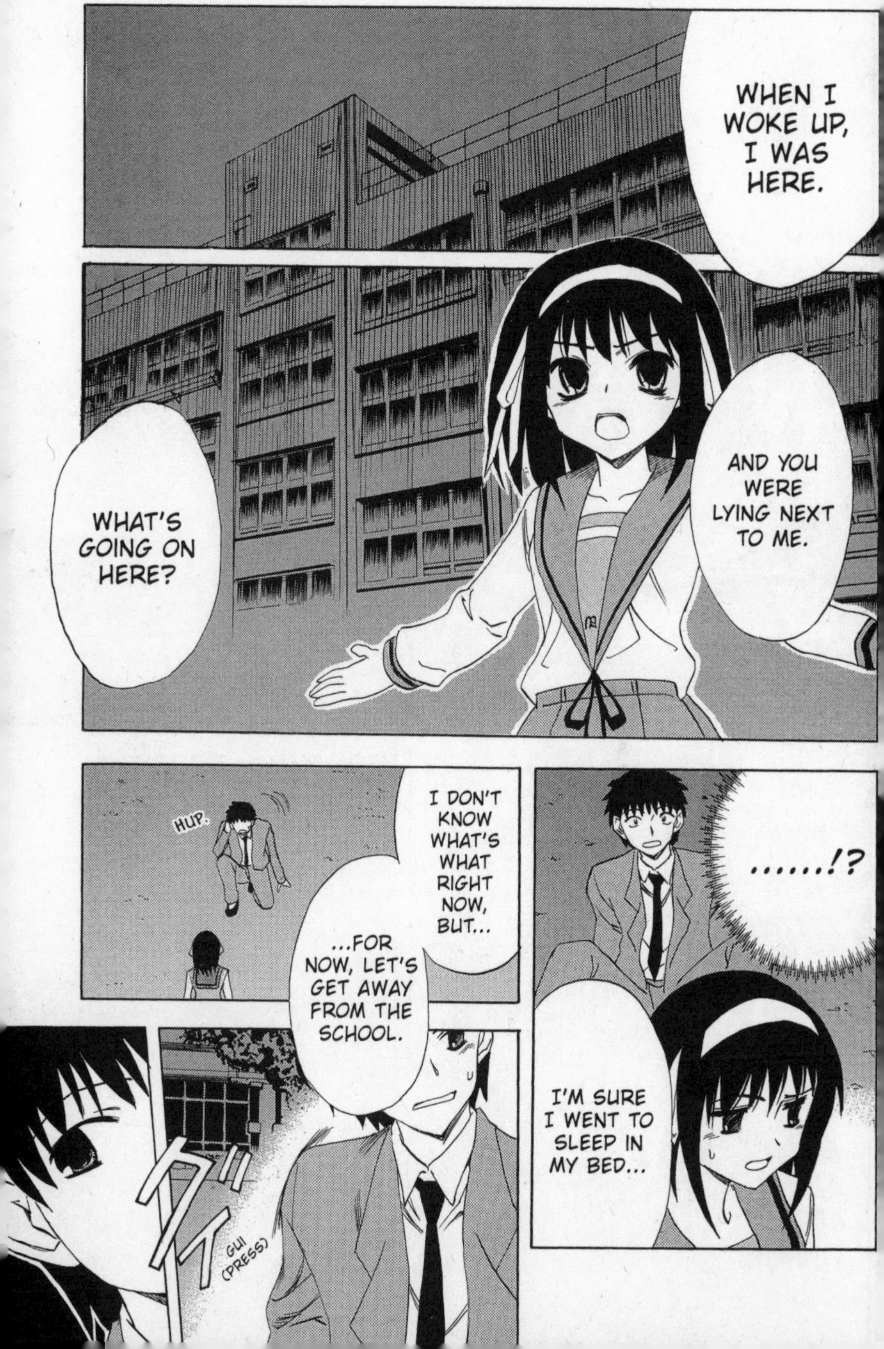
WHEN I WOKE UP, I WAS HERE.
AND YOU WERE LYING NEXT TO ME.
WHAT'S GOING ON HERE?
......!?
I'M SURE I WENT TO SLEEP IN MY BED...
HUP.
I DON'T KNOW WHAT'S WHAT RIGHT NOW, BUT...
...FOR NOW, LET'S GET AWAY FROM THE SCHOOL.
GUI (PRESS)

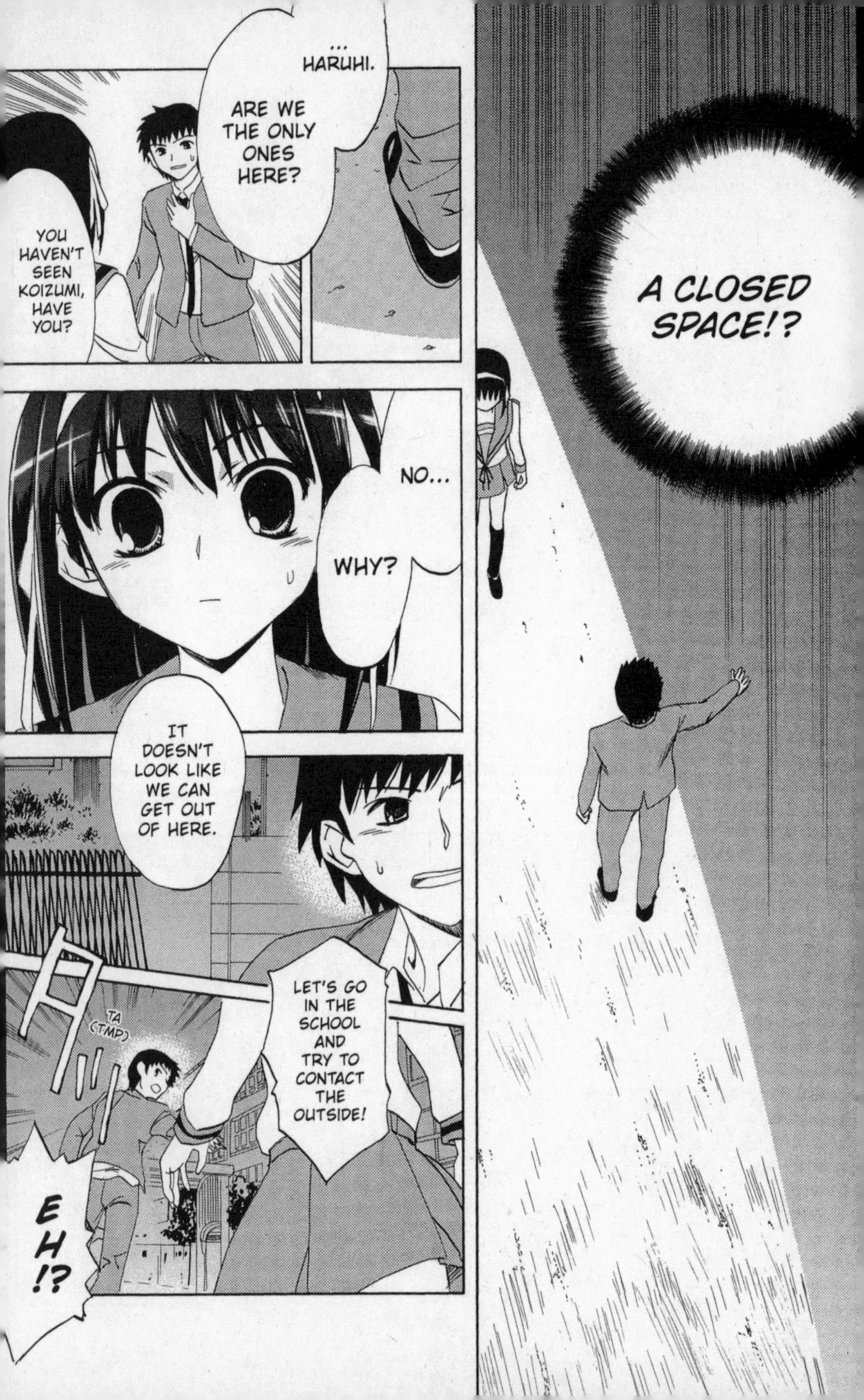
A CLOSED SPACE!?
... HARUHI.
ARE WE THE ONLY ONES HERE?
YOU HAVEN'T SEEN KOIZUMI, HAVE YOU?
NO...
WHY?
IT DOESN'T LOOK LIKE WE CAN GET OUT OF HERE.
LET'S GO IN THE SCHOOL AND TRY TO CONTACT THE OUTSIDE!
TA (TMP)
EH!?

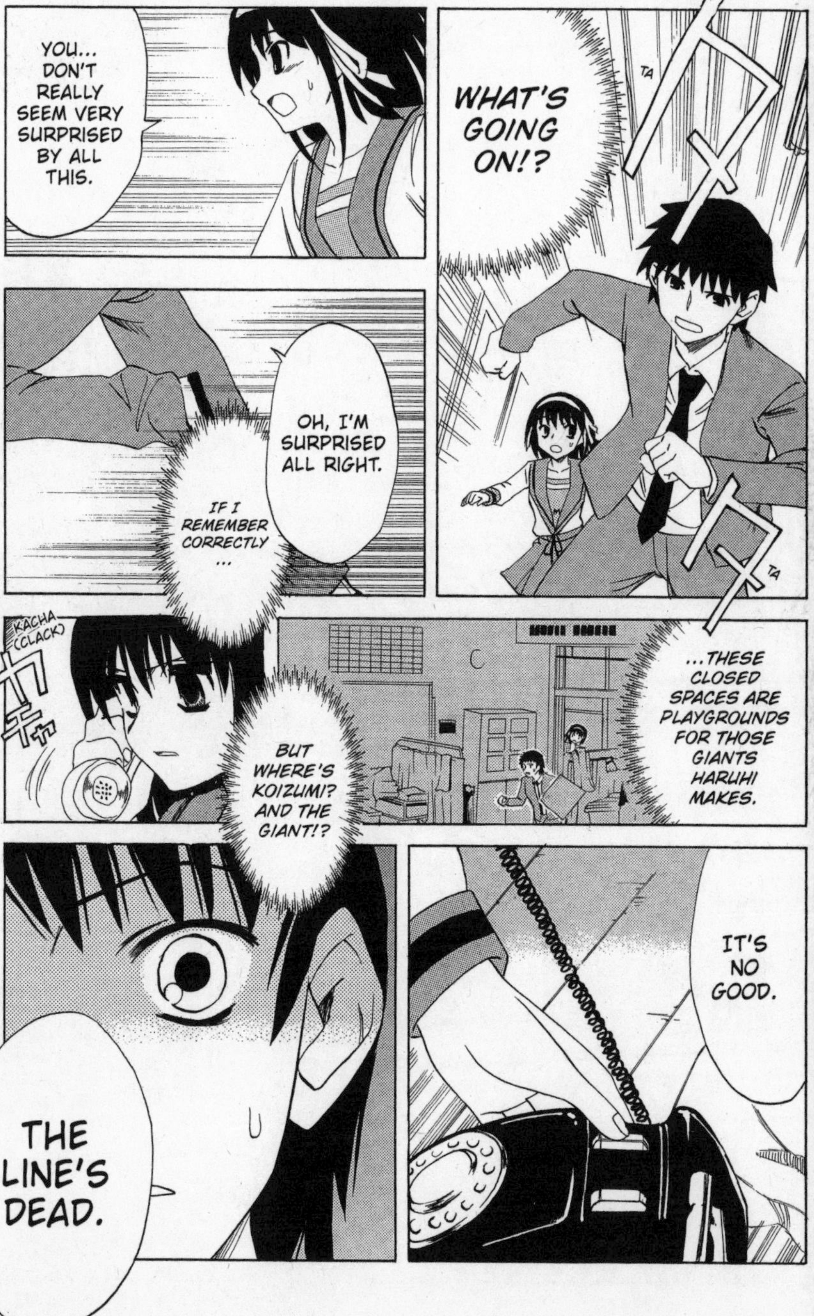
TA
WHAT'S GOING ON!?
YOU... DON'T REALLY SEEM VERY SURPRISED BY ALL THIS.
TA
OH, I'M SURPRISED ALL RIGHT.
IF I REMEMBER CORRECTLY ...
...THESE CLOSED SPACES ARE PLAYGROUNDS FOR THOSE GIANTS HARUHI MAKES.
BUT WHERE'S KOIZUMI? AND THE GIANT!?
KACHA (CLACK)
IT'S NO GOOD.
THE LINE'S DEAD.

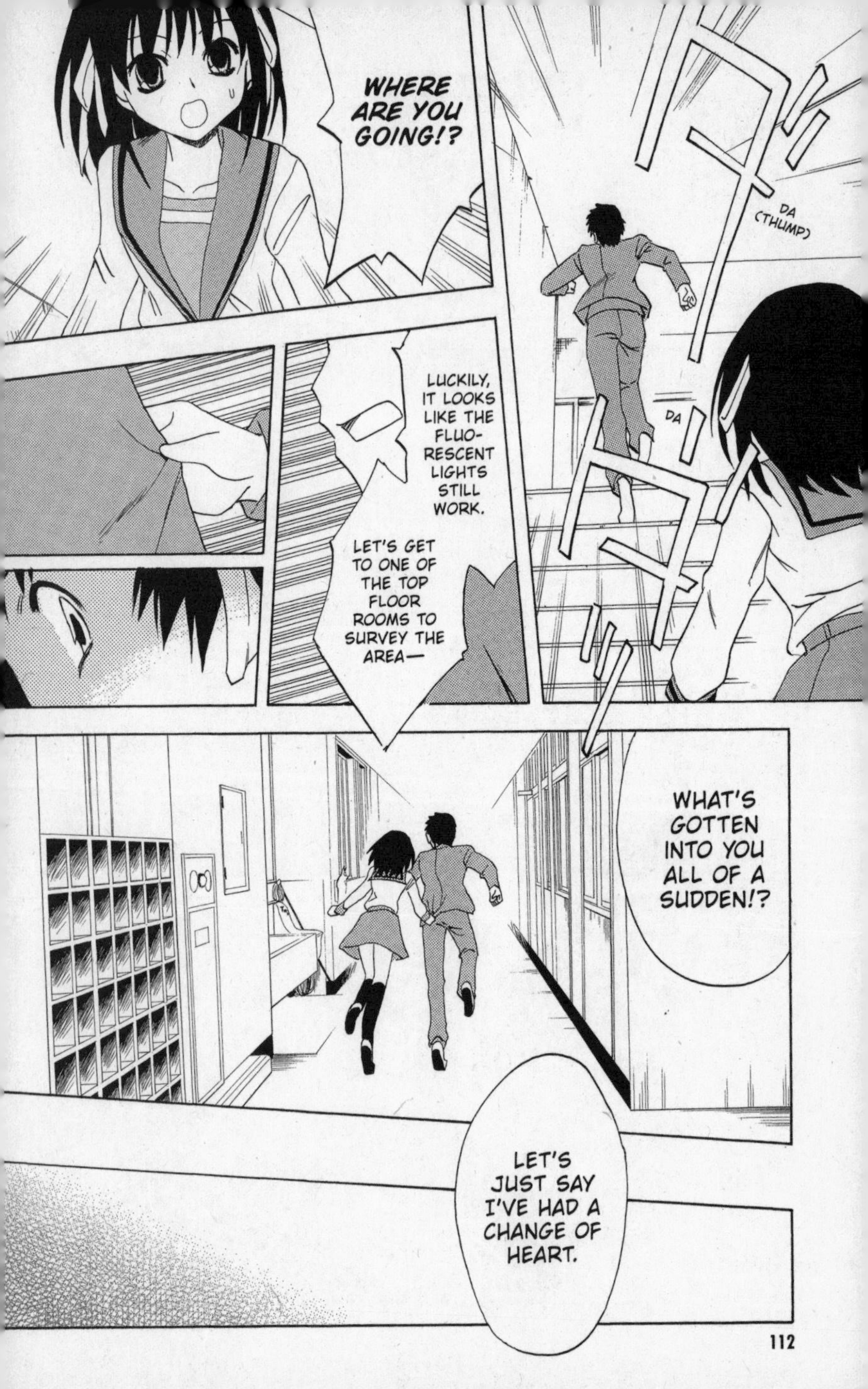
DA (THUMP)
DA
WHERE ARE YOU GOING!?
LUCKILY, IT LOOKS LIKE THE FLUO-RESCENT LIGHTS STILL WORK.
LET'S GET TO ONE OF THE TOP FLOOR ROOMS TO SURVEY THE AREA—
WHAT'S GOTTEN INTO YOU ALL OF A SUDDEN!?
LET'S JUST SAY I'VE HAD A CHANGE OF HEART.

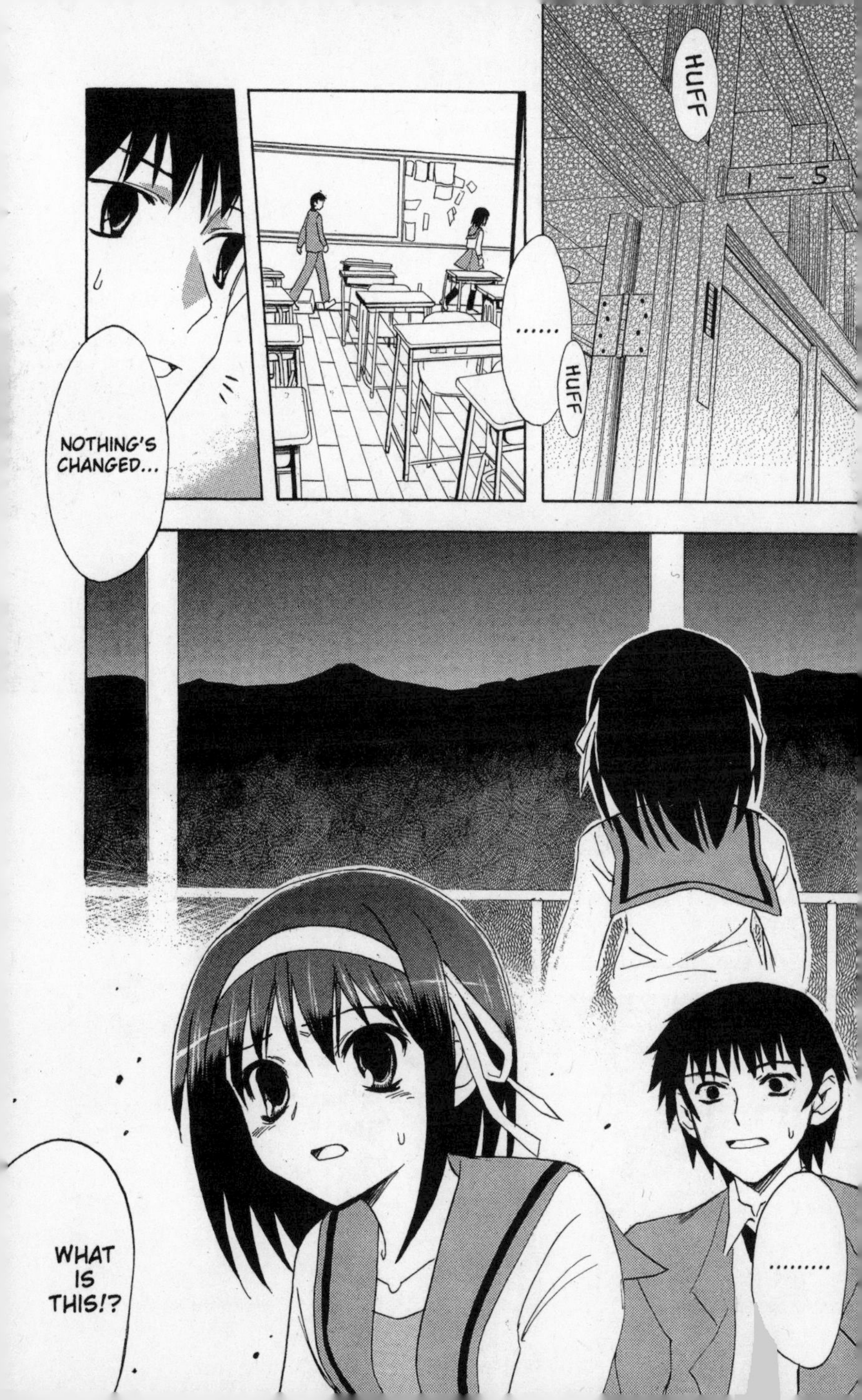
HUFF
......
HUFF
NOTHING'S CHANGED...
WHAT IS THIS!?
....

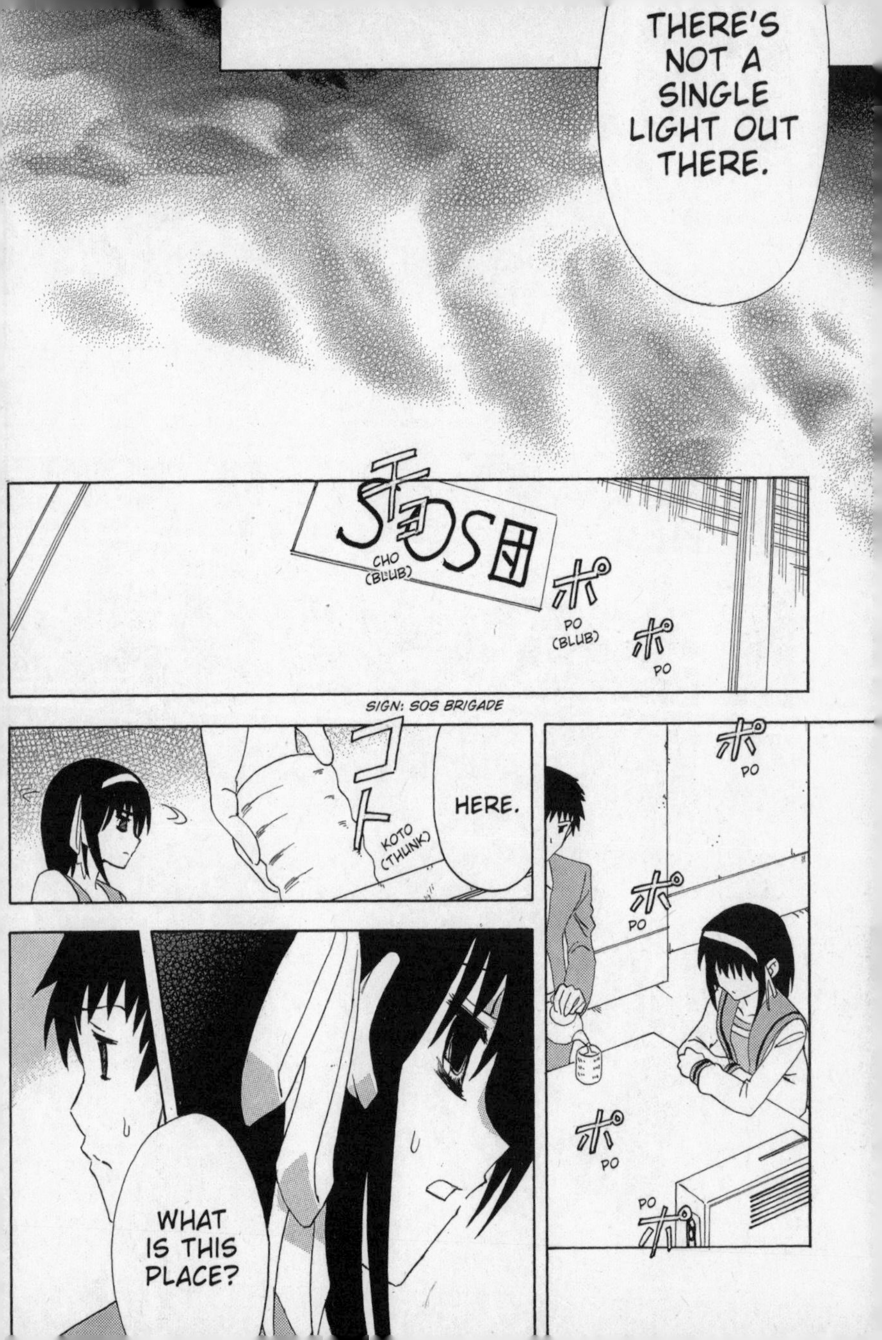
THERE'S NOT A SINGLE LIGHT OUT THERE.
SOS団
チョ
CHO (BLUB)
ポ
PO (BLUB)
ポ
PO
SIGN: SOS BRIGADE
ポ
PO
ポ
PO
ポ
PO
PO
ポ
コト
KOTO (THUNK)
HERE.
WHAT IS THIS PLACE?

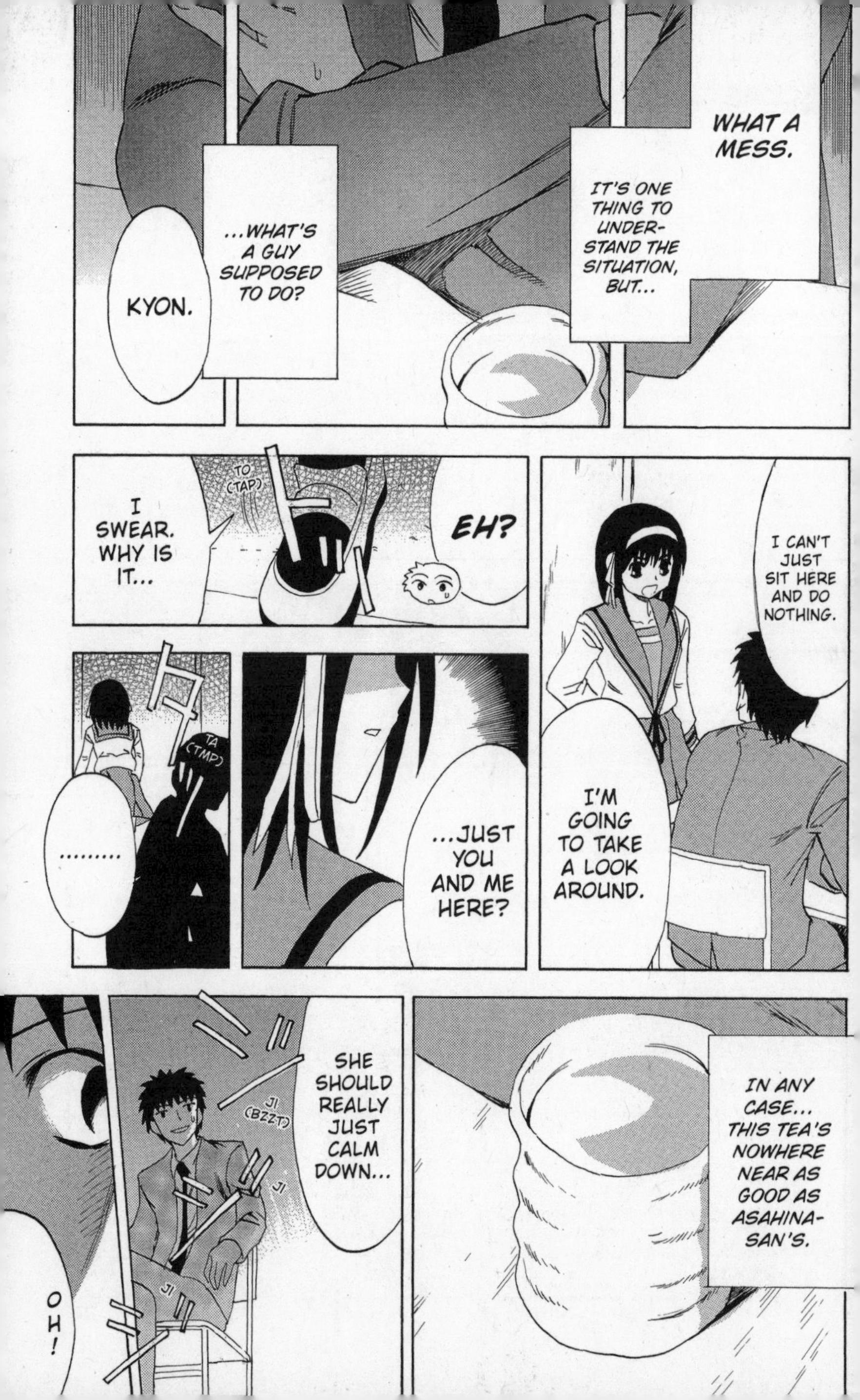
WHAT A MESS.
IT'S ONE THING TO UNDERSTAND THE SITUATION, BUT...
...WHAT'S A GUY SUPPOSED TO DO?
KYON.
I CAN'T JUST SIT HERE AND DO NOTHING.
I'M GOING TO TAKE A LOOK AROUND.
EH?
TO (TAP)
I SWEAR. WHY IS IT...
...JUST YOU AND ME HERE?
TA (TMP)
....
IN ANY CASE... THIS TEA'S NOWHERE NEAR AS GOOD AS ASAHINA-SAN'S.
SHE SHOULD REALLY JUST CALM DOWN...
JI (BZZT)
JI
JI
OH!

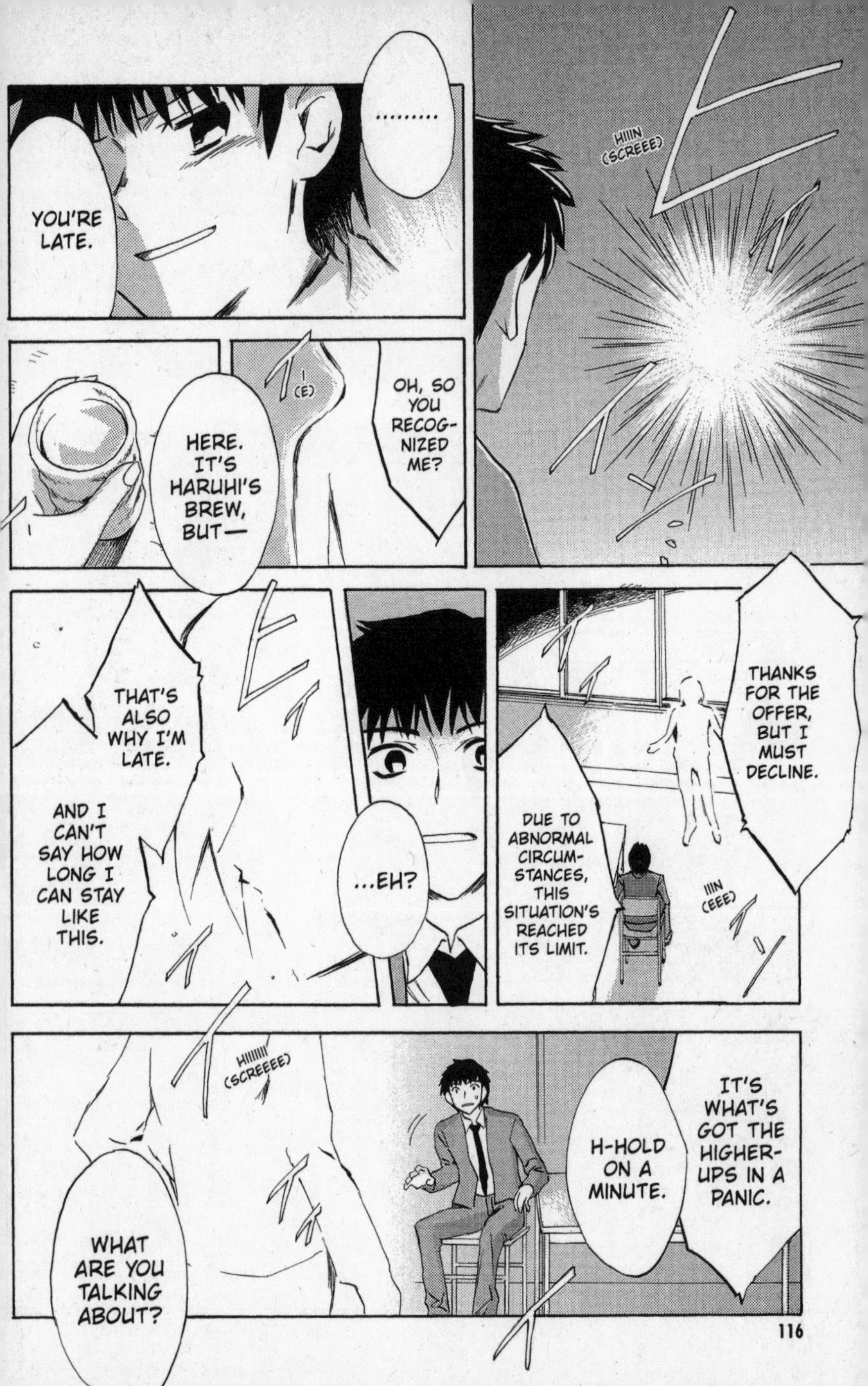
HIIIN (SCREEE)
....
YOU'RE LATE.
OH, SO YOU RECOGNIZED ME?
I (E)
HERE. IT'S HARUHI'S BREW, BUT—
THANKS FOR THE OFFER, BUT I MUST DECLINE.
DUE TO ABNORMAL CIRCUMSTANCES, THIS SITUATION'S REACHED ITS LIMIT.
IIIN (EEE)
...EH?
THAT'S ALSO WHY I'M LATE.
AND I CAN'T SAY HOW LONG I CAN STAY LIKE THIS.
IT'S WHAT'S GOT THE HIGHER-UPS IN A PANIC.
H-HOLD ON A MINUTE.
HIIIIIII (SCREEEE)
WHAT ARE YOU TALKING ABOUT?

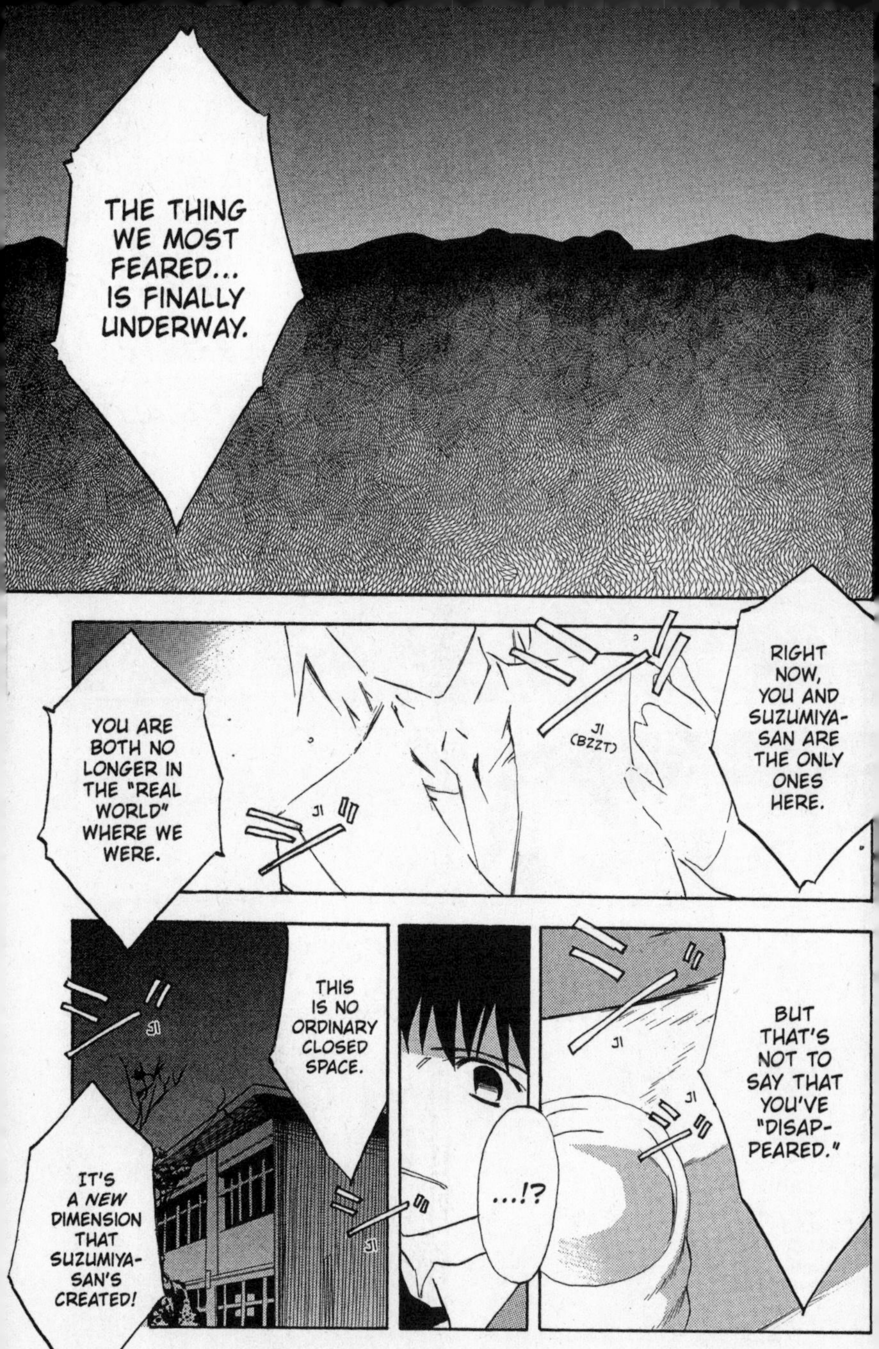
THE THING WE MOST FEARED... IS FINALLY UNDERWAY.
RIGHT NOW, YOU AND SUZUMIYA-SAN ARE THE ONLY ONES HERE.
JI (BZZT)
JI
YOU ARE BOTH NO LONGER IN THE "REAL WORLD" WHERE WE WERE.
BUT THAT'S NOT TO SAY THAT YOU'VE "DISAPPEARED."
JI
JI
...!?
THIS IS NO ORDINARY CLOSED SPACE.
JI
JI
IT'S A *NEW* DIMENSION THAT SUZUMIYA-SAN'S CREATED!

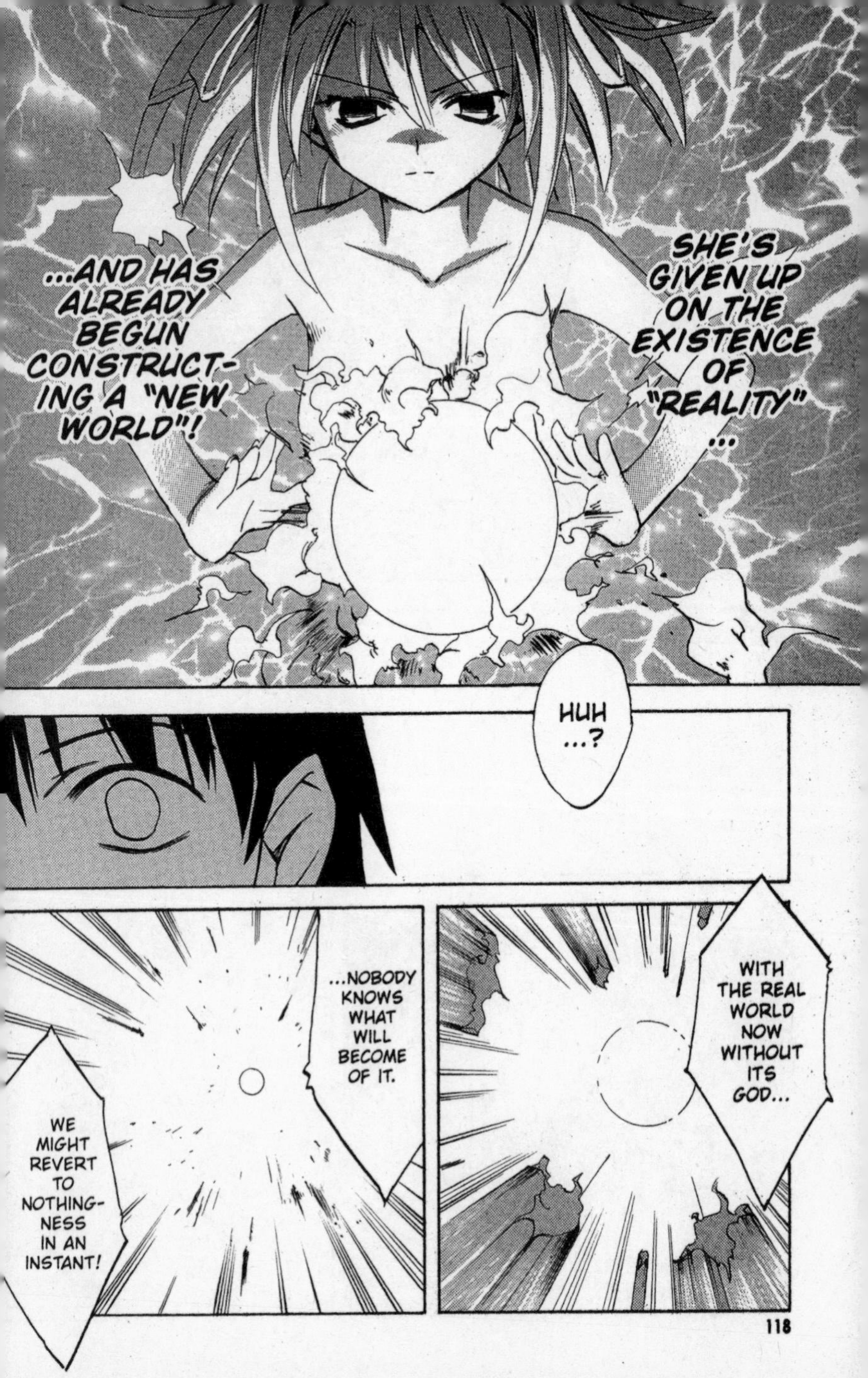
SHE'S GIVEN UP ON THE EXISTENCE OF "REALITY"...
...AND HAS ALREADY BEGUN CONSTRUCTING A "NEW WORLD"!
HUH ...?
WITH THE REAL WORLD NOW WITHOUT ITS GOD...
...NOBODY KNOWS WHAT WILL BECOME OF IT.
WE MIGHT REVERT TO NOTHINGNESS IN AN INSTANT!

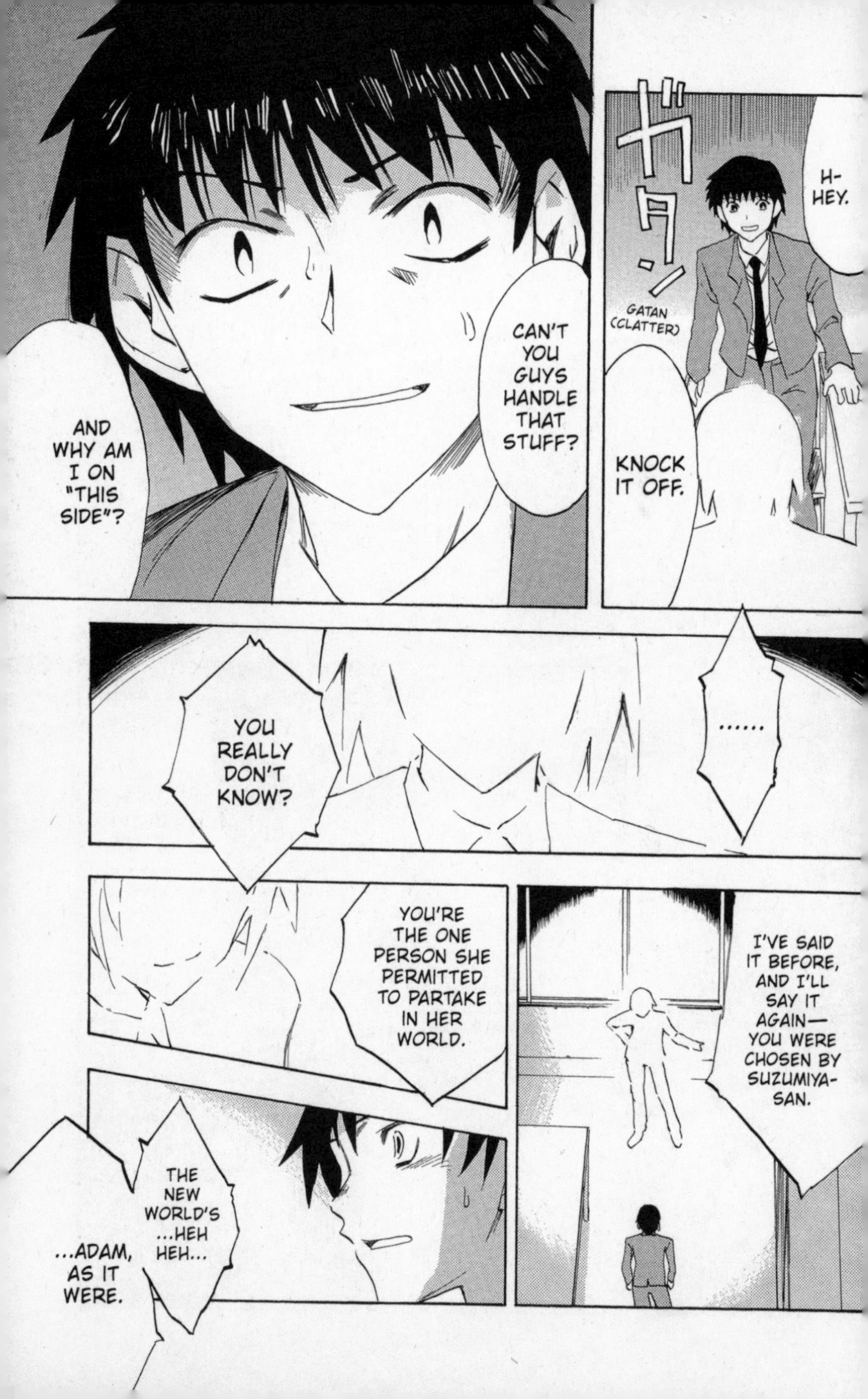
H-HEY.
GATAN (CLATTER)
KNOCK IT OFF.
CAN'T YOU GUYS HANDLE THAT STUFF?
AND WHY AM I ON "THIS SIDE"?
......
YOU REALLY DON'T KNOW?
I'VE SAID IT BEFORE, AND I'LL SAY IT AGAIN— YOU WERE CHOSEN BY SUZUMIYA-SAN.
YOU'RE THE ONE PERSON SHE PERMITTED TO PARTAKE IN HER WORLD.
THE NEW WORLD'S ...HEH HEH...
...ADAM, AS IT WERE.

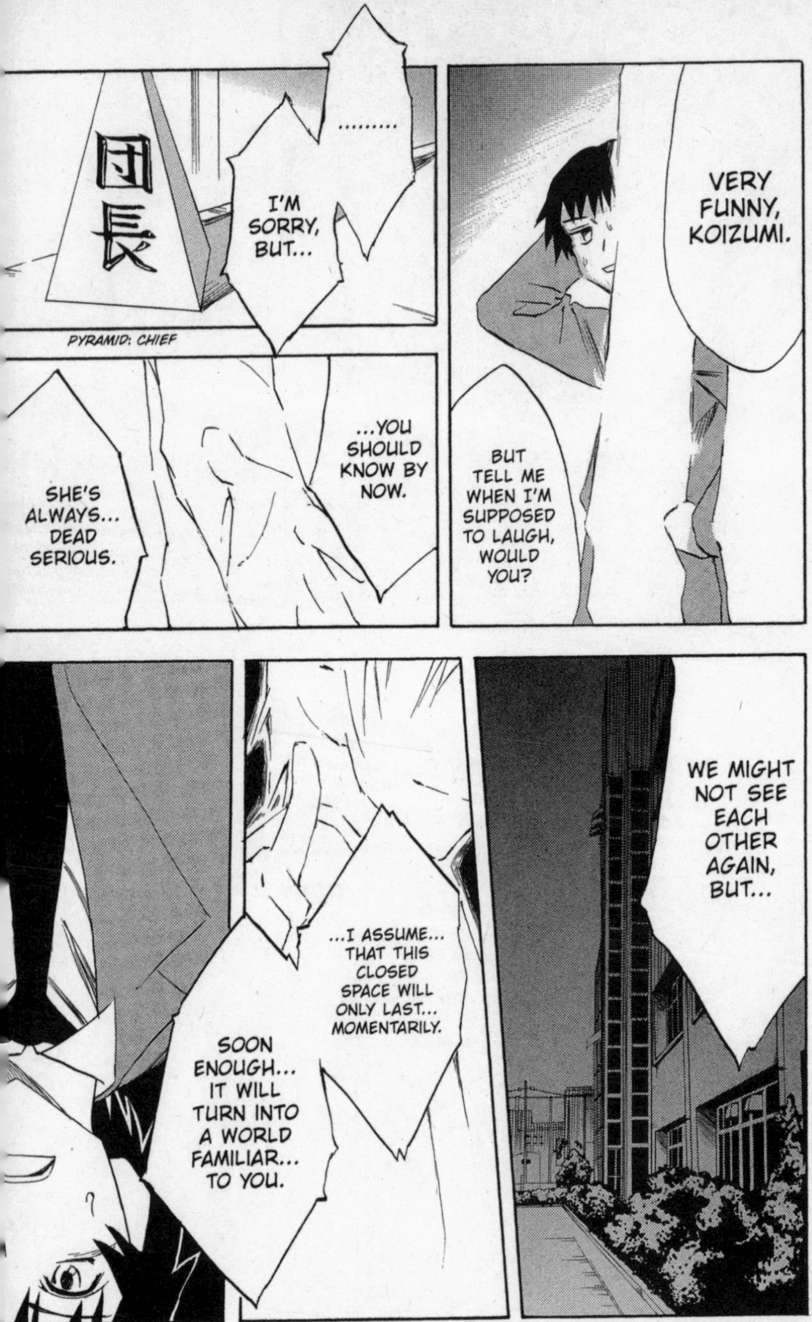
VERY FUNNY, KOIZUMI.
BUT TELL ME WHEN I'M SUPPOSED TO LAUGH, WOULD YOU?
....
I'M SORRY, BUT...
団長
PYRAMID: CHIEF
...YOU SHOULD KNOW BY NOW.
SHE'S ALWAYS... DEAD SERIOUS.
WE MIGHT NOT SEE EACH OTHER AGAIN, BUT...
...I ASSUME... THAT THIS CLOSED SPACE WILL ONLY LAST... MOMENTARILY.
SOON ENOUGH... IT WILL TURN INTO A WORLD FAMILIAR... TO YOU.

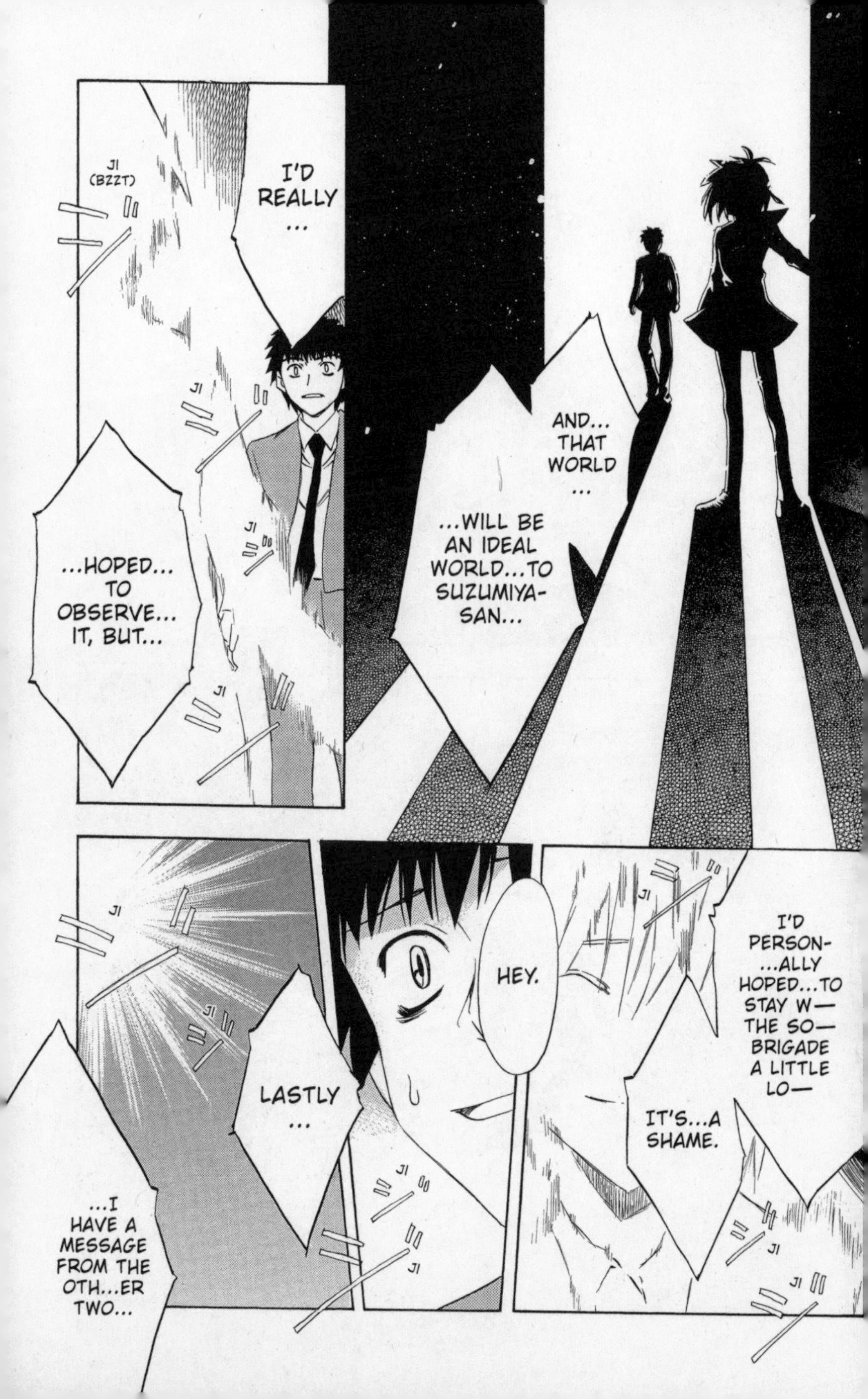
AND... THAT WORLD ...
...WILL BE AN IDEAL WORLD...TO SUZUMIYA-SAN...
JI (BZZT)
I'D REALLY ...
JI
JI
...HOPED... TO OBSERVE... IT, BUT...
JI
JI
I'D PERSON- ...ALLY HOPED...TO STAY W— THE SO— BRIGADE A LITTLE LO—
IT'S...A SHAME.
JI
JI
HEY.
JI
JI
JI
JI
LASTLY ...
...I HAVE A MESSAGE FROM THE OTH...ER TWO...

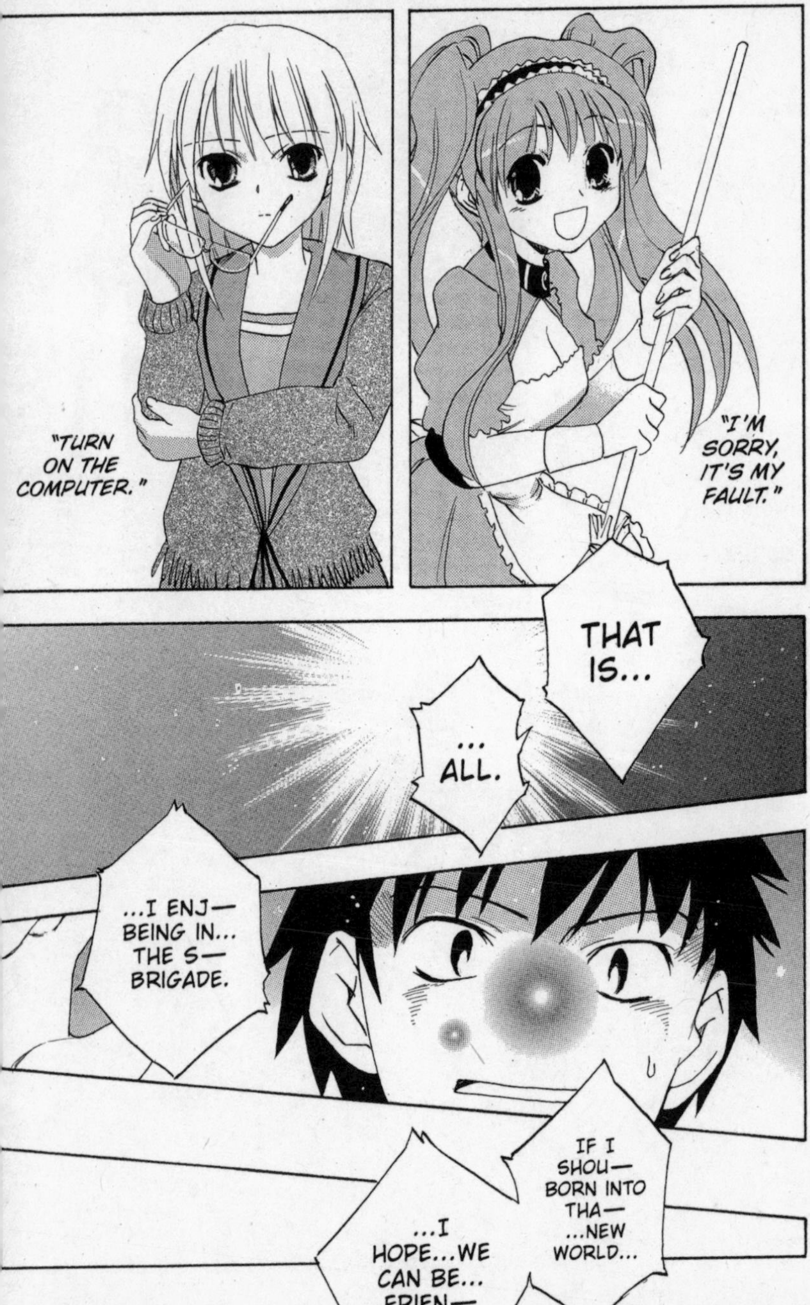
"I'M SORRY, IT'S MY FAULT."
"TURN ON THE COMPUTER."
THAT IS...
...ALL.
...I ENJ— BEING IN... THE S— BRIGADE.
IF I SHOU— BORN INTO THA— ...NEW WORLD...
...I HOPE...WE CAN BE... FRIEN—

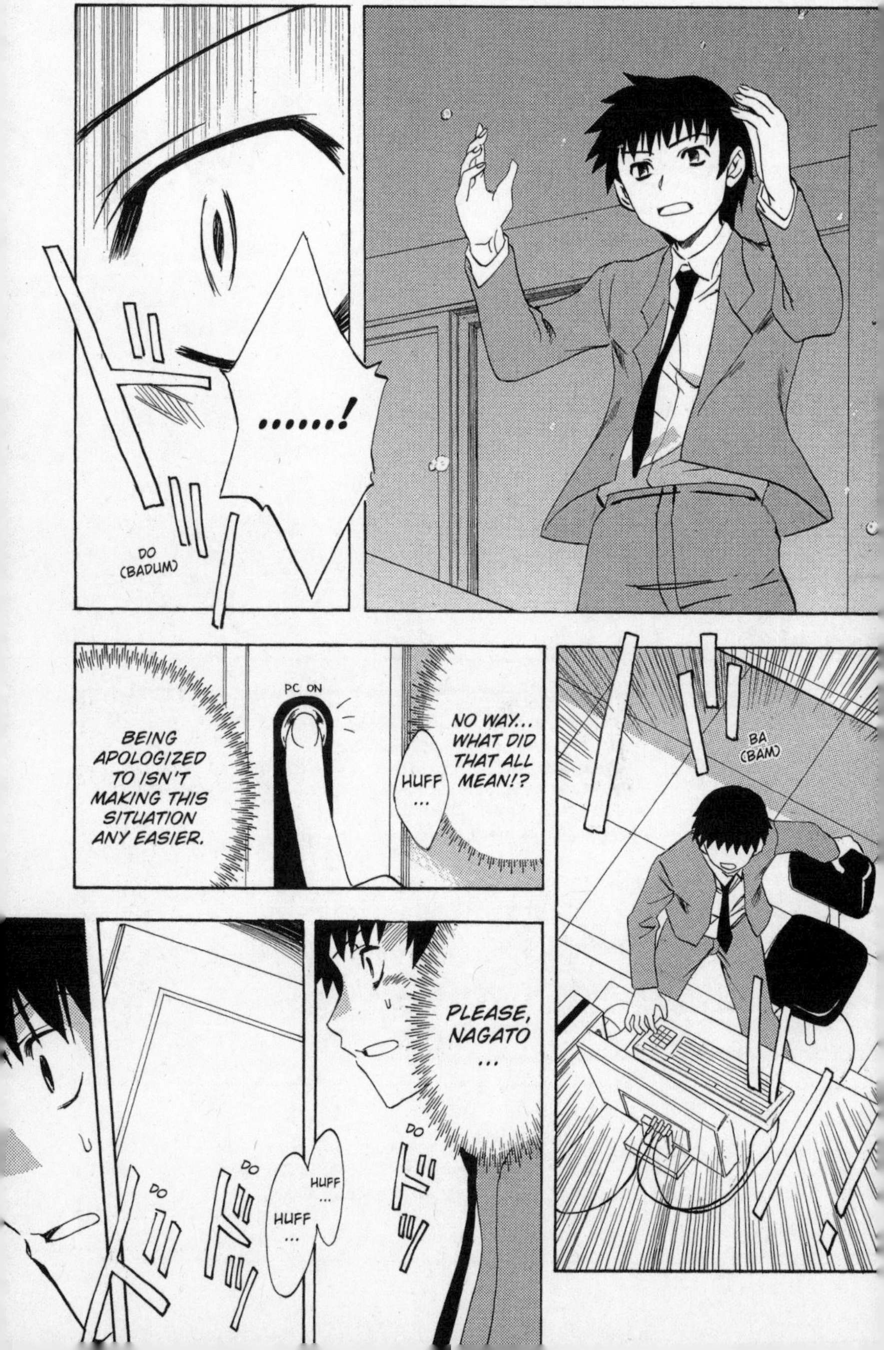
......!
DO (BADUM)
BA (BAM)
NO WAY... WHAT DID THAT ALL MEAN!?
HUFF ...
PC ON
BEING APOLOGIZED TO ISN'T MAKING THIS SITUATION ANY EASIER.
PLEASE, NAGATO ...
DO
HUFF ...
HUFF ...
DO
DO

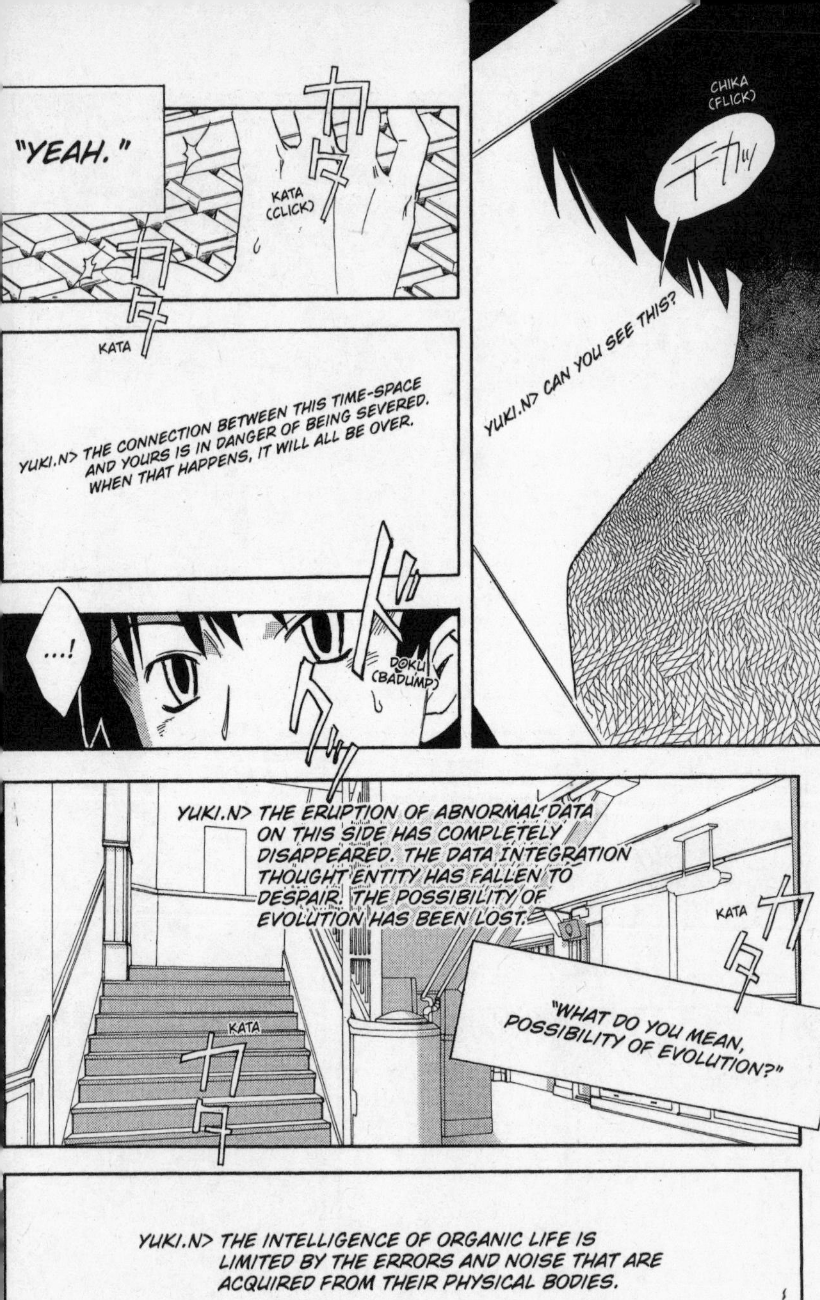
CHIKA (FLICK)
YUKI.N> CAN YOU SEE THIS?
"YEAH."
KATA (CLICK)
KATA
YUKI.N> THE CONNECTION BETWEEN THIS TIME-SPACE AND YOURS IS IN DANGER OF BEING SEVERED. WHEN THAT HAPPENS, IT WILL ALL BE OVER.
DOKU (BADUMP)
...!
YUKI.N> THE ERUPTION OF ABNORMAL DATA ON THIS SIDE HAS COMPLETELY DISAPPEARED. THE DATA INTEGRATION THOUGHT ENTITY HAS FALLEN TO DESPAIR. THE POSSIBILITY OF EVOLUTION HAS BEEN LOST.
KATA
"WHAT DO YOU MEAN, POSSIBILITY OF EVOLUTION?"
KATA
YUKI.N> THE INTELLIGENCE OF ORGANIC LIFE IS LIMITED BY THE ERRORS AND NOISE THAT ARE ACQUIRED FROM THEIR PHYSICAL BODIES.

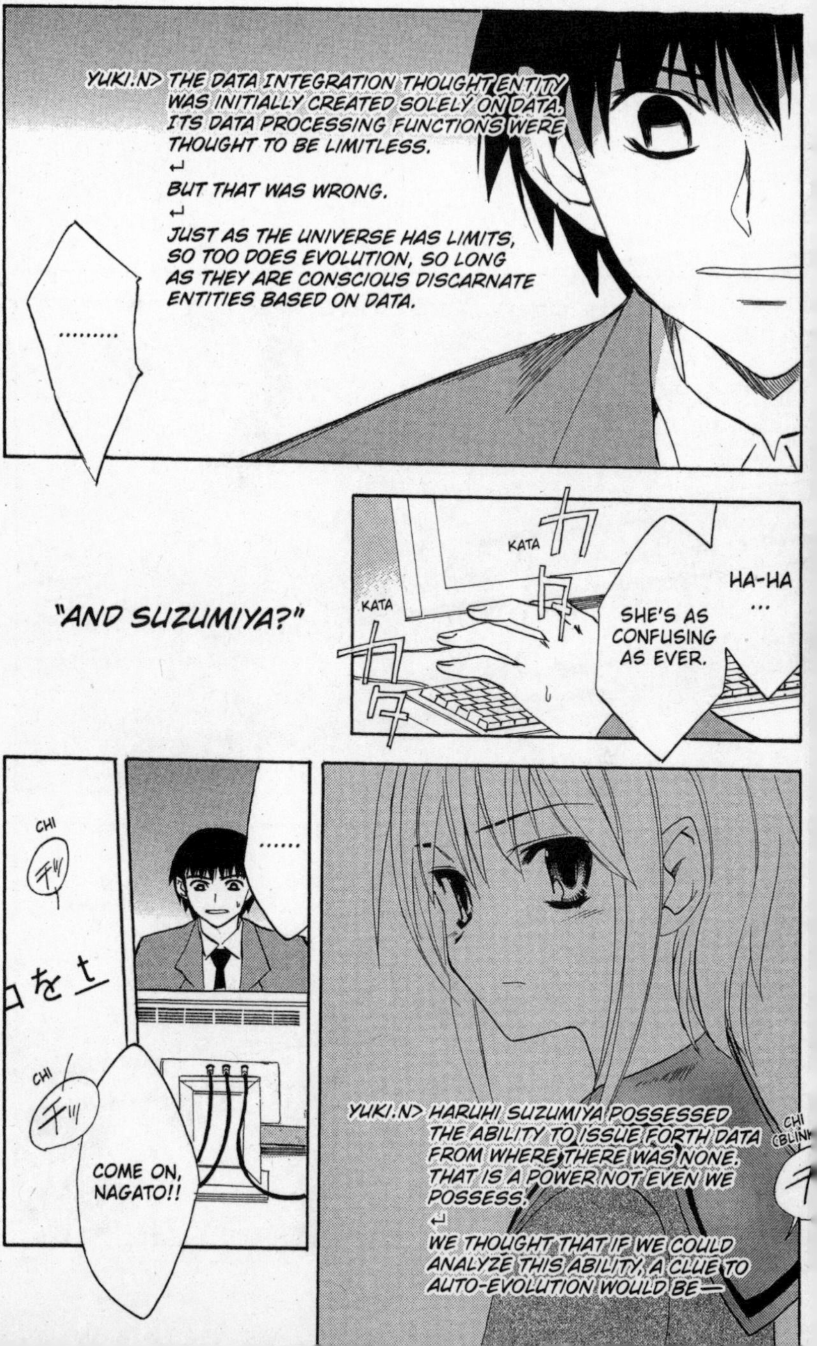
YUKI.N> THE DATA INTEGRATION THOUGHT ENTITY WAS INITIALLY CREATED SOLELY ON DATA. ITS DATA PROCESSING FUNCTIONS WERE THOUGHT TO BE LIMITLESS.
↵
BUT THAT WAS WRONG.
↵
JUST AS THE UNIVERSE HAS LIMITS, SO TOO DOES EVOLUTION, SO LONG AS THEY ARE CONSCIOUS DISCARNATE ENTITIES BASED ON DATA.
....
HA-HA ...
SHE'S AS CONFUSING AS EVER.
KATA
KATA
"AND SUZUMIYA?"
YUKI.N> HARUHI SUZUMIYA POSSESSED THE ABILITY TO ISSUE FORTH DATA FROM WHERE THERE WAS NONE. THAT IS A POWER NOT EVEN WE POSSESS.
↵
WE THOUGHT THAT IF WE COULD ANALYZE THIS ABILITY, A CLUE TO AUTO-EVOLUTION WOULD BE—
....
CHI
COME ON, NAGATO!!
CHI

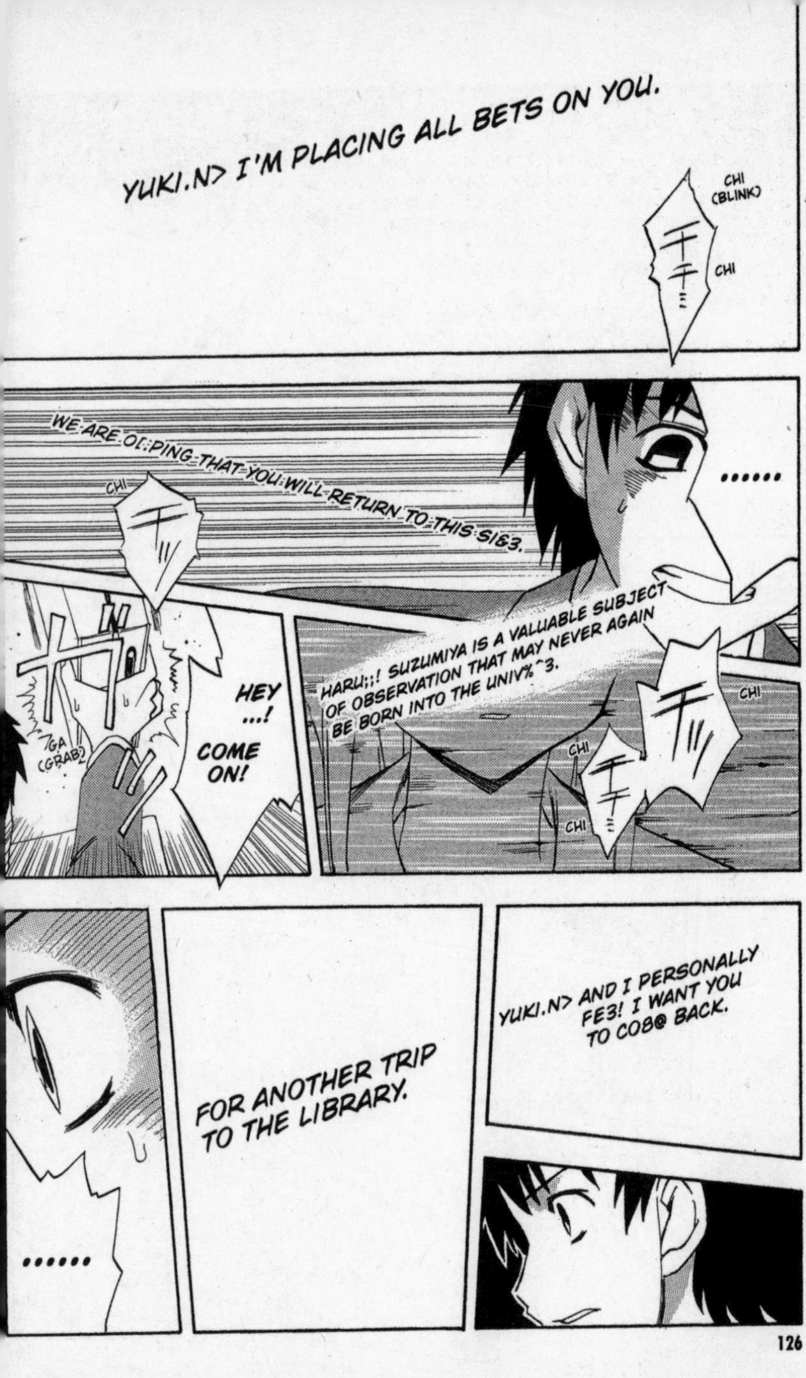
YUKI.N> I'M PLACING ALL BETS ON YOU.
CHI (BLINK)
CHI
......
WE ARE OI:PING THAT YOU WILL RETURN TO THIS SI&3.
CHI
HARU;;! SUZUMIYA IS A VALUABLE SUBJECT OF OBSERVATION THAT MAY NEVER AGAIN BE BORN INTO THE UNIV%^3.
CHI
CHI
CHI
HEY ...! COME ON!
GA (GRAB)
YUKI.N> AND I PERSONALLY FE3! I WANT YOU TO CO8@ BACK.
FOR ANOTHER TRIP TO THE LIBRARY.
......

YUKI.N> SLEEPING BEAUTY

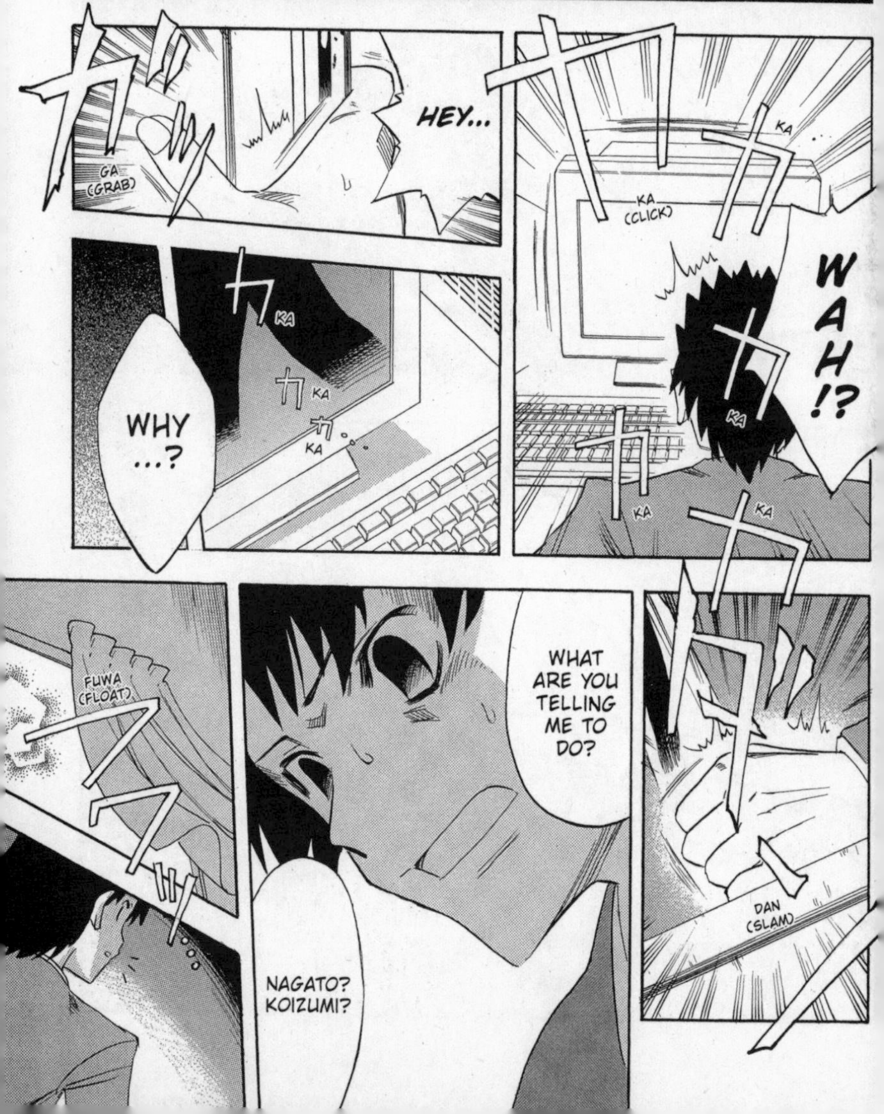
KA
KA (CLICK)
WAH!?
KA
KA
KA
GA (GRAB)
HEY...
KA
KA
KA
WHY ...?
DAN (SLAM)
WHAT ARE YOU TELLING ME TO DO?
NAGATO? KOIZUMI?
FUWA (FLOAT)

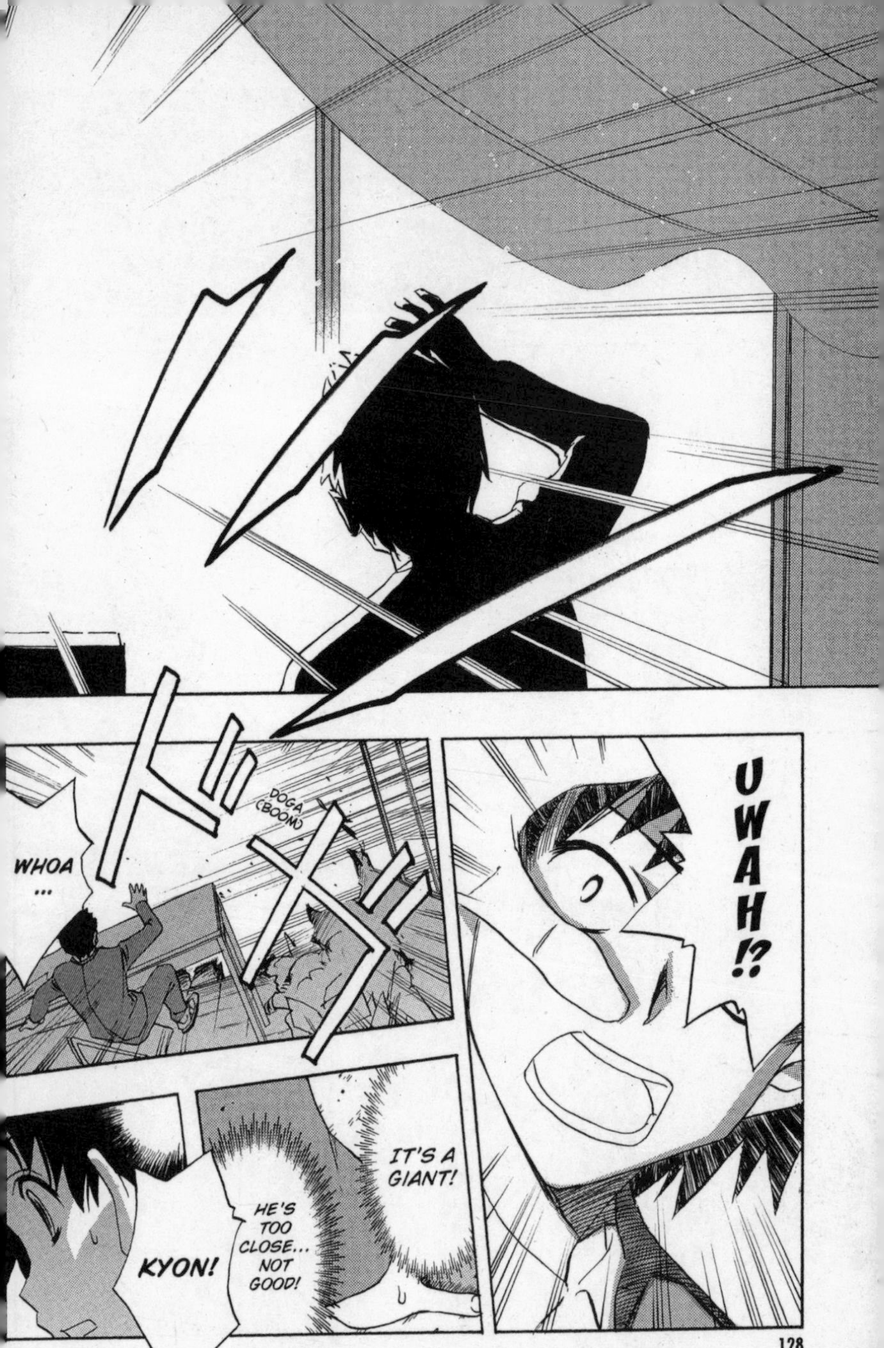
UWAH!?
DOGA (BOOM)
WHOA ...
IT'S A GIANT!
HE'S TOO CLOSE... NOT GOOD!
KYON!

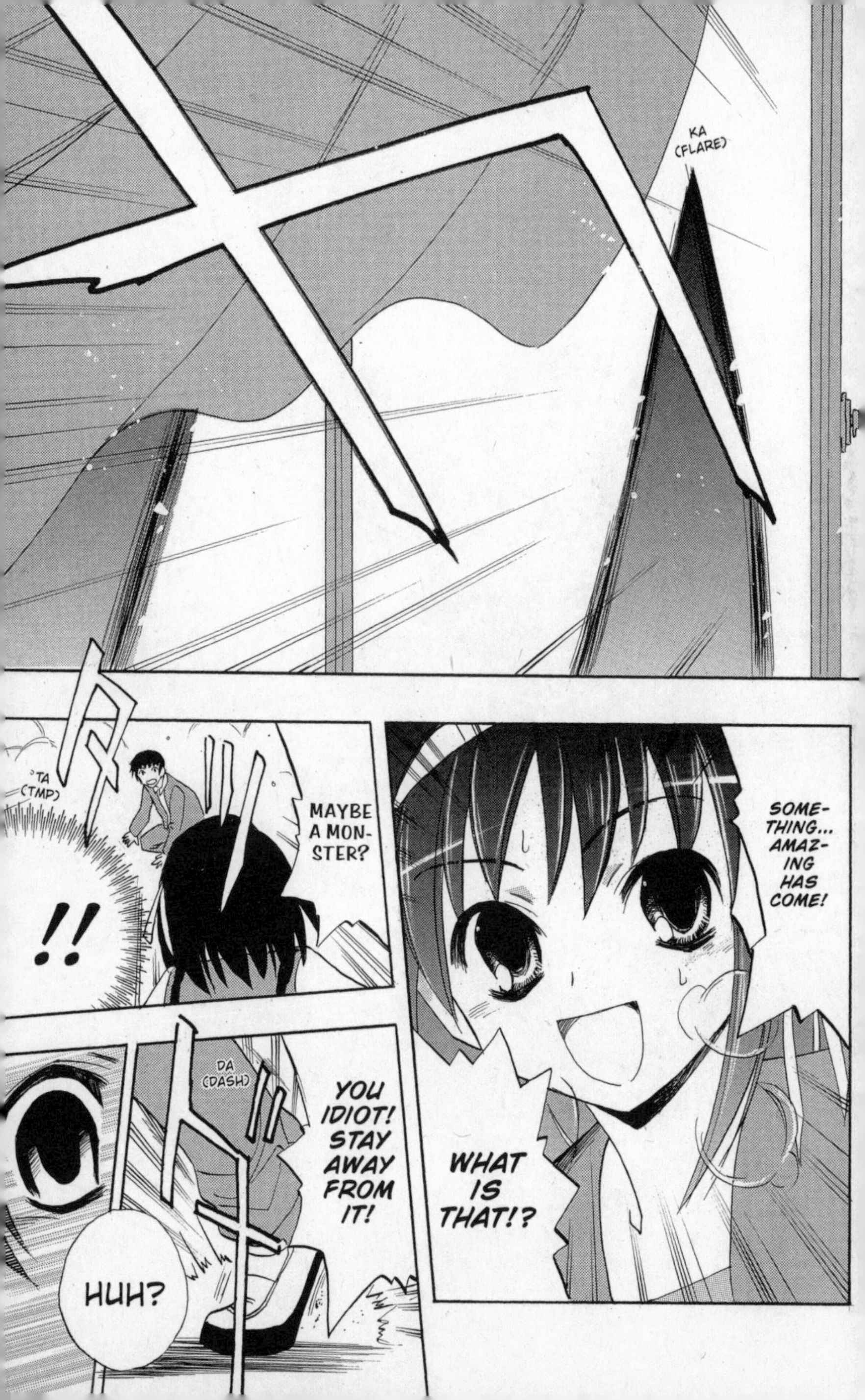
KA (FLARE)
SOMETHING... AMAZING HAS COME!
MAYBE A MONSTER?
TA (TMP)
!!
WHAT IS THAT!?
YOU IDIOT! STAY AWAY FROM IT!
DA (DASH)
HUH?

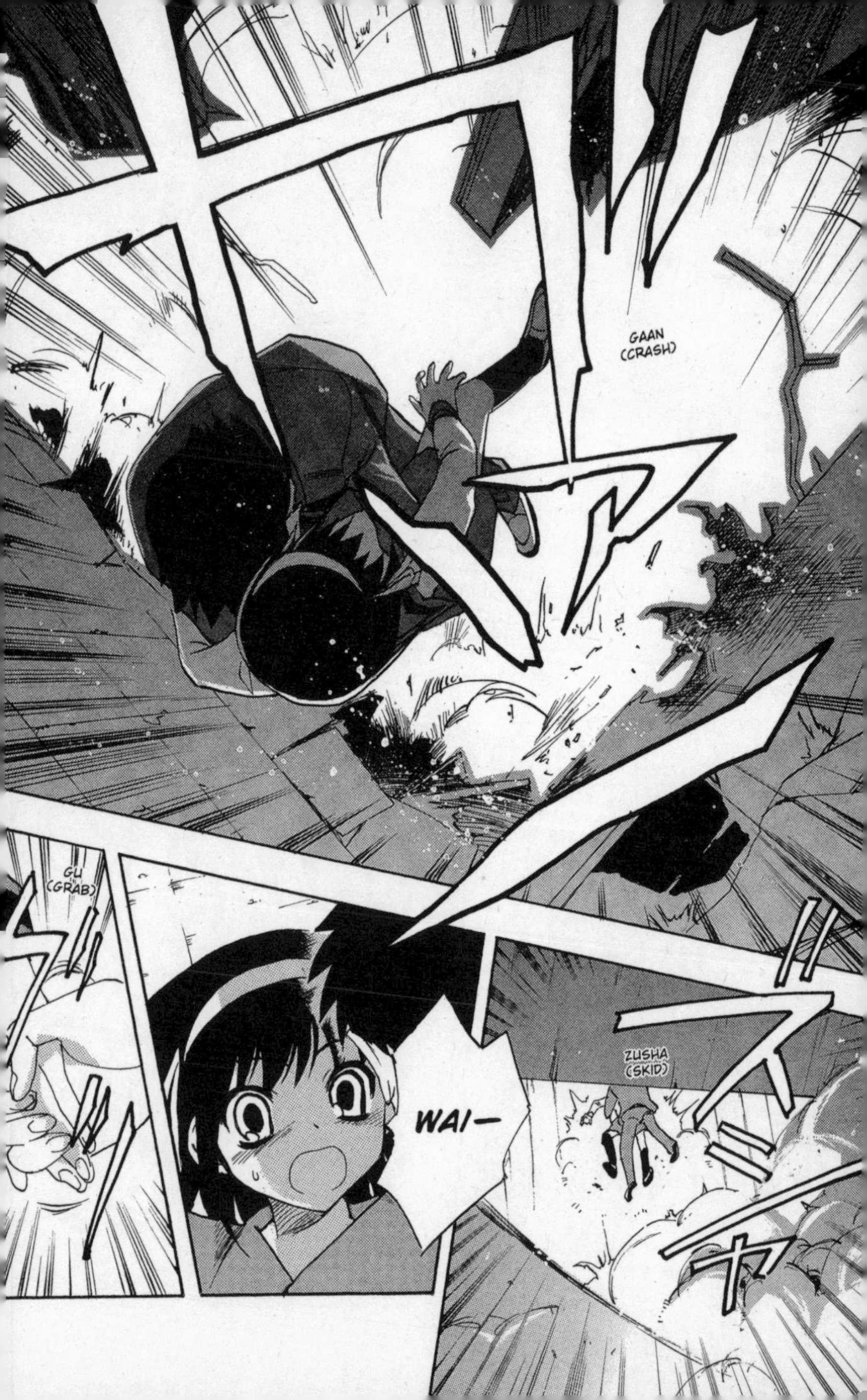
GAAN (CRASH)
GU (GRAB)
ZUSHA (SKID)
WAI—

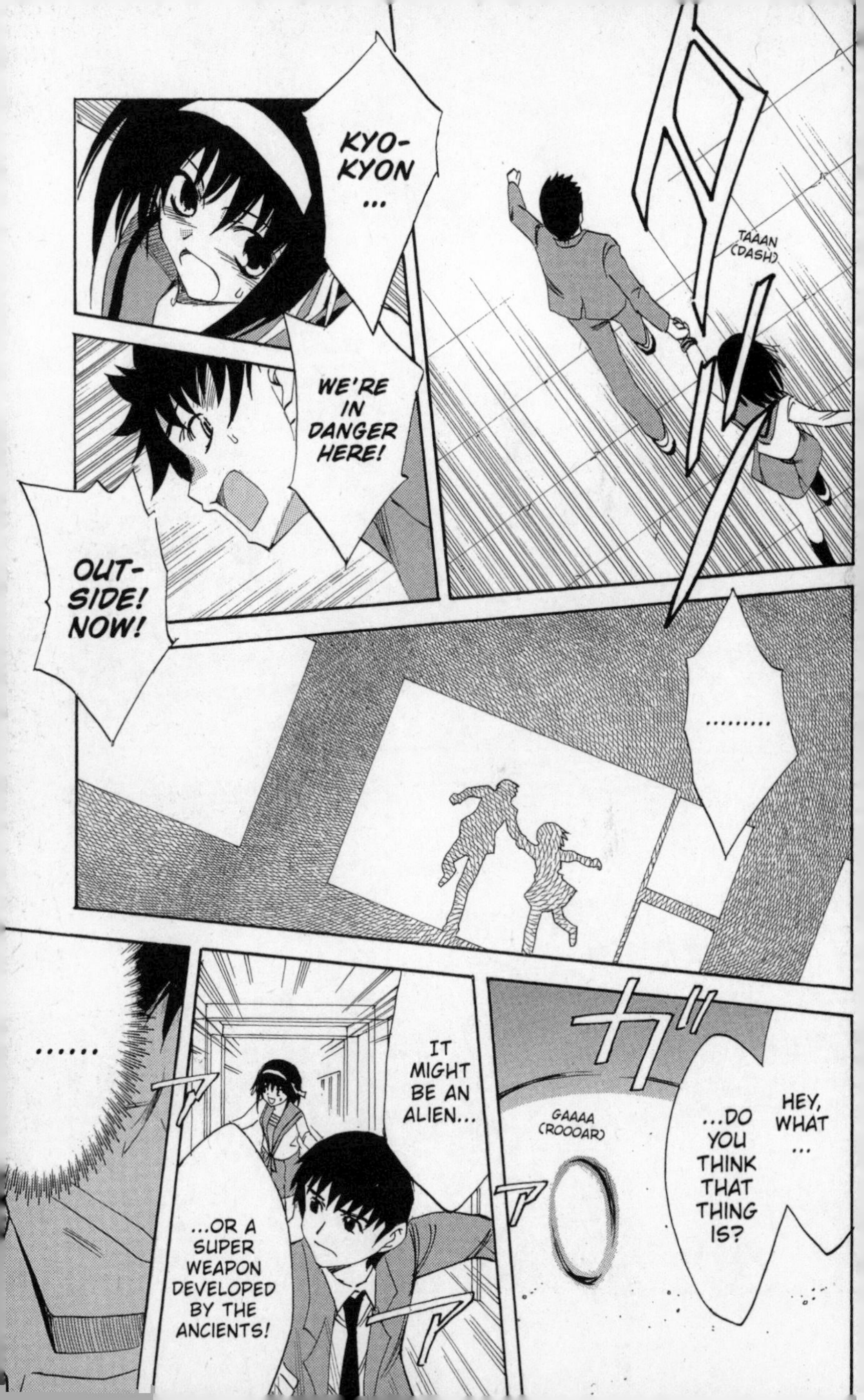
TAAAN (DASH)
KYO-KYON...
WE'RE IN DANGER HERE!
OUT-SIDE! NOW!
....
HEY, WHAT...
...DO YOU THINK THAT THING IS?
GAAAA (ROOOAR)
IT MIGHT BE AN ALIEN...
...OR A SUPER WEAPON DEVELOPED BY THE ANCIENTS!
......

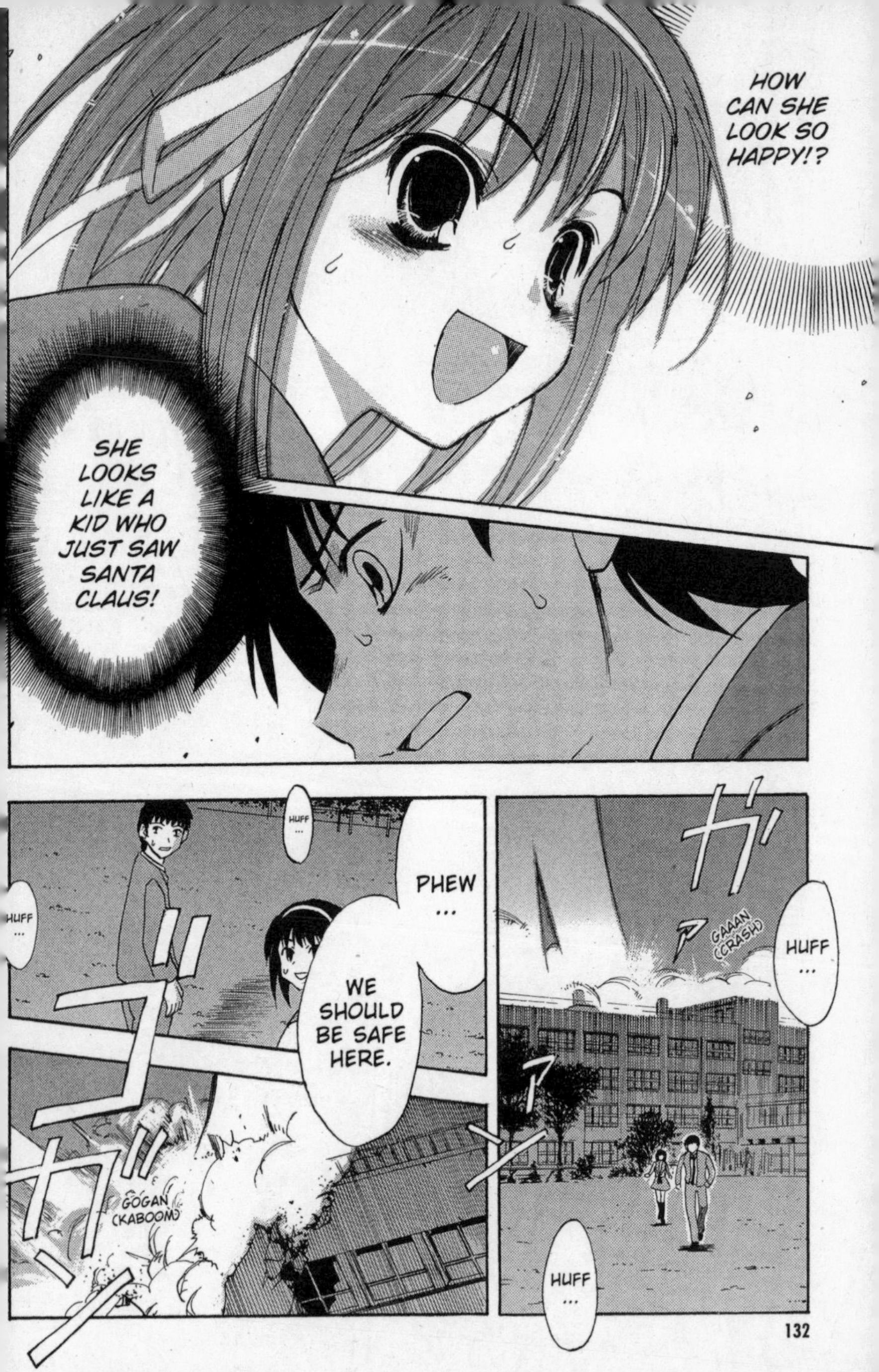
HOW CAN SHE LOOK SO HAPPY!?
SHE LOOKS LIKE A KID WHO JUST SAW SANTA CLAUS!
GAAAN (CRASH)
HUFF ...
HUFF ...
HUFF ...
PHEW ...
WE SHOULD BE SAFE HERE.
HUFF ...
GOGAN (KABOOM)

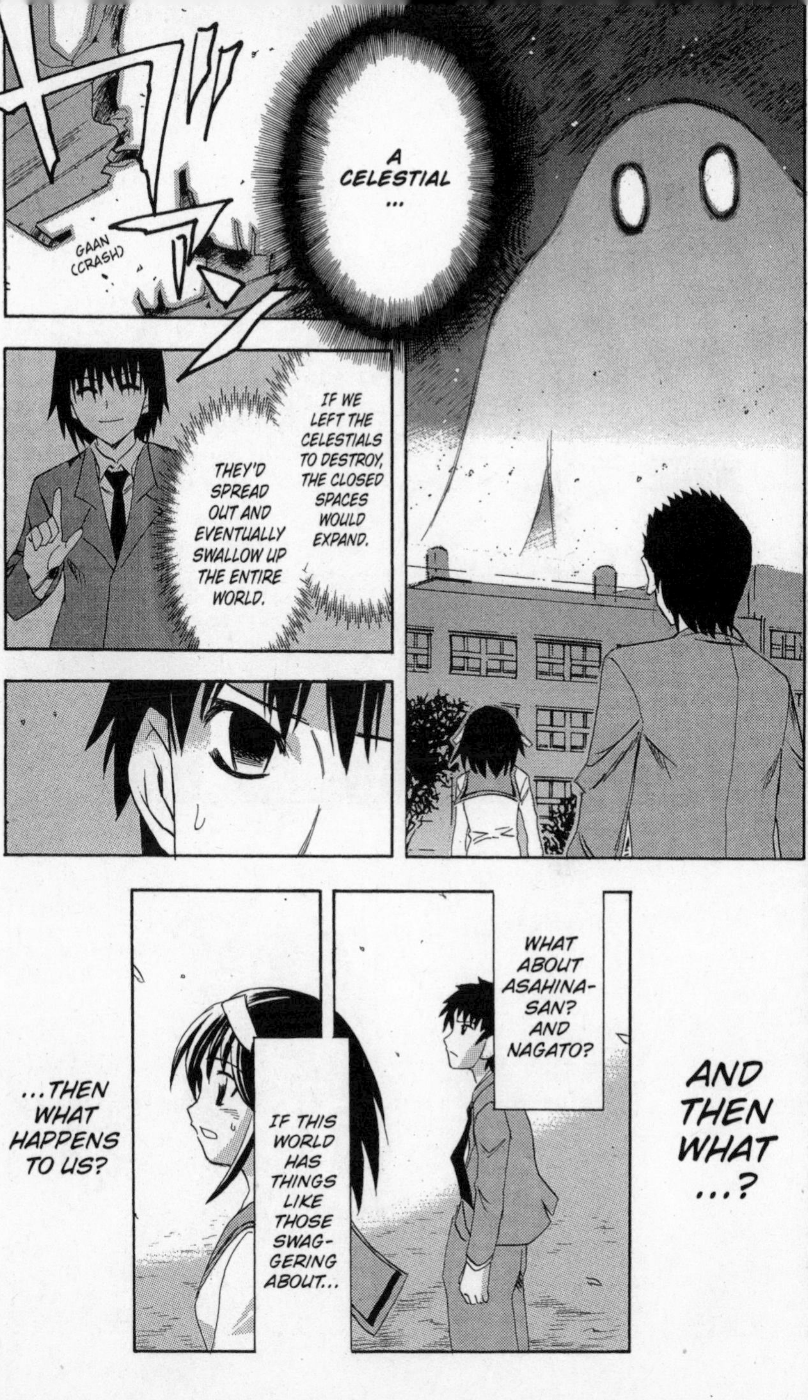
A CELESTIAL ...
GAAN (CRASH)
IF WE LEFT THE CELESTIALS TO DESTROY, THE CLOSED SPACES WOULD EXPAND.
THEY'D SPREAD OUT AND EVENTUALLY SWALLOW UP THE ENTIRE WORLD.
AND THEN WHAT ...?
WHAT ABOUT ASAHINA-SAN? AND NAGATO?
IF THIS WORLD HAS THINGS LIKE THOSE SWAG-GERING ABOUT...
...THEN WHAT HAPPENS TO US?

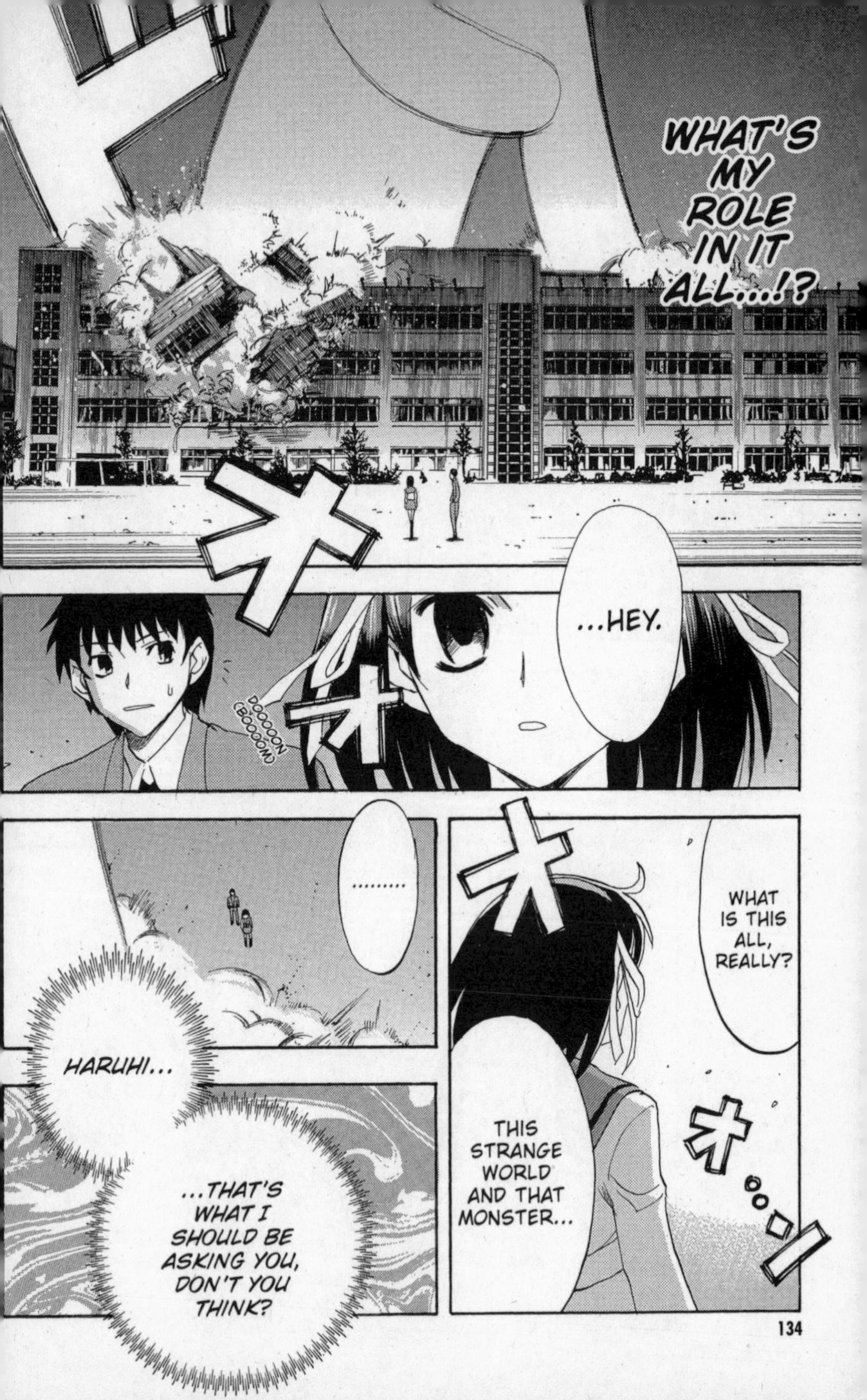
WHAT'S MY ROLE IN IT ALL...!?
...HEY.
DOOOOON (BOOOOM)
WHAT IS THIS ALL, REALLY?
THIS STRANGE WORLD AND THAT MONSTER...
....
HARUHI...
...THAT'S WHAT I SHOULD BE ASKING YOU, DON'T YOU THINK?

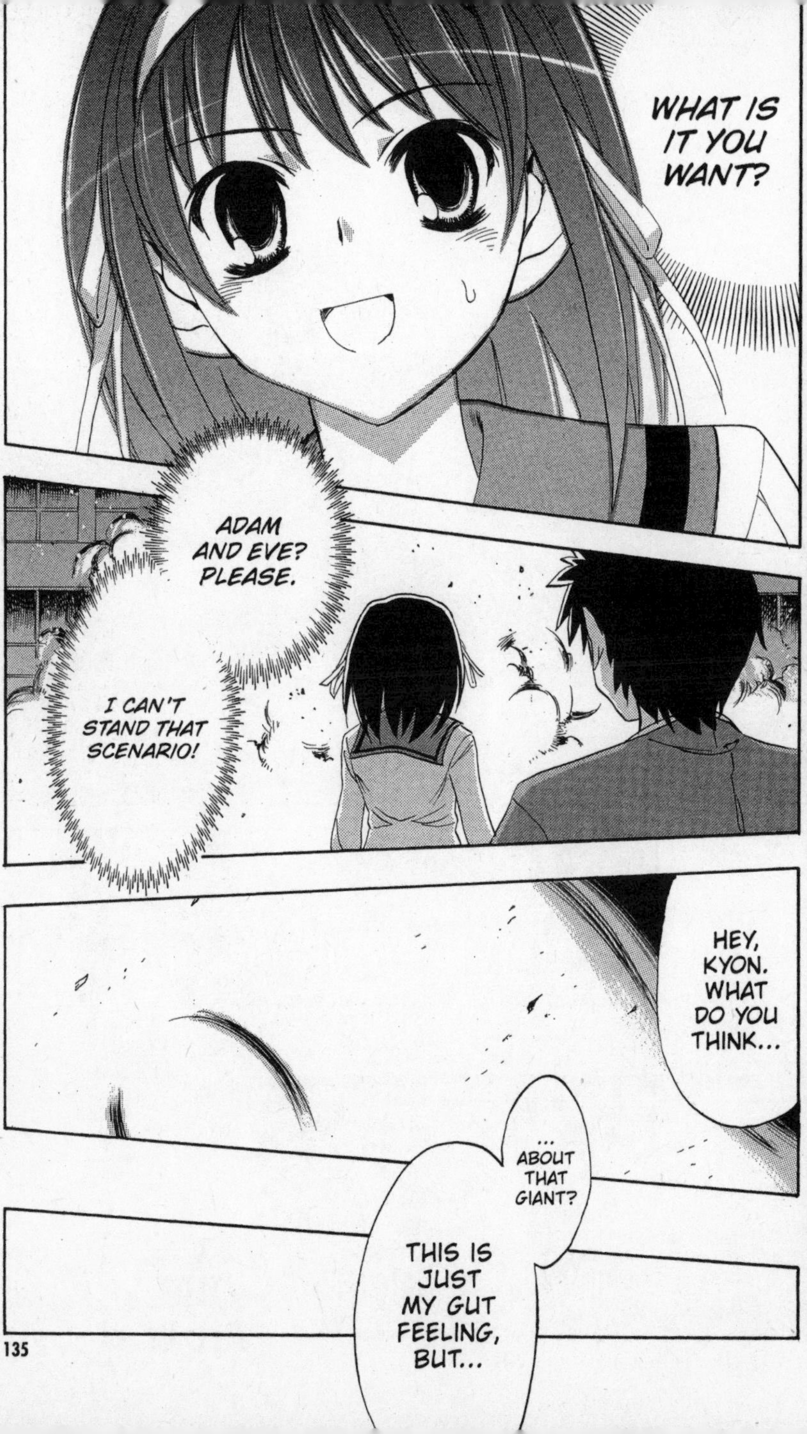
WHAT IS IT YOU WANT?
ADAM AND EVE? PLEASE.
I CAN'T STAND THAT SCENARIO!
HEY, KYON. WHAT DO YOU THINK...
... ABOUT THAT GIANT?
THIS IS JUST MY GUT FEELING, BUT...

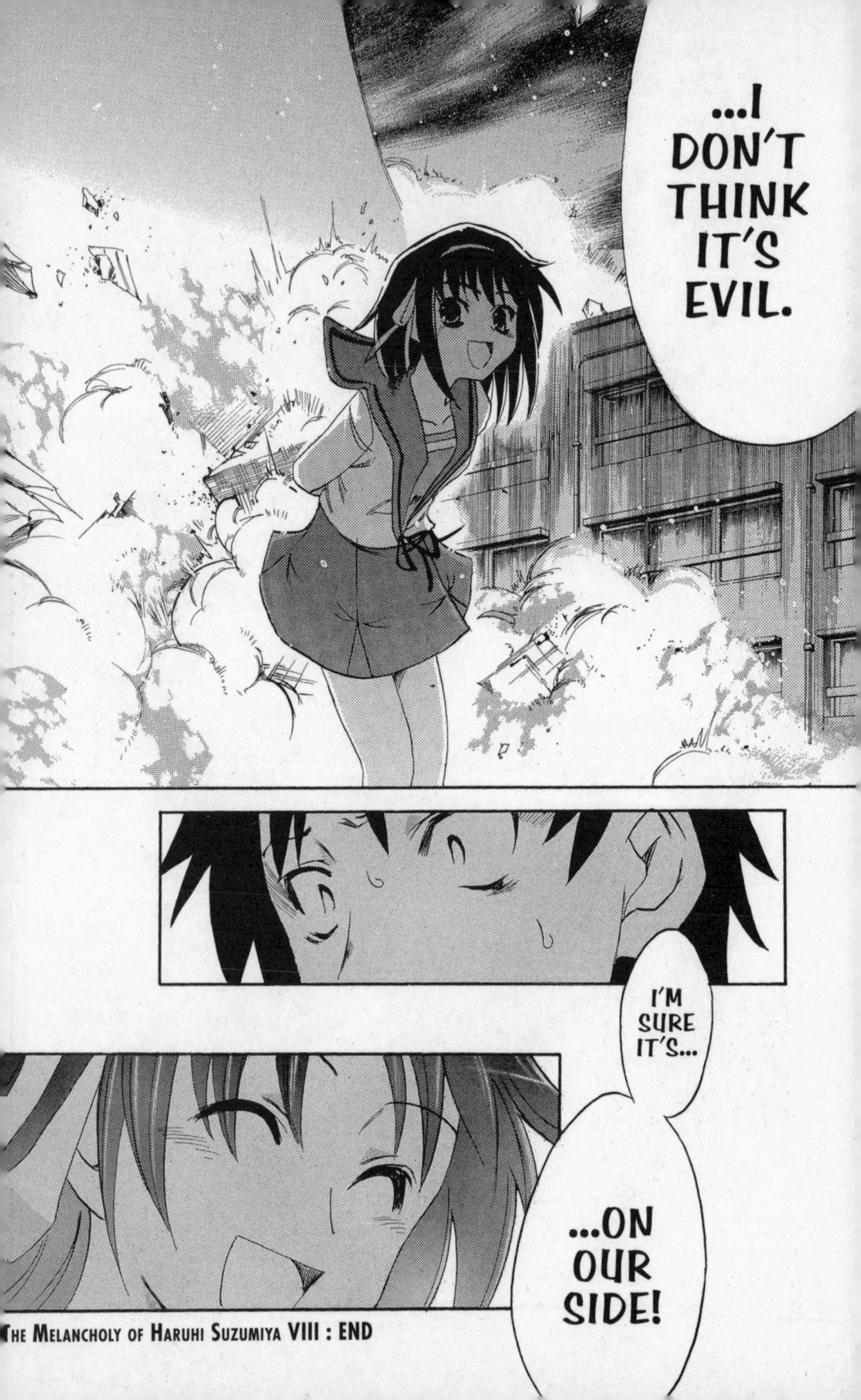
...I DON'T THINK IT'S EVIL.
I'M SURE IT'S...
...ON OUR SIDE!

THE MELANCHOLY OF HARUHI SUZUMIYA VIII : END

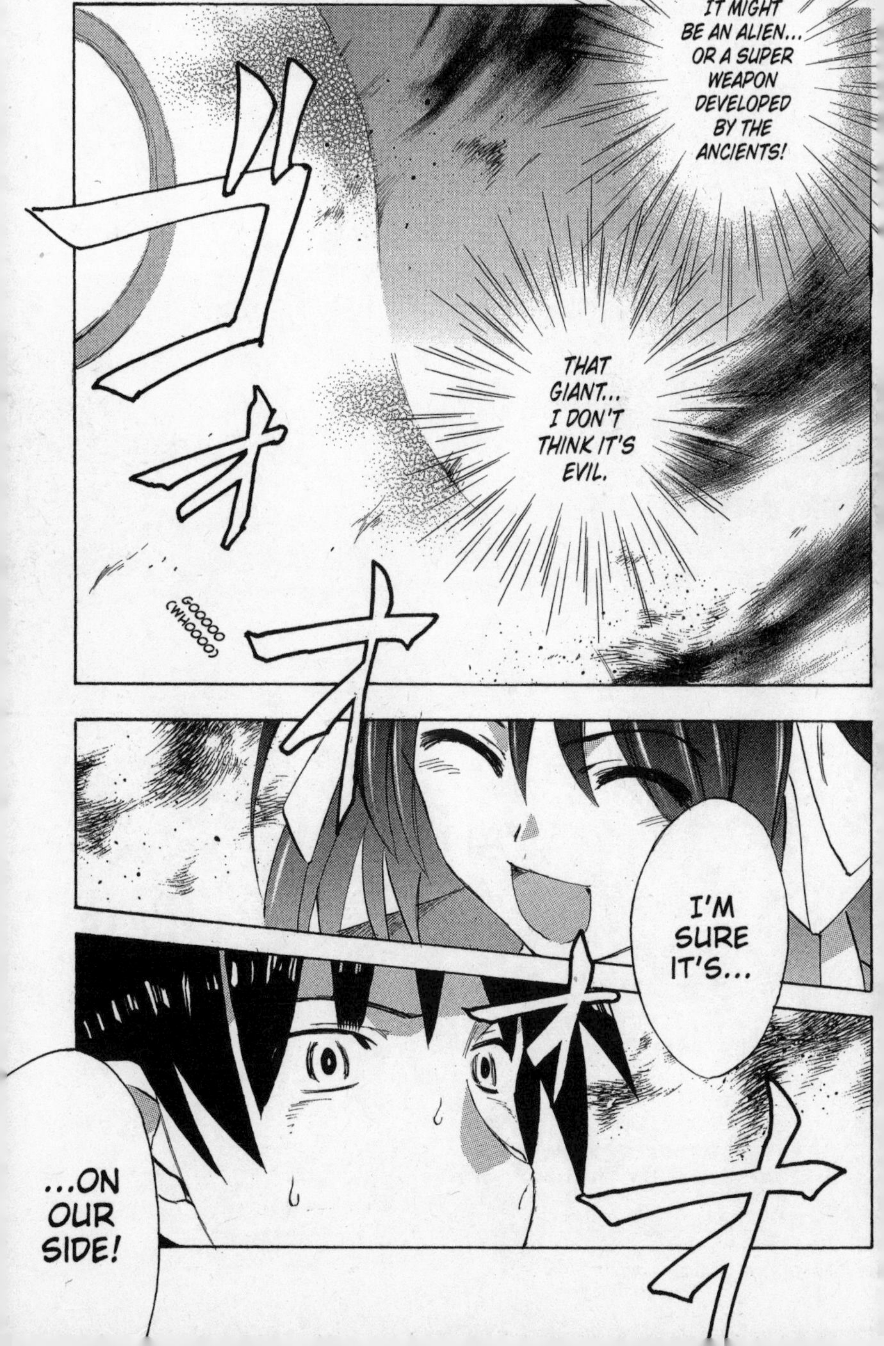
IT MIGHT BE AN ALIEN... OR A SUPER WEAPON DEVELOPED BY THE ANCIENTS!
THAT GIANT... I DON'T THINK IT'S EVIL.
GOOOOO (WHOOOO)
I'M SURE IT'S...
...ON OUR SIDE!

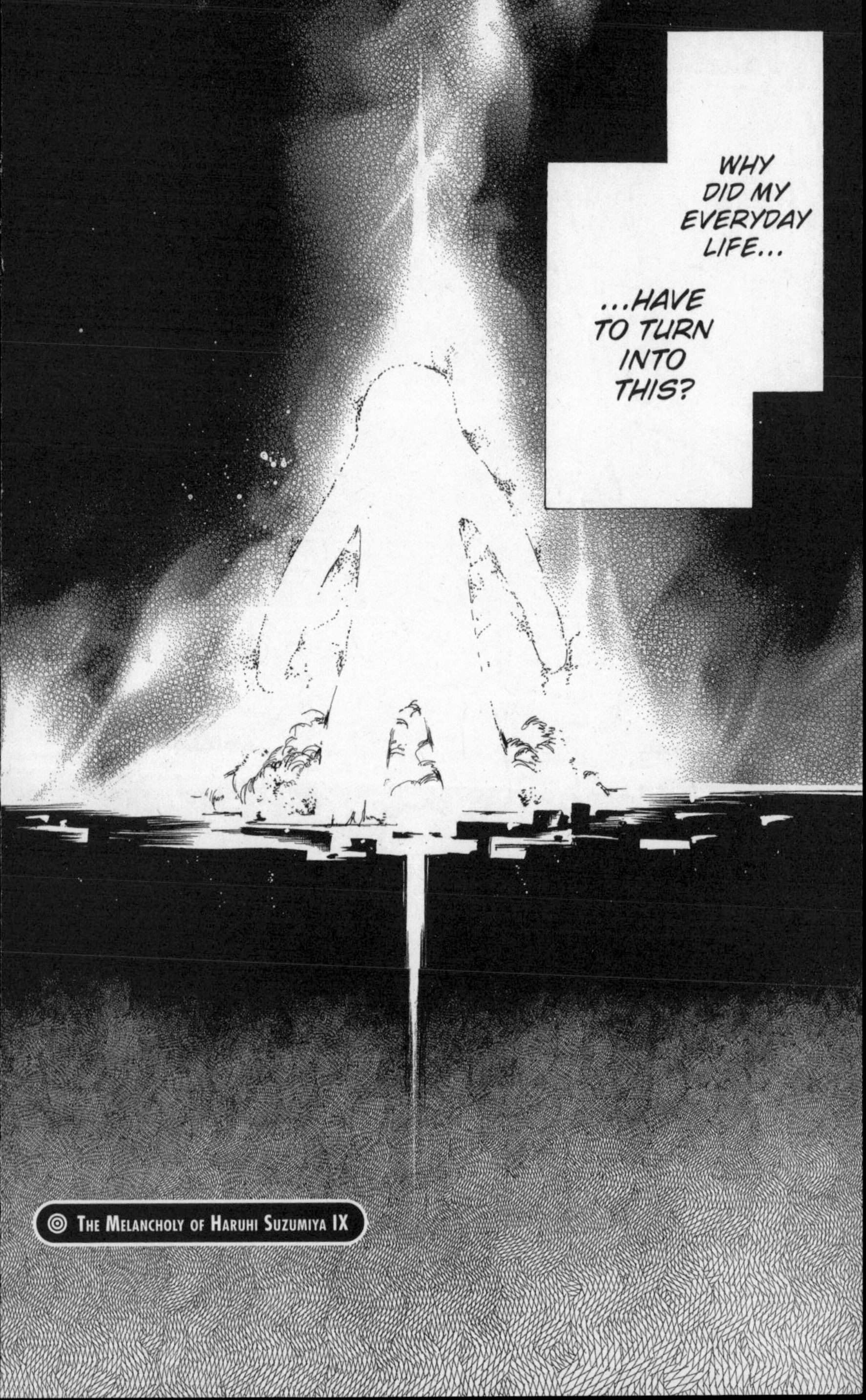
WHY DID MY EVERYDAY LIFE...
...HAVE TO TURN INTO THIS?
THE MELANCHOLY OF HARUHI SUZUMIYA IX

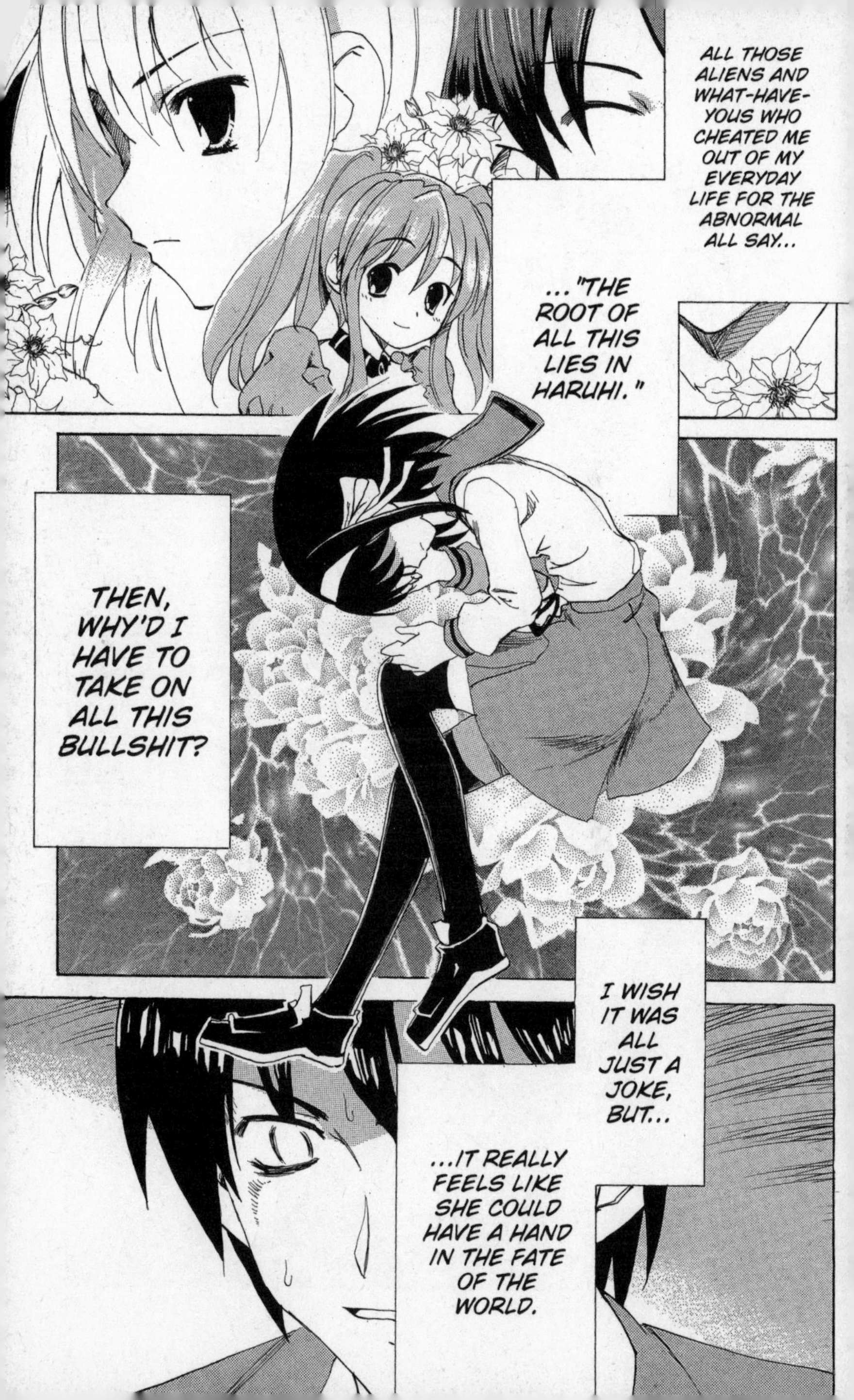
ALL THOSE ALIENS AND WHAT-HAVE-YOUS WHO CHEATED ME OUT OF MY EVERYDAY LIFE FOR THE ABNORMAL ALL SAY...
..."THE ROOT OF ALL THIS LIES IN HARUHI."
THEN, WHY'D I HAVE TO TAKE ON ALL THIS BULLSHIT?
I WISH IT WAS ALL JUST A JOKE, BUT...
...IT REALLY FEELS LIKE SHE COULD HAVE A HAND IN THE FATE OF THE WORLD.

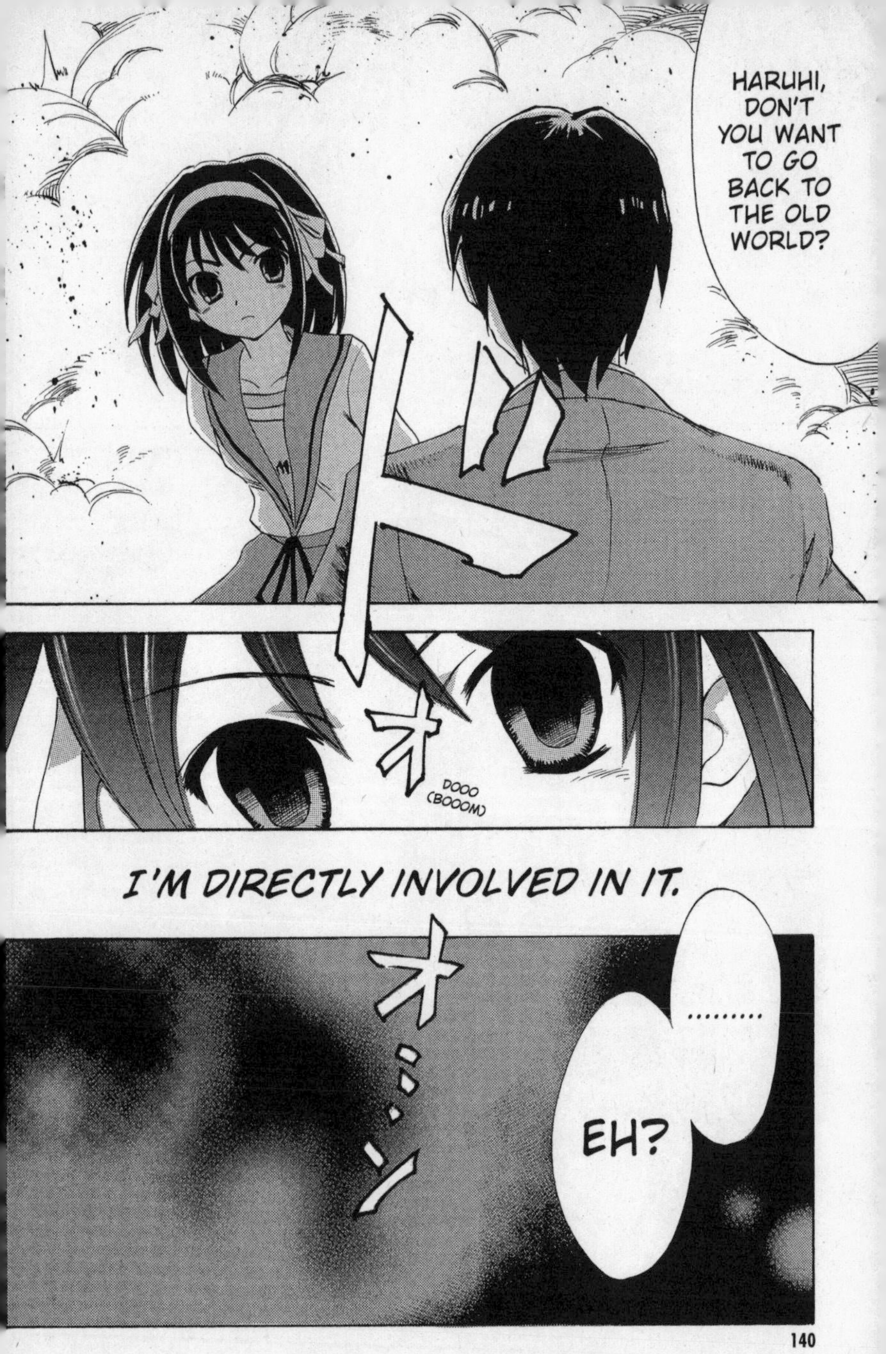
HARUHI, DON'T YOU WANT TO GO BACK TO THE OLD WORLD?
DOOO (BOOOM)
I'M DIRECTLY INVOLVED IN IT.
....
EH?

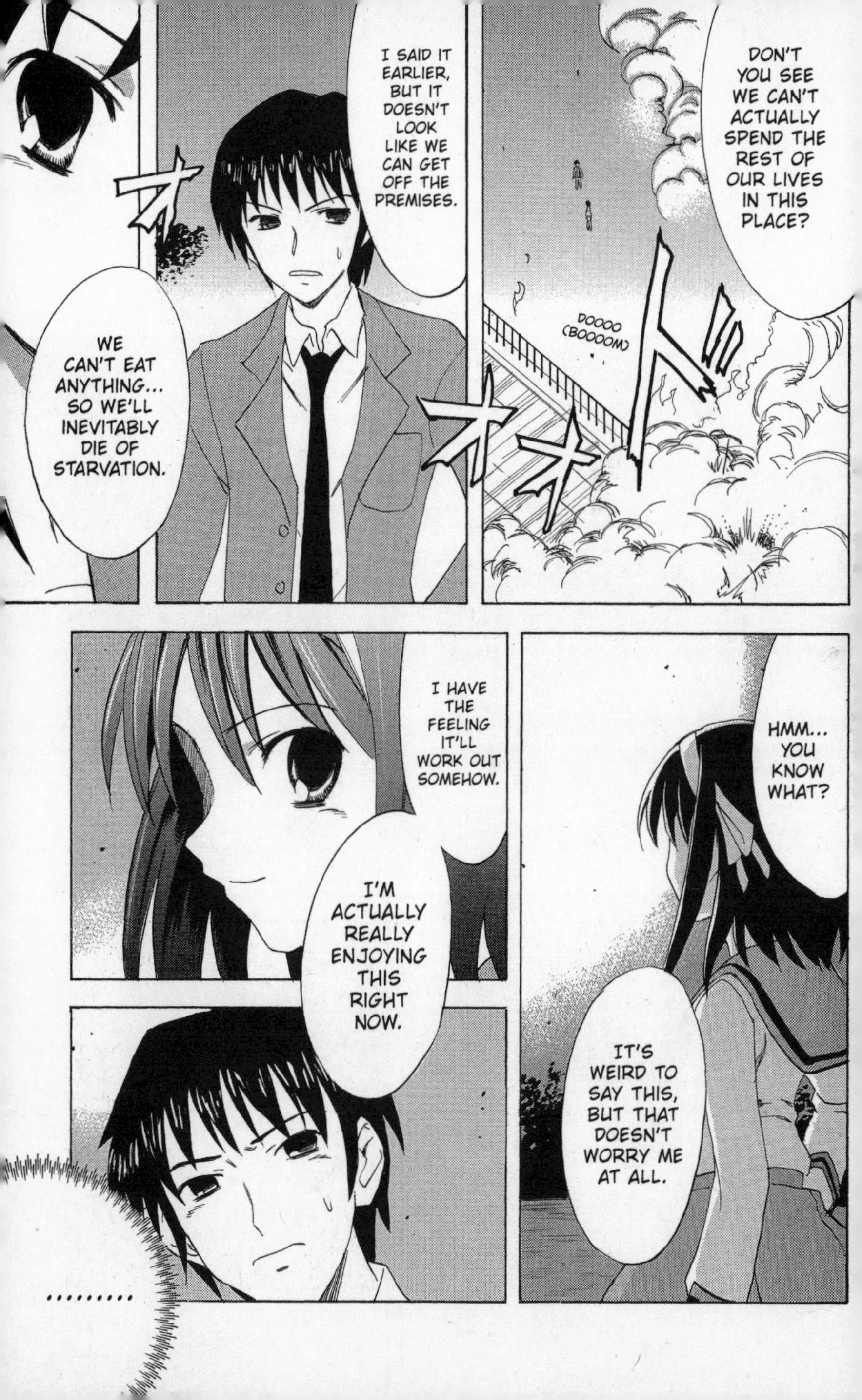
DON'T YOU SEE WE CAN'T ACTUALLY SPEND THE REST OF OUR LIVES IN THIS PLACE?
DOOOO (BOOOOM)
I SAID IT EARLIER, BUT IT DOESN'T LOOK LIKE WE CAN GET OFF THE PREMISES.
WE CAN'T EAT ANYTHING... SO WE'LL INEVITABLY DIE OF STARVATION.
HMM... YOU KNOW WHAT?
IT'S WEIRD TO SAY THIS, BUT THAT DOESN'T WORRY ME AT ALL.
I HAVE THE FEELING IT'LL WORK OUT SOMEHOW.
I'M ACTUALLY REALLY ENJOYING THIS RIGHT NOW.
....

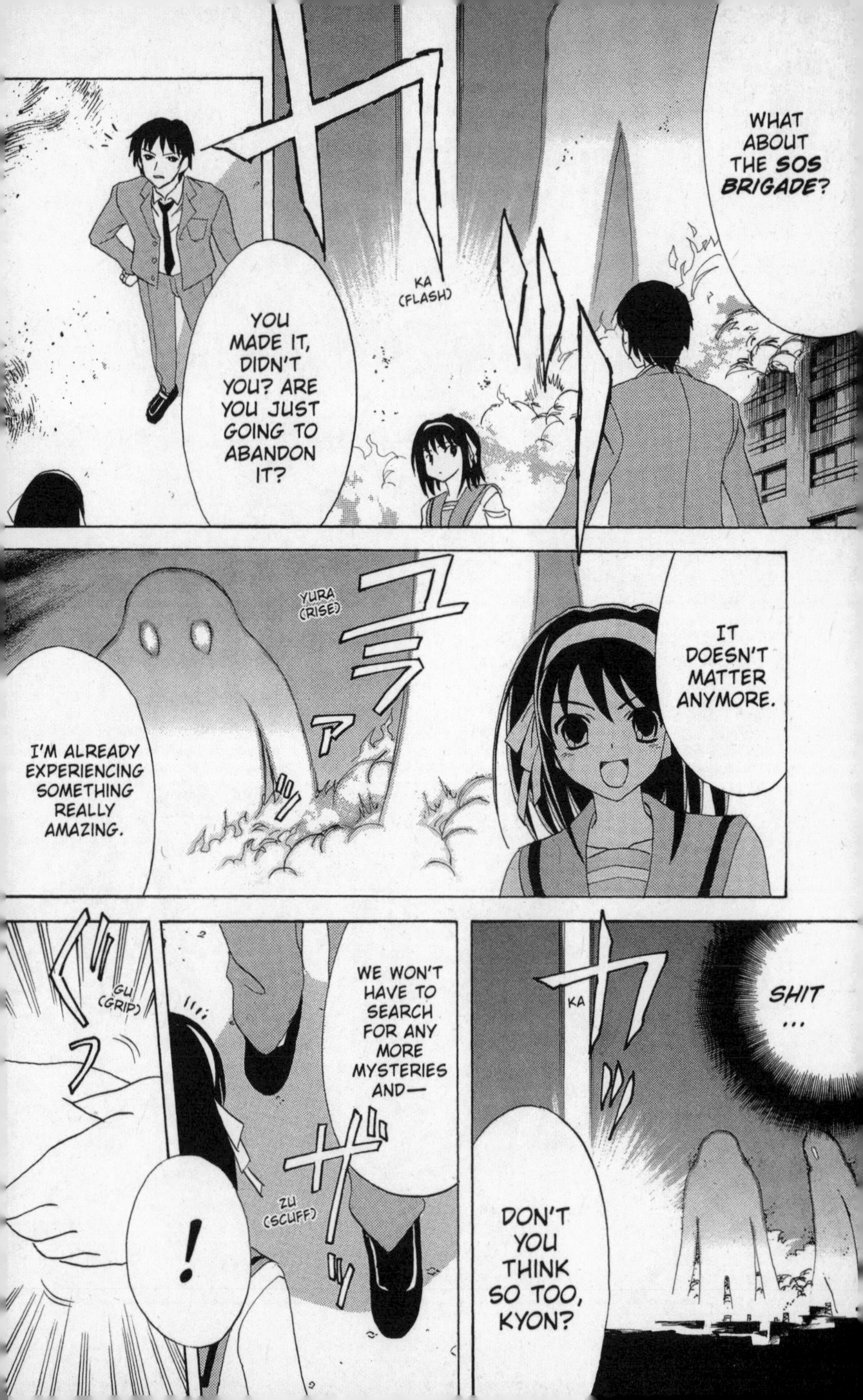
WHAT ABOUT THE SOS BRIGADE?
KA (FLASH)
YOU MADE IT, DIDN'T YOU? ARE YOU JUST GOING TO ABANDON IT?
IT DOESN'T MATTER ANYMORE.
YURA (RISE)
I'M ALREADY EXPERIENCING SOMETHING REALLY AMAZING.
SHIT ...
KA
DON'T YOU THINK SO TOO, KYON?
WE WON'T HAVE TO SEARCH FOR ANY MORE MYSTERIES AND—
GU (GRIP)
ZU (SCUFF)
!

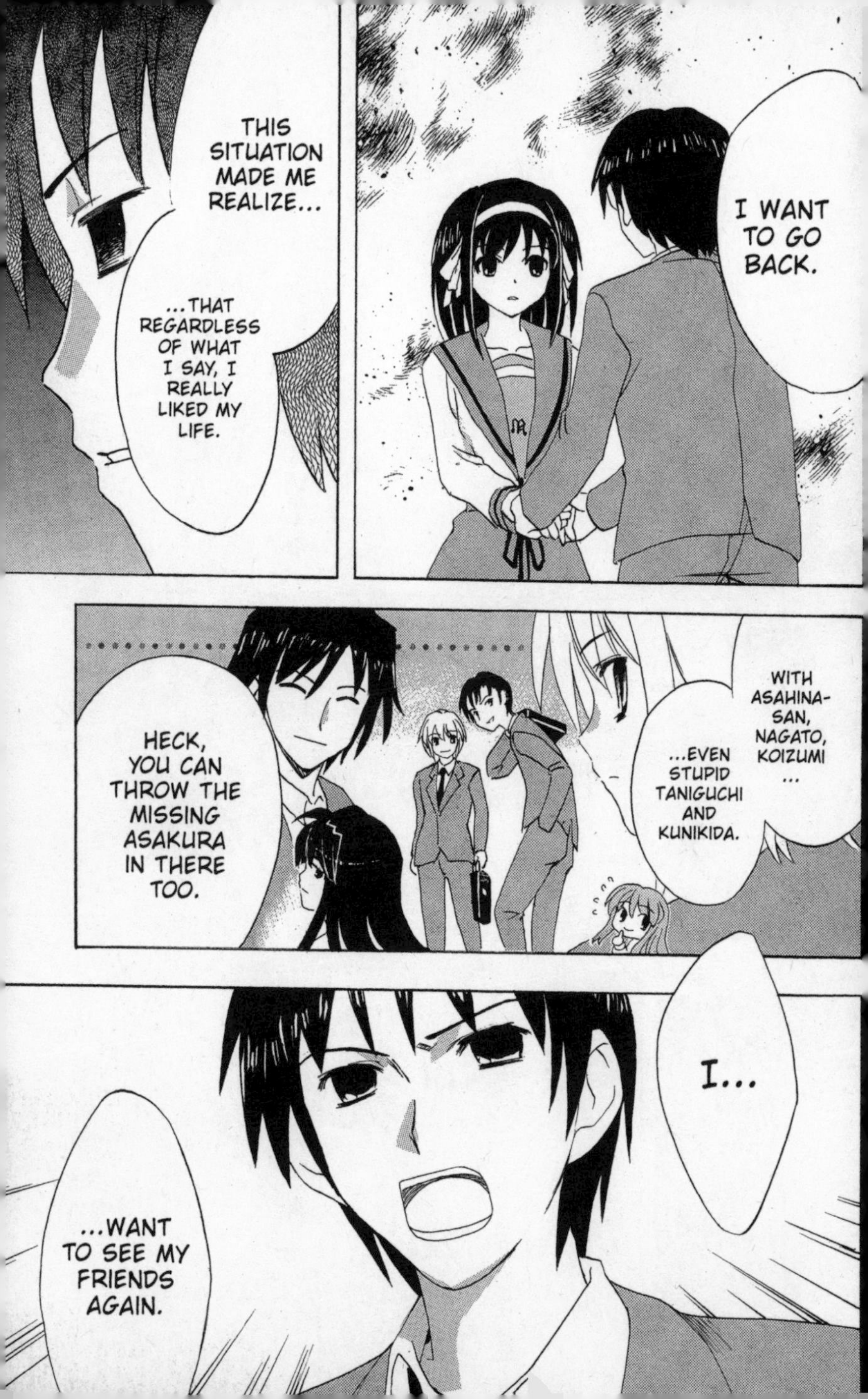
I WANT TO GO BACK.
THIS SITUATION MADE ME REALIZE...
...THAT REGARDLESS OF WHAT I SAY, I REALLY LIKED MY LIFE.
WITH ASAHINA-SAN, NAGATO, KOIZUMI...
...EVEN STUPID TANIGUCHI AND KUNIKIDA.
HECK, YOU CAN THROW THE MISSING ASAKURA IN THERE TOO.
I...
...WANT TO SEE MY FRIENDS AGAIN.

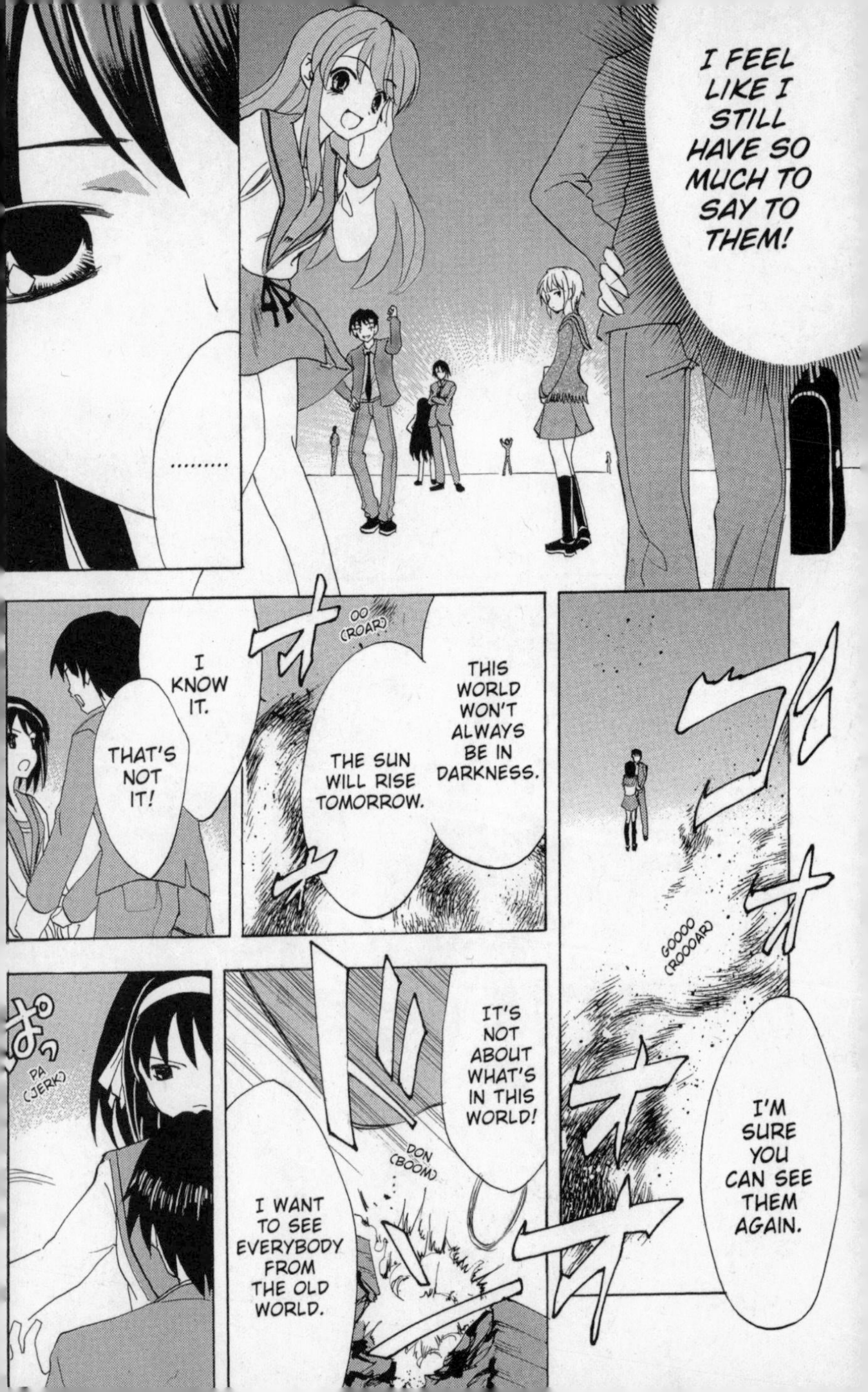
I FEEL LIKE I STILL HAVE SO MUCH TO SAY TO THEM!
....
GOOOO (ROOOAR)
I'M SURE YOU CAN SEE THEM AGAIN.
OO (ROAR)
THIS WORLD WON'T ALWAYS BE IN DARKNESS.
THE SUN WILL RISE TOMORROW.
I KNOW IT.
THAT'S NOT IT!
IT'S NOT ABOUT WHAT'S IN THIS WORLD!
DON (BOOM)
I WANT TO SEE EVERYBODY FROM THE OLD WORLD.
PA (JERK)

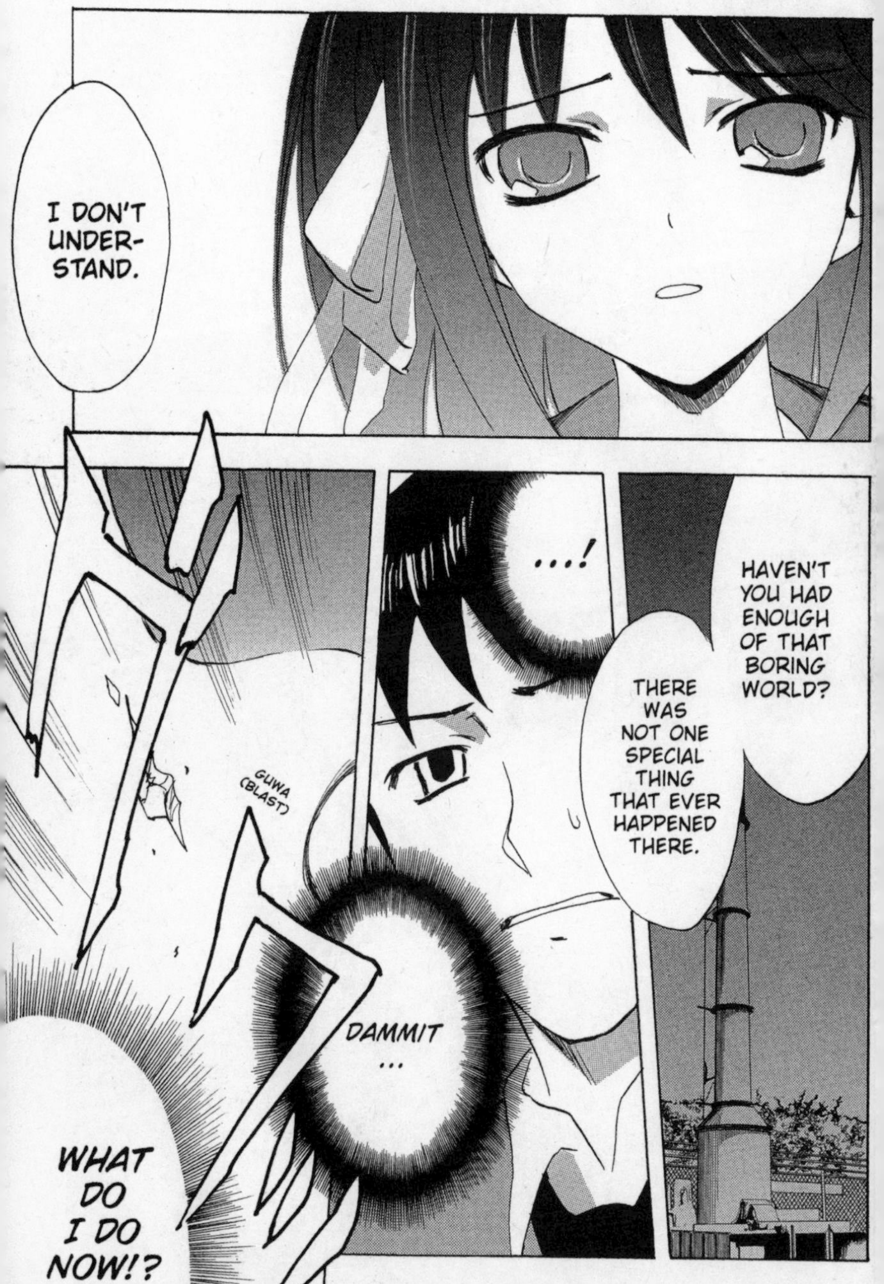
I DON'T UNDER-STAND.
HAVEN'T YOU HAD ENOUGH OF THAT BORING WORLD?
THERE WAS NOT ONE SPECIAL THING THAT EVER HAPPENED THERE.
...!
DAMMIT ...
GUWA (BLAST)
WHAT DO I DO NOW!?

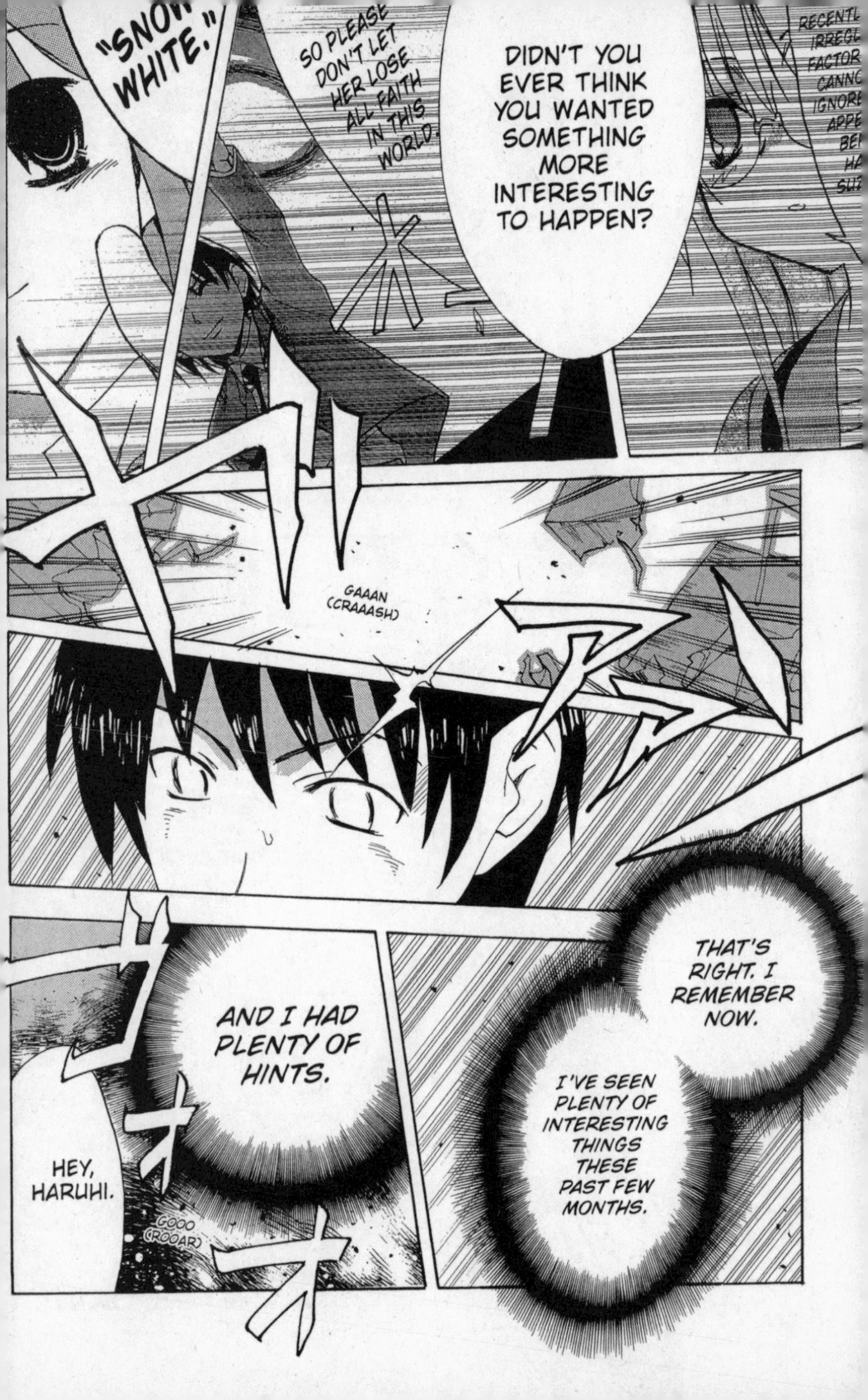
DIDN'T YOU EVER THINK YOU WANTED SOMETHING MORE INTERESTING TO HAPPEN?
SO PLEASE DON'T LET HER LOSE ALL FAITH IN THIS WORLD.
"SNOW WHITE."
GAAAN (CRAAASH)
THAT'S RIGHT. I REMEMBER NOW.
I'VE SEEN PLENTY OF INTERESTING THINGS THESE PAST FEW MONTHS.
AND I HAD PLENTY OF HINTS.
HEY, HARUHI.
GOOO (ROOAR)

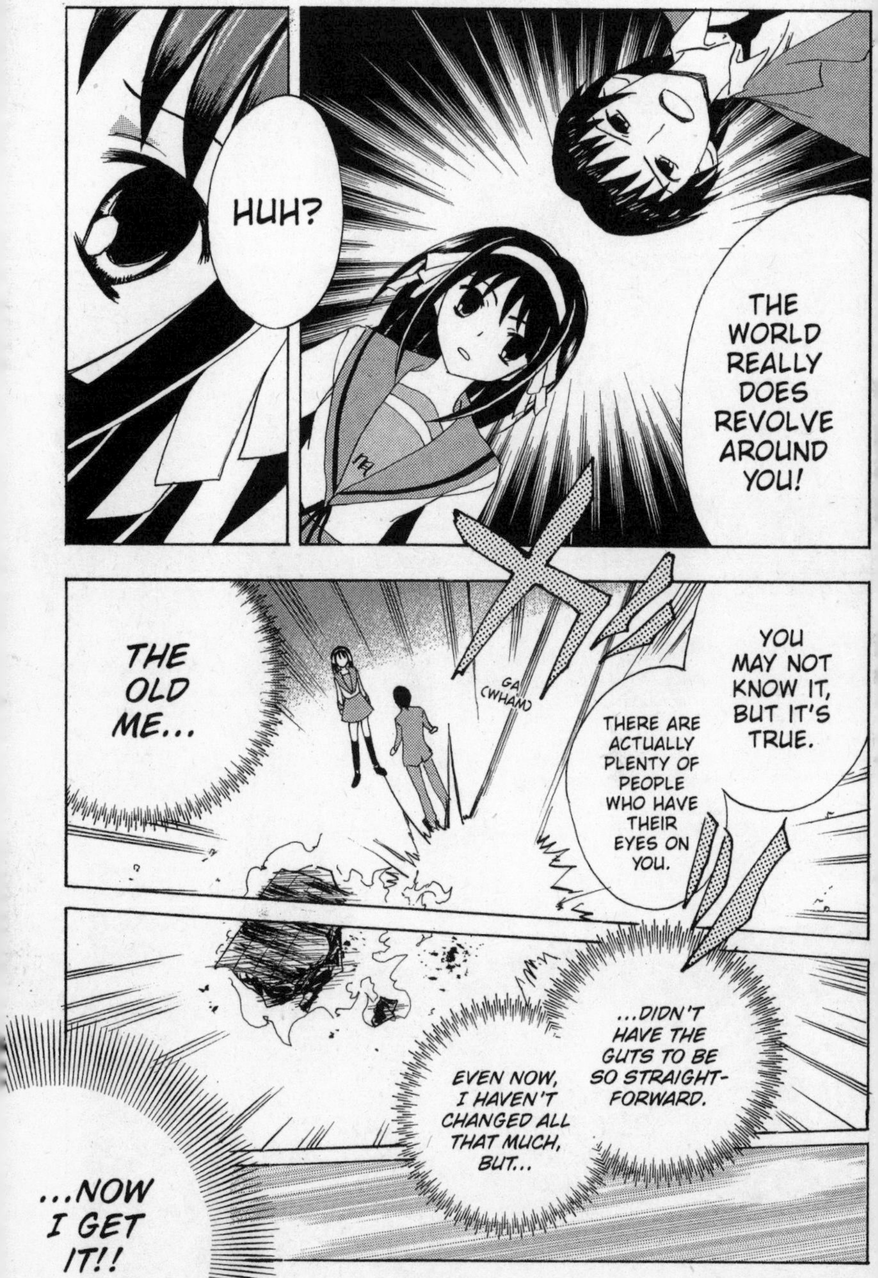
THE WORLD REALLY DOES REVOLVE AROUND YOU!
HUH?
YOU MAY NOT KNOW IT, BUT IT'S TRUE.
THERE ARE ACTUALLY PLENTY OF PEOPLE WHO HAVE THEIR EYES ON YOU.
GA (WHAM)
THE OLD ME...
...DIDN'T HAVE THE GUTS TO BE SO STRAIGHT-FORWARD.
EVEN NOW, I HAVEN'T CHANGED ALL THAT MUCH, BUT...
...NOW I GET IT!!

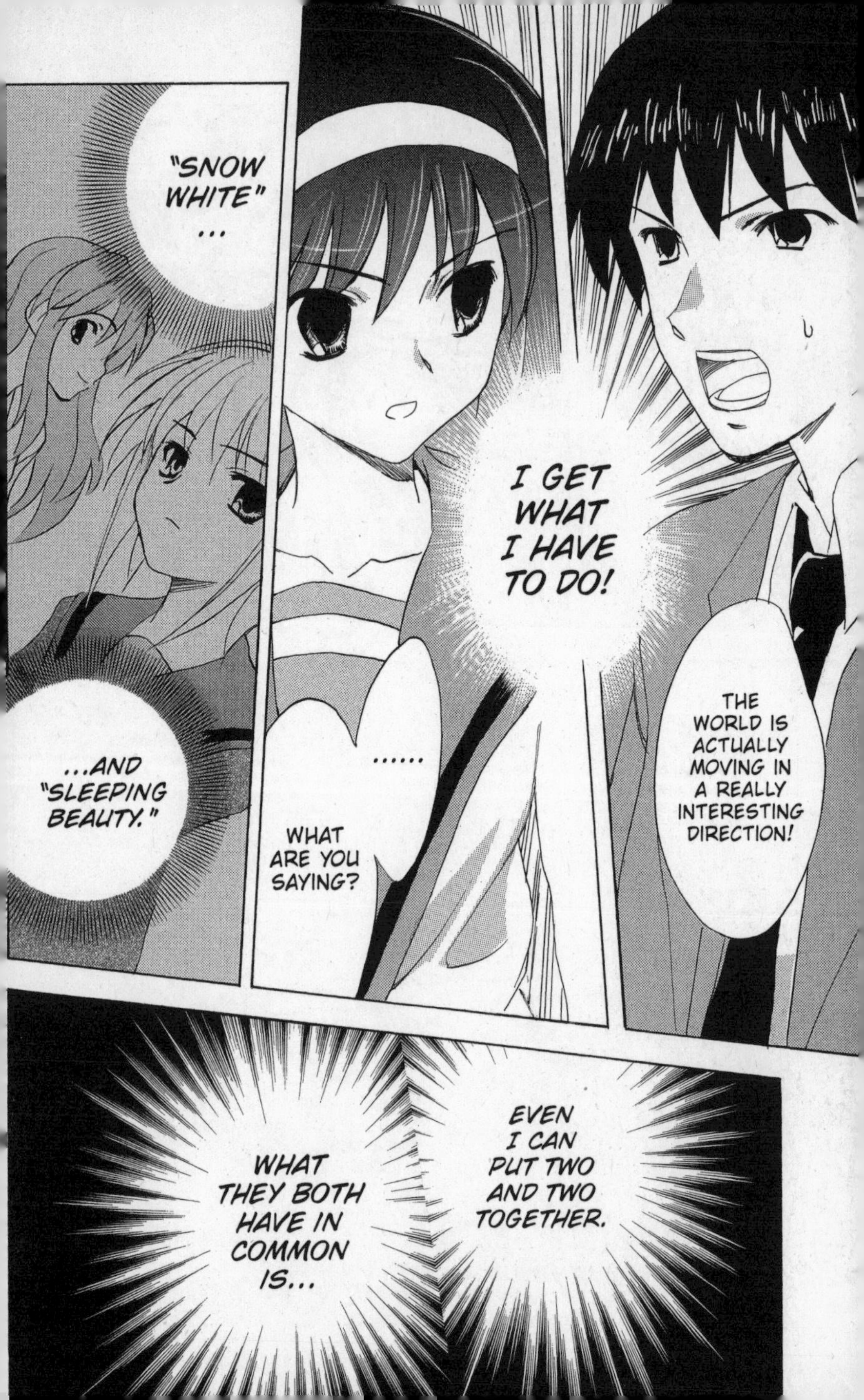
I GET WHAT I HAVE TO DO!
THE WORLD IS ACTUALLY MOVING IN A REALLY INTERESTING DIRECTION!
......
WHAT ARE YOU SAYING?
"SNOW WHITE" ...
...AND "SLEEPING BEAUTY."
EVEN I CAN PUT TWO AND TWO TOGETHER.
WHAT THEY BOTH HAVE IN COMMON IS...

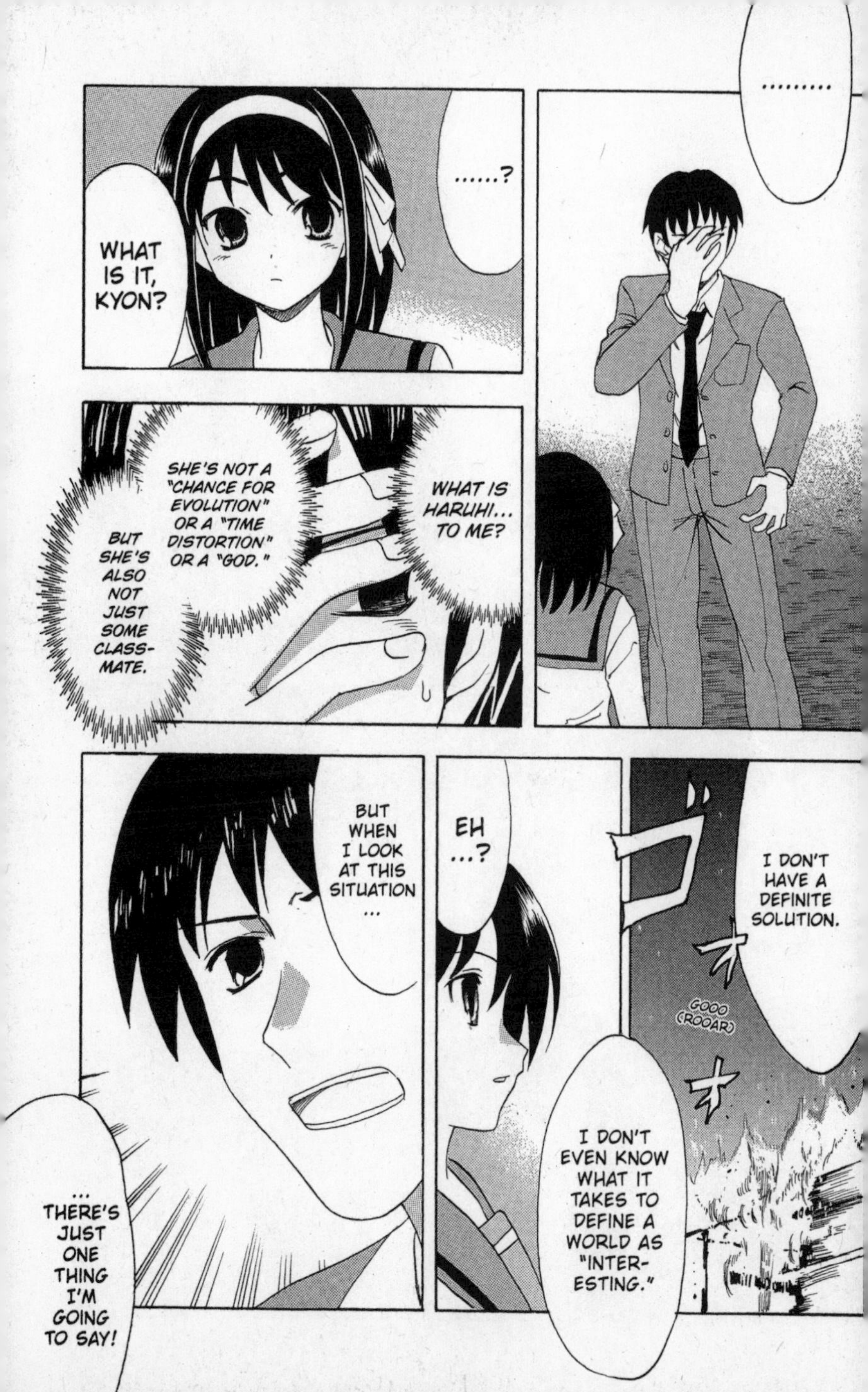
....
......?
WHAT IS IT, KYON?
WHAT IS HARUHI... TO ME?
SHE'S NOT A "CHANCE FOR EVOLUTION" OR A "TIME DISTORTION" OR A "GOD."
BUT SHE'S ALSO NOT JUST SOME CLASS-MATE.
I DON'T HAVE A DEFINITE SOLUTION.
GOOO (ROOAR)
I DON'T EVEN KNOW WHAT IT TAKES TO DEFINE A WORLD AS "INTER-ESTING."
EH ...?
BUT WHEN I LOOK AT THIS SITUATION ...
... THERE'S JUST ONE THING I'M GOING TO SAY!

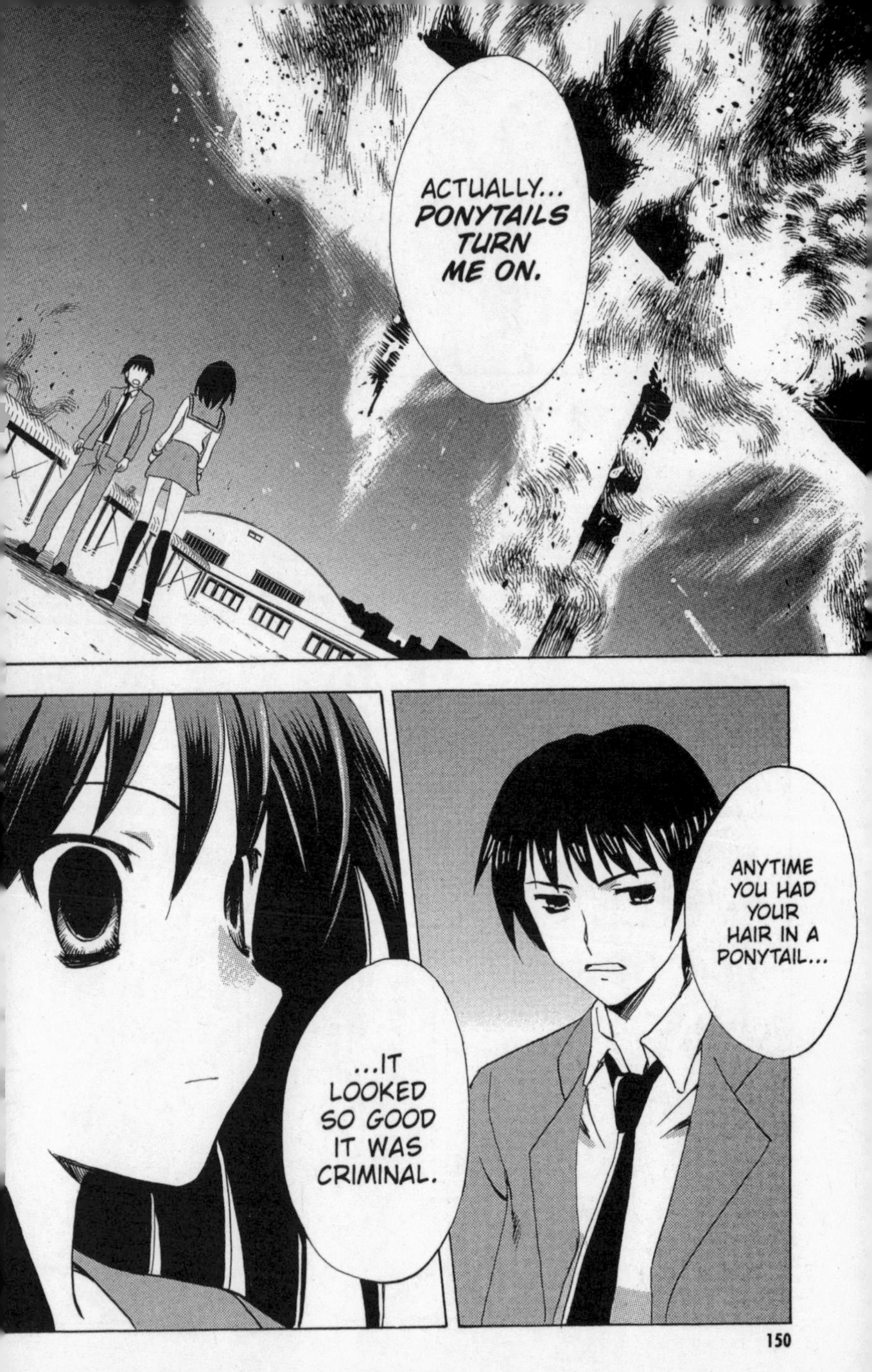
ACTUALLY... PONYTAILS TURN ME ON.
ANYTIME YOU HAD YOUR HAIR IN A PONYTAIL...
...IT LOOKED SO GOOD IT WAS CRIMINAL.

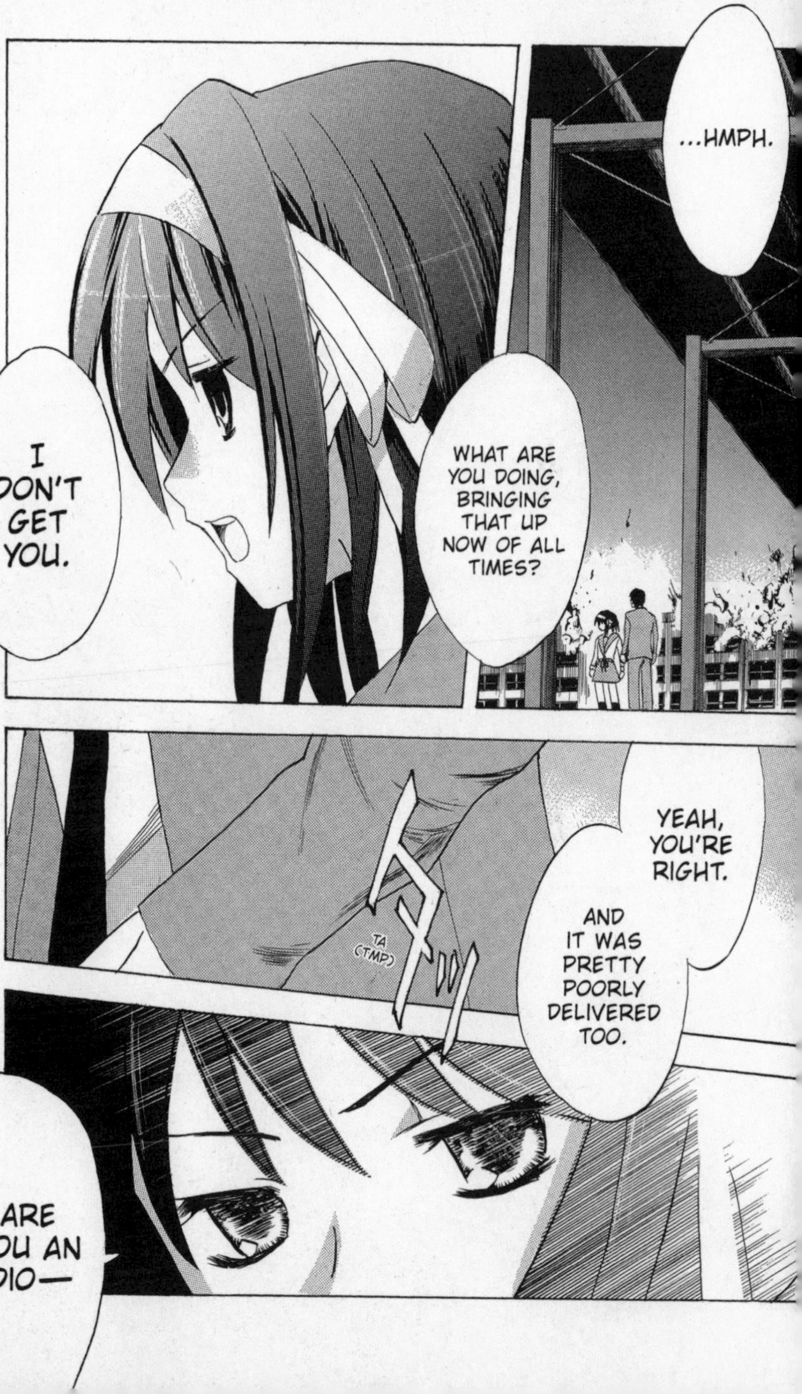
...HMPH.
WHAT ARE YOU DOING, BRINGING THAT UP NOW OF ALL TIMES?
I DON'T GET YOU.
TA (TMP)
YEAH, YOU'RE RIGHT.
AND IT WAS PRETTY POORLY DELIVERED TOO.
ARE YOU AN IDIO—

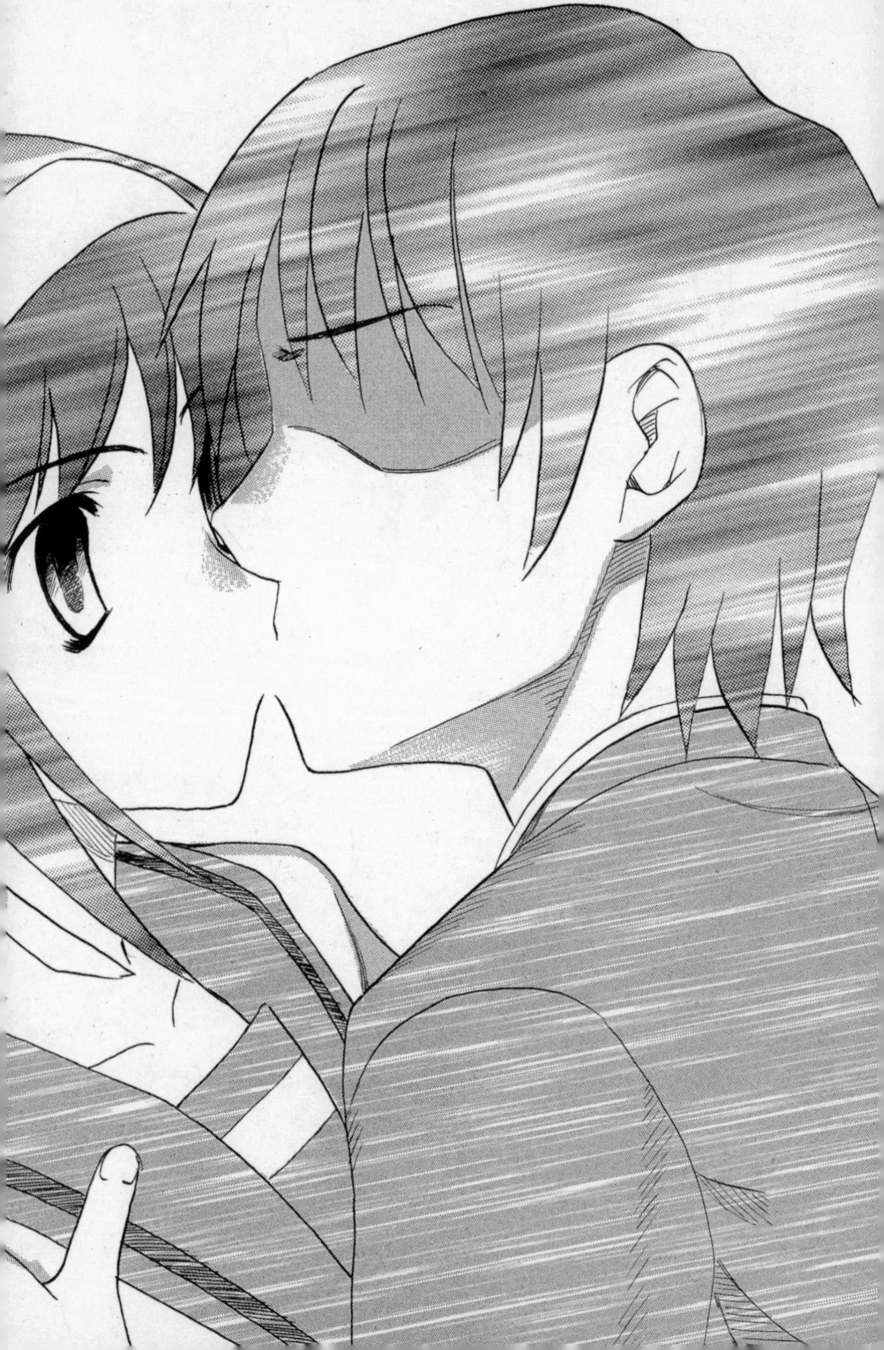

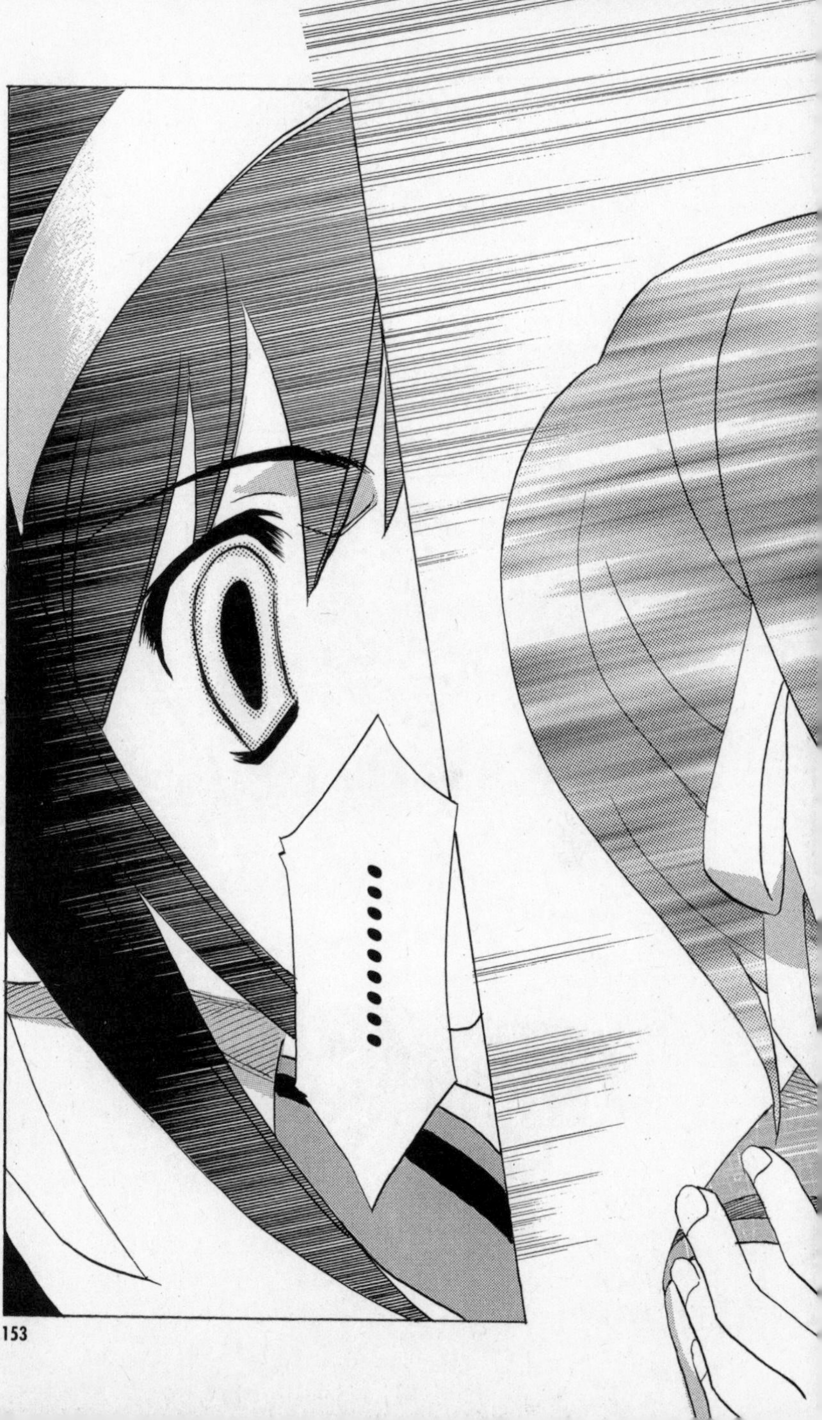
....

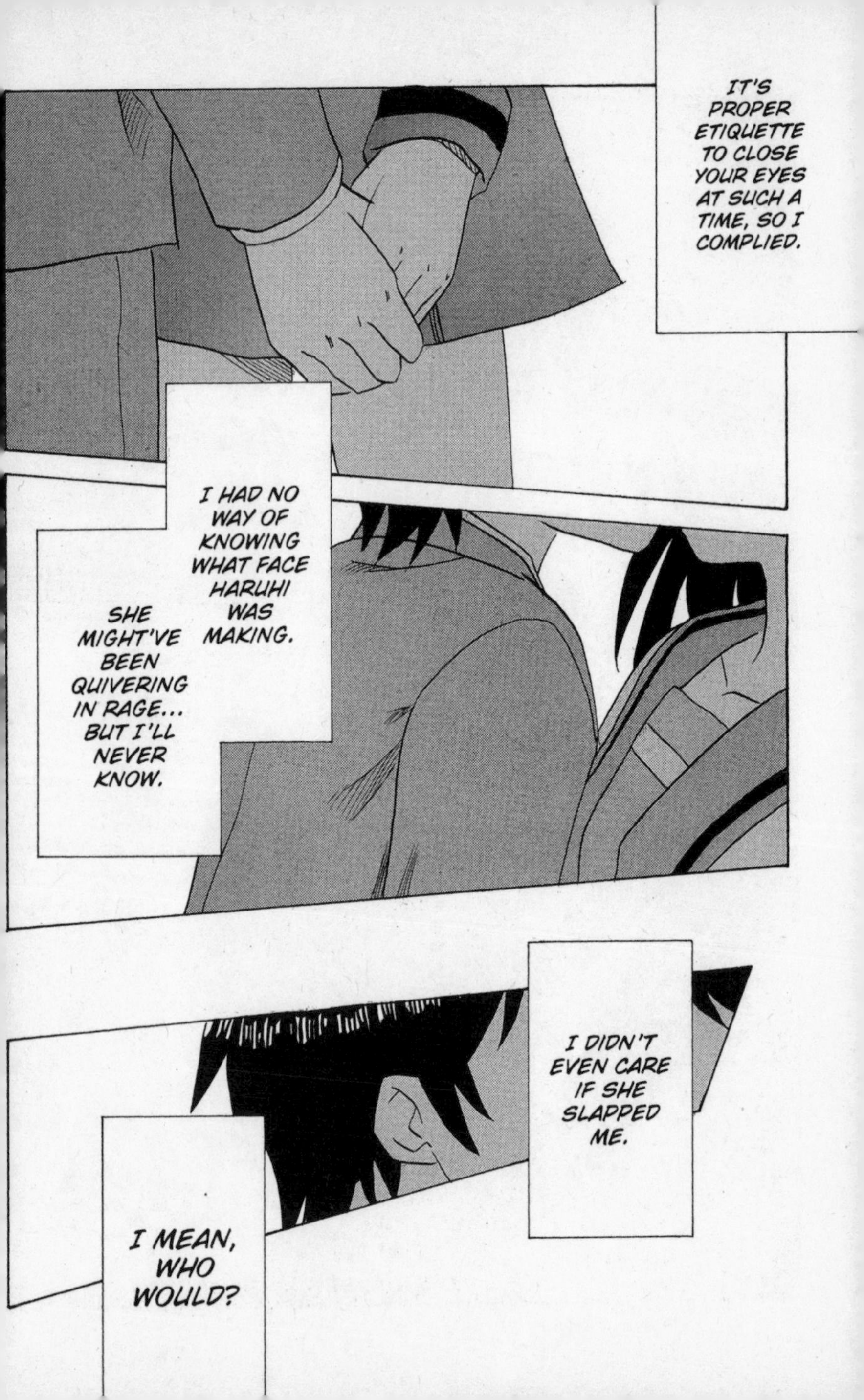
IT'S PROPER ETIQUETTE TO CLOSE YOUR EYES AT SUCH A TIME, SO I COMPLIED.
I HAD NO WAY OF KNOWING WHAT FACE HARUHI WAS MAKING.
SHE MIGHT'VE BEEN QUIVERING IN RAGE... BUT I'LL NEVER KNOW.
I DIDN'T EVEN CARE IF SHE SLAPPED ME.
I MEAN, WHO WOULD?

"I DON'T WANT TO LET GO FOR A WHILE."

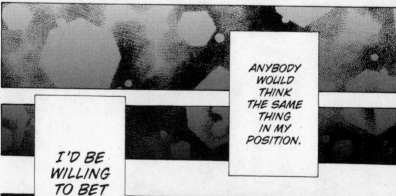

ANYBODY WOULD THINK THE SAME THING IN MY POSITION.

I'D BE WILLING TO BET ON IT.

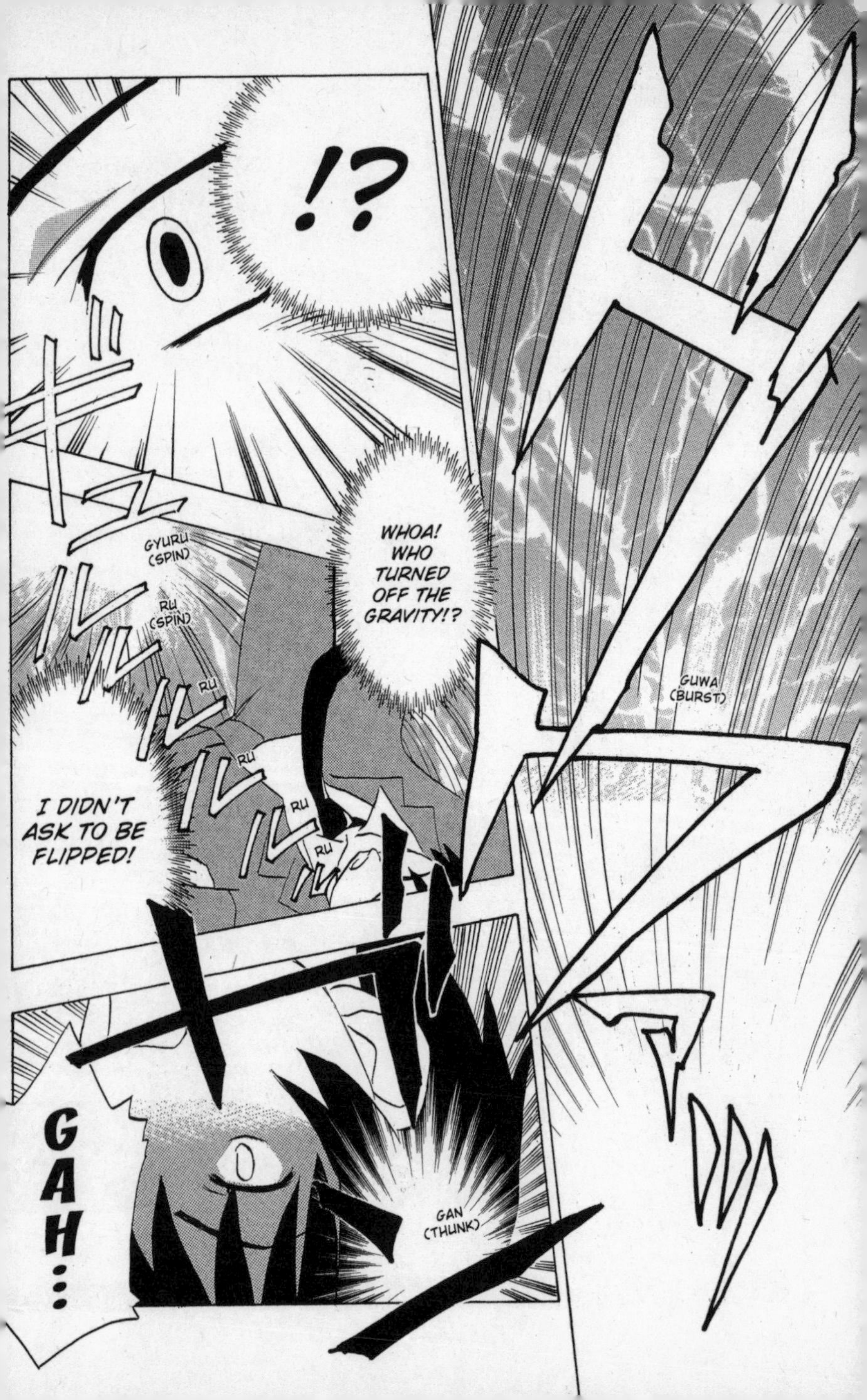
GUWA
(BURST)
!?
WHOA! WHO TURNED OFF THE GRAVITY!?
GYURU
(SPIN)
RU
(SPIN)
RU
RU
RU
RU
I DIDN'T ASK TO BE FLIPPED!
GAN
(THUNK)
GAH...

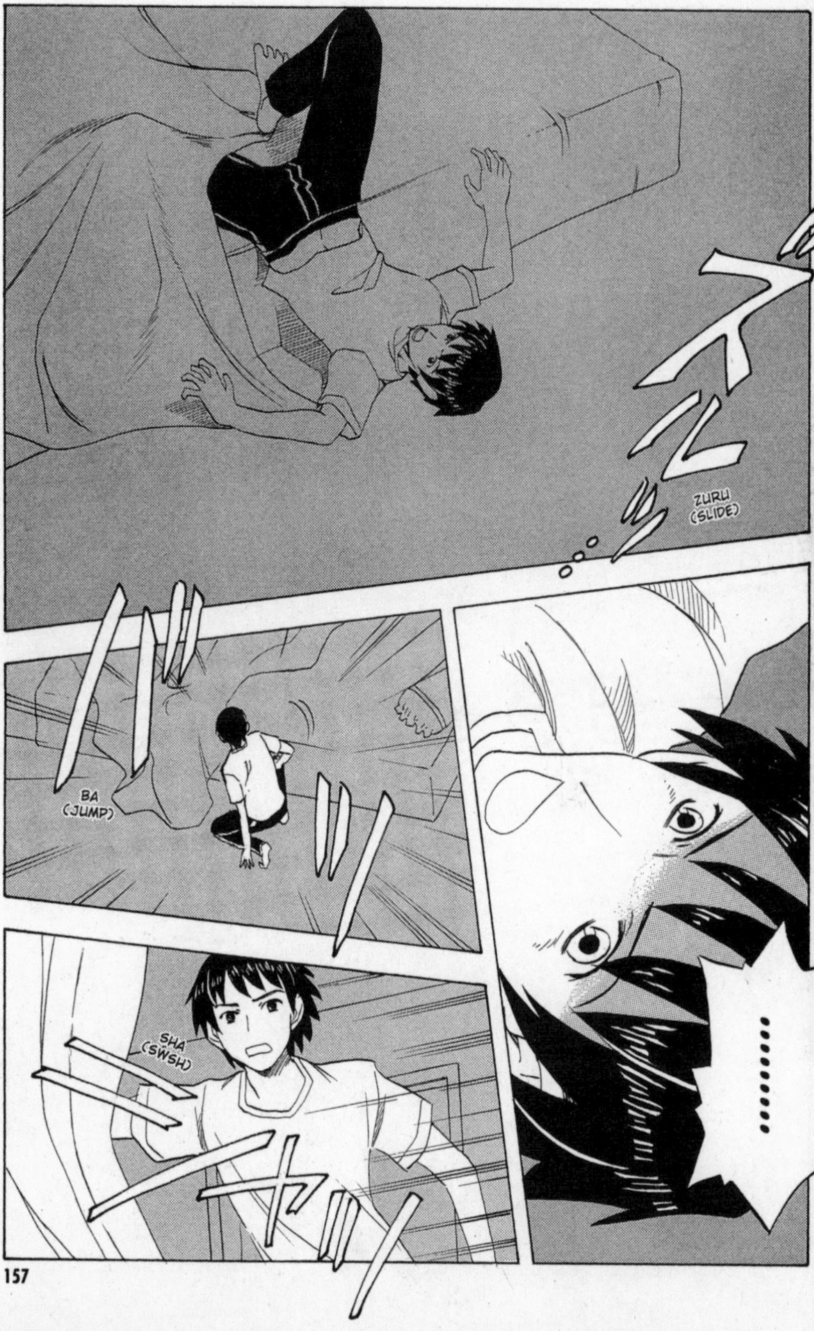
ZURU (SLIDE)
......
BA (JUMP)
SHA (SWSH)

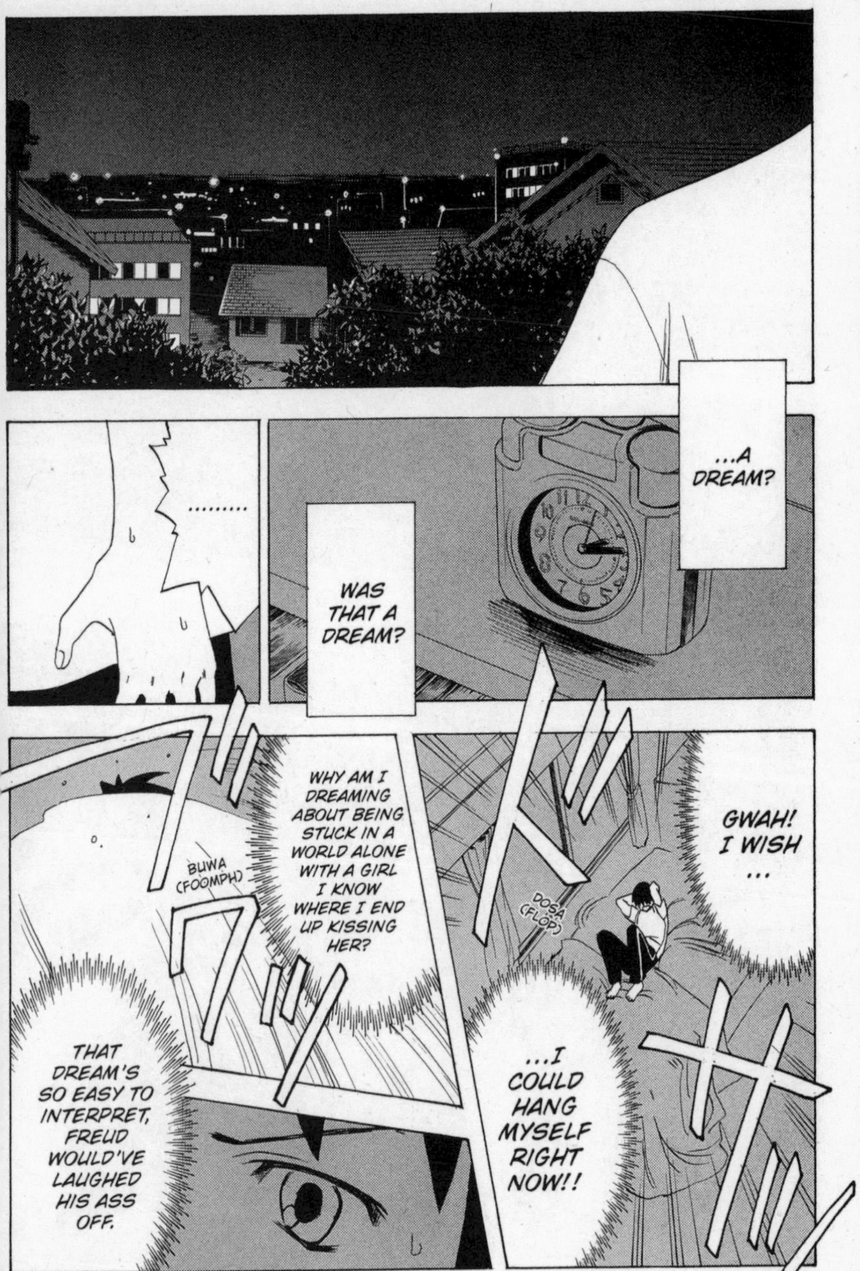
...A DREAM?
WAS THAT A DREAM?
....
GWAH! I WISH ...
DOSA (FLOP)
...I COULD HANG MYSELF RIGHT NOW!!
WHY AM I DREAMING ABOUT BEING STUCK IN A WORLD ALONE WITH A GIRL I KNOW WHERE I END UP KISSING HER?
BUWA (FOOMPH)
THAT DREAM'S SO EASY TO INTERPRET, FREUD WOULD'VE LAUGHED HIS ASS OFF.

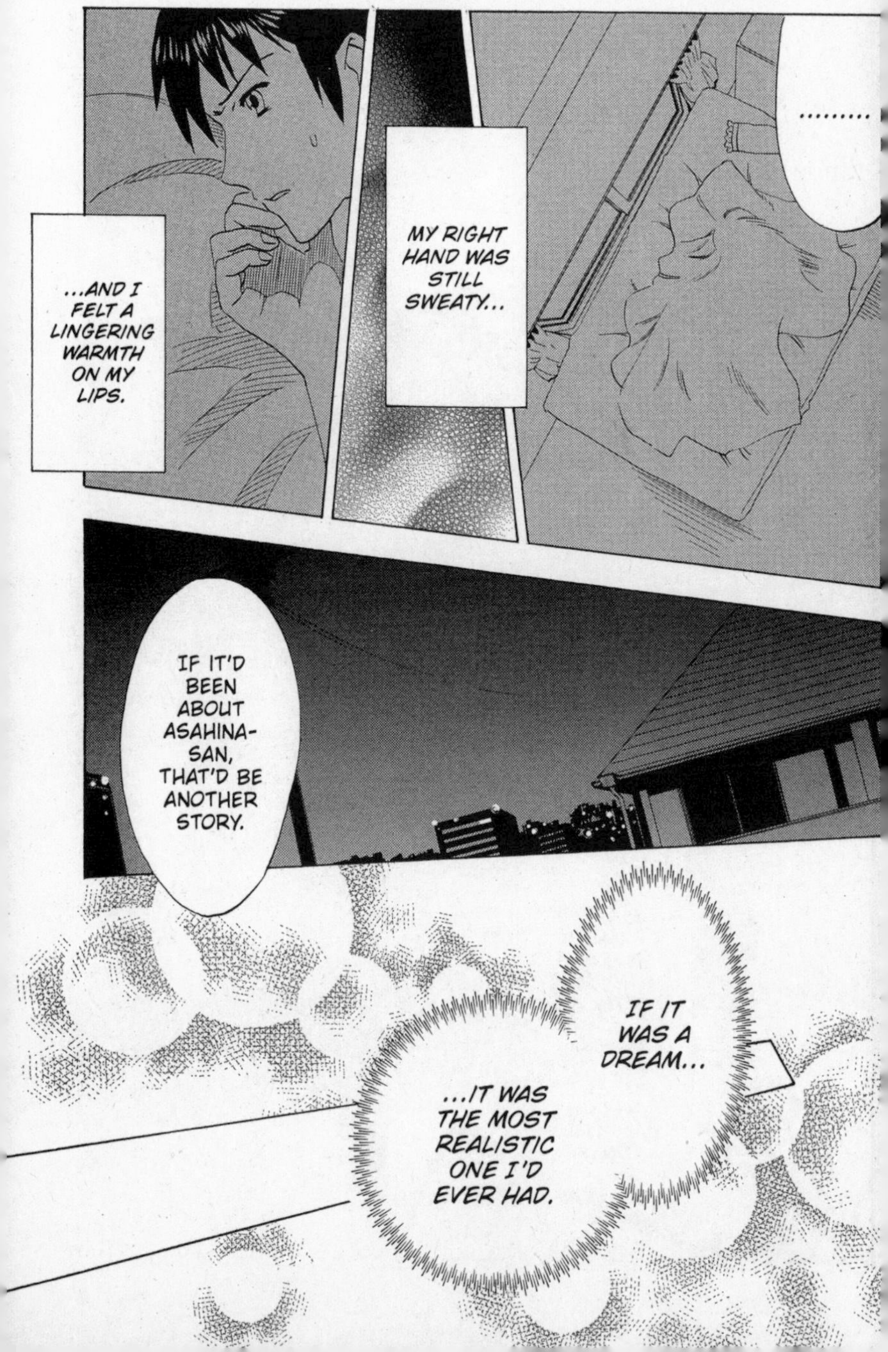
....
MY RIGHT HAND WAS STILL SWEATY...
...AND I FELT A LINGERING WARMTH ON MY LIPS.
IF IT'D BEEN ABOUT ASAHINA-SAN, THAT'D BE ANOTHER STORY.
IF IT WAS A DREAM...
...IT WAS THE MOST REALISTIC ONE I'D EVER HAD.

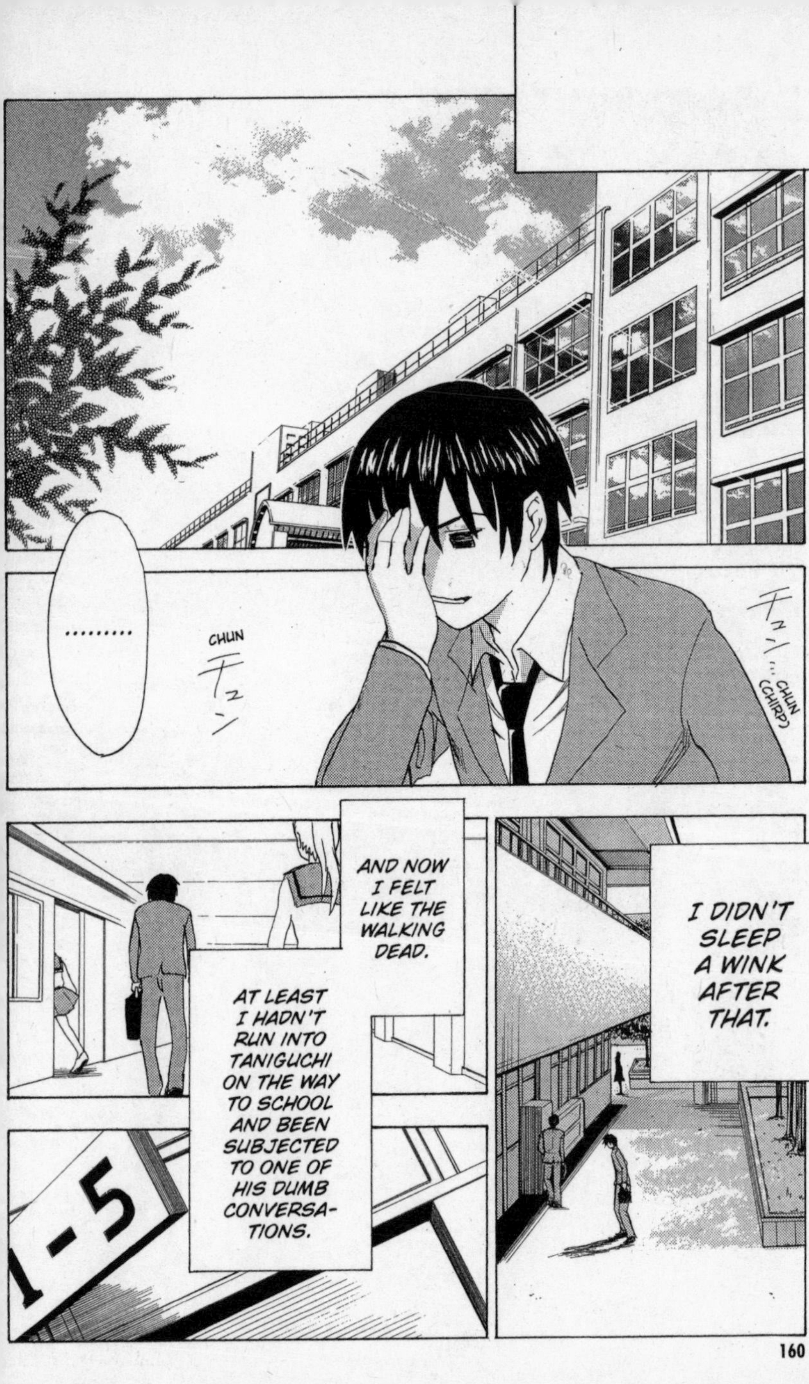
チュン... CHUN (CHIRP)
....
CHUN チュン
I DIDN'T SLEEP A WINK AFTER THAT.
AND NOW I FELT LIKE THE WALKING DEAD.
AT LEAST I HADN'T RUN INTO TANIGUCHI ON THE WAY TO SCHOOL AND BEEN SUBJECTED TO ONE OF HIS DUMB CONVERSA-TIONS.
1-5

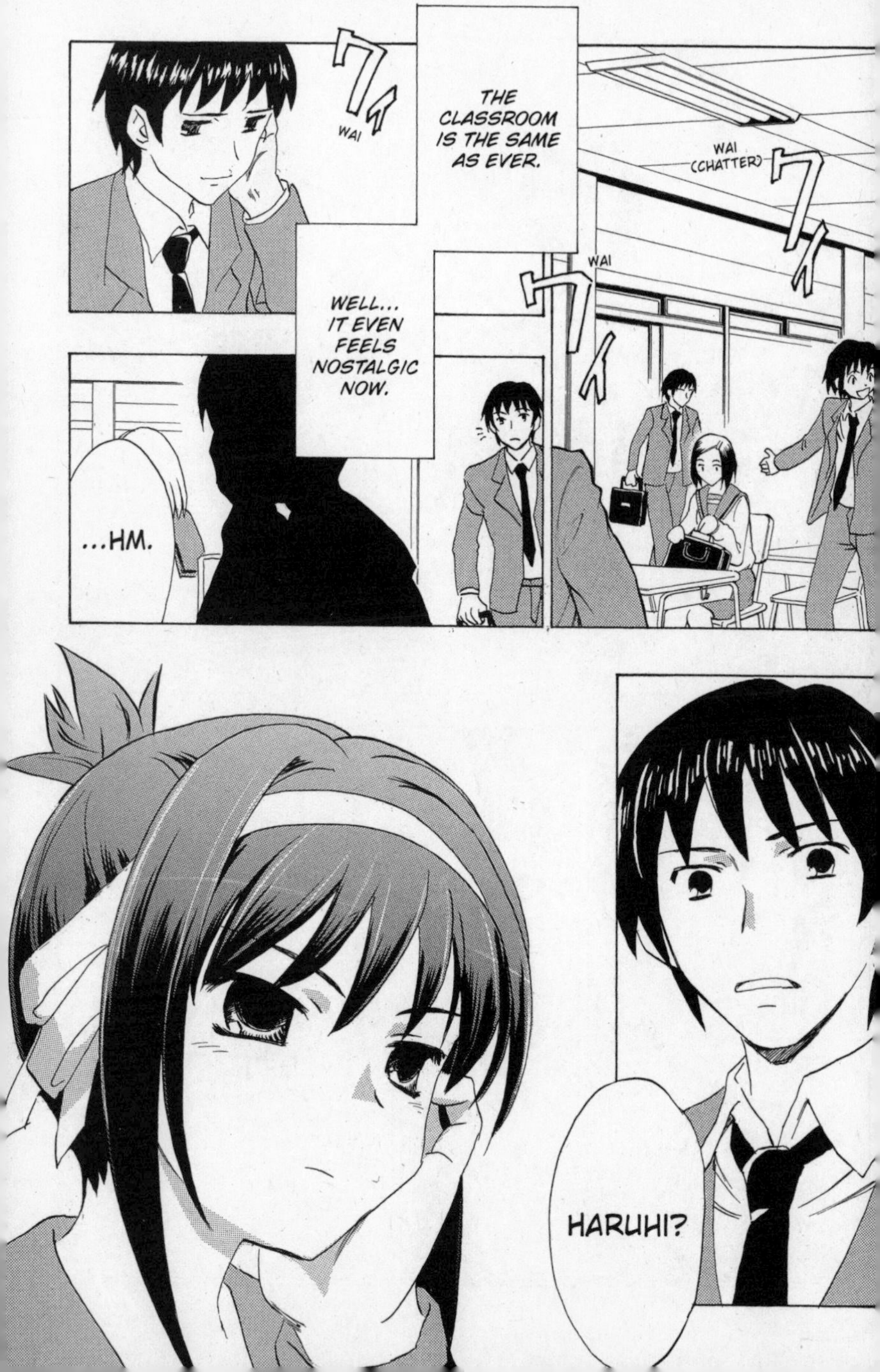
WAI (CHATTER)
THE CLASSROOM IS THE SAME AS EVER.
WAI
WAI
WELL... IT EVEN FEELS NOSTALGIC NOW.
...HM.
HARUHI?

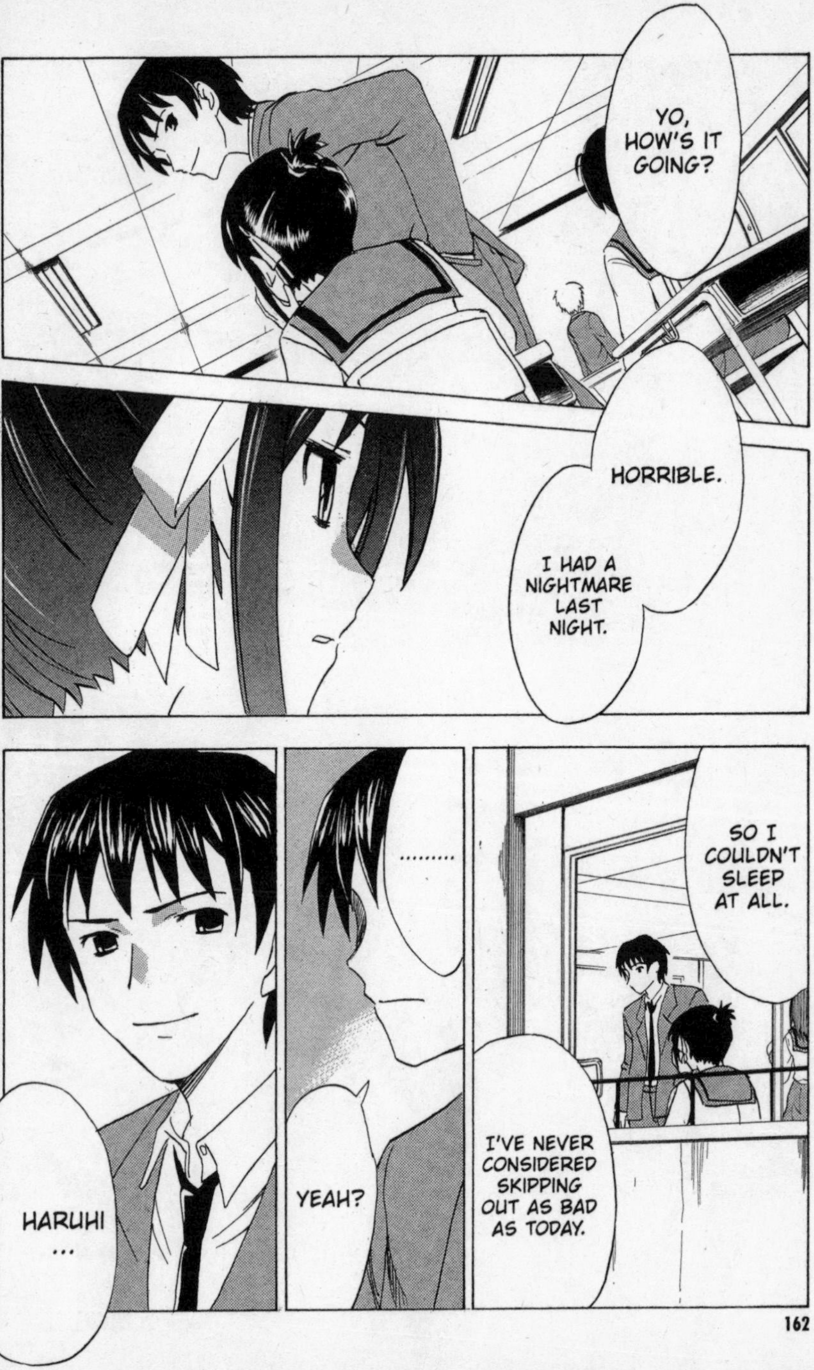
YO, HOW'S IT GOING?
HORRIBLE.
I HAD A NIGHTMARE LAST NIGHT.
SO I COULDN'T SLEEP AT ALL.
I'VE NEVER CONSIDERED SKIPPING OUT AS BAD AS TODAY.
....
YEAH?
HARUHI ...

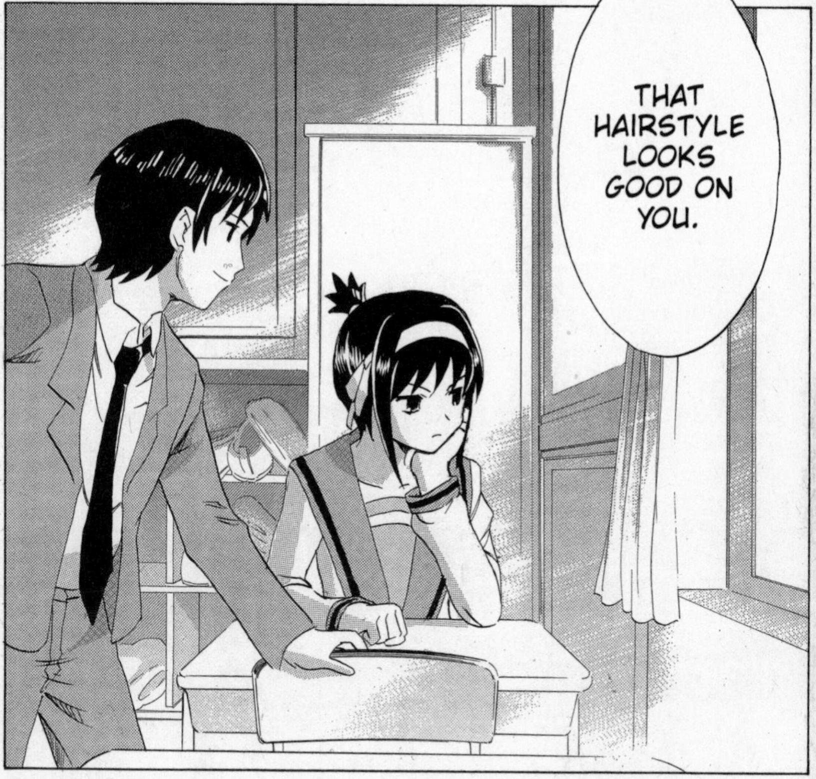
THAT HAIRSTYLE LOOKS GOOD ON YOU.

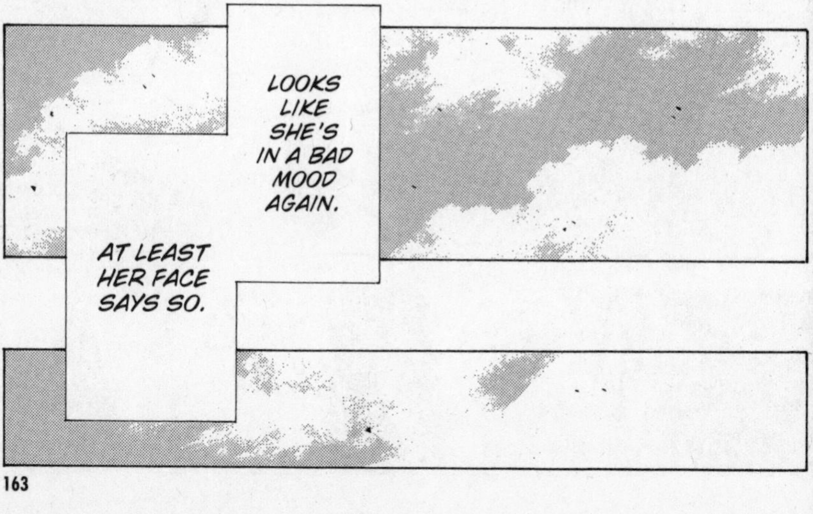
LOOKS LIKE SHE'S IN A BAD MOOD AGAIN.
AT LEAST HER FACE SAYS SO.

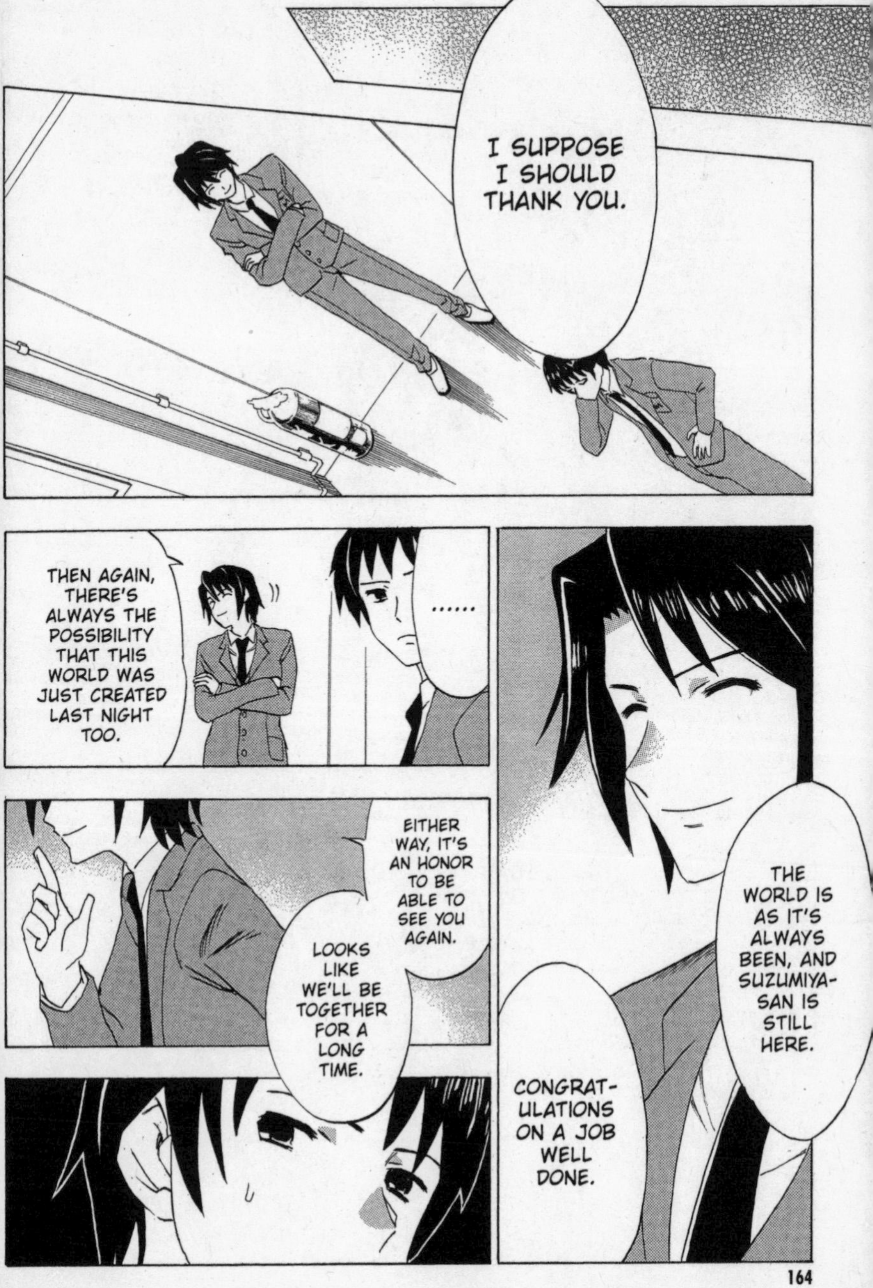
I SUPPOSE I SHOULD THANK YOU.
THE WORLD IS AS IT'S ALWAYS BEEN, AND SUZUMIYA-SAN IS STILL HERE.
CONGRAT-ULATIONS ON A JOB WELL DONE.
......
THEN AGAIN, THERE'S ALWAYS THE POSSIBILITY THAT THIS WORLD WAS JUST CREATED LAST NIGHT TOO.
EITHER WAY, IT'S AN HONOR TO BE ABLE TO SEE YOU AGAIN.
LOOKS LIKE WE'LL BE TOGETHER FOR A LONG TIME.

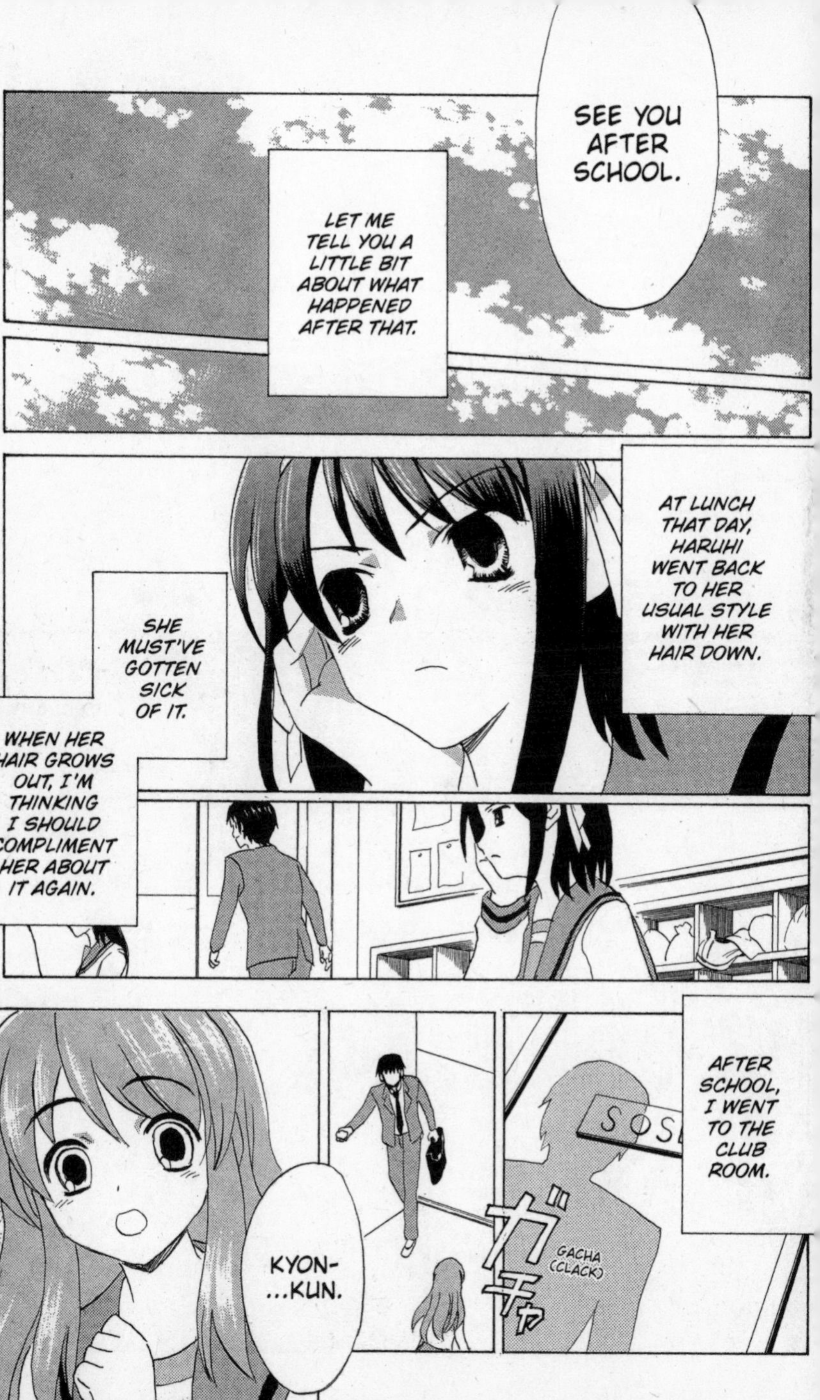
SEE YOU AFTER SCHOOL.
LET ME TELL YOU A LITTLE BIT ABOUT WHAT HAPPENED AFTER THAT.
AT LUNCH THAT DAY, HARUHI WENT BACK TO HER USUAL STYLE WITH HER HAIR DOWN.
SHE MUST'VE GOTTEN SICK OF IT.
WHEN HER HAIR GROWS OUT, I'M THINKING I SHOULD COMPLIMENT HER ABOUT IT AGAIN.
AFTER SCHOOL, I WENT TO THE CLUB ROOM.
GACHA (CLACK)
KYON-...KUN.

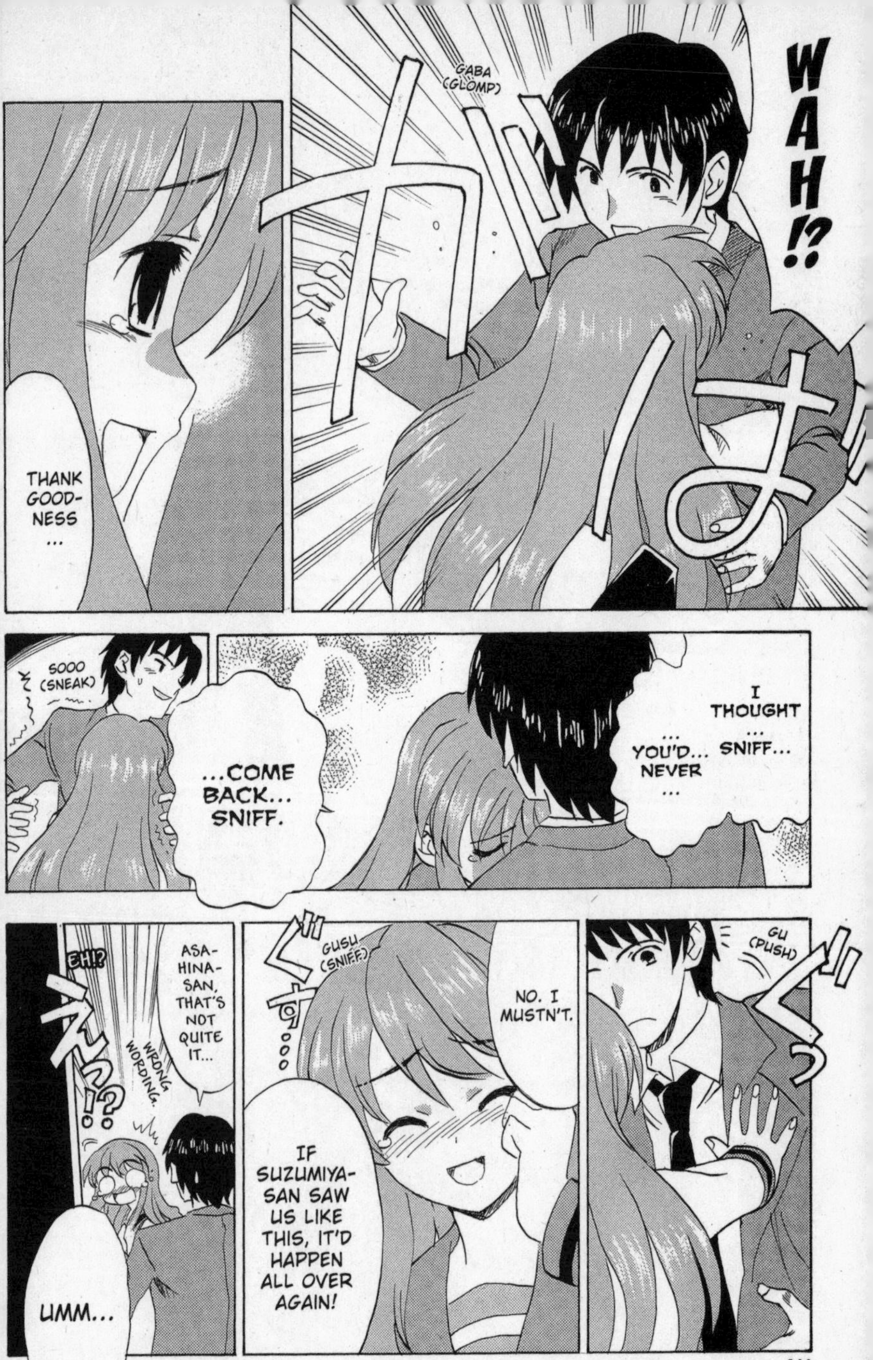
WAH!?
GABA (GLOMP)
THANK GOOD-NESS ...
I THOUGHT ... SNIFF...
... YOU'D... NEVER ...
SOOO (SNEAK)
...COME BACK... SNIFF.
GU (PUSH)
NO. I MUSTN'T.
GUSU (SNIFF)
IF SUZUMIYA-SAN SAW US LIKE THIS, IT'D HAPPEN ALL OVER AGAIN!
EH!?
ASA-HINA-SAN, THAT'S NOT QUITE IT...
WRONG WORDING.
UMM...

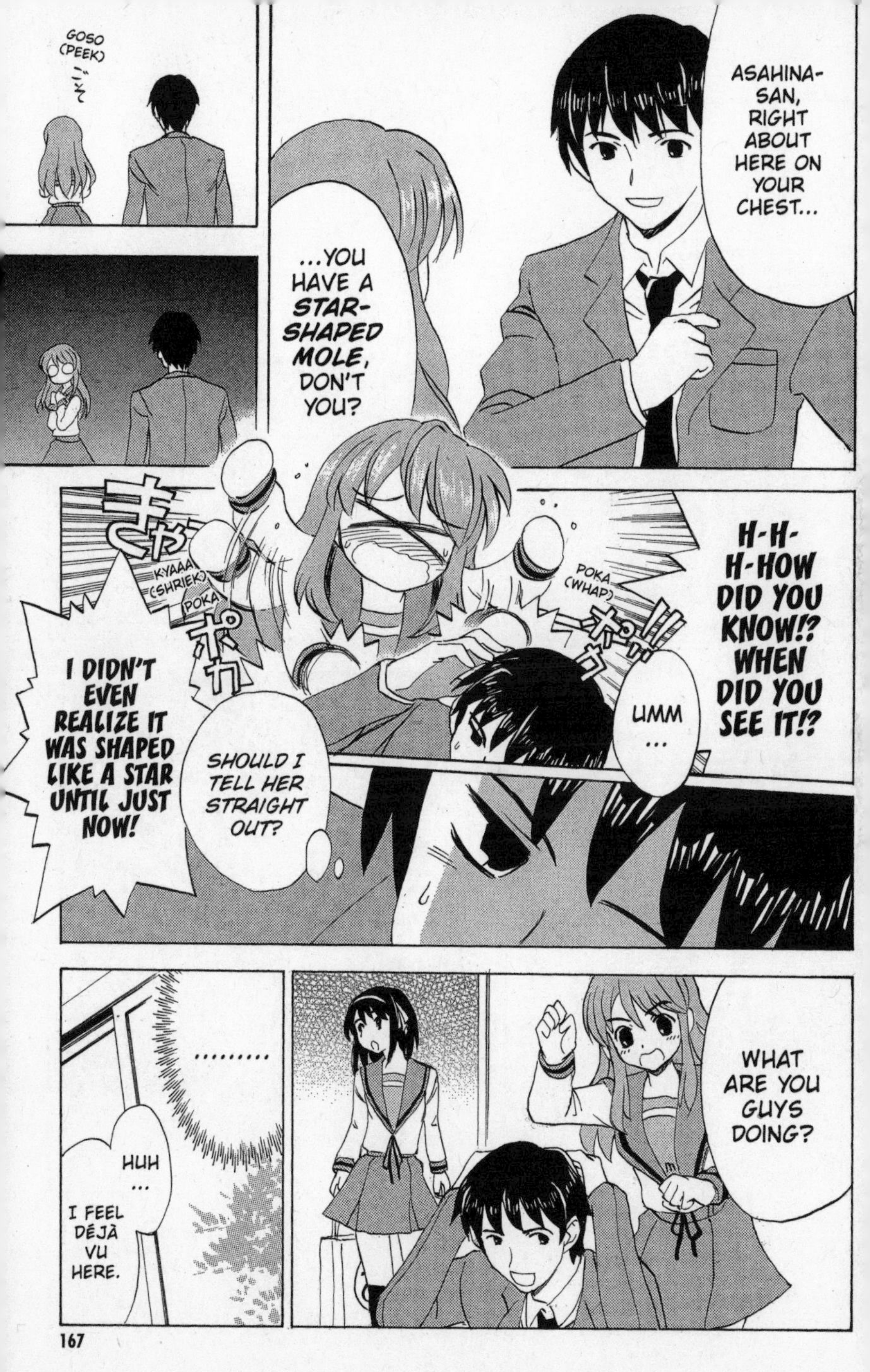
ASAHINA-SAN, RIGHT ABOUT HERE ON YOUR CHEST...
...YOU HAVE A STAR-SHAPED MOLE, DON'T YOU?
GOSO (PEEK)
H-H-H-HOW DID YOU KNOW!? WHEN DID YOU SEE IT!?
POKA (WHAP)
KYAAA (SHRIEK)
POKA
UMM ...
I DIDN'T EVEN REALIZE IT WAS SHAPED LIKE A STAR UNTIL JUST NOW!
SHOULD I TELL HER STRAIGHT OUT?
WHAT ARE YOU GUYS DOING?
....
HUH ... I FEEL DÉJÀ VU HERE.

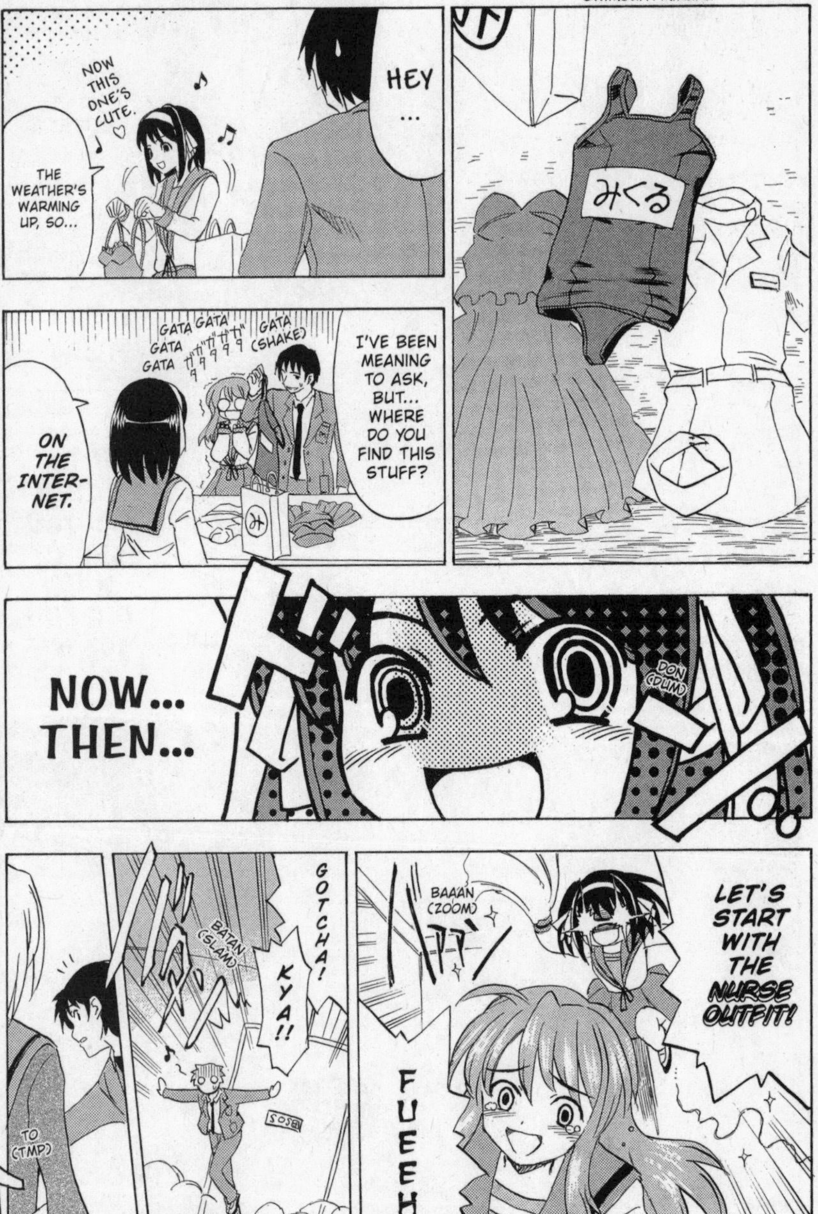
みくる
HEY ...
NOW THIS ONE'S CUTE. ♡
THE WEATHER'S WARMING UP, SO...
I'VE BEEN MEANING TO ASK, BUT... WHERE DO YOU FIND THIS STUFF?
GATA GATA GATA GATA (SHAKE)
ON THE INTER-NET.
DON (DUM)
NOW... THEN...
LET'S START WITH THE NURSE OUTFIT!
BAAAN (ZOOM)
FUEEH!?
GOTCHA!
KYA!!
BATAN (SLAM)
TO (TMP)

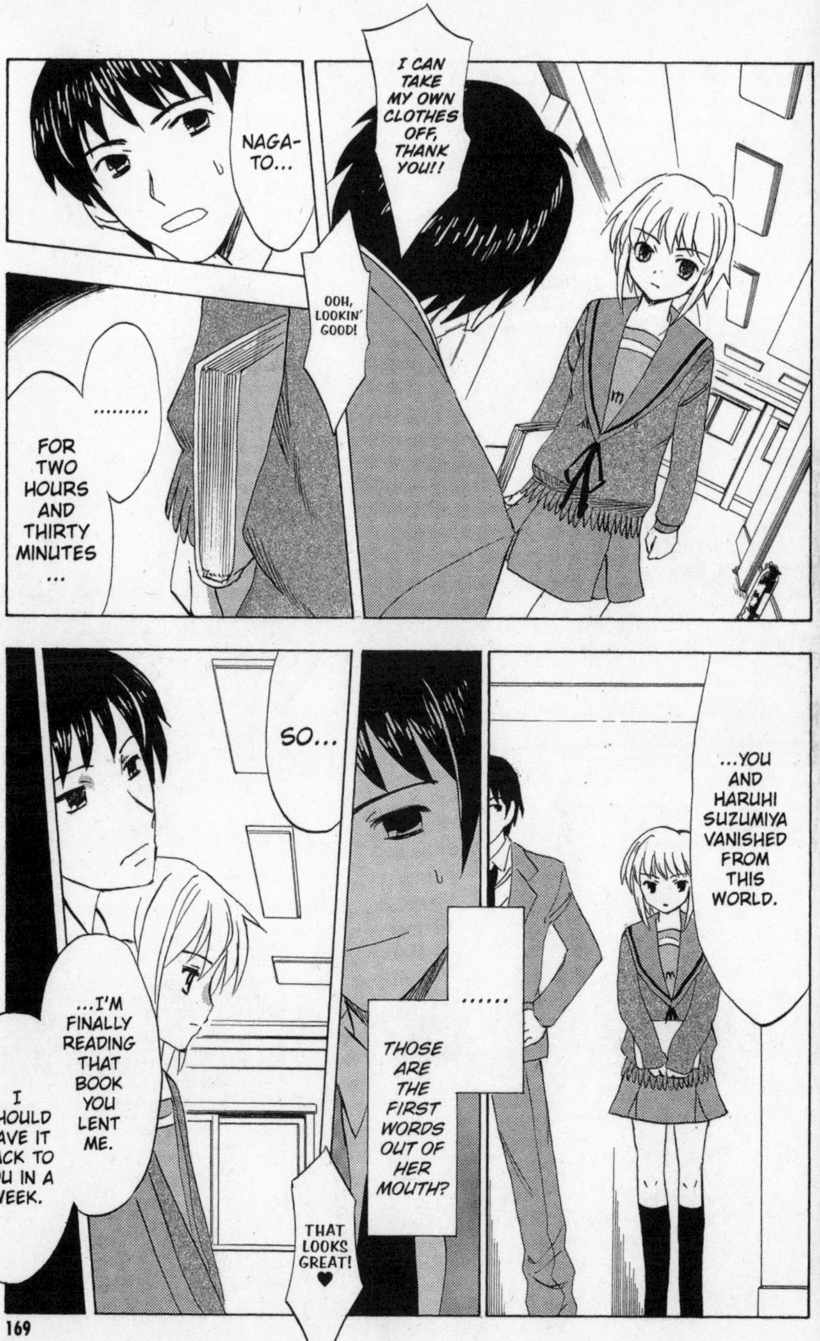
I CAN TAKE MY OWN CLOTHES OFF, THANK YOU!!
OOH, LOOKIN' GOOD!
NAGA-TO...
....
FOR TWO HOURS AND THIRTY MINUTES ...
...YOU AND HARUHI SUZUMIYA VANISHED FROM THIS WORLD.
......
THOSE ARE THE FIRST WORDS OUT OF HER MOUTH?
THAT LOOKS GREAT! ♥
SO...
...I'M FINALLY READING THAT BOOK YOU LENT ME.
I SHOULD HAVE IT BACK TO YOU IN A WEEK.

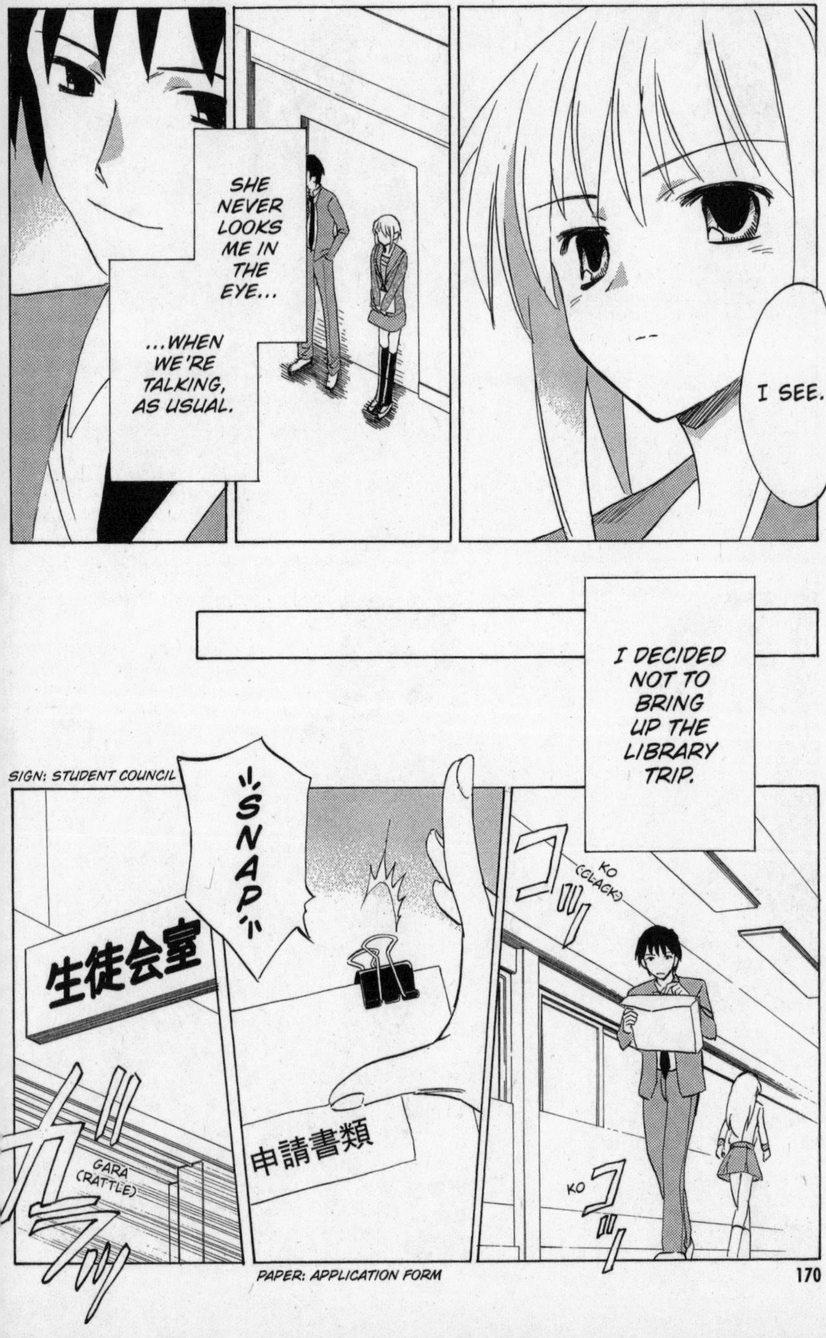
I SEE.
SHE NEVER LOOKS ME IN THE EYE...
...WHEN WE'RE TALKING, AS USUAL.
I DECIDED NOT TO BRING UP THE LIBRARY TRIP.
KO (CLACK)
KO
SNAP
生徒会室
申請書類
GARA (RATTLE)

SIGN: STUDENT COUNCIL

PAPER: APPLICATION FORM

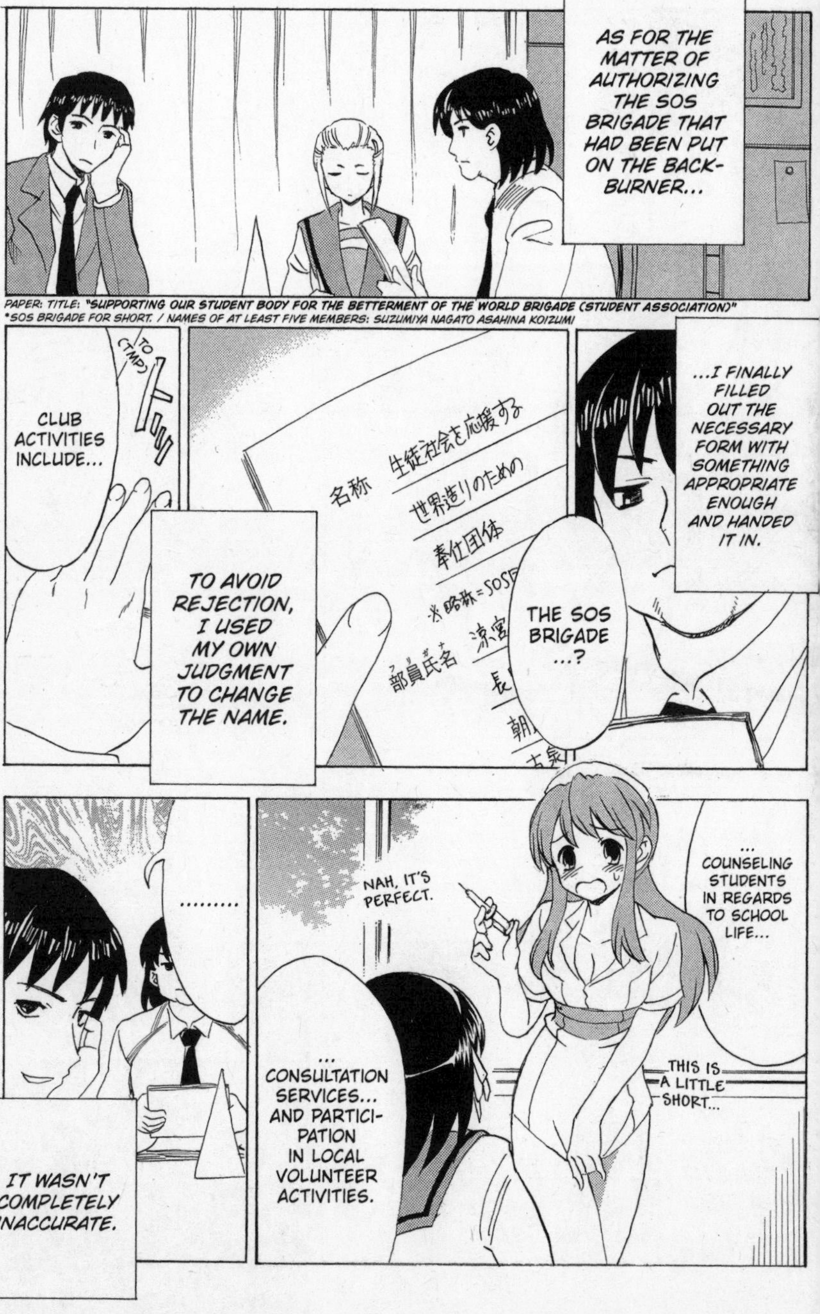
AS FOR THE MATTER OF AUTHORIZING THE SOS BRIGADE THAT HAD BEEN PUT ON THE BACK-BURNER...
PAPER: TITLE: "SUPPORTING OUR STUDENT BODY FOR THE BETTERMENT OF THE WORLD BRIGADE (STUDENT ASSOCIATION)"
*SOS BRIGADE FOR SHORT. / NAMES OF AT LEAST FIVE MEMBERS: SUZUMIYA NAGATO ASAHINA KOIZUMI
...I FINALLY FILLED OUT THE NECESSARY FORM WITH SOMETHING APPROPRIATE ENOUGH AND HANDED IT IN.
THE SOS BRIGADE ...?
名称
生徒社会を応援する
世界造りのための
奉仕団体
※略称＝SOS
部員氏名
涼宮
古泉
TO AVOID REJECTION, I USED MY OWN JUDGMENT TO CHANGE THE NAME.
TO (TMP)
CLUB ACTIVITIES INCLUDE...
... COUNSELING STUDENTS IN REGARDS TO SCHOOL LIFE...
THIS IS A LITTLE SHORT...
NAH, IT'S PERFECT.
... CONSULTATION SERVICES... AND PARTICIPATION IN LOCAL VOLUNTEER ACTIVITIES.
....
IT WASN'T COMPLETELY INACCURATE.

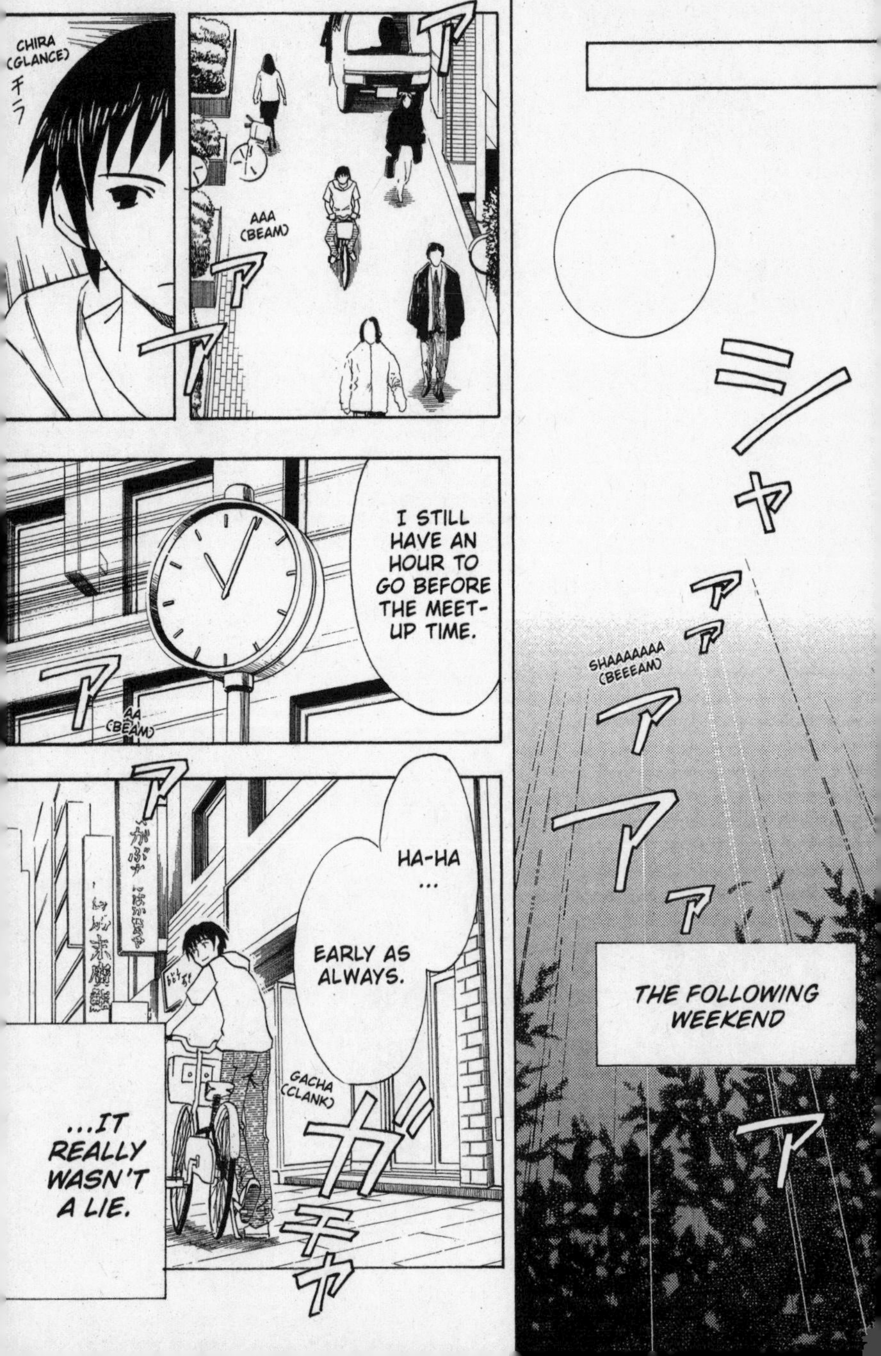
SHAAAAAAA (BEEEAM)
THE FOLLOWING WEEKEND
AAA (BEAM)
CHIRA (GLANCE)
チラ
I STILL HAVE AN HOUR TO GO BEFORE THE MEET-UP TIME.
AA (BEAM)
HA-HA ...
EARLY AS ALWAYS.
GACHA (CLANK)
...IT REALLY WASN'T A LIE.

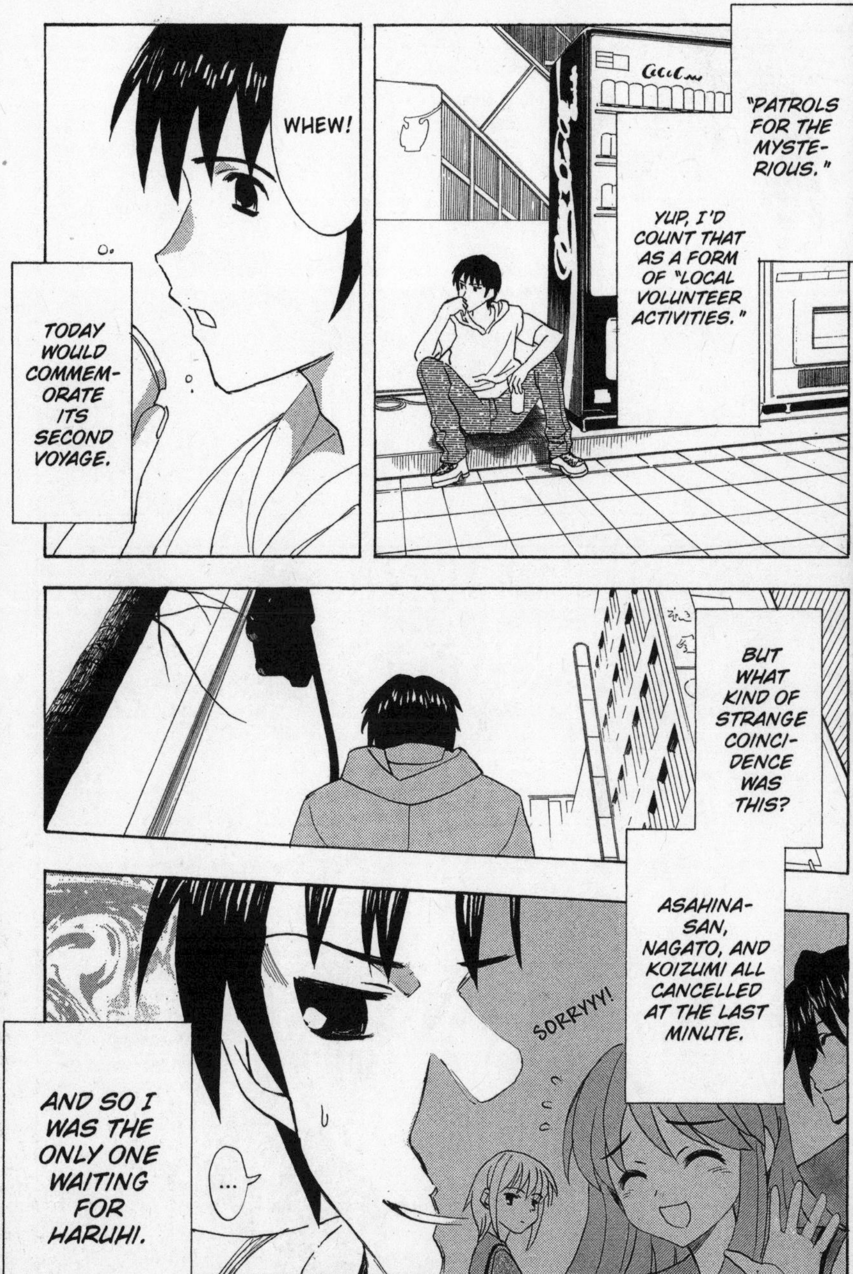
"PATROLS FOR THE MYSTERIOUS."
YUP, I'D COUNT THAT AS A FORM OF "LOCAL VOLUNTEER ACTIVITIES."
WHEW!
TODAY WOULD COMMEMORATE ITS SECOND VOYAGE.
BUT WHAT KIND OF STRANGE COINCIDENCE WAS THIS?
ASAHINA-SAN, NAGATO, AND KOIZUMI ALL CANCELLED AT THE LAST MINUTE.
SORRYYY!
...
AND SO I WAS THE ONLY ONE WAITING FOR HARUHI.

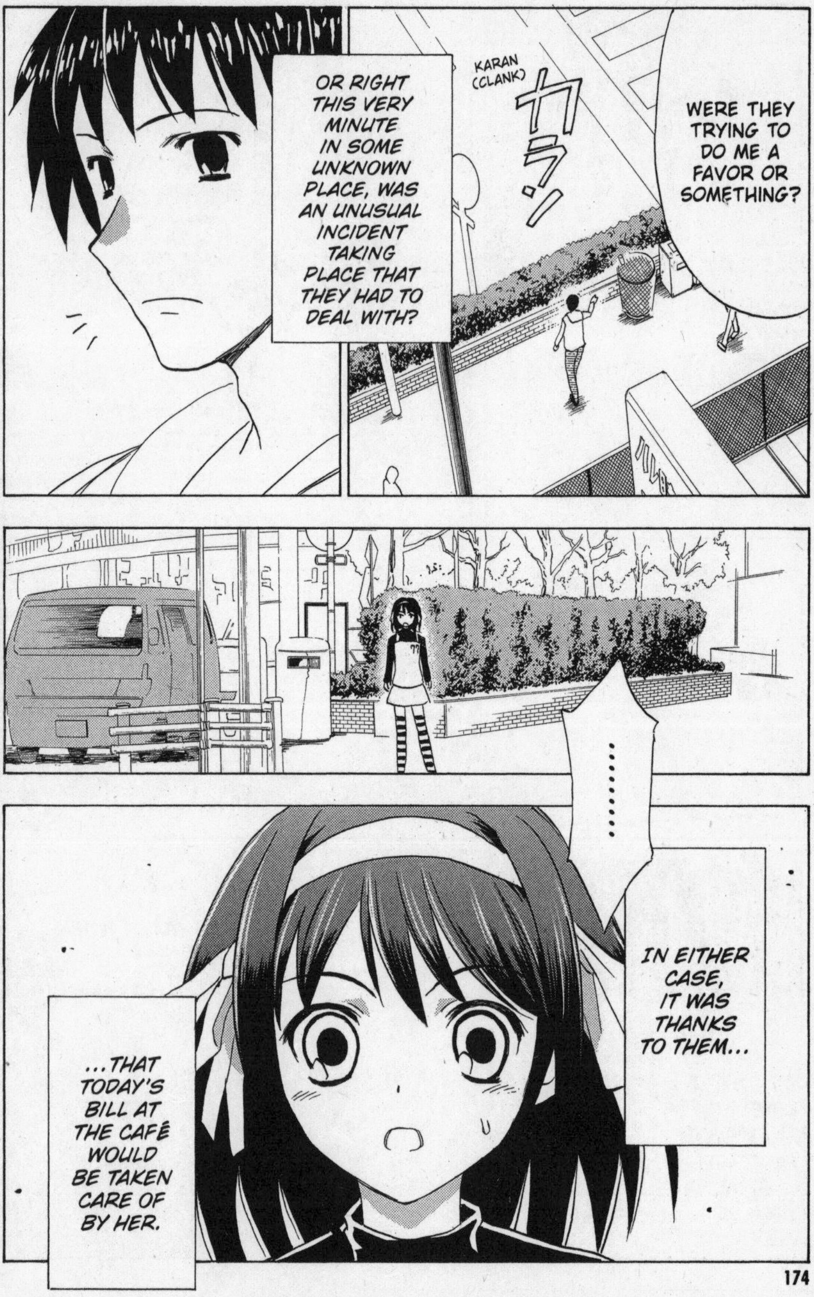
WERE THEY TRYING TO DO ME A FAVOR OR SOMETHING?
カラン
KARAN (CLANK)
OR RIGHT THIS VERY MINUTE IN SOME UNKNOWN PLACE, WAS AN UNUSUAL INCIDENT TAKING PLACE THAT THEY HAD TO DEAL WITH?
......
IN EITHER CASE, IT WAS THANKS TO THEM...
...THAT TODAY'S BILL AT THE CAFÉ WOULD BE TAKEN CARE OF BY HER.

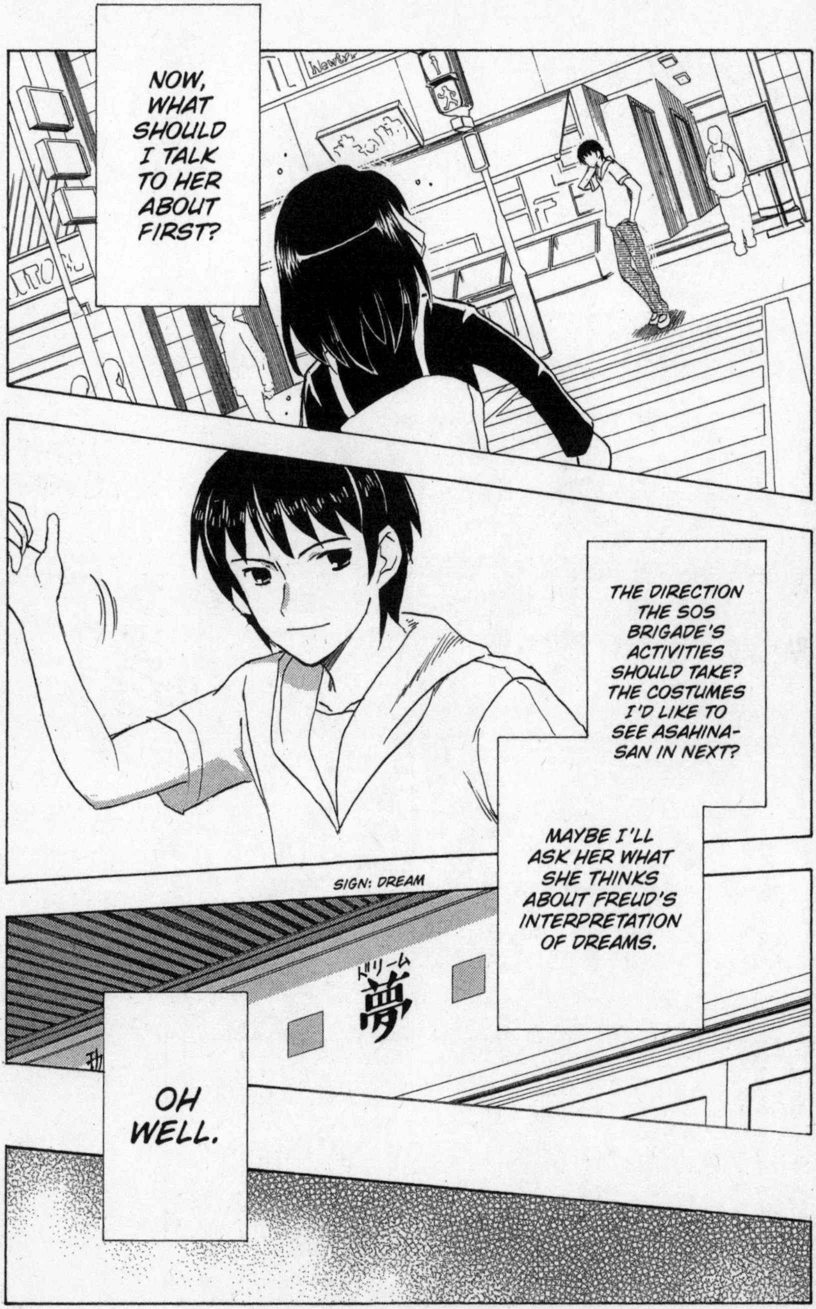
NOW, WHAT SHOULD I TALK TO HER ABOUT FIRST?
THE DIRECTION THE SOS BRIGADE'S ACTIVITIES SHOULD TAKE? THE COSTUMES I'D LIKE TO SEE ASAHINA-SAN IN NEXT?
MAYBE I'LL ASK HER WHAT SHE THINKS ABOUT FREUD'S INTERPRETATION OF DREAMS.
SIGN: DREAM
ドリーム
夢
OH WELL.

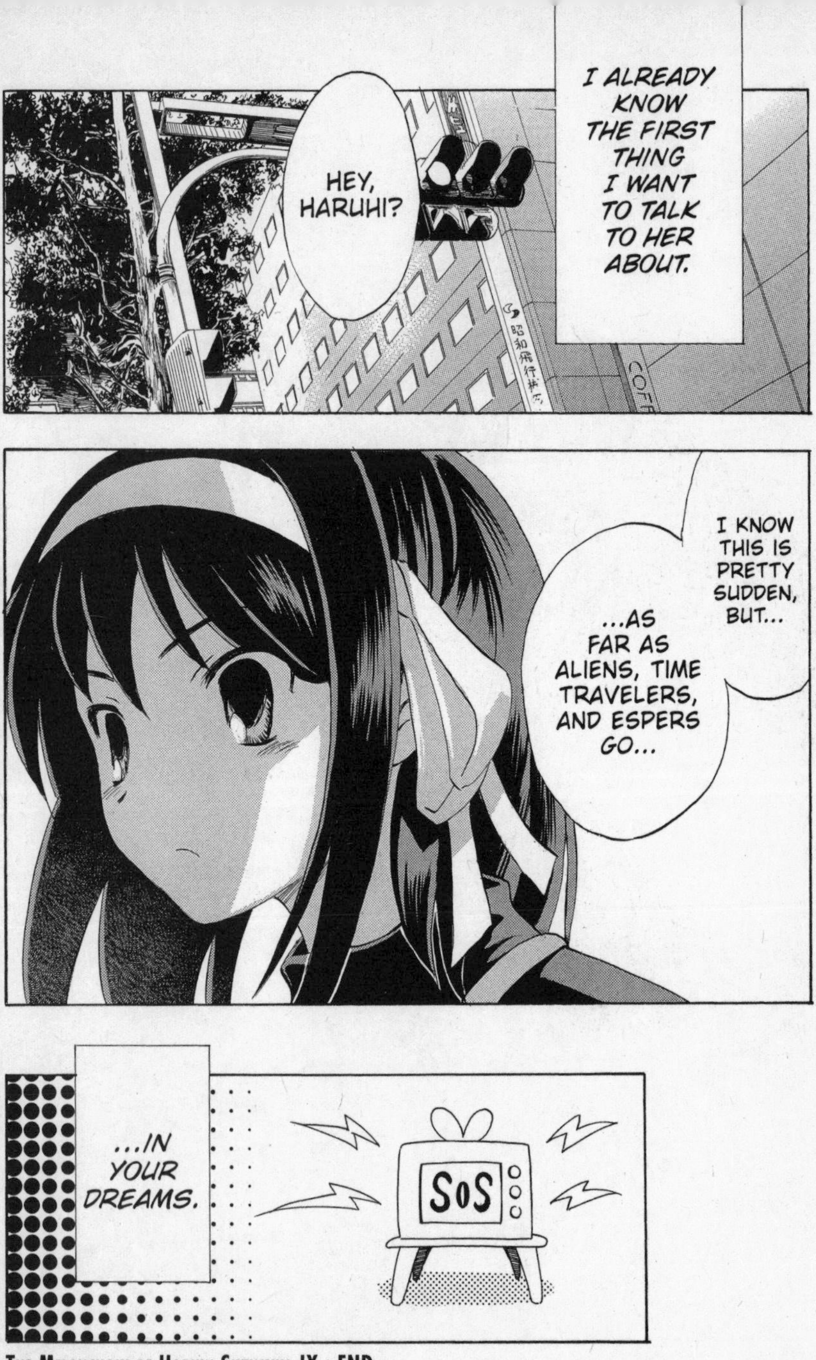
I ALREADY KNOW THE FIRST THING I WANT TO TALK TO HER ABOUT.
HEY, HARUHI?
I KNOW THIS IS PRETTY SUDDEN, BUT...
...AS FAR AS ALIENS, TIME TRAVELERS, AND ESPERS GO...
...IN YOUR DREAMS.
SOS

THE MELANCHOLY OF HARUHI SUZUMIYA IX : END

TO BE CONTINUED

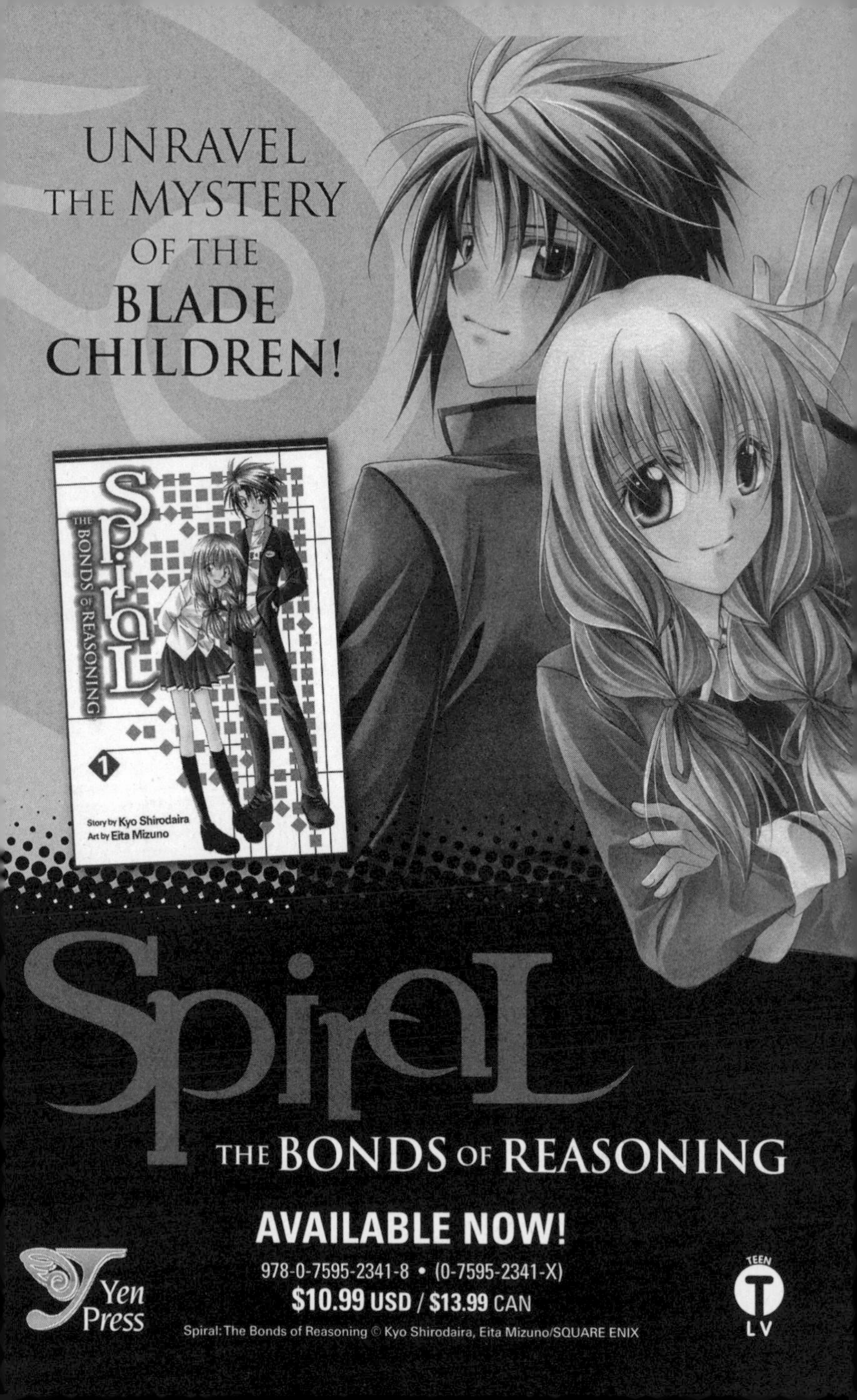
UNRAVEL THE MYSTERY OF THE BLADE CHILDREN!
Spiral THE BONDS OF REASONING 1
Story by Kyo Shirodaira
Art by Eita Mizuno
Spiral
THE BONDS OF REASONING
AVAILABLE NOW!
978-0-7595-2341-8 • (0-7595-2341-X)
$10.99 USD / $13.99 CAN
Spiral: The Bonds of Reasoning © Kyo Shirodaira, Eita Mizuno/SQUARE ENIX
Yen Press
TEEN T LV

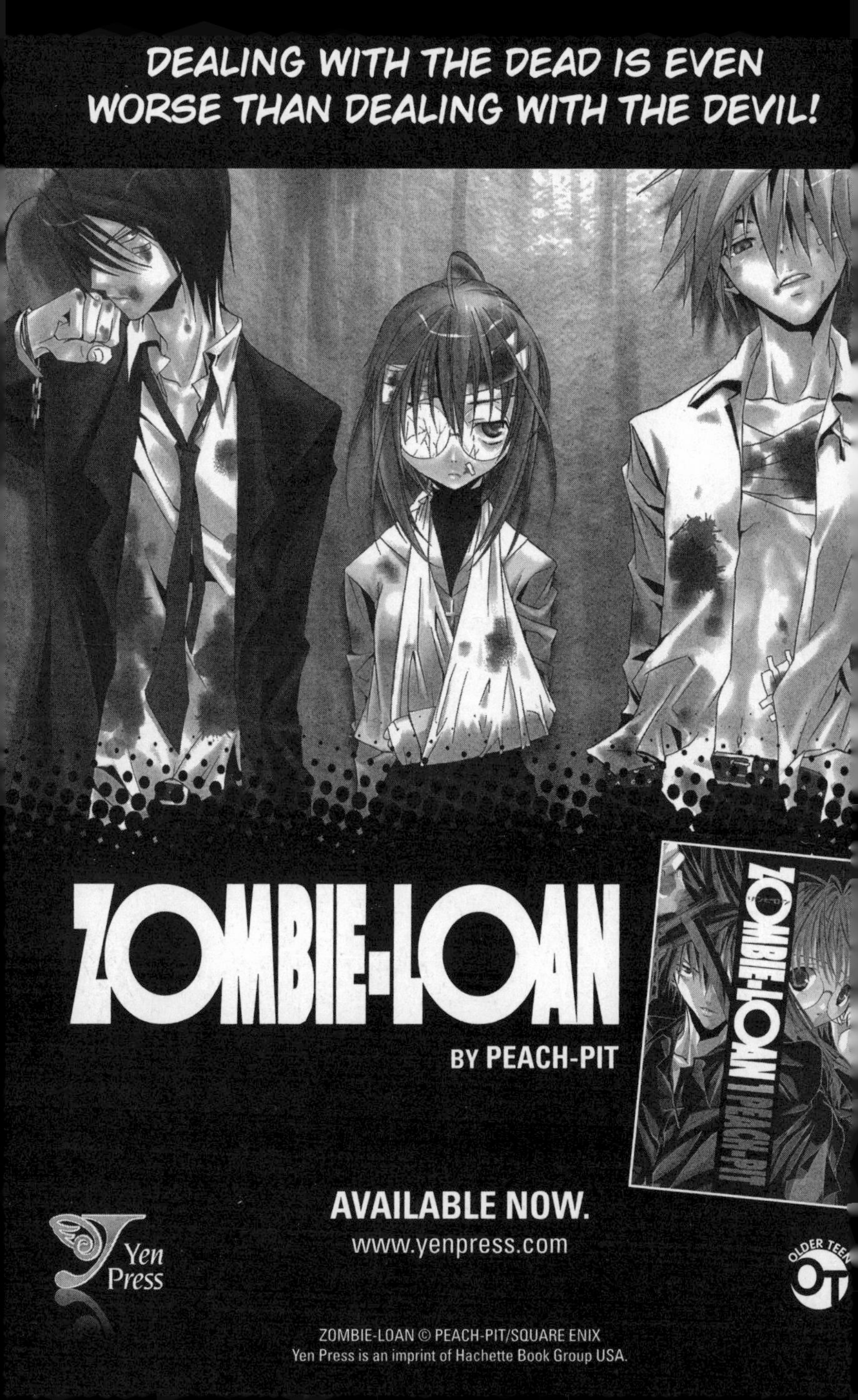
DEALING WITH THE DEAD IS EVEN
WORSE THAN DEALING WITH THE DEVIL!
ZOMBIE-LOAN
BY PEACH-PIT
ZOMBIE-LOAN 1 PEACH-PIT
AVAILABLE NOW.
www.yenpress.com
Yen Press
OLDER TEEN
OT
ZOMBIE-LOAN © PEACH-PIT/SQUARE ENIX
Yen Press is an imprint of Hachette Book Group USA.

THE MELANCHOLY OF HARUHI SUZUMIYA
2

Original Story: Nagaru Tanigawa
Manga: Gaku Tsugano
Character Design: Noizi Ito

Translation: Christine Schilling
Lettering: Alexis Eckerman

SUZUMIYA HARUHI NO YUUTSU Volume 2 © Nagaru TANIGAWA • Noizi ITO 2006 © Gaku TSUGANO 2006. Edited by KADOKAWA SHOTEN. First published in Japan in 2006 by KADOKAWA CORPORATION, Tokyo. English translation rights arranged with KADOKAWA CORPORATION, Tokyo, through TUTTLE-MORI AGENCY, INC., Tokyo.

Yen Press
Hachette Book Group
1290 Avenue of the Americas, New York, NY 10104

www.HachetteBookGroup.com
www.YenPress.com

Yen Press is an imprint of Hachette Book Group, Inc. The Yen Press name and logo are trademarks of Hachette Book Group, Inc.

First Yen Press Edition: March 2009

ISBN: 978-0-7595-2945-8

10 9 8 7 6

BVG

Printed in the United States of America